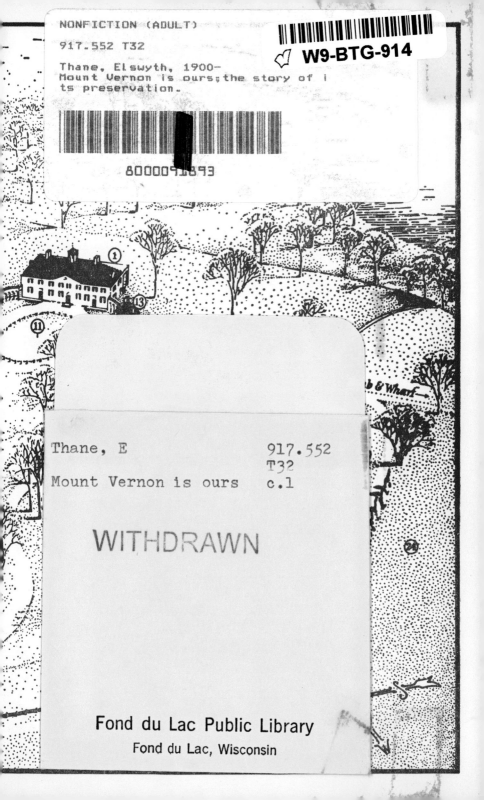

MOUNT VERNON
IS OURS

Books by ELSWYTH THANE

FICTION

RIDERS OF THE WIND

ECHO ANSWERS

CLOTH OF GOLD

HIS ELIZABETH

BOUND TO HAPPEN

QUEEN'S FOLLY

TRYST

REMEMBER TODAY

FROM THIS DAY FORWARD

MELODY

THE LOST GENERAL

LETTER TO A STRANGER

THE WILLIAMSBURG NOVELS

DAWN'S EARLY LIGHT

YANKEE STRANGER

EVER AFTER

THE LIGHT HEART

KISSING KIN

THIS WAS TOMORROW

HOMING

NONFICTION

THE TUDOR WENCH

YOUNG MR. DISRAELI

ENGLAND WAS AN ISLAND ONCE

THE BIRD WHO MADE GOOD

RELUCTANT FARMER

THE FAMILY QUARREL

WASHINGTON'S LADY

POTOMAC SQUIRE

MOUNT VERNON IS OURS

PLAYS

THE TUDOR WENCH

YOUNG MR. DISRAELI

MOUNT VERNON IS OURS

THE STORY OF ITS PRESERVATION

By ELSWYTH THANE

DUELL, SLOAN AND PEARCE New York

First edition

DUELL, SLOAN & PEARCE
AFFILIATE OF
MEREDITH PRESS

Library of Congress Catalog Card Number: 66-10911
MANUFACTURED IN THE UNITED STATES OF AMERICA

TO
THE REGENT
MRS. FRANCIS BEIRNE
AND
THE CURRENT VICE-REGENTS
OF
THE MOUNT VERNON LADIES' ASSOCIATION
OF THE UNION

FOREWORD

I have been greatly privileged in writing this book. The Association opened its library to me, so that I have been permitted to make use not only of the earliest correspondence between the founding sisters but of the Minutes of Council—without which it would not have been possible to comprehend and appreciate the continuous chain of remarkable women who for over a hundred years have labored for and cherished Washington's home. Many of them bore historic or distinguished names. Most of them were unusual in character and ability. Some of them were always in frail health. In the fading ink of those early letters they left their own portraits—unconsciously preserving as in amber the zeal, the humor, the charity, the occasional bitterness and dissension, above all the indefatigable, undefeatable common effort, the united strength behind the plough to which they had set their hands.

It has been an inspiring experience to make their acquaintance, from the tragic, tormented, dedicated Ann Pamela Cunningham to the gracious, delightful woman who is the ninth and current Regent. The present staff, headed by the fourth Superintendent, who is now called Resident Director, prefer to remain anonymous and invisible, behind the walls of the simple red brick administration building, dating from 1929, which stands behind a white fence and a tall hawthorn hedge facing the salesroom which is in the Quarters in the North Lane. They consider themselves, as the Director once put it to me, merely stage managers, reconstructing and preserving the authentic environment which George Washington created, and functioning mainly behind the scenes—and they see to it that the now complex machinery does not clank. They have accomplished perhaps too well their avowed intention, so that to the outer world Mount Vernon appears almost to run itself, in the temporary absence of its original master. Many of its visitors assume that some more publicized organization is responsible for its present perfection, whereas the Mount Vernon Ladies' Association antedates the D.A.R. and the Colonial Dames by more than thirty years, while the Williamsburg Restoration is its junior by some seventy years, and the National Park Service, which has done so well for nearby Arlington House, dates from 1916. Ever since Mount Vernon ceased to belong to Washingtons, in 1858, it has been owned by the Association. And a more hospitable, helpful, and good-humored company than its present officers and staff would be hard to find. To them, as much as to the undersigned, the reader is indebted for this glimpse into enchanted territory.

E.T.

CONTENTS

FROM THE ADDRESS by the first Regent, Ann Pamela Cunningham, at the first meeting of the Grand Council at which she presided, November 19, 1866:

"Looking back from our present assured stand-point of an *accomplished fact*, my memory cannot fail to recall the early vicissitudes, the oft-discouraging progress of our labor of love, in redeeming from oblivion and sure decay the home and grave of the immortal Washington! Then we lived on hope! We *would* not yield to despair. Now we can rejoice, with intense satisfaction, to know that *Mount Vernon is ours*—the Nation's! And well may I feel almost overpowered to find myself, at this moment, in the midst of ladies representing the varied sections of our country, pledged to guard that sacred spot *forever*. . . ."

MOUNT VERNON
IS OURS

THE RESCUE
1853–1860

I

"Mount Vernon is open to the public every day in the year, from 9 o'clock."

It takes only a dozen words to encompass the achievement of a little miracle. But in that simple statement resides a great dream come true, accomplished by more than a hundred years of dedicated effort by an organization of remarkable women, assembled one by one from nearly every state in the Union.

The Mount Vernon Ladies' Association is not sponsored by nor beholden to the Federal Government or the State of Virginia. It stands alone, its original charter having been granted in 1858, when ladies were not supposed to be capable of conducting anything like public affairs, and it was the creation of one resolute woman who at the age of thirty-seven acquired what even her friends at first considered an impracticable obsession. She had made up her mind that the home which George Washington loved should not be allowed to fall down in ruins from neglect. Not the uncooperative Washington family, the skeptical Virginia Legislature, nor her own condition of chronic invalidism could daunt her, nor swerve her from her apparently impossible purpose. As an example of sheer grit and courage, laced with Southern charm, Ann Pamela Cunningham remains unique.

The story of Mount Vernon's rescue is simple to read in the guide-books. The thing was done, and it has stayed done, superbly

3

well. But after one hundred and twelve years, the struggle and
the disappointments, the stubborn hope and repeated despair, the
strength and the flame of this one woman's spirit demand to be
contemplated.

Moreover, she was not alone for long. She had the faculty and
the good fortune to gather round her other gallant women who
caught fire from her—women as diverse as the actress Anna Cora
Mowatt, whom a romantic second marriage had brought to
Richmond as the wife of William Ritchie; Mrs. James Chesnut
of South Carolina, who as a young girl had strewn flowers in
Washington's path at Trenton on his way to the Presidency in
1789; Mary Morris Hamilton, grand-daughter of both Alexander
Hamilton and Robert Morris; and a grand-niece of Washington
who had married a nephew of Napoleon and was living on a
plantation in Florida.

Miss Cunningham was however no blind idealist, and she knew
that there would have to be masculine know-how somewhere
when it came to matters of publicity, which she shrank from,
finance, and legalities. Again she chose and got the best. Edward
Everett is not much remembered now, but in the 1850's a man
with his wide experience and gift of oratory could not fulfill all
the requests for his presence on lecture platforms before cultivated, enthusiastic audiences hungry for entertainment in a world
where theaters were scarce and dubious, transportation difficult,
and a new volume of Dickens read aloud to the family around
the lamp in the evenings was a treat. The professional lecturer
in those days held an enviable place in society, and Everett was
well qualified in the great tradition of Daniel Webster, with
many imitators to come, right down to Burton Holmes and his
travel talks. The London *Quarterly Review* in 1840 had described him as "one of the most remarkable men living," and in
his ready response to the Mount Vernon cause, his generosity, his
wisdom, and his willing labor, he became the rod and staff without which even Miss Cunningham must have failed.

Shall we go back to the beginning?

As everyone ought to know, George Washington died at Mount Vernon in 1799, and Martha followed him in 1802. He had had not quite three years at home after the end of his second term as President—during which time he had managed to repair in some degree the inevitable dilapidation which his absence from the estate always entailed, and to initiate some of the new projects which were always simmering in his mind, even in the middle of a war.

It is necessary to comprehend the feeling which Washington had for the home he cherished for more than forty years, and which may have compensated in a way for his childlessness. *Home* is an essentially English word. Many other languages are without its exact equivalent, even French, from which we borrow so many subtle shades of meaning. A house is not quite the same thing—as he demonstrated by calling the Mansion itself, in his *Diaries,* the Home House, and the acres which lay closest to it, the Home Farm. Washington was, in his blood and bones, all English. To him this plot of land on the west bank of the Potomac, and the simple white dwelling which crowned the green bluff overlooking the River, were the fairest he ever saw. Other men's houses had finer carved walnut staircases and panelled rooms, more impressive plasterwork ceilings and marble mantelpieces. But it is doubtful if any one of them moved him to anything like envy or desire.

His love for Mount Vernon, his pride in its every aspect, his affectionate attention to its smallest detail, are almost pathetically revealed in his writings and in his daily habits when he was at home. He carried in his head a map of its fields and farms, and at Valley Forge and Morristown in the terrible winters of the war he could find comfort in writing long letters to the man he had left in charge, requiring from him long letters in return to report how many lambs and colts had been born, how the fencing and hedging and harvest went, how the workmen progressed with repairs and additions, which slaves were ailing, what had been done about wells and necessaries. When he was at home he rode every day around the whole estate to see for himself, jack up the help, and on occasion take off his coat and work beside his men. He never stopped planning, improving, repairing, beautifying—cherishing—his place.

What the cost was to him in self-sacrifice and self-discipline when he left it again to undertake the Presidency after having already lost eight years to the war, can be seen in his letters too —and his touching jubilation when at last he got home again in 1797, with another ordeal ended. But he was sixty-five then, and he was always aware that the Washingtons were not a long-lived family. Mount Vernon's future must have lain heavy on his heart. The nieces and nephews and step-grandchildren who were always under his feet had proved with only a few exceptions to be disappointing liabilities. His favorite nephew, George Augustine Washington, son of his brother Charles, had married Martha's favorite niece, Fanny Bassett, and after a few years of failing health had died at the age of thirty, leaving four small children. Looking about the crowded field for an heir worthy of Mount Vernon, Washington chose another nephew, Bushrod, son of John Augustine, who was the best of his three brothers and closest to the General during all his life.

Bushrod, at the time Washington made his will in the summer of 1799, was thirty-seven, and had recently been appointed a Judge of the Supreme Court by President Adams. He had always been a studious, steady man, unlike some of his cousins, and was fond of music and "a temperate glass," according to his friend Horace Binney, who left a memoir. One thing must have troubled Washington as he made his decision. Bushrod was fourteen years married to Ann Blackburn of Rippon Lodge down the River— his wife was an invalid, and the marriage was childless. Mr. Binney has recorded that Judge Washington always adjourned court precisely at three o'clock, even if some one was in the middle of a sentence, and that he gave the following explanation one day as they walked away from the court together:

"The sound of that clock is as distinctly heard by Mrs. Washington at our lodgings as it is by us in the court-room; and if I am not in her parlor within five minutes afterwards, she imagines some evil has befallen me, and her nerves are disordered for the rest of the day. . . . I give the whole of the evening to reading aloud to her such books as will amuse and interest her, until drowsiness comes on. I look at neither book nor paper in the cause until the next morning, and then, by early hours, I endeavor to redeem the time."

Mrs. Washington's taste in reading matter is said to have been confined to innocuous novels, and her shattered health was laid to shock at the death of her sister, from which she had never recovered. Judge Washington's good-tempered connubial slavery endured for over forty years, and his death caused hers, before his funeral could take place. He had one brother, Corbin, who had married a daughter of Richard Henry Lee and died in the same year as George Washington, leaving three sons in Bushrod's care.

The General's will dispersed many of his belongings by bequests —his swords to his nephews, his writing-desk to his old friend Dr. Craik, his walking-sticks to the Chotank cousins, and so on. Martha's will three years later scattered the contents of the house still further, among her grandchildren, and the remainder was auctioned off for the benefit of the estate. Bushrod left it on record that in order to live at Mount Vernon in any kind of comfort, he and his wife had brought in some furnishings of their own, but his duties at the Court in Washington necessitated many absences. His ownership lasted twenty-seven years, embracing the war of 1812 and the sentimental pilgrimage to America of the aging Lafayette and his son in 1824. Bushrod was always over-generous with souvenirs, and gave away many priceless papers and trinkets to his friends and visitors.

He left Mount Vernon to the second surviving son of his brother Corbin and Hannah Lee—named John Augustine for his grand-

father—who was then thirty-seven, married, and father of a
family. Owing to the early death of Corbin, when John A. was
seven, he and his elder brother had been brought up by their
Uncle Bushrod and were often at Mount Vernon during their
boyhood. When he was old enough John A. managed the place
during Bushrod's absences. He had however about 1820 built a
handsome house called Blakeley, near Charlestown, in what is
now West Virginia. Built of brick, with a white-columned portico
and a balustrade, it faced his brother's house, Claymont, across a
rolling valley.

Whether or not John A. anticipated his inheritance of Mount
Vernon, he now found it necessary to spend at least part of his
time at the Potomac house, while his brother (Bushrod II) remained undisturbed at Claymont. In this generation the two
Washington brothers had married Blackburn sisters, nieces of
Judge Washington's wife. John A. owned Mount Vernon only
three years, dying in 1832 at the age of forty. His elder son John A.
Jr. was then twelve, and Richard was ten. He left Mount Vernon
in his wife's hands, with a codicil providing for its purchase as a
public trust by Congress or the State of Virginia if desired—which
it was not.

So now began the long twilight of slow decay, under the
widow's tenure. Her source of income is doubtful. There must
have been some colored servants about the place, but skilled labor
for repairs and upkeep may have been beyond her means. Her
privacy was at the mercy of the steady stream of visitors who even
during General Washington's lifetime had regarded his home as
some sort of show place, or shrine, so that he once in exasperation
described it as resembling a tavern. It was not obligatory on the
current Mrs. Washington to provide meals and stabling for all the
strangers who came down from Washington City to see the home
and tomb of the first President, but the demands on her hospitality just by accredited visitors with introductions were heavy.

The prevailing magnetism of Mount Vernon is thought-provok-
ing. To be sure, it sheltered and then symbolized a beloved public

hero, an historical figure—it was fairly available from the capital city, though for a long time the roads to it were so bad that the water route was the only comfortable way to reach it—it was in itself a lovely sight, on its green bluff above the tranquil River— and the tomb is there. But is that all? It seems as though the house in its very fabric possessed some magic of its own, which enslaved first the heart of its master all his life, and then through the love and care he lavished on it drew to itself more love, more homage, even from strangers. For Washington, certainly, the house was nearly alive in the devotion it inspired in him. Something of that vitality seems to have endured. It lived again for Miss Cunningham, demanded and received her devotion. But in the years between, it was barely able to save itself for its destiny.

The widow Washington should not be blamed, supposedly. She was dependent on what inferior help she possessed while her sons were small. Being a Blackburn, with Virginia traditions behind her, she must have felt a responsibility, she must have recognized a daily deterioration before her eyes. A portrait of her, painted in the 1830's, shows a matronly woman in a widow's cap, surrounded by her three children and a nephew of her husband's, seated with a book in her lap.

In 1835 the greenhouse burned down, and with it the best lodging for servants—the greenhouse which was built with such anxious thought by George Washington in the easy days soon after the war, when he thought he had come home for good, before the Presidency began to loom. John A. Jr. was fifteen when the fire occurred, and it must have been a time of considerable excitement and distress. In 1837 his mother wrote to him, presumably from Blakeley, about repairs: "The portico and pavement round the House at Mount Vernon should be immediately laid —many of the flagstones are broken and much defaced—there are more than eno' to replace them in the Burnt Hothouse; the rubbish must be removed and have them carefully taken up."

In 1840, when John A. Jr. was twenty, and old enough to see for himself what ought to be done, Mount Vernon was visited by the French Minister, the Chevalier de Bacourt, who left a pitiless indictment:

"All is as shabby as possible; the park is grown over with weeds; the house tumbling down; everything dirty and in a miserable condition. The whole country ought to do something for a place which gratitude should make sacred in their eyes. It would cost very little to give this resting-place of General Washington the dignity which is due to it. He was the greatest man of the country, the only brilliant point in American history. The United States owe their existence and prosperity to his genius; and he lies forgotten amidst uncultivated bushes, and near his house, which will soon be in ruins!"

In 1846 a memorial was submitted to Congress by a group of politicians, asking the Government to purchase and preserve Mount Vernon. Attached to it was a statement that the descendants of Washington had for nearly half a century maintained the house and had been overrun by visitors to the tomb to the average annual number of 10,000, in spite of bad roads and lack of nearby inns. Mrs. Washington was asking $100,000 for 150 acres and some dilapidated buildings, including the Mansion and tomb— it was too much, of course, but the alternative, it was pointed out. was that the estate might fall into the hands of "some Turk or other foreigner, who would have the power to exact *tribute,* or levy a tax in the shape of admission *fees* on all persons visiting those consecrated grounds."

This project died of inanition, as the memorialists did not sufficiently bestir themselves in support of their convictions. Meanwhile, the Washington Monument in the city across the Potomac, begun two years later, remained an unfinished stump until 1876.

John A. Jr. at twenty-two married Eleanor Love Selden of Loudoun County and brought her to Mount Vernon, where all but one of their seven children would be born. His mother had given

Blakeley to his younger brother Richard when he turned twenty-one that year, but although John A. was the acknowledged heir to Mount Vernon she still retained it in her possession. About this time a passenger on one of the river steamers published an indignant account of the scene at the landing-place:

"On deck a bustling man, a photographer, was running hither and thither, calling in a loud voice to those who wished to have their pictures taken at the tomb of Washington, to follow him; leading the way ashore over the gang-plank to a tiny shanty built for his convenience near the old tomb. Negro boys clamorously cried their wares: 'Walking-sticks from the trees that Washington planted!'—while Negro women, carrying trays, vociferously offered their refreshments for sale. . . ."

It was said that the public carried off anything available for souvenirs, and wandered freely and intrusively about the grounds and the house, without regard for the family's feelings. The Washingtons got an agreement that the boat was to land passengers on only two days a week, and they received a percentage of each passenger's fare from the company. In the summer when the tourist traffic was heaviest they seem to have migrated back to Blakeley—one wonders who was left to cope with the public then —and it is not surprising that at least in their absence the Negroes sold souvenirs, and vandals chipped away the tomb and stole even a stair-post from the Mansion hall. There was at one time a gate across the bottom of the staircase to keep intruders from the bedrooms. The question naturally arises—were there no locks to the outer doors—no one responsible care-taker to stand guard at the tomb?

Finally the elder Mrs. Washington relinquished Mount Vernon into her son's care, though she had another three years to live. It was now 1852, and Miss Cunningham was only a year away.

John A. Jr. at thirty-two remains a dim and perplexing figure.

He had at this time four children, all girls, and some sort of law practice in Alexandria. Every impecunious gentleman seems to have had some sort of law practice somewhere. It is his apparent lifelong resignation to the status quo that is the riddle. There are photographs which show haycocks on the front lawn above the River, and bare, unfinished timbers propping up the piazza where some of the square white columns had failed—the piazza where Martha had dispensed tea from a little table set on the flagstones at the north end, where the breeze was, while the enchanted artist Latrobe from England sketched the young Nelly Custis in a classic gown and ringlets, posed against a pillar. And the rather ramshackle porch which Bushrod had built on to the south end in front of the covered way to the kitchen now needed paint and some work with a hammer and nails.

Inside the house—long stripped of Washington's desk and bed, Martha's writing-table and china, and Nelly's harpsichord—the Houdon bust remained, and the terrestrial globe ordered from London by Washington in 1789, and the key to the Bastille sent as a gift by Lafayette to his one-time general, still hanging in its glass case on the wall at the foot of the stairs where Washington had placed it. The more practical furnishings must have been odds and ends, from Bushrod's tenancy, from Blakeley, perhaps from Woodlawn a few miles down the road—that splendid brick house which Nelly had deserted more than ten years before to live at her son Lorenzo's place, Audley, near Winchester; perhaps even from Arlington, where George Washington Parke Custis, grandson to Martha, still lived at seventy-two in impoverished splendor and reflected glory. Mount Vernon was the poor relation now, wrapped in sorrow for its lost grandeur.

Degrading offers for its purchase by speculators as a recreation area, implying further exploitation and indignities, came in occasionally and were refused by John A. Jr. Half-hearted negotiations for its sale to the Federal Government or the State of Virginia were all abortive. The price had gone up. John A. Jr. wanted

$200,000, and seemed prepared to hold out for that, while the house fell apart around him.

At Christmas time in 1853 a letter arrived at Mount Vernon, addressed to Mrs. Washington, and signed Ann Pamela Cunningham. They had never even heard of her.

2

She was a South Carolina lady, no longer young, and like Elizabeth Moulton Barrett in England, who had only recently escaped from her father's bleak household in Wimpole Street by eloping with Robert Browning, she had been injured in girlhood by a fall from her horse. There would be for Ann Pamela Cunningham no masterful poet liberator, no miraculous recovery—but her legacy to the world is in its way comparable to the incandescent *Sonnets from the Portuguese* which had barely had time, in 1853, to cross the Atlantic.

Her home was Rosemonte in Laurens County, built of Saluda timber on the model of the ancestral mansion in England, and famous for its gardens. Her mother was related to the Pennsylvania Bird family, and to the Daltons of Alexandria—a woman of great beauty and "refinement." Her father was a South Carolinian— handsome, courtly, wealthy, and "vehement." She was the only daughter, educated by a governess and at fashionable boarding-schools in Columbia and Philadelphia, in the usual preparation for a brilliant social career and a suitable if not a romantic marriage. The riding accident caused a painful injury to her spine which was beyond the skill of local physicians, so she was taken to Philadelphia and placed in the care of Dr. Hugh Hodge, a surgeon specialist in women's diseases. He required a series of treatments which provided some relief and necessitated frequent sojourns in Philadelphia, but were far short of a cure.

During the autumn of 1853 her mother had again accompanied her to Philadelphia and established her in lodgings convenient to the routine with Dr. Hodge, with a Miss Campbell, who was an old friend, nearby for company. Mrs. Cunningham then returned

South for the winter, as was apparently their custom—travelling by boat down the Potomac and along the coast to Charleston, and thence via Columbia to Rosemonte—a journey which must always have been an ordeal for her invalid daughter. Writing back to Philadelphia to announce her safe arrival at home, she unwittingly lit the flame which was to burn so brightly for the rest of that daughter's life.

The steamboats plying up and down the Potomac maintained a tradition which was said to have been begun by a British naval officer when Washington City was occupied in 1814, and some of its public buildings set afire, including the President's house. Yet this hard-bitten Navy man, when sailing past Mount Vernon, apparently ordered the bell of his flagship to toll in respect for the tomb of the American general who less than a generation before had severed the colonies from the mother country, with which the new nation was again at war. Whoever did it first, the American boats now followed the custom of tolling their bells in salute to the late owner of the long white house on its green eminence above the River.

Aroused by the bell that winter night in 1853, Mrs. Cunningham had gone out on deck. The winter moon was bright—so bright that she fancied she could see by its light the signs of decay at Mount Vernon—shabby scattered huts and outhouses, shaggy undergrowth and broken trees, and the tumbledown wharf. She had spent much of her youth at Alexandria, and her maternal grandmother would have been of the generation of Daltons which was often at Mount Vernon in the General's lifetime, as mentioned in his *Diaries*. Having herself been born in the late 1770's, Louisa Cunningham might well have seen Washington in the streets of Alexandria, and been a visitor with her elders to Mount Vernon as a girl. Traditionally, her daughter Ann Pamela was taken there during her childhood, by which time Mrs. Cunningham, at least, would have noticed the progressive dilapidation, which was now brought to her mind again as she stood on the deck of the River steamer at the end of 1853.

"I was painfully distressed at the ruin and desolation of the home of Washington," she wrote to her daughter in that now historic letter, "and the thought passed through my mind: Why was it that the women of his country did not try to keep it in repair, if the men could not do it? It does seem such a blot on our country!"

According to Miss Campbell's reminiscences, she found Ann Pamela Cunningham already alight with purpose when she looked in for her daily visit to one whom she considered an almost hopeless invalid. Miss Cunningham had composed a letter to the editor of the *Charleston Mercury*, the most influential newspaper in the South, which she read aloud to her caller. It was addressed to "Ladies of the South," and it urged in naive enthusiasm very movingly expressed, "that by your combined efforts, in village and country town, and city, the means may be raised, from the mites of thousands of gentle hearts upon whom the name has yet a magic spell, which will suffice to secure and retain the home and grave as a sacred spot for all coming time!" It was signed, as became one who was herself a lady in every sense of the word, by the seemly anonymity, "A Southern Matron."

Miss Campbell pointed out with amusement that the writer was not a matron—to which Miss Cunningham replied that her mother was one, and that after all it was her mother's idea, and anyway she herself didn't want to be recognized as the writer.

The *Mercury* published the letter, which ran to two columns, on December 2d, 1853. Other papers, like the *Mobile Herald and Tribune,* copied it. The ladies of the South responded warmly. The crusade was on.

In mid-December Miss Cunningham composed the difficult letter to the resident mistress of Mount Vernon. She had heard, she wrote, that the estate was for sale—and the women of the South had undertaken to raise the money to buy it, if only the present owners would allow them sufficient time before closing a contract with some other purchaser—"When you reflect on the

rare nature of this enterprise and the results which must follow
its success, I trust Mr. Washington and yourself will not only
return a favorable answer to our appeal for time, but will determine in your hearts that no other shall be allowed to possess
Mount Vernon, not even Congress, should they apply at last—
until failure attends warmer hearts and purer patriots," she wrote.

The answer, which was delayed, was anything but favorable.
Mr. Washington wrote, for his wife, that he preferred not to sell
Mount Vernon except to the Federal Government or the State of
Virginia. But Miss Cunningham did not take this nor later re-
fusals as final, and somehow remained convinced that if the
purchase price was raised, no matter by whom, it would be
accepted.

Some time during the spring of 1854 the first meeting of what
was to become the Mount Vernon Ladies' Association took place
at a little church near Rosemonte. Mrs. Louisa (Bird) Cunningham presided, and headed the subscription list with $100. She was
later to deplore the demands made on her daughter's time and
strength by the project, but in the beginning she was a zealous
promoter of it.

Money actually began to come in, in spite of the discouraging
attitude of Mr. Washington. Years later, in May of 1866, in a
letter to a friend Miss Cunningham wrote an account of the four
years between her first appeal in the *Mercury* and the actual
signing of the Mount Vernon contract, which took place in
Richmond in April, 1858. Allowing for lapses of memory in the
interval, this remains the best guide to the long campaign which
took so much of her strength and determination.

"We published appeals and hammered away from December,
1853, till July, 1854," she wrote, "held meetings in Savannah,
Georgia, and Laurens, South Carolina—my own district; several
hundred dollars were subscribed. Collections were made in Augusta by Mrs. Eve. In July, I think, through friends I got up a
meeting in Richmond, Virginia, where a committee was formed

and Mrs. Ritchie (then a bride) made secretary of it. By this time editors north of the Potomac began to take notice; and some of my Northern friends made overtures to me to open the matter to the North and have it made national.

"Collections went on slowly because there was doubt of success and no organization, and though the 'Southern Matron' was known as the moving spirit she was like a myth. Nobody could give person or locality. I took care to send all letters I wrote under cover to Mrs. Eve to mail, to allow no clue, and announced publicly that all communications for the Southern Matron were to be sent to the committee at Augusta (Mrs. Eve being the committee); she did not wish her name out either. So little did I imagine that I would ever be caught. . . ."

Within four months of the original *Charleston Mercury* letter, a second appeal signed "Southern Matron" appeared in the *Washington Union*, and other papers. Her desire to avoid personal publicity, and the very feminine simplicity of the first conception —which was "simply to raise $200,000 and give it to Virginia to purchase and hold title" to two hundred acres of Mount Vernon property, including the Mansion and the tomb, "Virginia to keep it for a public resort, the ladies to have charge of it and adorn it if they could have the means"—had caused some bewilderment and uncertainty among more worldly-minded people who were willing and anxious to contribute if they knew where and how the funds were to be administrated.

The gallant editor of the *Mobile Herald and Tribune* had written a stirring article for his paper, which she now quoted in part in her second appeal:

"The purchase of Mount Vernon by women impresses me as a most admirable way to secure the property and set it solemnly apart to the guardianship of the hero's grave. The form of the tribute, hallowed by womanly affections and executed by womanly devotion, is the most fitting it can assume. There will be a *soul* in the thing that will be felt—a soul of life and love that will throb its own high thoughts into every pilgrim who wanders amid the shades of Mount Vernon."

At the same time he suggested some improvements in the original procedure, which Miss Cunningham willingly adopted and which she detailed in the *Union* letter. The organization would have a central head for each State—and to "prevent jealousy" as to where that central honor and power should reside, she specified that "to the place or person first evincing decided action, or issuing an address as its *avant courier*, there the ruling belongs. We are gratified to announce," the *Union* letter read, "that the cause we had the honor to present to you last December for your patriotic support is now exhibiting a life and vitality which bid us hope it will have the power at last to reach Mount Vernon. Three States are interested and proportionately active."

The three at this time were South Carolina, of course, Georgia, and Alabama. In Georgia, both Savannah and Augusta already had Mount Vernon Associations—the "first action" having taken place in Augusta by Mrs. William Eve, who was "cousin" to the Cunninghams by marriage, her father being a Georgia physician named Casey who had married Sarah Berrien of the New Jersey family in whose Princeton mansion, Rocky Hill, George Washington had passed the last endless-seeming months of waiting for the peace treaty which would release him from the army in 1783. The connection was a marriage between Mrs. Eve's aunt and Miss Cunningham's uncle—near enough in the South to be called "coz." She was three years younger than Miss Cunningham, and her first name was Philoclea. She is mentioned in Miss Cunningham's later summary of the whole Mount Vernon undertaking as having been her "first ally," when she herself had "only intended to pull the wires behind the scenes, and pass the cause on to others' hands when the public was fully aroused." She remained a faithful friend and counsellor throughout Miss Cunningham's lifetime, and her comfortable home at Augusta was always a welcome way-station on the long journeys between Philadelphia and Rosemonte.

Soon after the *Washington Union* letter appeared, Mrs. Eve published an appeal of her own, in May of 1854, deploring the evidence that Washington was being forgotten by the nation he had created: "Many of us claim, with pride, descent from those who bore arms under him, in our glorious Revolution. It is our greatest boast. This is America's patent of nobility. How can we forget?"

Among the outstanding contributions to the fund in these early years was that of Mrs. Tubman of Augusta, who during the first week after Mrs. Eve's published appeal sent in $300—in honor, she explained, of the State where she was born, the State where she was married, and the State where she now lived. By May of 1860, Augusta had given $3000, a sum equivalent to 25¢ for every man, woman, and child in the city.

At Richmond in July of 1854 the real record begins, with the Diary of Mrs. Susan Pellet, the widow of a Massachusetts doctor who since her husband's death in 1838 had conducted a select girls' school in the Virginia capital. She was now forty-seven, and an old friend of Miss Cunningham's, who had been her guest when visiting Richmond. As a consequence, Mrs. Pellet was one of the first Virginia ladies to respond. Conscious of history being made, she kept a brief journal of the proceedings, to supplement the Minutes kept by the secretary. And at Richmond, the extraordinary Anna Cora Mowatt Ritchie took, as was her custom, the center of the stage.

Before her marriage to the editor and publisher of the *Richmond Enquirer*, she had been for years an actress of international fame. Her somewhat baroque story begins with her birth at Bordeaux, France, three years after Miss Cunningham's at Rosemonte. Her father was Samuel Ogden, a New York merchant who had retreated to France after having "speculated unsuccessfully" in a South American adventure designed to free Venezuela from Spanish rule. Although he had suffered heavy financial losses, he soon established a profitable new connection with the French wine industry, and maintained his family of nine children in a late Renaissance chateau complete with terraces, gardens, and a grotto. Her mother was the daughter of Francis Lewis, one of the Signers of the Declaration of Independence. When Anna Cora, who was always called Lily by her family, was brought back to America at the age of six, she spoke better French than English.

A terrible voyage to New York, during which one of her brothers was washed overboard and the cabins were constantly deluged, was said to have begun the chronic bronchial and lung weakness which was her lifelong affliction. Her frequent illnesses provided opportunity for reading, writing, and study, and Lily became a brilliant scholar. Established in a comfortable home in Warren Street in New York, the family eventually stretched to fourteen, of whom Lily was the ninth. Their greatest amusement was always amateur theatricals, for which they had a full company, and at the chateau in France they had had a small theater where they performed everything from Shakespeare to their own original compositions, for their father's guests. Lily's first appearance there was at the age of four. At fourteen in New York she dramatized, staged, and acted in Voltaire's tragedy, *Alzire*, the scene of which was laid in Peru.

Her own life thereafter pursued a melodramatic course equal to anything in the plots she read or wrote. Still a schoolgirl, slender and pale, with chestnut hair and blue eyes, she had caught the attention of one of her elder sisters' callers, James Mowatt. He was twenty-eight, a lawyer of position and substance in New York. From the first day he saw her he became, as it were, possessed. He sent her books and flowers, corrected her writings, directed her reading, and the morning after the performance of *Alzire* he proposed marriage. Her first reaction was to run out of the room calling for her sister. The next day he put it in writing. Her father considered it a trifle premature, and advised waiting till Lily was seventeen. But within a few weeks Mowatt persuaded her to elope with him, in October, 1834. She was forgiven at home, and he bought her a charming little house at Flatbush, and her younger sister May came to live with them and keep her company.

Under Mowatt's guidance she continued to learn, and to stage concerts, readings, and *tableaux vivants* in her own home. A severe bronchial attack resulted in a long European tour for the sake of her health. While they were abroad Mowatt was stricken with a painful eye disease from which he never fully recovered. It destroyed his earning power, and speculation absorbed his resources, and after they returned to America the house at Flatbush had to be given up.

Their positions were now reversed. Necessity for funds turned Lily to the thing she did best, and she began to give professional readings, the first one taking place at Boston with a program which included Sir Walter Scott and *Woodman, Spare That Tree*. She was twenty-three, a touching young lady reduced by circumstance to display her talent in public. Her audiences forgave her, and applauded, though the *Ladies' Companion* denounced her for setting a precedent that would lead to the dissolution of homes, as other well-bred ladies began to offer "readings and recitations in the style of Mrs. Mowatt."

After a program at the Society Library in New York City she was approached by the manager of the Park Theater for an engagement as an actress, but this was considered socially quite impossible, and she refused. Over-use of her voice, her chronic weakness of the lungs, and nervous fatigue brought on a collapse, the first of many, and she turned to mesmerism, which worked a miraculous improvement, and for years to come she resorted to treatments of this kind to restore her strength. Mesmerism—Transcendentalism—Swedenborgism—she tried them all, and seemed to benefit from them.

During the periods of invalidism she now resorted to writing for publication, in the desperate drive to earn money. Her stories and essays appeared in *Godey's, Graham's,* and the *Ladies' Companion*. She wrote a novel called *The Fortune Hunter*, which won a $100 prize, and went on selling. She wrote a play called *Fashion*, the first American comedy of manners, which was produced at the Park Theater with brilliant success even among the critics— though Edgar Allan Poe was inclined to quibble, and said that it derived from *The School for Scandal*, of which he had a poor opinion anyway. *Fashion* had an unprecedented run for a new play, and the royalties all disappeared into Mowatt's debts.

In June, 1845, at twenty-six, after intensive coaching from her professional leading-man, she undertook to act at the Park Theater the role of Pauline in *The Lady of Lyons*, Bulwer-Lytton's shop-worn vehicle for every female star of the generation. She was an astounding hit—the critics, who had come to jeer, praised her "naturalness," her "rich, ringing voice," her grace of movement, her smile. She had achieved the impossible. An amateur, she bore comparison with Charlotte Cushman and Fanny Kemble.

Her career was launched by that début. An occasional misanthrope among the critics complained of her unorthodox methods—they said she moved about too much—they said she moved directly from upstage downstage, instead of on the more graceful diagonal—and she spoke hackneyed lines with new readings. The audiences loved her. Plagued by ill health, with the ailing Mowatt attempting to function as her manager, she trouped the country in a growing, murderous repertoire of plays—Boston, Charleston, Savannah, Mobile, Montgomery, New Orleans, Philadelphia, Buffalo, Baltimore—and westward to Cincinnati and St. Louis. She appeared in everything from her own play, *Fashion*, in which she detested her part, to *Romeo and Juliet*, besides a number of lesser vehicles which have now been forgotten.

In the autumn of 1846 she came to Richmond, where the widower of one of her many sisters resided as a school teacher. *Ingomar* was the play performed at Richmond, and except that its heroine, Parthenia, wore classic robes, the only account of it seems to be in her own *Autobiography*. "Somebody has laughingly called *Ingomar* a covert 'woman's rights drama,' " she wrote, and added that in the second act "she weaves a garland while she prattles to the savage, who is becoming Parthenia-ized as he watches her."

Present in the audience at Richmond was William Foushee Ritchie, whose father was the owner of the *Richmond Enquirer* and in some way acquainted with Lily's father, so that young Mr. Ritchie could with propriety make himself known to her. Like Mowatt more than ten years before, he had taken one look at Lily and become possessed. However, she was accompanied by a devoted husband, she was in the middle of a tour, she was at the high tide of her career, which would take her the following year to England. There she triumphed over the initial skepticism and hostility of the British professionals who had intended to freeze her performance, and won the admiration of Macready, the leading figure on the London stage at the time. He offered her a co-starring engagement in his company, but she had the courage—or the wit—to refuse, aware that the great tragic roles of Lady Macbeth and Queen Katherine in his repertoire were not suited to her limitations.

While she was in England, Shakespeare's birthplace at Stratford-on-Avon was rescued from public auction by an association hastily formed to save it as a national monument, and this made a lasting impression on the visiting American. Lily was convinced that in the rooms where great men had passed their daily lives "there still lingered vibrations through which lesser men with spirits properly attuned could strike contact with the yet living presences."

The London profits all went in an unfortunate business partnership, and Mowatt died there in February of 1851. Lily came home —to another triumph at Niblo's new theater in New York, and a winter tour like a royal progress. The first engagement of 1852 brought her back to Richmond, where her brother-in-law still lived—six years, since she had played Parthenia in a white gown and dazzled tall, red-haired young Mr. Ritchie.

It no doubt appeared to him providential that she had returned a widow, while he himself had never married. His father had now turned the *Enquirer* over to him and his brother. For the ten days of Lily's Richmond engagement Ritchie conducted a whirlwind campaign—love letters, flowers, gifts, and columns of praise in the newspaper. Lily could hardly have failed to be impressed, but the tour carried her on, to Baltimore, Washington, Providence, Boston —Ritchie followed her to Baltimore and Washington, and sent telegrams and gifts to meet her the rest of the way.

Such a headlong courtship had not passed unnoticed, and there were rumors of an engagement between them. Lily was thirty-four, and touring was always a tax on her strength. But she was accustomed to the life, and to her own earning power. To marry into Richmond society, to settle down, to take root, without money of her own—it must have been a hard choice, even though she could always go on writing, as Ritchie's wife.

When she reached New York in midsummer of 1852 he came there, but she sent him away, and embarked on another winter tour, during which she went down with malaria at New Orleans and collapsed in the middle of a performance of *The Stranger.* She was taken by boat to one of her married sisters in Philadelphia. Both Ritchie and her father rushed there, and conveyed her to her father's house on Long Island. During her convalescence she began to write her autobiography—Mowatt had often urged her to do so. Ritchie, who lingered at her bedside, read the chapters as they came from her pen, well qualified himself to praise or criticize, as Mowatt had always done. Once again he was forced to leave her and return alone to Richmond. *The Autobiography of an Actress* was published in the autumn of '53, and was an immediate success, commended for its candor, simplicity, and humor. Over a hundred years later, it is still a readable, ingratiating book.

Lily made one of her mysterious recoveries and was in "resplendent beauty" when in November of '53 she began what was announced as a farewell tour. The rumors of her impending marriage and retirement made the demand for seats so great that at Boston they had to be auctioned to the highest bidders. At

Cincinnati in April she caught her usual late winter cold, and the usual fatigue set in. For ten years she had travelled and performed with pitiless self-discipline. Mowatt was gone, she had neither his encouragement nor his dependence. She had not for years had a home, security, nor a consuming love like Ritchie's. By the time she reached her final benefit performance at Niblo's in New York the wedding had been set for the following month. Along with his triumph, Ritchie must have been almost as incredulous as any of them, that the event would actually take place.

The marriage of Anna Cora Mowatt to William Foushee Ritchie was a social milestone in the New York season of 1854. The ceremony was held at her father's house, and the press gave it considerable space. Among the guests were Senator Stephen A. Douglas, and five other members of Congress, and an ex-Cabinet member. There were six bridesmaids, and Lily wore white with a veil of Honiton lace, and the bridegroom's gift to her was a pearl necklace. It was the wedding the frightened fourteen-year-old girl, eloping with James Mowatt twenty years earlier, had had to forego. The Swedenborgian service was used, there was a band from New York, and "dancing and champagne until a late hour." The bridegroom's family was in mourning for his brother, and no member of it was present.

The Ritchies were not enormously wealthy, but they were comfortable, and William Foushee drew a salary as editor of the paper. He brought her home to a modest frame house on the outskirts of Richmond—Lily always called it "the cottage." His sister had married a Harrison of Brandon, where there was more style. No one in Richmond society had ever married an actress, and Lily at first was regarded with some suspicion that her friendly ways and her warm-hearted interest in good works were just another role she was playing among them. Ritchie was forty-one, and had been a confirmed bachelor with a bright eye for pretty women. People felt that some sorcery had been at work—and then succumbed to it themselves.

It is probable that Lily—she was called Cora now, in Richmond

—had heard about Miss Cunningham and the Mount Vernon Association before she came to Richmond in the summer of 1854 as Ritchie's bride. She had been on tour in the South at the time the Charleston and Mobile papers published the first "Southern Matron" letter. And she had never forgotten Stratford.

As editor of the *Enquirer*, Ritchie was also aware of Miss Cunningham's progress in her undertaking, and was doubtless already acquainted with her. According to Mrs. Pellet's journal, he was present, along with other gentlemen of distinction, including Governor Johnson, at the first Richmond meeting in July of '54, soon after arriving home with his wife. In November, Miss Cunningham published a circular letter to the ladies of Richmond, providing for a central Virginia committee for the Association, which had as its president the "Southern Matron," with a lady from each interested State as Honorable Members. It was not until the July meeting a year later, in 1855, that Mrs. Ritchie's name appeared in the Minutes as Virginia's Secretary.

Her acquaintance with Miss Cunningham—who was not present at that Richmond meeting—had begun with an impulsive letter addressed to her from Philadelphia in January of '55, after Miss Cunningham had read the *Autobiography*, lent to her by a friend. She had at once recognized in the writer of the book "the very mind and spirit and qualities so needed to carry to a triumphant end this or any other inspiring enterprise," she wrote—and she rejoiced to know that Mrs. Ritchie was already one of the Richmond committee. Mrs. Ritchie of course replied warmly, and an affectionate correspondence ensued, though they did not meet until the autumn of '55 when Mrs. Ritchie stopped in Philadelphia on her way back from a visit to her father on Long Island. By the following spring they were "Dearest Pamela" and "My dear Cora" to each other, in a friendship which was for years one of the most colorful and sustaining things in Miss Cunningham's circumscribed invalid life.

Money continued to dribble in, as difficulties multiplied. Mr. Washington remained impervious to blandishment by letter, and would give no satisfaction whatever about even entertaining the idea of selling Mount Vernon to a group of unkown women. The birth of his first son, named Lawrence in the Washington tradition, during the past year may have stiffened his resolve with the certainty of another male heir. The Pennsylvania Committee balked at Virginia's retaining even a nominal ownership of Mount Vernon, having supposed that the United States would hold title, but the Government could not own land in any State until the State ceded the title, which Virginia would not do. There was no alternative, Miss Cunningham explained to Pennsylvania, "unless by raising the money we could change Mr. Washington's mind and get the place ourselves!"

And so, apparently without blinking, she contemplated that staggering solution. Raise the money. Change Mr. Washington's mind. Possess Mount Vernon themselves. There was just one other small snag. The Association had no legal status, and so could not itself acquire property. It must first have a charter, and no organization of women had ever held a charter before. Mrs. Eve's uncle, Judge Berrien of Georgia, recently U.S. Senator, advised them to apply at once to the Virginia Legislature for a charter to the Association, which though the title had still to be vested in Virginia, should satisfy the sectional feeling in Pennsylvania and elsewhere in the North—and this was done.

But even Ann Pamela Cunningham must have realized sometimes, in the middle of the night, that without some gift from the gods, $200,000 was an impossible sum.

The gods therefore obliged, with Edward Everett.

3

He was sixty-one, with a distinguished public career and a recent bitter set-back behind him. Born in 1794, son of a Boston clergyman, his youth had been halcyon. The youngest of his class to enter Harvard—thirteen—he was a Phi Beta Kappa and a B.A. at seventeen, and entered the ministry. Two years later he became pastor of a fashionable Boston church—the brown-painted brick Unitarian Church in Brattle Street, which had served as barracks to the British in '75, and the night before the evacuation was struck by a cannon-ball, which on its reconstruction was left in the brickwork, so that Oliver Wendell Holmes wrote that it

> "Wore on its bosom, as a bride might do,
> The iron breast-pin that the British threw."

In an era of unbridled rhetoric Everett was soon famous for his sermons. "All his speech was music, and with such variety and invention that the ear was never tired"—but there are always carpers, and one of them said that he was "too rich for common use." At the end of 1814 a chair of Greek Literature was endowed at Harvard, including a two-year period of study in Europe as preparation—and they offered it to Everett. He found the idea irresistible, and left the church after only fourteen months, which caused some resentment there.

The war with England known as 1812 had just ended when he sailed, and the pilot who came aboard at Liverpool brought the news of Napoleon's escape from Elba. Everett was in London— in conversation with Lord Byron—when Waterloo was won, and he proceeded at once to the Continent. He spent two years at

Göttingen University, subsisting on six hours' sleep a night, while
his industry bore out his old Harvard nickname of Ever-at-it.
Having won the first diploma of Philosophy ever awarded to an
American at Göttingen, he wrote to Harvard asking for two more
years, which were granted. A winter in Paris, where he was received by everyone from Mme. de Staël to the Duchesse d'Angou-
lême, and from Lafayette to Louis XVIII, was followed by a
summer in England, after a rough Channel crossing—("There
was a lord, in the company, whose title afforded him so little
protection that he was much the sickest on board," Everett's
journal recorded. "There was soon, however, little room for in-
vidious comparisons. I succeeded by dint of peppermint lozenges,
in sustaining my stomach some time. . . .")

He spent enviable days as a member of Sir Walter Scott's household at Abbotsford—went back to the Continent and on through
Rome to Greece—(at last!)—to Constantinople, and via Hungary
to Vienna, Paris, London, and home. His first caller after his
somewhat belated arrival at Cambridge in the autumn of 1819
was his one-time schoolmaster, Daniel Webster. The young professor was twenty-five, and at once made his own Greek grammar
for the use of his students.

His energy continued to be colossal. In addition to his duties
at the College, he did a course of lectures on *Boston Antiquities*
—he took the editorship of the *North American Review*—he
wrote articles, and some poetry which became recitation classics,
such as *The Dirge of Alaric,* the Visigoth who plundered Rome
in 410 A.D. This was a favorite on school platforms for years to
come—

> "My course is run, my errand done,
> I go to him from whence I come,
> But never yet shall set the sun
> Of glory that adorns my name,
> And Roman hearts shall long be sick
> When men shall think of Alaric. . . ."

College life as a professor bored him, and he began to think
of studying law. He married the daughter of a well-to-do Boston
merchant, who settled a comfortable income on them, and made
it possible for Everett to buy his way out of Harvard by returning the advance for his years abroad. He went into Congress
under Webster's wing, and by 1835 he was Governor of Massachusetts, and in great demand as a speaker on public occasions—
it was about this time that Whittier unjustly called him "pomp-
ous."

After four terms as Governor he was defeated for a fifth, and
took his family abroad—an entourage, including five children
and a nurse. He rented a villa near Florence which had been
built by a de Medici—slept in the room where Lorenzo was said
to have died at the early age of forty-four—called on the exiled
Bonapartes—and became friends with the American sculptor
Horatio Greenough, who with his wife lived nearby and was
at work on a statue of George Washington commissioned for
the Capitol at Washington City.

While at Florence, Everett was appointed Minister to the
Court of St. James's, and proceeded to London. He took a house
in Grosvenor Place, and there his social circle was enriched by
Disraeli, Peel, Carlyle, Macauley, Wordsworth, and Sydney Smith.
He and Mrs. Everett made several memorable visits to Windsor
Castle as the guests of Queen Victoria and Prince Albert—card
games were not permitted, but in the evening the Queen gave out
pretty ivory letters to be put together into words. In 1846 he returned to Boston on the new Cunard steamship *Britannia,* after
more than five years abroad. Awaiting him was a unanimous
request from Harvard to accept the Presidency of the College.

He was reluctant; he knew better; life at Cambridge had been
irksome to him twenty-five years before, in the relative freedom
of a professorship, and student discipline had deteriorated since
then. "A man would be in a hornet's nest," he wrote prophetically.
But he was persuaded, and moved his family into Wadsworth
House, where the President always lived. Longfellow at thirty-

nine, ten years a member of the faculty, and at this moment at work on *Evangeline,* was happily established with his second wife in a large yellow-painted mansion with white pilasters, set in broad lawns running down towards the River Charles. Everett and his wife had spent their early married life there when it was an expensive boarding-house kept by the Widow Craigie, whose husband had made a fortune as apothecary-general to the Continental Army, and spent it all on lavish hospitality. Mrs. Craigie's charges were so excessive that she was known as Miriam the Profitess. But the yellow house was haloed by the fact that during the first winter of the Revolution, deserted by its Tory owner and confiscated, it had served as General Washington's headquarters.

Everett made an auspicious beginning on what was to prove his least successful undertaking. Ralph Waldo Emerson, a long-time admirer, was present at his Harvard inauguration, and wrote: "Nature has finished this man. He seems perfectly built, perfectly sound and whole; his eye, voice, hand exactly obey his thought. His quotations are a trifle trite, but saved by the beautiful modulation and falls of the recitation."

Harassment, confinement to uncongenial surroundings, and his habitual overwork soon told on Everett's health, and his wife's gave way entirely into years of invalidism. He was too formal, too reserved, and too easily annoyed to win the affection of the students. After three years he resigned again—to be succeeded by Jared Sparks—and retired into literary and family life, for despite his cold exterior he was a devoted and humorous father. His daughter Charlotte had married a Navy man and was living in Washington. "I enclose a note to Aunt Lucy," he wrote her in December, 1850. "As it contains a check, I will thank you not to do up your hair with it. . . ."

Ominous words were now being heard in the political world— secession—abolitionist—compromise—underground—and again, secession. Fillmore became President after Zachary Taylor's unexpected death—by exposure to a hot sun during the ceremonies at the laying of the cornerstone of the Washington Monument— and Fillmore signed the Fugitive Slave law, which raised more storm clouds. Drawn back to the public scene by his friendship with Daniel Webster, Everett succeeded him briefly as Secretary of State—a satisfaction quickly submerged in another failure as Senator from Massachusetts. Buffeted between extremists of both North and South, regarding secession as the supreme horror to be avoided at all costs, baffled and defeated, he retired once more into his study, while what seemed the probable break-up of the Union affected him like a nightmare. He became convinced that his work was all done, and that he would be henceforth a useless semi-invalid in a household already darkened by his wife's hope-less condition.

But he was still in demand as a speaker, for his platform presence was still an impressive memory to all who had heard him. In the autumn of 1855 he was invited by the Mercantile Library Association of Boston to appear as the first speaker of a new lecture course. He thought he wasn't interested, but various members of his large family were in a chronically insolvent state, and he needed money for them. Casting about in his mind for a subject, he recollected that 1856 was the centenary of George Washington's first visit to Boston as a young Virginia colonel with a mission to the British Governor Shirley. He offered to prepare a discourse on the character of Washington and deliver it on February 22d, and the Mercantile Library eagerly accepted.

The lines are drawing in.

His Washington oration lasted nearly two hours, and was a great success. Possibly a sample of this popular form of rhetoric is pertinent here. More people knew Everett by this one oration than by any other, and it provided him with a springboard to appeal for national unity in troubled times, a subject very close to his heart. He was not by any means a spur-of-the-moment speaker—he left nothing to inspiration. It was all written out

beforehand, as though for the printer. After careful study, he
relied on his memory for delivery. He always carried his manuscript on to the platform with him, and then never referred to
it. People complained sometimes that he was too perfect. It went
like this:

"A great and venerated character like that of Washington,
which commands the respect of an entire population, however
divided on other questions, is not an isolated fact in history to
be regarded with barren admiration—it is a dispensation of
Providence for good. It was well said by Mr. Jefferson in 1792,
writing to Washington to dissuade him from declining a second
nomination: 'North and South will hang together while they
have you to hang to.'

"Washington in the flesh is taken from us; we shall never behold him as our fathers did; but his memory remains, and I say
let us hang to his memory. Let us make a national festival and
holiday of his birthday; and ever, as the 22d of February returns,
let us remember, that while with these solemn and joyous rites
of observance we celebrate the great anniversary, our fellow-
citizens on the Hudson, on the Potomac, from the Southern
plains to the Western lakes are engaged in the same offices of
gratitude and love. Nor we, nor they alone—beyond the Ohio,
beyond the Mississippi, along that stupendous trail of immigra-
tion from East to West, which, bursting into States as it moves
westward, is already threading the Western prairies, swarming
through the portals of the Rocky Mountains and winding down
their slopes, the name and the memory of Washington on that
gracious night will travel with the silver queen of heaven through
sixty degrees of longitude, nor part company with her till she
walks in her brightness through the Golden Gate of California,
and passes serenely on to hold midnight court with her Australian stars. There, and there only, in barbarous archipelagos, as
yet untrodden by civilized man, the name of Washington is un-

known; and there, too, when they swarm with enlightened millions, new honors will be paid to his memory."

Let us hang to his memory. It needed to be said. It needs to be said now.

Word of the oration naturally spread. New Haven wanted to hear it, and New York, and Baltimore. Meanwhile he had seen in a newspaper an account of the Mount Vernon Association, when he was on the point of refusing an invitation to speak at the Richmond YMCA in favor of engagements nearer home. He wrote instead to a friend in Richmond suggesting that he might repeat his Washington lecture for the benefit of the fund.

The offer was passed on to Mrs. Ritchie, who wrote to Miss Cunningham in Philadelphia, and an invitation was sent to Mr. Everett by the Richmond Committee. He replied that it would give him great pleasure to accept, and remained their "obedient, faithful Servant, EDWARD EVERETT." The 19th of March was agreed on as a date, following his appearance at Baltimore.

So now Mount Vernon had laid claim to him. The strange partnership between the invalid spinster and the fading politician would begin.

Everett's journal establishes that on his way to the Baltimore and Richmond engagements he stopped in Philadelphia, where Miss Cunningham was undergoing treatment with Dr. Hodge, and their first meeting took place there on March 10th, 1856:

"I called very early on Miss Cunningham, the Southern Matron, who has been principally active in getting up the Ladies' Mount Vernon Association. She is a confirmed invalid and confined to her chamber; but by great mental energy has contrived with infinite embarrassment and disgusts to collect subscriptions to a large amount. Promised I would repeat the address in Philadelphia for the benefit of the fund.

"An invalid maiden lady seems the last person to manage a

difficult business affair, but I believe this poor little woman, dropping into the grave with a spinal complaint, has done all that has been done for the purchase of Mount Vernon."

Miss Cunningham was nearly twenty years from her grave, and he was on the threshold of a whole new career. They had work to do.

4

Miss Cunningham left her own account of that first meeting in Philadelphia, in her 1866 letter about the origin of the Association:

"Mr. Everett called to see me en route to Richmond," she wrote, "and the spirit moved me that day! I wondered at myself, when the excitement was over; but the end was gained. He consecrated that address from that moment to Mount Vernon! All was now prosperous. . . ."

The Mount Vernon crusade had become nation wide. The publicity it had already received in the newspapers swelled Everett's audiences, just as his Washington oration swelled the contributions to the fund. Moreover, the first two volumes of Washington Irving's popular *Life of Washington* had appeared in '55—he had been working at it off and on for years—and the third was due soon. Irving at seventy-three had been present at the delivery of the Washington oration in New York and was much moved by it. He had visited Mount Vernon as long ago as 1842, during the tenure of John A. Sr.'s widow, just before his departure for Spain as American Minister there, and he would himself contribute handsomely to the fund within a few months.

During the next three years Everett delivered his Washington address one hundred and twenty-nine times, travelling from Boston to Wilmington, North Carolina, westward to St. Louis, and northward to Detroit. The receipts, for he paid his own expenses and made no deductions, came to around $55,000.

Coincidence is frowned upon in works of fiction, as is inconsistency in the behavior of fictitious characters. History has no

37

such artificial inhibitions, and concocts coincidence with almost monotonous regularity, while as for inconsistency in human beings—who has escaped it?

Everett, the great recruit, arrived on cue in Richmond at a theatrical moment in Mount Vernon's story, just as the battle for the Association charter had come to a showdown. The necessary document had been drawn up and an influential member of the Virginia House, Mr. Langfitt, had promised to present the bill at the first opportunity. As Miss Cunningham remained confined to her room in Philadelphia, Mrs. Ritchie was in charge of the Richmond campaign, largely social, to break down the opposition in the Legislature. On February 29th she had written to Miss Cunningham:

"Now I must give you some scraps of good news.—I have been *electioneering,* and very successfully. Night before last I gave a musical soirée, and desired my husband to invite as many of the Senators and members of the Legislature as the house would hold. Our small but very expansive rooms were well crowded.— Everyone declared he had had a delightful evening. The music was excellent, and the supper good. Then came the grand *coup.* As the ladies began to retire, Mrs. Pellet commenced the subject with Governor Floyd, and I soon managed to make it general. Governor Floyd *pledged* himself to use his best endeavors to pass our bill *and at once*—so did all the other members and Senators present. After all the ladies had left, the gentlemen still remained and talked to me, and some were actually warmed into enthusiasm. . . ."

But by the middle of March, with the session moving to its close, no action had been taken, and the bill was always mysteriously bypassed. It was Mrs. Ritchie, well accustomed after her many years in the theater to dealing with masculine obtuseness in any form, who sparked the dramatic descent of some ladies of the Richmond committee—Mrs. Pellet, Mrs. Cabell, Mrs. Robinson, and herself—on the Governor and Mr. Langfitt as they finished their Sunday dinner at the Exchange Hotel. The Governor capitulated on the spot, the Speaker was routed out to give his consent, and Mr. Langfitt was promised the floor at eleven o'clock the following day to present the bill.

The delegation took to its separate carriages to alert all the other members of the Association in the city, and many of them assembled at Mrs. Pellet's on Monday, from where they proceeded in a body to the Capitol a little before eleven, and filed into the gallery. It was spring. One can picture the floating ribbons and the rustling flounces and the flowered bonnets, at a period when women's clothes were at their most impressive, and there was an astonished silence in the House, even before the Speaker's gavel fell. He made a courtly speech with reference to the ladies who had honored the Assembly with their presence, and asked if the gentlemen would set aside other business until the ladies' bill was attended to. Most of the replies were "Certainly, certainly," with a few murmurs of "Outrageous," which were ignored, and Mr. Langfitt spoke. Under the bright, attentive gaze of their militant womenfolk, the members gave their Ayes and Noes. There were only two dissenting votes.

The ladies then crossed, with an escort, to the Senate, which kept them waiting only a few minutes before the bill was again presented. One misguided soul got up and made a short speech, apparently in dissent—but nobody paid any attention to him, and he wilted into a unanimous vote. The Mount Vernon Ladies' Association was now incorporated.

"Victory! Victory! Beloved friend and fellow worker!" Mrs. Ritchie wrote to Miss Cunningham the same day. "Heaven smiles upon our efforts. I have just returned from the Capitol. Our bill has gloriously passed both Houses. But after what troubles— what exertions—*it has passed!* Think, think, imagine if you can, how we felt. I was perfectly overpowered with joy. Many of the members and senators talked to us, and assured us again and

again that the bill would never have passed but for the presence
of the ladies. Now, if I can collect myself, let me write of other
subjects.

"Mr. Everett arrives here today. My husband has just made his
toilet and gone to meet him, and will afterwards dine with him,
at the Governor's. I believe it is quite a large dinner party.

"The tickets are $1, and already there is a great demand. I
must close. I am very, very weary, but so happy. Mount Vernon
is secure—*is ours!* We may be sure of that. All praise and honor
be to you—"

Thus it was on the evening of that exciting day that Everett
delivered his Washington oration in Richmond—the first of the
hundred and twenty-nine performances whose receipts went bodily into the Mount Vernon fund.

Mrs. Ritchie's jubilation was premature. The charter had no
sooner been granted than Mr. Washington took exception to it,
and withdrew the estate from sale. Apparently the charter as
drawn seemed to him to provide loop-holes for political chicanery
—and by his written word he had no faith whatever in the ability
of the ladies to raise $200,000—and even if they could, it may
have hurt his pride to contemplate taking the money from
women. The enigma of John A. persists. At Mount Vernon he
lived uncomfortably in an unpainted house with a leaking roof
and sagging floors, its grounds fast becoming a wilderness—and
he allowed this national treasure to go on decaying under him
while he held out for his price, in the face of widespread public
criticism and chronic legislative indifference. Various charitable
explanations of his obstinate course have been devised—such as
the discouraging example of the unfinished stump of stone designed to be the Washington Monument, which had been at
least a suitably masculine enterprise, and was now apparently
abandoned for lack of funds and interest in its completion. He
had a large family to provide for, it is true—but $200,000 in 1856
was worth something like $800,000 nowadays, which seems some-

what excessive. Even Miss Cunningham failed to provide any
convincing apologia, even when she had made the journey from
Philadelphia to Mount Vernon herself, and after a fashion won
his friendship. This she would actually accomplish in June of the
same year, accompanied by a woman friend and a maid named
Grace.

Word had got round very quickly during the spring that Mount
Vernon was not for sale after all, and contributions dropped off.
Miss Cunningham refused to give up. They must simply change
his mind. Mrs. Ritchie was involved in domestic crises and poor
health—her marriage to the dynamic, demanding Ritchie was
not altogether a success, and her father, to whom she always remained unusually devoted, was not well, and she intended to
spend the summer with him in the North. But someone had to
do something.

Miss Cunningham wrote to Mr. Washington, proposing to
come to Mount Vernon, and asking that a chair be provided to
convey her from the steamer to the house, as it would be impossible for her to make the steep ascent on foot. It does not appear that at this time they had ever met, though her Alexandria
background provided mutual acquaintance, and her parents had
apparently known his wife's parents. Her account of the visit
leaves tantalizing gaps in the story, but it is all we have:

"Of course we could do nothing with the public when they
believed that Mr. Washington *would not sell!*" she wrote in
1866. "I proposed to Mrs. Ritchie to go to Mount Vernon and
charm the bear (as I thought him then.) She urged that *I* should
go; she was sure I should succeed. Mr. E[verett] coincided and
urged also. I had not for years been on a railroad. The motion
made me ill. I found I could get to Baltimore by canal boats, and
then the railroad ride would be short. Dr. H[odge] threatened
to put me in a strait jacket, but finally yielded.

"Mrs. Mitchell [a Philadelphia cousin] and Grace and I set
out. I was carried up to Mount Vernon in a chair, on an awful

hot day in June, 1856, after being very sick on the steamer—
saw the family, was received kindly—but all my arguments failed,
though Mr. Washington promised to meet me in Washington.
When I got to the wharf the boat had gone and left me! We
could just see it. I was put into a sail-boat and towed into the
stream, expecting to catch the mail-boat, but waited in vain.
When I got back to the bank I was nearly dead, but the moment
I saw I was left, I said *Mount Vernon is ours!!* I was just as sure
in my heart as if we had it then!

"I lay in my room till evening, and was carried down to the
parlor at night. I couldn't walk then, up or down a step. I talked
pleasantly, telling of various incidents connected with Mr. Everett
and his Washington lecture, and enlightened the family in a
roundabout way as to our proceedings and the interest felt. I
could see their amazement. It was a side of the shield they had
not seen, and I saw I had gained *Mrs.* Washington, and I hoped
she would give a caudle lecture. I shook hands with Mr. Washington and told him it was leap-year, woman was bound to have her
way, he might resist with all his might, but I knew I was to be
the victor, and must counsel him to follow the example of his
illustrious ancestor, who never acted upon a grave affair without
having slept on it.

"Next morning we had a regular talk. The spirit moved me
as it never had before, never has since, and never will again. I
never spoke to mortal as I spoke to him. I told him that the Isles
of the Sea would send up their tributes for Mount Vernon—that
he would live to see it, though I would not. (We both did! For
Havana and the Sandwich Islands sent us contributions!)

"When I saw I could not shake his resolution not to let Virginia have a chance to buy Mount Vernon, for he was very indignant at that, and considered it would be mean in Virginia to
accept the purchase money—I went so far as to point out to him
the light in which coming generations would view his conduct
in preventing our tribute to Washington. I told him his descendants would mourn having descended from him, and I dared say

these things because I felt that I, by starting this movement, had
been instrumental in placing him in this unpleasant position. He
thanked me—said he knew it—but he was firm as a rock, though
he was deeply moved.

"The carriage was waiting—and I had to go—the cause was
lost! I turned to him mournfully, expressed my grief, but that I
could not leave him without putting myself in proper position.
I told him I knew the public had behaved abominably toward
him—that the Virginia Legislature had done so in framing a
charter contrary to the terms he had expressed himself willing
to accept—that as soon as I saw the charter, I realized it was not
what would be agreeable to him. I consulted a lawyer in Philadelphia, got him to mark out such alterations as would make it
comply with Mr. Washington's terms, and immediately wrote to
this effect to the Chairman of the Mount Vernon Committee and
begged he would make the alterations, but they seemed to pass
it over his head (to quote their own words.) I assured him I believed all the ladies concerned felt as I did—while we wished to
succeed in our beautiful tribute, we were grieved that his feelings
had been so repeatedly insulted because of it.

"I looked up to him as I said this. What a change in his face!
Unawares, I had at last touched the sore spot, the obstacle no
money could have removed. I now found that he believed the
whole thing had been arranged between the Association and
Virginia to put an indignity upon him!! His feelings were
wounded, goaded, and lo! in explaining my feelings I had shown
him his error! I then told him if he would consent to overcome
minor objections that I would prove to the country what were
the feelings of the Association by going before the Legislature
and asking it to make every change he required—but he must
let the Association pay the money and not feel that his State or
himself were lowered by the act. I held out my hand, he put his
in mine. Then, with quivering lips, moist eyes, and a heart too
full for him to speak, our compact was closed in silence. His
little son was brought to me; a lock of hair was clipped for me.

I started at eleven o'clock—the day was awfully hot. I nearly died
from the heat before I got to Alexandria; every breath was a
groan for two miles. The heat *stunned* me, like the pricking of
millions of pins! None but God can know the mental labor and
physical suffering that Mount Vernon has cost me!"

Only Miss Cunningham could have drawn so vivid a picture
of that momentous interview between the sensitive, touchy, defeated man and the valiant woman expending every ounce of her
strength on her unalterable purpose. After a perilous landing at
the crumbling wharf, she had been *carried* up past the tomb to
the house—by whom?—in the heavy riverside heat. On the way
she had seen the uncut lawns, the choked shrubbery, the rickety
south porch added by Judge Bushrod, the sway-back piazza
propped up with timbers—inside, the rooms were shabby and
run down. She had been confronted by the family—John A.,
bearded, defensive, coldly courteous to what he doubtless considered an extremely tiresome visitor—his wife, now about thirty,
with smooth, straight hair parted and banded over her ears and
rolled into a neat knot behind, chiseled eyelids, and a thin, un-
humorous mouth—their six children, the eldest girl twelve, the
youngest a baby—the only boy, now two years old. They must
have offered her refreshments, in the heat.

She had come back from the sail-boat experience so obviously
shaken that they apparently repented of the inhospitality which
had allowed her to attempt it, and in the circumstances they
could only ask her, and Mrs. Mitchell and Grace, to stay the
night. She was shown to a bedroom where she rested till evening,
when she had gathered sufficient strength to charm them with
stories, bringing surprise and laughter into their somewhat cheer-
less lives. *Mrs.* Washington began to thaw—and perhaps when
they had all retired for the night she did question her husband's
decision, as Miss Cunningham hoped, but without changing it.
(The expression, "caudle lecture," so casually used by her, derived
from a character created for *Punch* in a series of humorous

sketches by Douglas William Jerrold, and published in book
form in 1846. Mrs. Caudle was a voluble scold, whose curtain-
lectures addressed to her long-suffering husband when he wanted
to go to sleep, were lengthy exhortations on his faults and obligations.)

The next morning they provided a carriage to take her to
Alexandria, aware that she had had enough of the boat. She
tried again, probably at the breakfast table—but John A. was
submerged in his own doubts and obstinacy and some hidden,
inarticulate grievance, until out of her own disappointment she
had been inspired to sympathize with *him*. Public comment on
his behavior had certainly not been kind, either as to the condition he had allowed the place to come to, the price he was asking,
or the difficulties he made about selling. She looked *up* at him,
she remembered, years later—she was frail and feminine and
sorry—she promised she would have the charter changed to suit
him, she agreed that it was not what he wanted—he seemed to
melt, he took her hand. But remember, he did not speak. Within
a few months he would backslide, and make another attempt to
get the State to purchase the house, independently of the Association. Again the State refused to take an interest, and the Association still refused to be discouraged. It is difficult to see where he
preferred the money to come from and why—except that the
Association was female.

There were further more or less fruitless interviews and some
correspondence during that summer, while she was at Willard's
Hotel in Washington with her parents, and after she had retreated to Cape May to recover at the seaside from the exhaustion
and frustration of her Mount Vernon visit. She got from him in
this way some further indication of his objections to the charter
as drawn, and his requirements for a new one.

Mrs. Ritchie went to Mount Vernon in July, but he escaped
her more experienced persuasiveness by being absent. Mr. Ritchie
wrote to him from Richmond, with the weight of the *Enquirer*
behind the letter, and received a chilly reply, in which Mr. Wash-

ington expressed his conviction that after "a period of languid mismanagement" by the Association the estate was sure to fall into the possession of Virginia anyhow, by forfeiture of the charter, which would entail a no doubt unpleasant altercation—and that even if they did find the purchase price, the Association would never be able to raise the additional sum required annually for the maintenance of the place—for to suppose, wrote Mr. Washington, that the small admission fees would ever produce enough for that purpose was "simply preposterous."

5

"Our position was painful," Miss Cunningham would recall. "The public felt itself deceived—was not willing to give without a surety. Our first charter made payment of Mr. W. depend on the success of the Association. Mr. W. required that *Virginia* pay him. (I found it hard work to get him to consent to Virginia doing so)—how were we to get Virginia to do this for us—risk her chance of being paid unless we had enough money beforehand to justify her confidence? The North behaved very ungenerously in this extremity. After having asked to join the work, she now refused to give a dollar until she was sure Mount Vernon would be sold, and she could not gain this surety but by having the money given to us. The South, then, with the aid of Mr. Everett, won the battle. . . .

"Well! With stout hearts we set to work. I had been removed on an air-bed from Philadelphia to Charleston in October, '56. In March, '57, we began. I had enlisted enthusiastically an influential gentleman in Charleston, whose glowing 'appeals' in the *Courier* (which I broadcast all over the South) did us infinite good. William L. Yancey took up our cause in Alabama. Wherever his law practice carried him, he spoke for us; took up collections. Thus was raised $1500 in a short time. We started interest again in Virginia, North Carolina, South Carolina, Georgia, Tennessee, and Alabama, but it took time. Old Charleston City awoke, and on the 4th of July her noblest citizens formed a band to relieve each other by turns and remained in the City Hall all day to receive contributions. I was proud. Meanwhile, I had overworked, and Dr. G. told my father I must die unless I gave up working. But the ball was now rolling, the action of Charleston had started the country, and I could take a rest, as we had high

47

hopes of going on swimmingly in the autumn; Mr. W. had declared that the matter must be decided at the meeting of the next Legislature [1858] so you see we were under whip and spur, especially after the course the North took. . . ."

Tennessee and Alabama brought two more unusual women into the field of endeavor. Mrs. Francis Fogg at Nashville issued a stirring address to "Sons and Daughters of Tennessee!" and collected $200 in two days. "I know some rich old codgers in this town," she wrote, "who have no children or are bachelors, and whose State pride shall be worked on by every argument, and whose purses shall be tapped by the finger of skill till they are exalted to a higher position in the scale!" Miss Cunningham's return to Charleston may have led to this appointment, as Mrs. Fogg was a South Carolina Rutledge, the grand-daughter of Edward, and of Arthur Middleton, both of whom had signed the Declaration of Independence.

Her father was Henry Rutledge, who inherited the 75,000 acres of western land granted to Edward by the Government for services rendered, and he married Septima Sexta Middleton—who had a sister named Emma Philadelphia—daughters of the magnificent Arthur of Middleton Place, outside Charleston. Henry settled with his bride at Janesse on the Ashley River, two miles above his father-in-law's estate, and their daughter Mary was born there in 1801. Some time during her childhood her father moved the family, bag and baggage and slaves, to Tennessee, transporting the family silver, portraits, library, wardrobe, and Mrs. Rutledge's harp, in an impressive cavalcade which ended at a log house on the Duck River, where he established a new estate called Chillhowie—erecting a boarded, painted mansion whose interior had all the elegance of mahogany, candlelight, crystal, silk gowns, and music its mistress had known in the Low Country. She even required that on one day of the week nothing but French would be spoken, so that her children would not forget the training they had received from their tutor, a Mr. Willing of Philadelphia. Her daughter's education ended there, but one of her sons attended the University of Nashville, and the other went to West Point.

In 1824, when Ann Pamela Cunningham was eight years old, Mary Rutledge married Francis Brinley Fogg, who had come to Tennessee a few years earlier from Brooklyn, Connecticut. He was the devout son of an Episcopalian minister, and an authority on canon law. As his wife, Mary Middleton Rutledge Fogg was always active in local charities and parish affairs, and wrote a book for young people on the catechism. She was a tall, handsome woman, taller than her husband, and her portrait shows an elaborate headdress with a turban and tassels. Of her three children, the eldest son died in 1848, on the eve of his marriage, and her only daughter died three years later at twenty-three. Mrs. Fogg turned to poetry to express her grief, and also wrote a novel called *Mary Ashton, or the Beauty and Triumph of Christian Principle,* in the "Elsie books" tradition of blue-eyed innocence and virtue sorely tried.

During a tour of the country in 1829 Edward Everett had spoken at a banquet given in his honor at Nashville, and had doubtless met the Foggs at that time. Since then they had travelled in New England, and Everett had in his library two of her books inscribed to him. This friendship was probably also a factor in Miss Cunningham's choice of the Vice-Regent for Tennessee, and at their invitation he delivered his Washington address at the Tennessee State Capitol—under what was believed to be the largest chandelier in the world.

Mrs. Fogg would now have been fifty-six years old, and on the way to becoming the character described by one who knew her in later years when she had "snowy curls" and arrived at church always carrying a black silk bag of keys, the mark of a good housekeeper, which clanked as she set it down in the pew. She was accustomed to make audible corrections and comment if the rector read out her Parish Aid announcements wrong, and her clear, strong voice soared away from the choir in her own rendition of the hymns.

During the war which was so soon to come, Mrs. Fogg would lose her only surviving son, who volunteered on the Confederate side, with which his Connecticut-born father was not in sympathy, and died at thirty-one in a skirmish on the Cumberland River. Unbroken by repeated family tragedy, Mrs. Fogg adopted a niece to bring youth into the house on Church Street with its box-garden and well furnished library, did valiant service in the Nashville hospitals among the sick and wounded, and was still writing books at the age of seventy.

Alabama was represented by Octavia Walton LeVert, whose grandfather, George Walton, also signed the Declaration of Independence, went out to get into the fight, and was wounded and taken prisoner at the fall of Savannah in 1778. He was later Governor of Georgia, and she was born at the family estate, Meadow Garden, outside Augusta, about 1810. She wrote in later life that her first remembrance was of the devotion of all around her—that contradiction was never breathed to any of her words, while praise was lavished on her every action. "Even while decked in her little white apron, lovers came thronging to her," said her reminiscences, written in the third person and not for publication. An unkind word never met her. By some fortunate quirk of character, this wholesale adoration roused in her a resolution to be worthy of it, and inspired her to long hours of study and serious thought "too deep for one of her sex."

Mother and grandmother together, full of family pride, determined that their treasure should be known as the greatest belle of them all. But a reverse in her father's fortunes caused him to remove his family in the early 1820's to Pensacola, Florida, where he was appointed territorial agent and acting governor, and young Octavia became the admiration of the cosmopolitan naval base there.

Educated by those two great ladies, her mother and grandmother, and an old Scotch tutor, she learned "the humanities"—grammar, rhetoric, and poetry, with Greek and Latin—and when she was twelve spoke French and Spanish by daily custom so well that she was often sent for to translate at her father's office, and by further study she acquired German and Italian. An old Seminole Indian became attached to her, calling her "the white dove of peace," and must have added to her collection of languages—for when she was asked to suggest a name for the new capital city she christened it Tallahassee, a Creek Indian word meaning Old Town, as the chosen site was that of a former mission town. She was presented to Lafayette at Mobile during his 1824 tour of America, substituting at fourteen for her mother, who was too ill to appear; and he predicted for her a brilliant future, remarking that she had conversed with him "with intelligence and tact in the purest French."

While still in her teens she was taken to the fashionable Virginia Springs, where her talent with a guitar and the Spanish love songs picked up at Pensacola turned the heads of the gentlemen. In 1827 at Baltimore she encountered Edgar Allan Poe, only a year older than herself, though his first volume of poems, called *Tamerlane,* was published that year. Young Mr. Poe was no exception, and wrote in her album a sentimental verse which ended—

> "But Octavia do not strive to rob
> My heart of all that soothes its pain,
> The mournful hope that every throb
> Will make it break for thee!"

It was 1833 and she had turned twenty before the family finances permitted Octavia's début in Washington and her entrance into Eastern society. Escorted by her mother and brother, she somewhere travelled in the same stage-coach with Washington Irving, then in his charming fifties and recently returned from seventeen years abroad, three of them as attaché to the American

Legation at Madrid, where the American Minister was Alexander
Everett, elder brother of Edward. Already a celebrity for many
years, and having recently published his *Alhambra* and *Tales of
a Traveller,* Irving had begun to think of the *Life of Washington*
which was to occupy him off and on for another twenty years,
and meanwhile was acquainting himself with his native land,
much as Everett had done nearly ten years before. The immediate
result of this journey was Irving's *Tour of the Prairies,* and a
correspondence with Miss Walton. She visited him at Sunnyside
more than once—that tiny castle he had built on the east bank
of the Hudson—her first visit possibly occurring after her sojourn
at Saratoga later that same year of '33, and the last probably during another tour of the North shortly before the Civil War began.
Irving, who was certainly a qualified judge, pronounced her "such
a woman as occurs but once in the course of an empire."

In Washington that winter, she sat each day in the gallery at
Congress, taking notes in her journal while Clay, Webster, and
Calhoun debated President Jackson's unpopular policies, and she
was highly regarded by all of them as a reporter. She was painted
by Thomas Sully, wearing a rose pink silk gown and accompanied
by her guitar—being listed in his register as "Miss Walton of
Pensacola." This portrait, taken twenty years before she became
a Vice-Regent, is ample evidence for her lifelong reputation for
irresistible charm. And when the Washington season ended and
she went on to Saratoga and Newport, a smitten society reporter
wound up his account: "She floats through the rooms, with a
radiant smile for her acquaintances. . . . We do involuntary
homage to those matchless powers, such as in other lands made
the undying fame of a de Staël, a de Genlis, or a Maintenon. At
the same time, the grace and high-bred manner in which she
receives homage remove her as far from the hackneyed everyday
belle as the stars are above the earth." It would go on like that,
at home and abroad, for another thirty years.

Soon after her return to Pensacola, the family moved to Mobile,

ANN PAMELA CUNNINGHAM. Founder and first Regent of the
Mount Vernon Ladies' Association. From a portrait by Stolle.

Mount Vernon As It Appeared Just Before the Civil War. From a photograph taken at that time.

"Mount Vernon Is Ours." With the summer temperature in the high 90's, the line of patient people waiting to go through the mansion stretches from the door back to the gate. From a photograph taken by the author in June, 1964.

THE GREENHOUSE. The ruins of Washington's building as sketched by Benson Lossing in the 1850's. And the reconstruction by the Association, completed in the 1940's after a careful study of the physical and documentary evidence.

JOHN AUGUSTINE WASHINGTON, JR. Last private owner of Mount Vernon.

EDWARD EVERETT. From a crayon portrait by R. M. Staigg, made about 1850.

"The Gorgeous Mrs. Ritchie," about 1860. First vice-regent for Virginia.

Miss Mary Morris Hamilton. First vice-regent for New York.

Left: Mme. Octavia Walton Levert. First vice-regent for Alabama. From a portrait by Thomas Sully made about 1833. Courtesy the Walton-LeVert Collection, Mobile. *Right:* Mrs. J. Scott Laughton. (Lily Macalester, Mme. Berghmans.) First vice-regent for Pennsylvania, second Regent.

Miss Sarah Tracy. First secretary, 1859–1868.

New York
Nov 1st 1860

My dear Miss Cunningham,

I am so tired that I can scarcely guide my pen, but neverthe-less, if you will put on your patient spectacles and remember that you often receive & harrowing looking documents from me, I will try to tell you all the news I can, & my doings and Miss Hamilton's doings — In the first place, I saw Mrs Frank D. Goodwin who informed me that Mrs Mary B. L— left early Saturday morning for Connecticut, so my advisers were reduced to this Hamilton, but so you rely so much on her judgment, I kept my

MISS TRACY TO MISS CUNNNINGHAM, from New York, November 1, 1860. It is mainly from letters like this one that the story of the Mount Vernon Ladies' Association has been reconstructed.

UNION SOLDIERS AT MOUNT VERNON. From the *New York Illustrated News,* December 16, 1861.

where she became acquainted with the young French surgeon whom she married in 1836. Henry LeVert must have been an unusual man, to capture the darling of so many rivals. His father had come to America with Lafayette in 1777, and had acted as surgeon to Rochambeau at Yorktown. After the war he married and settled in America, and when he died his widow and two sons made their home in Mobile. Young Mme. LeVert's "Mondays" were soon famous, the nearest thing to a *salon* America had ever seen. During the Mobile Season, she received in a white and gold drawing-room in an elegant house in Government Street from 11 A.M. till 11 P.M., and the élite from all over the South as well as from abroad flocked there to admire and to pay their respects to one of the most attractive bluestockings of her day. Again the press went into raptures— "The walls of the principal drawing-room, adorned by portraits of distinguished persons, were wreathed with garlands of rich flowers then in luxuriant blossom; and in the midst of the roses stood the accomplished lady receiving her guests. What sculptured beauty in that rounded form! Her face is Madonna-like, brown waves of hair parting from a broad, high forehead; her eyes are blue, and seem to melt with thought, and her chiseled lips are tinted like a delicate sea shell. She has made you think just by her manner and her few felicitous words, that you are the very being she is most delighted to see. . . ."

And that, of course, was the magic.

Among her visitors was that passionate traveller, the widowed Lady Emmeline Stuart-Wortley, second daughter to the Duke of Rutland, accompanied by her twelve-year-old daughter Victoria, who was supposed to be "delicate." They were nevertheless on their way to Mexico and Peru, and arrived in Mobile from New Orleans in time for New Year's Day of 1850. While waiting for the steamer which would take them to Vera Cruz, they were the guests of Mme. LeVert, whom Lady Emmeline thought "one of the most delightful people in the world." They had, of course, a mutual friend in Edward Everett. In the inevitable book describing her travels, Lady Emmeline recorded her enjoyment of the carriage drives around Mobile, with her hostess's black coachman on the box, and a little black page boy riding behind—through tall magnolia groves whose branches dipped almost to the blue water of the Bay, past bowers of Cherokee roses and picturesque Indian *chumpa* girls with their loads of pine wood, to visit the Choctaw camp where young Victoria made sketches of the flattered Indian remnants of a once great tribe, who donned pathetic finery to pose for her.

The hospitality Mme. LeVert bestowed on Lady Emmeline was amply returned when she herself went abroad in 1853, accompanied by her father, her young daughter Octavia, and a devoted colored maid, Betsy; she went again in 1855, when her husband attended her, as she was then the accredited representative of Alabama to the Paris Exhibition. One always marvels at the sheer mileage accomplished by these indefatigable travellers of the mid-eighteen hundreds. Mme. LeVert had now turned forty, and she wore the cumbersome women's costume of the period, when dresses weighed a considerable poundage and were tightly laced. Yet she travelled by steamer, railway, diligence, ferry-boat, and even ox-team, through England, France, Germany, Switzerland, Italy, and Spain, and never did her interest or her spirits—or her health—appear to flag. Returning home for the second time in the autumn of 1855, she wrote two engaging little volumes about her experiences—Lamartine in Paris had urged her to do so—which were published in 1857. "I have received the copy of your work, which has made me once more your fellow traveller," Washington Irving's acknowledgment began. "A veteran cosmopolitan as I am, I have well been able to keep you company on your European travels; but as I read your bright and sparkling narrative, and see what a continual fairyland your buoyant spirits and happy temper spread around you, I feel how greatly you have the advantage of me in catching the most favorable view of every picture. . . ."

It is difficult to choose only a few passages from Mme. LeVert's *Souvenirs* for repetition, so lively, so good-natured, and so vivid are they. She carried, of course, innumerable letters of introduction, which were generously responded to, and she would have been a most rewarding guest. At the further risk of too long a pause, consider for a few minutes what it was to be a well-connected American lady of means on a European tour a hundred years ago.

In London, Rachel was appearing at the St. James's Theater —she would not permit an orchestra to distract the attention of the audience from her performance, even in the intervals. "The tones of her voice are exquisitely musical," wrote Mme. LeVert, "and the utterance of *one word* seemed the revelation of the whole scene." Lady Emmeline's mam*ma,* the Duchess of Rutland, invited Mme. LeVert to the family seat at Belvoir Castle, and to social evenings in London where she met Disraeli, now turning fifty and recently Chancellor of the Exchequer, and was charmed with his conversation. Queen Victoria sent her a card to a State ball, obviating the formality of a presentation, a most unusual honor. While making her curtsey there to the Queen, Mme. LeVert found her much handsomer than her portraits— "There is such an air of honest, earnest goodness about her," she wrote, "a genial manner, so lovely and so lovable. . . . She looks exceedingly young. No one would suppose her to be the mother of eight children." Prince Albert was in uniform, with a slung jacket and Orders, and very graceful in the dance.

At Paris, when asked what the products of Alabama were, "I can but point to Octavia," she recorded, with a mother's pride. After Paris and Brussels they visited the Field of Waterloo in a stage-coach, besieged by beggars and guides, and walked for several miles, following the course of the battle. "The growth of wheat, the guide told me, was particularly luxuriant over the places where the bodies of the soldiers were buried," she recalled. They went down the Rhine by steamer, past Coblenz with its fairytale castles, and Bingen, where she did not overlook the opportunity to quote Caroline Norton's lachrymose poem in full—

"I dreamed I stood with *her,* and saw the yellow sunlight shine
On the vine-clad hills of Bingen—fair Bingen on the Rhine—"

thence to Mannheim, where they left the steamer—to Baden-Baden, where she saw for the first time the febrile fascination of the gambling-rooms—to Strasbourg, Basle, and back to Paris, in time for the fête-day of the Emperor, Napoleon III. "The Empress is a beautiful, fair, delicate woman, with an expression of exquisite sweetness and genial kindness. She was attired in a dress of India muslin covered with fleecy clouds of Brussels lace, and a bonnet of white adorned with roses and buds," she noted.

It was on the second tour that from Geneva, via the Castle of Chillon—not, we may be sure, without some one chanting Byron's imperishable "My hair is grey, but not with years"—they crossed the Simplon in a horse-drawn diligence, through the galleries and under the water-falls to Italy. At Verona, the legendary House of the Capulets was found to be a wretched little inn, and the Mansion of the Montagues was a lodging-place for donkey-drivers. At the Venice customs house the Austrian inspectors read every note and hotel bill, shook out every dress and petticoat, unrolled the stockings, felt in the fingers of the gloves—for what?—and took down the statistics of every member of the party, including Betsy, who was styled by them, to her indignation, a Moor. Mme. LeVert noticed with disapproval that there were *omnibus*-gondolas, but was mollified when the party was serenaded that night by floating musicians with a guitar.

At Florence she spent an evening with the Brownings at Casa Guidi. Elizabeth was then the "happy mother of a lovely little boy," and Robert was "an amiable man, frank, cheerful, and charming, said to be the most captivating conversationalist on the Continent. . . . Their union seems perfect in happiness, the mind as well as the heart having met its affinity." At Ferrara she visited the humble home of the author of *Orlando Furioso,* with which epic poem she was, of course, familiar in her Italian studies, though it was written fifty years before Shakespeare began. And we are not so far off the subject as might appear, for at Ferrara she wrote:

"The house of Ariosto belongs to the Government, and a neat old woman and her pretty little niece were its guardians. No article of furniture has been removed from the position it occupied when the 'immortal poet' (as the Italians call him) lived within it. In his studio, upon the writing-table, the inkstand remains as he left it, and the chair where he was often seated, writing those exquisite poems still so dear to his countrymen. In this room there was a noble bust of Ariosto by Canova. He must have been an uncommonly handsome man. The forehead was gloriously intellectual, and the mouth sweetly expressive of tender feelings. His small garden, with its cool grotto and vine-covered arbors, appeared carefully tended.

"As I remarked the watchful attention bestowed upon this house, I thought of Mount Vernon, the home of our Washington. Why should not that sacred spot be the object of a love as unceasing? It should indeed be the nation's property—a Mecca, where pilgrims from all the vast regions between the Atlantic and the Pacific shores might come, and there, as at a holy altar, swear a new oath of faithfulness to the Union that his patriotism created and preserved."

When Mme. LeVert addressed her Mount Vernon appeal to the Ladies of Mobile, it had a somewhat more professional turn of phrase than the effusions of some of her associates:

"Your hearts are enlisted in Washington's behalf," she wrote. "We hear, already, that whispering has taken place among you on this subject. Raise your voices, ladies, and fear not. Call a meeting; elect a president, a treasurer, and all the other necessary officers. Issue circulars, open subscription lists—and the scheme is under way! You have time, talents, and patriotism enough among you, if you would only give them to this noble cause. But some of you are so eager to be thought helpless and feminine that you would faint at the idea of doing anything spirited! And some of you are so modest that we never hear you lisp out your 'aversions to being conspicuous' without thinking of the young lady who vowed 'she would never get married—no, never! It would shock her to see her name in the newspapers!' "

Cajolery—charm—wit—good-nature—inevitably she was "the favorite of every society she enters." She was small, and graceful —"that little worldly lady"—she was lively and brilliant besides. Her jewels were a famous set of turquoises. At a fancy dress ball at Newport she appeared as Nourmahal, Light of the Harem, "blazing with jewels, in a short dress with Turkish trousers and silver anklets."

Some of her more articulate friends attempted to describe her, or pin down her magnetic quality—and there was no one of importance in America who had not felt it at one time or another, from Longfellow in the cloistered Cambridge circle, to Webster and Henry Clay in the Washington political hurly-burly, and men of the world like Washington Irving and Edward Everett. Clay said: "She was made up without antipathies, and in place of them has a large adaptation and tolerance." An anonymous Mobile gentleman impressed on his daughter the peculiar magic noted before: "When you had been with her a half hour you left feeling flattered that so famous and charming a woman had been so interested in what you had to say. Then, when you tried to remember what you had said that was so brilliant, you realized that you had said nothing; she had done all the talking, but she had made you think you had." And the great Unitarian divine, Henry Bellows, wrote to her in 1855: "I have tried to think what it was that brought so many of all ages to your feet. My mature observation instructs me now that your social success is due to the sympathetic power which enables you to fling yourself into everybody's place, or feelings, to become interested in every human being and give them that most flattering and engaging of all gifts, your attention. We may talk of presence of mind, but there is a still rarer quality, *presence of heart.*"

Thus, after more than a hundred years, the fragrance of this enchanting woman remains.

Mrs. Dickinson of North Carolina, in contrast to Mme. LeVert, preserved an even stricter anonymity than Miss Cunningham's. In December, 1858, she sent in a statement of collections amounting to over $5000 and soon after resigned to devote herself to an invalid sister. She was immediately succeeded by Mrs. Letitia Harper Walker, who had been born at Guildford Courthouse and had two uncles in the battle there in 1780. Mrs. Walker proved to be a tower of strength for years, and lived to become the dean of them all, until 1908. As time went on it became her almost annual duty to read the eulogy for some junior member of the group, as one by one the founding sisters who could remember with her the early struggles and anxieties dropped away.

6

Miss Cunningham was exhausted by the journey South after the summer's unusual activity, and remained in Charleston during the winter of '56–57 to be near a physician. She spent the following summer in a darkened room on Sullivan's Island near by, and in the autumn of '57 returned to the city.

During all this time she continued to bombard Mr. Washington with long letters full of argument, expostulation, and appeal. The charter which was to be presented to the Virginia Legislature during the spring session, to replace the one rejected by Mr. Washington in March, '56, required a Constitution for the Association, and this was being drawn up by a distinguished South Carolina lawyer, Mr. James Petigru, who was said to have a manner which was "hearty, even hilarious, but courteous," and an unusually beautiful speaking voice. This no doubt stimulating supporter also prepared the By-laws, and designed a handsome Certificate of Appointment to be issued to the Vice-Regent of each State—the Constitution providing to all States equal privileges in the purchase and possession of Mount Vernon, and stipulating that the Association should be presided over by a Regent (Miss Cunningham) and that each State should be represented by a Vice-Regent appointed by her. Convinced that they would somehow get round Mr. Washington's scruples and crotchets, they began issuing monthly reports of each State's contributions, which "excited a generous rivalry."

A subscription book had been placed in Independence Hall at Philadelphia, where travellers visiting that historic building could add their mite towards the preservation of another valuable shrine. A copy of that list sent to Miss Cunningham showed the signatures of a Glasgow clergyman, a Cuban planter, and well-wishers from Nebraska Territory, California, Texas, Wisconsin, and Vienna, Austria.

There was still a considerable outcry against Mr. Washington's price, which was admittedly exorbitant, and Mrs. Ritchie was stung into replying to that in a letter which was widely circulated:

"If the price is deemed too great for the actual value of the estate," she wrote, "let us remember that it is to be paid for by the whole nation, and to the nation Mount Vernon is priceless. We can put no market value upon a nation's attestation of gratitude, no price upon hallowed memories and holy associations—no price upon the footprints of Washington—and these give to Mount Vernon its value!"

The autumn of 1857 found the whole country in the grip of a financial panic, the worst in twenty years—banks were closing, mercantile houses were failing, private fortunes were being wiped out, after years of the mounting prosperity which usually precedes a bust.

In the midst of it, Everett went cheerfully on with his self-imposed task of touring the country for the cause, and somehow continued to collect funds as he went, and to record in his journal and letters the varied experiences which he viewed always with humorous equanimity. At Detroit he must speak from the pulpit in a church, so that applause was interdicted, which was a let-down—in Kentucky he made a night voyage on a river steamer with a life-preserver beside every pillow—at Niagara he left his favorite cane in the cars—at Buffalo he spoke in a tent, with most of the audience standing for two hours in the open air on a chilly autumn day. He went back to Detroit for an engagement at Ann Arbor, travelling from Buffalo in a superb lake steamer where he occupied "what is absurdly called the bridal chamber," eleven feet by twenty in size, "as I ascertained by actually pacing it," and which contained besides the usual furniture a card-table, sofa, four chairs, a washing apparatus supplied by a pipe, and a water-

closet. At Toledo his pocket was picked of his precious watch—
("I could have cried when I found it out, but what good would
that do?")—at Cleveland "every inch of sitting-space was filled."
And everywhere, in dimes and quarters and half-dollars, the
money dribbled in.

Moreover it was at about this time that he took on a tremendous
additional labor, by pledging himself to contribute a weekly article
for one year to *The New York Ledger*, which had a circulation
of three hundred thousand. The editor made no restrictions as to
the subject matter of the fifty-three papers—that was left entirely
to the writer, and in the end they ranged far, in anecdote and
reminiscence, from the house on the Potomac. But once he had
committed himself to write them, he received from the *Ledger* a
check for $10,000 which he paid over immediately to the Associa-
tion funds. He was aware that he was in danger of overworking,
and he had accepted the offer with hesitation, "but I could not
resist the temptation to add $10,000 at once to the fund," he wrote
Miss Cunningham when she expressed solicitude for his health.
The *Ledger* articles were the scholarly *Mount Vernon Papers*
which were eventually gathered into one volume and sold under
that title.

The correspondence between Everett and Miss Cunningham
raises again the odd analogy between the Regent and Elizabeth
Barrett, who while sofa-bound and without hope of recovery, in
the prison of her father's London house, won the dynamic devotion of Robert Browning through the letters they exchanged, and
escaped into a happy marriage. A dim echo of Elizabeth Barrett
is present in the letters Ann Pamela Cunningham wrote to
Edward Everett from Philadelphia and after her return to Charleston in the winter of 1856-7. "I have and do count the days till
your return," she confessed, after their second meeting, which was
at the time of his Philadelphia address in April, '56, "and in the
interim shall be happy to be employed in what may procure ever
so small a gratification to one to whom I look up with the grate-

ful, reverential feelings of a child!" And again—"You do not, cannot, realize how much I dreaded meeting you—the earnest persuasions of others compelled me to be so courageous I could scarce account for it. But all such feelings vanished the first moment I saw you—a *childlike* feeling came over me, for the second time in my life, which made it impossible for me to speak or act but with the frank confidingness of one. May I not venture to ask you to judge of what I do or say as the imprisoned invalid, who is of life as you know it almost a thing apart."

He had perhaps remarked upon her dedicated tenacity of purpose, her serious mien, feeling no doubt in her presence a dearth of the sophisticated humor and light touch he was accustomed to find in women like Mrs. Ritchie—and she was quick to feel that she had somehow disappointed him. "Pardon me, Mr. Everett, if I do not smile in the customary manner of others," she wrote. "Sorrows and suffering have riven me from the world, confinement and separation almost entirely from gay, formal society have broken the shackles such forge, while indifference and impaired memory make me too forgetful, I fear, of their nature in my intercourse with those under their influence, and too much guided by the simple and earnest life I lead." From Charleston early in '57 she wrote: "Your letter seemed like a sunbeam penetrating the clouds and shadows which darken the dawn of my New Year and I could but hope it was sent to remind me that its closing might be brighter than its sad beginning."

She wrote almost illegibly always, often lying down, presumably with a lap-board—usually on outsize sheets of rather rough paper which was sometimes dull blue in color. Her handwriting was small and cramped, and she often mentioned her "shaky fingers" and tortured eyesight. Her crowded pages, covered on both sides, with no margins and the last sentences squeezed in sidewise along the edges and crosswise at the top, must have caused him many a sigh, for his own eyes often gave trouble. But for all her frailty, Miss Cunningham obviously was alight

with the indescribable Southern charm, and he responded warmly
to the open admiration of one to whom his practiced platform
personality and cosmopolitan polish must indeed have seemed
from another world. The childlike attitude—it was not to be
called a pose—came naturally to her, with her slight figure and
lack of normal social background. She always alluded to Dr.
Hodge as her second father. Everett now became her pa*pa,* with
the accent on the second syllable, of course.

He had for years lived with the domestic frustration of a
chronically invalid wife, whose mind was also failing, and he
must in his varied social scene have encountered many more high-
powered votaries than the delicate Miss Cunningham. But at
sixty-three and a grandfather, Mr. Everett was soon beginning his
letters to the Regent "My dearest daughter," or "My dear little
Pam," and signing himself "Your poor old Papa."

George Washington Parke Custis died in October at Arlington
House, and the estate passed to his daughter, who was Mrs. Robert
E. Lee. Since the death of his sister Nelly in 1852, he was the sole
surviving member of Washington's household. His collection of
Washington relics filled the rooms of his mansion, and he always
welcomed visitors who wished to view them, wrote articles and
speeches, and left a rather miscellaneous book of *Reminiscences.*
Colonel Lee was on duty with his cavalry on the Texas frontier,
but his wife, who was crippled by rheumatism, was at Arlington
with the younger Lee children when her father died, and the
Colonel returned home on leave to cope with the Custis estate.

Miss Cunningham had told Mr. Washington, that memorable
June day at Mount Vernon, that when the next Virginia Legis-
lature convened in the spring of 1858, she would herself present
to it the revised charter, and this she now prepared to attempt.
There was still a political faction in Richmond which opposed
the Association with one hand while opposing purchase by the
State with the other. In the last week of December, 1857, she left
Charleston for Richmond with the Constitution and By-laws,

ready to do battle again. She was accompanied by her mother, brother, and the maid Grace, and a manservant, and her health was so precarious that a clause had been inserted in the Constitution empowering her to appoint her successor in case she died before the organization was completed. "My physician told me to take my coffin and leave my trunk," she wrote, many years later.

7

"I got to Richmond alive," her narrative continued, "but looking so awfully that the ladies were alarmed and, after consultation without consulting me, employed a physician to be at my bedside daily. I have never been the same person since that journey, and the wear and tear of that winter's campaign."

In spite of the obstinate laggards in the Legislature and at Mount Vernon, the ball was rolling in earnest now. In February the Grand Secretary of the Grand Lodge of Virginia Masons enclosed in a letter to Miss Cunningham the resolutions of the fraternity in support of the Association, the plan being for each Mason in the United States to contribute a dollar to the fund, in honor of their "illustrious Brother."

Edwin Booth, son of the great Junius and elder brother of the still unknown John Wilkes, had recently become the new idol of the American theater. Billed with the usual managerial hyperbole as "the hope of the living drama," he was now a slender, dark-eyed, very handsome man of twenty-five, playing most of his father's famous roles, and inheriting with them the old rivalry between his father and the aging, embittered Edwin Forrest. Although he was a professional, brought up in the rant-and-rave school of his father's heyday, young Edwin was reaching for new readings to old parts—the quieter, more reflective, character-building approach with which Mrs. Ritchie in her amateur way had startled the critics a dozen years before, in sharp contrast to Forrest, who "shook the scenery with his voice."

An Australian tour and an engagement in Hawaii, besides his triumphs in Boston and New York, were already behind Booth when he took his own company on tour with a substantial repertoire. He arrived in Richmond late in February of 1858, and addressed the ladies of the Mount Vernon Association:

"Entertaining an earnest wish for your success in the noble and patriotic cause you are engaged in, and unwilling to be thought wanting in zeal to promote that cause, I beg to offer you my humble services to contribute to the fund you have established to purchase the sacred ground of Mount Vernon, where rests the ashes of our beloved Washington. My stay in Richmond is short, and with your favor, I would propose to give a 'Matinee' at the theater on any morning during next week you shall propose, when I shall be happy to appear, either in tragedy or comedy as you may determine.

"Messrs. Kunkel & Co. have in the most liberal manner informed me that they will tender the use of the theater, free of charge, and the Dramatic Company, together with the Orchestra and attachees of the Theater will gladly volunteer their services to further your noble object.

"Hoping my humble petition will meet with your favor, I subscribe myself, Your servant, EDWIN BOOTH."

The Ladies accepted, and left the selection of the performance to his "well known good taste." His repertoire at that time included the first production of *Henry V* to be performed in the United States, besides the usual stand-bys such as *Hamlet, Othello, The Merchant of Venice, The Stranger, Richelieu,* and something called *Little Toddlekins.* But for his generous gesture to the Mount Vernon Ladies' Association, he elected to perform some version of *The Taming of the Shrew* entitled *Catherine and Petruchio.*

On February 17th Mme. LeVert forwarded from Mobile the sum of $1010, and about this time addressed Mrs. Ritchie as "Darling Cora" in a letter where she was able to state with pride that "Not one single person has aided me in anything I have done. Alone I have planned and arranged the pageant of the 22d, induced the orator to come, obtained the theater, etc., etc. Now I can just imagine you will take me in your dear arms and say 'Well done, brave and energetic little woman!' Read my note to dear Pamela and give her my tender love." Her acquaintance with Mrs. Ritchie doubtless dated back to the days when Anna Cora Mowatt fulfilled her engagements at the Mobile theater. Writing in 1866, Miss Cunningham mentioned that she had known Mme. LeVert when she was at school in Philadelphia, a Cunningham cousin being a mutual friend—Mme. LeVert was six years older than the Regent. Everett, acknowledging a copy of the *Souvenirs* sent him by its author, said it reminded him of "auld lang syne," and signed himself "Your old friend."

He reappeared at Richmond in February of '58, having been invited to the dedication on Washington's birthday of Thomas Crawford's equestrian statue of Washington, executed in Rome and cast at Munich, which was to adorn the Capitol Square. Mme. LeVert during her travels abroad had visited Crawford's studio in Rome and admired the unfinished work, and thought the sculptor "a fine, intellectual-looking man, with a frank and self-possessed manner." He was not present, having died in London the previous year.

On February 23d Everett was presented with one of Washington's canes, on behalf of the Association, in a ceremony at the Richmond theater, attended by a distinguished audience which included four State Governors, General Winfield Scott, who was Commander-in-Chief of the Army and a Virginia man, ladies of the Mount Vernon Association, and Miss Cunningham herself, who was again the guest of Mrs. Pellet. He repeated the Washington oration then, and again on the 26th. The sums so far accruing from his labor had been invested as they came in by a board of trustees set up by him, and once Mr. Washington could be brought to sign a contract for the sale of Mount Vernon, the money would be paid over to the Association.

His correspondence with Miss Cunningham was now reinforced

by another meeting, after an interval of more than a year, during which time her idealism of him may have grown, and her naive pleasure at the reunion in Richmond would have both touched and flattered any man, even one so accustomed as he had no doubt become to feminine susceptibility. That his Richmond stay was cut short is evident in a letter written from Boston on March 25th:

"My dearest daughter—

"I was very much grieved to leave Richmond without seeing you again, but I did not make up my mind to do so until the last moment. I reached Boston safely last evening. I found my poor wife had been much worse than my son had written me, he having wished to spare me as much anxiety as possible. She has, as I believe you are aware, been a confirmed invalid for some years. Ten days ago most of her symptoms underwent a marked and sudden change which has resulted in the almost total prostration of reason, which requires vigilant watching night and day. Greatly as I deplore the postponement of my engagements, I am thankful I came home. The care and responsibility incident to her present condition are too great to fall upon my son, aided only by nurses, though they have done all that duty or affection can prompt. The moment I am able to do so, I will return to the South to fulfill my appointments, but this cannot be until some decided change in my wife's condition takes place.

"I hope you did not think me discouraging in my remarks about contracting immediately with Mr. Washington. I spoke under the impression that if judiciously and cautiously dealt with he could be induced to abate a good deal from the really *exorbitant price* which he demands, and that some risk would be incurred of the loss of what we advance him by inability to raise the balance within the time stipulated. But situated as I am, I feel that I ought not to oppose anything you decide to do, and I can only repeat that everything held here is unreservedly at your service, at a day's notice.

"I hope, dearest Pamela, that your precious health will not give way under your labor and anxieties, for if that fails, the purchase of Mount Vernon fails, at least for this generation. Give my kindest remembrances to Cora when you see her, and tell her I shall write to her very soon. For a day or two I am overwhelmed by the mass of letters to be attended to. With sincere affection, your friend and father, EDWARD EVERETT."

Meanwhile, she faced the fight for the second charter without his immediate support. Mrs. Ritchie was of course at her side in Richmond, Mrs. Eve was due to arrive from Georgia, and the Vice-Regent for Missouri, Mrs. Walton, had come down from Washington where she was apparently paying a visit with her husband. She was a typical Victorian beauty, with a dimple in her enigmatic smile, and was the only Vice-Regent who succeeded in getting the Legislature of her State to contribute officially to the fund. They had voted $2000 in a lump, and this sum figured in the only swindle encountered by the Association.

A man representing himself as "Judge" Underwood of Kentucky, with a burning desire to emulate Senator Yancey of Alabama in collecting money for the cause, had somehow got to the Governor of Missouri and without any authority whatever obtained possession of the $2000, "while he (the Governor) was intoxicated." The money was repaid by the Governor, who admitted that he was at fault—after it was discovered that "Judge" Underwood had disappeared and taken the $2000 with him. An order for his arrest went out, and an article appeared in the *National Intelligencer* in Washington denouncing him as an impostor and cautioning the other Vice-Regents against him. The whole affair caused singularly little excitement, and seems very odd. The Regent expressed herself as "much annoyed," but added that she thought they were fortunate it should be the only instance of an attempt at fraud.

Tension rose in Richmond as the time for a vote on the second Mount Vernon bill approached, and the strange, hostile element

whose motive remains largely a political riddle mustered their
forces against it.

"I was allowed but little time to rest," Miss Cunningham recollected, "for we had too little money and must make it up by
woman's influence! I had a noble coadjutor, Mrs. Ritchie. We
two had it all on us! I had to receive gentlemen in bed! I was
very low physically, but my spirit seemed to soar on wings! Mrs.
R. did the outside work, I did the within. Before a month passed
all Richmond was excited as never before. We gained friends so
fast, it was said we 'bewitched the men.'

"This excited the ire of Mr. Pryor, member of Congress—he
hated the Ritchies and vowed to injure them; he thought, I suppose, to do so by defeating Mrs. Ritchie's hopes for Mount Vernon,
so, with a most *plausible* article in the paper, he warned the
Legislature not to be carried out of its propriety by *sentiment* and
female witchery; to look to the purse of the Association. He stated
that, 'though the ladies acted in good faith, they could not get the
money unless the people gave it, and if Virginia paid Mr. W., as
he required, the public would be very indifferent about bestowing
money to refund Virginia after they had got their object, viz.,
Mount Vernon.'

"There was truth in this, and it acted like magic. I was called
upon to answer it immediately. I was very sick. I took laudanum
—put my feet in mustard water, wrapped my head in hot cloths
till my face was purple—and I dictated to Mrs. Pellet. I did not
mean to be severe (but satire is my forte.) I only meant to give
facts and a refutation. But the article was so annihilating that
over the whole South there was intense satisfaction that the bully
Pryor, who had killed so many in duels, had met his match and
got a castigation which he could not revenge.

"As you may suppose, the reply I gave caused intense excitement; in next day's paper Mr. Pryor retorted and yielded in a
gallant spirit, apparently, but he was so enraged that he swore he
would defeat the Association! He was a Hunter man, the Ritchies

were of the Wise party; it became a political matter. Spies were put upon all our movements—the parties were pitted against each other. Pryor did defeat us by log-rolling, as it is called. We lost our bill!"

This colorful passage naturally alerts the researcher to what would appear to be prejudice or exaggeration on Miss Cunningham's part. The facts are found to be by no means drab, and lead to the conclusion that the explanation of the otherwise unaccountable defeat of the charter on the first vote in '58 lies right here.

Roger Pryor, born in Petersburg, Virginia, in 1828, and therefore a prime thirty years of age at this time, has a scorching record even in *Appleton's Cyclopedia*. He was successively on the staff of both the *Washington Union* and the *Richmond Enquirer*, where his enmity for the Ritchies doubtless began. He then established his own daily paper, *The South*, at Richmond. Bear with *Appleton* verbatim, in support of Miss Cunningham's opinion: "His aggressive course, and the intense utterance of his convictions led to several duels. He was elected to Congress in 1859 to fill a vacancy, and was re-elected in 1860, but did not take his seat. While in that body he made various fiery speeches, and in the excited condition of the public mind preceding the civil war was often involved in passionate discussions with his Northern opponents. One of these, John F. Potter, replied to him with similar acrimony, and was challenged. Mr. Potter named bowie-knives as the weapons, and the Virginian's seconds refused to allow their principal to fight with arms so barbarous. This challenge created an uproar throughout the country, and was accompanied with severe and characteristic comments on the principals from the Northern and Southern press. Mr. Pryor was eager for war, and visited Charleston to witness the firing on Fort Sumter, and its surrender. . . ."

So there you have Mr. Pryor, except for his actual score in the duels.

Virginia had now refused again to purchase Mount Vernon, even with the Association's money. Miss Cunningham, undaunted, wrote again to Mr. Washington, and on the 14th of March received the following frosty reply:

"Madam

"Your letter of March 12th has been received, in which you inform me that the bill providing for the purchase of Mount Vernon by Virginia has been defeated in the House of Delegates —and in the name and on behalf of the Mount Vernon Association you renew your offer to purchase this place.

"Heretofore I have only been willing to dispose of Mount Vernon to the United States or to Virginia, as I believed that in the hands of one or the other it would be better protected and preserved than in the possession of any individual or association. The events of the past seven years, however, seem to indicate that neither Virginia nor the United States wish to acquire the place.

"Under the circumstances, and believing that after the two highest powers in the country, the women of the land will probably be the safest, as they will certainly be the purest, guardians of a national shrine, I am willing so far to comply with your request as to await for a reasonably limited period of time the propositions you may wish to make to me on behalf of the Association over which you preside.

"And I assure you that unless these proposals are inconsistent with what I believe to be my duties upon the occasion I shall be inclined to give them the most favourable consideration.

"With assurances of the highest respect, I have the honor to be, Your obdt. servt., JOHN A. WASHINGTON."

Miss Cunningham overlooked this letter in her later account, but it must have caused considerable excitement when it arrived —the first crack in the wall of his defensiveness. Within a very few days of receiving it, she somehow got him to Richmond, and even in a friendly mood.

"I sent a gentleman to Mount Vernon to beg him to come to me," she related, having seized on only the purport of the letter, which was chiefly that he didn't say No again. "I had, during all our progress, sent him papers to show the extent of feeling enlisted in the work, and I hoped to prove to him that we should succeed if he would trust us and give us time—he came to tell me that we should have the title—I suppose he felt that if we failed no harm was done, as Mount Vernon would still be his. There was company in my room, and he whispered his intention, and I whispered in reply that he had made me the happiest woman in the world. He pressed my hand. I was bound to strict secrecy. We soon entered another bill, and carried it by acclamation."

So she had changed his mind. The Association had got the place themselves. All they needed now was $200,000.

The Association's charter as finally granted by the Virginia Legislature required that its Constitution should receive the approval of the Governor. Thanks to Mr. Petigru, this document was ready and waiting. The Governor formally approved it— it was filed in the office of the Secretary of the Commonwealth —and the Mount Vernon Ladies' Association was at last organized and legal. This original charter stood until 1963, when according to the present Director it "was deemed obsolete and flawed by a technicality," and new Articles of Incorporation were drawn up.

On March 29th, Miss Cunningham sent a receipt to Edward Everett for $2696, representing his contribution to that date. Mr. Washington was invited to come back to Richmond, sign the papers, and receive the down payment agreed upon. This he did, with as good grace as possible, on April 6th, 1858.

"But the wear and tear of the long struggle had been too much for me," Miss Cunningham wrote, "and on the day appointed for Mr. W. and the lawyers and the two Vice-Regents present to meet and witness the signing of the papers in my room, I woke with a struggle for breath and passed from one convulsion to another for hours. The house was horrified, and Mrs. Ritchie too, for fear that I should die before all was signed. After the lawyers had waited a long time, even offered to postpone and leave, my system was calmed. One of their number was sent to judge whether I was now in a sound mind!

"They assembled, Mrs. Ritchie kneeling beside my bed, me resting on her shoulder. All the papers were read in due form and then a gentleman knelt beside my low couch, and held the 'papers' for my signature; my lifeless fingers could hold the pen but a few moments, could only make two or three letters at a time—the pen was watched and caught 'ere it could fall, my hand must be rubbed and pinched to life and then try again! Finally all was got through—the 'papers' with my fearful scrawl were carried to the Archives of the State, and the long agony was over. Mrs. Ritchie was sick after it. I was in a mental stupor for three weeks. Has not Mount Vernon been bought with a price?"

The gold pen used by Miss Cunningham was the gift of her good friend and "second father," Dr. Hodge of Philadelphia, and is now in the possession of Mount Vernon.

The terms were all that even Mr. Washington could wish. He received $18,000 on the spot, and the remaining $182,000 was to be paid in four installments, payable on or about February 22d of the next four years. The Washington family was to retain possession of the estate till the full payment of all the bonds and interest had been made, although the Association undertook to pay the taxes. Provision was made to convey the property earlier than the designated four year interval if the ladies were successful in raising the purchase price sooner and wished to take possession.

In case of default on their part the down payment was forfeit and Mount Vernon remained with the Washington family.

Mr. Washington took his $18,000 and began to prepare a new home for his family at Waveland, near Warrenton. The first bond of $57,000 was due in less than a year's time. If he thought it would all come to nothing with a forfeit, or if he thought that he would hold Mount Vernon for the full four years, he thought wrong.

8

Miss Cunningham might well have gone into "a mental stupor for three weeks," as she recorded, but she had set herself another impossible goal in a determination to make the full payment by the 22d of February, 1859—ten months away —and take possession then.

By mid-summer she decided to return to Philadelphia where she could be in Dr. Hodge's care, and where she would be better able to discover Vice-Regents for the Northern States. Her first need was a private secretary to do the endless writing involved, though the Association would not need an official secretary until the collections had been made and the Councils began to meet. Mrs. Pellet, who had acted in that capacity in Richmond, could not leave the city, and "moreover was not fitted." It was here that Miss Christie Johnson entered the Regent's already burdened life.

Miss Johnson was, it appears, an unsuccessful teacher of elocution in a Washington female seminary, and a protégée of Mrs. Ritchie's—"darling Cora's" warm heart and outgoing nature attracted lame ducks and indigent relatives in swarms. Miss Johnson was either in Richmond at the time as Mrs. Ritchie's guest, or she was sent for, to accompany Miss Cunningham to Philadelphia and remain with her there. She proved to be an unfortunate choice, and as her eccentricities grew upon her, she would in about a year's time have to be dismissed, in unhappy circumstances.

The Vice-Regents for the other States must now be selected— which Miss Cunningham as Regent found a heavy responsibility —so that the drive for funds could go forward all over the country as fast as possible. Everett had nominated as Treasurer to the Association his friend George Washington Riggs, a banker of international reputation, conveniently located in Washington City, and Miss Cunningham at once wrote to him. Mr. Riggs's gallant letter of acceptance was dated May 7th, 1858.

"My dear Madam—

"It would give me great pleasure to do anything in my power to promote the success of the Mount Vernon Ladies' Association, and if as you intimate in your letter, you wish my services, I shall be happy to perform the duties of Treasurer of the Association, with the understanding that there is to be no compensation or salary attached to the office. With great respect, Madam, Your faithful Servant, GEO. W. RIGGS."

Without his kindliness and unlimited generosity and resources, the Association could not have weathered the grim war years so soon to begin.

Mrs. Ritchie was of course named Vice-Regent for Virginia, though she protested that some native-born Virginian ladies might feel slighted, and they did—and while the Regent had Mr. Everett's counsel on the choice of the Northern representatives, Mrs. Ritchie's own wide acquaintance there would have been of great value. They had also consulted Samuel Ruggles of New York, lawyer, trustee of the Columbia Library, and Commissioner of the Erie Canal. Mr. Ruggles lived in Union Square, and in 1831 had laid out and named Gramercy Park, presenting it to the nearby property-holders, and it was he who suggested the name for the Avenue known as Lexington. Writing to Miss Cunningham in May he summed up the ideal Vice-Regent:

"The office requires a rare combination of qualities—fitness of character, personal acceptability to her State, Revolutionary connection, if possible, freedom from cares of a young family, sufficient health, pecuniary (affluence), knowledge of accounts, knowledge of women—and of men too. All these are not often combined in one individual. Many individuals possess many of them, but few of them combine all. . . . Recollect, the choice is like that of a wife—for life; for better, perhaps for worse. In some respects young unmarried ladies are preferable, if possessing sufficient maturity and dignity. . . ."

He congratulated them on securing for New York State Miss Mary Morris Hamilton, granddaughter of Alexander, great-granddaughter of Robert Morris, who filled Mr. Ruggles' specifications almost to the letter, including the years of discretion—she was turning forty. Everett, who knew everybody, and may have suggested the appointment, wrote, "I do not know her superior in all the qualities that adorn and enoble our nature."

Miss Hamilton acknowledged the receipt of her Certificate of Appointment on May 11th, and opened an office at the Cooper Institute, where she had already done good works among the less fortunate women in New York City, and where she now held regular meetings of her lady managers, and from where she sent out her appeals. Mrs. Ritchie, having gone North on one of her inevitable family visits which so tried the patience of her husband, called at Miss Hamilton's office and sent back such a complimentary account to the Regent that it served as a description of a model organization.

Among the contributions soon reported by Miss Hamilton was a check for $500. "Since I wrote to you, we have received a noble contribution from Mr. Washington Irving, our much loved author and neighbor," Miss Hamilton wrote to the Regent—her home was at Dobbs Ferry not far from Sunnyside. "This evinces his future confidence and interest in our project, for he is not a man of wealth."

Although they were unlikely to have met at this time, a cordial correspondence soon flourished between Miss Cunningham as Regent and her New York representative. Attended by Miss Johnson, she was now settled in at a comfortable boarding-house in Philadelphia, where she intended to make her headquarters "until Mount Vernon is secured," and with Mrs. Ritchie no longer within reach, felt the need of a knowledgeable confidante.

"Accept my grateful thanks for your kindness in aiding me to fulfill worthily the very solemn and responsible duty of appointing Vice-Regents," she wrote to Miss Hamilton in August. "I say solemn and responsible; for on the Vice-Regents depend the future of Mount Vernon and all the moral influence our Association can exert for our country. Even if my time and strength would permit me to express to you the opinions I entertain in reference to the *nature* and *extent* of the latter, I would not venture to do so; for you would regard me as an enthusiast—a dreamer—unless like myself the present had receded from you, and you had lived for three long years only in the future, and saw and felt on the subject as those will see and feel who live a century hence."

This theme recurs again and again in Miss Cunningham's writings—her extraordinary projection into the future, her unfailing sense of permanence and continuity, in the thing she wanted to do. And we who have seen the flowering of the centenary of which she was always so certain and so aware, can only marvel at her prescience. She was of course besieged by the usual climbers and snobs, eager for the local social prestige of an appointment as Vice-Regent, and this confused and annoyed her, as she confided to Miss Hamilton:

"It would be safer and *better* for my country to add no more Vice-Regents to our number than to make unfortunate selections —an *irremediable* evil. Yet I am deeply sensible of the importance of having the citizens of each State in our strong bonds to Mount Vernon, and then having a representative among its guardians as soon as it *can* be done judiciously. From this you may be enabled to realize how very, very valuable your assistance will be to myself and to our noble cause.

"I am compelled to rely upon the judgment and representations of others, as to the qualifications of the ladies proposed to me; but I frankly confess to you that I am aware that there are *very few* upon whose judgment I can do so *safely*; for there are very few of either sex who, in this fast age, take time—if they have the ability—to reflect, to reason closely, and to study, to take in, any subject *in all its bearings*. Yet this is necessary in advisors, to secure the best appointment in each State.

"Permit me to say that I feel that I can turn to you for counsel, with the assurance that I may safely appoint any lady whom you may recommend from your *personal* acquaintance; and where that does not exist, may I not ask you to use all the sources for obtaining information which you may possess (greater than any other Vice-Regent, for New York is the mart of the Union) in order to investigate thoroughly the individual qualifications of the ladies under discussion. *Social position* and *family influence* in a State cannot be dispensed with, but except for the temporary purpose of raising the purchase fund, these are of very slight importance in the Grand Council, as they do not impart legislative ability, nor the wisdom, judgment, and clear perception necessary for the safe and prudent exercise of the power of voting in the Grand Council. Yet *on these votes* the future of our Association depends. Can you, my dear Miss Hamilton, be surprised at my hesitation to 'do the deed' *on which so much hangs?*

"From the time that I signed the Contract, every influence has been brought to bear upon me to hasten the appointment of Vice-Regents, but ill health—the very inefficient means I had at command to carry on such a vast work, and the consideration of the responsibility, caused me to proceed slowly. Latterly, however, I have been overwhelmed with demands made upon me on every side.

"None do I feel more keenly than the one from South Carolina. On the appearance of our report, an editorial appeared in my own organ [the *Charleston Mercury*] asking: 'Why the fair daughters of the Banner State had not yet been represented by a Vice-

Regent?' My native State has not only gallantly espoused our cause, but showered every honor and eulogy on one they kindly style 'the patriot daughter of the Palmetto State.' From gratitude I had determined that she should be represented by a lady who, I knew, had no superior in the United States—Harriet Rutledge Holbrook; but her health is so precarious at this time that I knew success depended on the postponement of the application; and I thought South Carolina would be patient, as the office of Regent could be claimed by her. . . .

"I perceive that you only require books of funds on the 1st of February. I regret this very much. It is of the utmost importance to pay the first installment as soon as possible, in order to acquire the privilege of paying small sums as collected; this stops the interest. Thus, in the Southern States, all money as collected is sent on at once, and put out at interest by Mr. Riggs until the $57,000 is accumulated. I mention this now, my dear Miss Hamilton, in order that you may give the necessary directions to your correspondents; as I am sure you will not be willing that the Empire State should make no sign until February."

It is illuminating to read, at this length, a letter so uncompromising, so far-sighted, and so cognizant of practical business matters—and then consider that apart from what advice she could absorb from men like Petigru, Everett, and Riggs, the last of whom she had probably not yet met, Miss Cunningham on her sofa in Philadelphia had a grasp of the whole undertaking which would have done credit to any one of her masculine confreres.

She realized too that this inspired union of the highest feminine influence in each community, North and South, just at this time might contribute in many subtle, behind-the-scenes ways to the over-all union of States, which was becoming more and more threatened by wedges of political controversy and social dissension on the issue of secession, which arose from the issue of slavery. She herself was a Southerner, Everett was a Bostonian, and Riggs in Washington was at the hub—and they all hoped that their common cause might form bridges, bonds, and friendships across the widening fissures in the national scene.

Miss Cunningham's dilemma regarding the appointment for South Carolina was not resolved till 1860, when she gave up hope of getting Harriet Rutledge Holbrook, and chose Mrs. James Chesnut, who was eighty-five, and the only one of them all who had actually conversed with Washington himself. She had been one of the flower-girls at the gala reception at Trenton in 1789. Later, as the débutante Miss Mary Coxe of Philadelphia, she attended Mrs. Washington's receptions, and as one of Nelly Custis's friends came under the benign attention Washington bestowed on pretty young ladies. Lastly, she had been present at his birthday ball in Philadelphia in 1796. That memorable day had begun with a peal of bells at one minute past midnight, a cannon salute at dawn, cannon again at mid-day, and chimes at intervals all afternoon, while the entire Congress led the crowd of well-wishers which flowed through the Presidential mansion all day to pay their respects and partake of cake and punch. After supper at Oeller's Hotel, there was a grand ball at Rickett's Amphitheater, decorated for the occasion with transparencies and symbolic paintings and countless candelabra. Five hundred citizens attended, though the circular room would only accommodate a hundred and fifty dancing couples at one time. The ladies wore white, with plumes on their heads. And Mrs. Chesnut, in the bloom of her twentieth year, had been there, and touched his hand.

Soon after, she married James Chesnut, a wealthy young South Carolina planter recently graduated from Princeton. Her sister married Bushrod Washington's friend Horace Binney, whose *Memoir* of Judge Washington was now published in '58, on the Mount Vernon tide. Mrs. Chesnut on her bridal trip had driven from Philadelphia to her new home near Camden in a cream-colored chariot and four, with outriders, bringing with her a tremendous amount of wedding silver. She was now enjoying a serene old age in her armchair at Mulberry plantation in her

adopted State. Her son James, Jr., was a member of the South
Carolina Legislature, and the United States Senate, till the war
began. In 1840 he had married seventeen-year-old Mary Boykin
Miller, from a neighboring plantation, and brought her to his
parents' house to live. It was this junior Mrs. Chesnut whose *Diary*
would become a classic source-book for the Confederate story of
the war, and we are indebted to it also for glimpses of "old Mrs.
Chesnut" and her devoted husband, who was several years older
still.

"Mrs. Chesnut, my mother-in-law, praises everybody, good and
bad," the younger Mary wrote in June, 1861. "'Judge not,' she
says. She is a philosopher; she would not give herself the pain to
find fault." She had a mind of her own, however. "My mother-
in-law, Mrs. Chesnut, has been sixty years in the South, and she
has not changed in feeling or taste one iota. She cannot like
hominy for breakfast, or rice for dinner, without a relish to give
it some flavor. She cannot eat watermelons and sweet potatoes
sans discrétion, as we do." She had become quite deaf, and her
husband's stentorian tones shook the window-glass during their
morning conversations in her bedroom, while her own voice remained always notably soft and sweet, her replies inaudible. She
was very sensitive to odors. "Candles have to be taken out of the
room to be snuffed," young Mary recorded without animus.
"Lamps are extinguished only in the porticoes, or farther afield.
She finds violets oppressive; can only tolerate a single kind of
sweet rose. A tea-rose she will not have in her room."

Old Mrs. Chesnut's over-active nose gave rise to a midnight
alarm in June, 1861, when young Mary was wakened by loud
calls, tramping feet, lighted candles in the yard and passages, and
a bellowing from the top of the stairs. They were jumpy days,
just before Manassas, and she could only suppose the disturbance
meant the arrival of some terrible news, a battle, perhaps, or an
accident—half-dressed, she rushed out to find the old Colonel
roaring orders from the piazza, and the yard alive with people
carrying lights, and she asked nervously for tidings. "No, no, only

Mamma smells a smell," the Colonel reassured her. "She thinks something is burning somewhere." Being so deaf, his wife was "totally innocent of the storm she had raised, and in a mild, sweet voice was suggesting places to be searched for fire. I was weak enough to laugh hysterically," young Mary admitted. "The bombardment of Fort Sumter was nothing to this."

Much of the Vice-Regent duty was of course done by the daughter-in-law, although no mention of Mount Vernon occurs in her *Diary* except a rather cryptic remark about what appears to have been a family argument during the same summer of 1861: "Mrs. Chesnut, born in Philadelphia, cannot see what right we have to take Mount Vernon from our Northern sisters. She thinks that ought to be common to both parties. We think they will get their share of this world's goods."

Mrs. Chesnut was quite right. Mount Vernon remained neutral ground.

When she died in 1864 her son was heartbroken, and months later her husband was accidentally seen through a half-open door by the younger woman, on his knees by the empty bedside in tears. Mrs. Lucy Pickens was appointed Mrs. Chesnut's successor in 1866.

Maryland too was long in acquiring its Vice-Regent, though Miss Cunningham's chosen candidate met Mr. Ruggles' specifications of being unmarried, not too young, with Revolutionary connections, and plenty of money—but Miss Emily Harper, granddaughter of Charles Carroll of Carrollton, was bringing up young nieces and nephews, and felt she could not accept any additional duties at the time the first proposal was made to her in 1858. True to her principles, the Regent chose to wait for the right person, and though many other names were mentioned there was no Vice-Regent for Maryland until Miss Harper was finally secured in 1866.

During the early summer of 1858 Everett toured the South with his oration, and made a visit to the Ritchies at Brandon, where he wrote Miss Cunningham that he was treated by Cora and her husband's family "like a beloved, petted grandpapa"—he was twenty-five years older than Cora, twenty-two years older than Miss Cunningham. In June he was back in Boston, submerged in vexatious domestic and pecuniary affairs, writing to thank her for the "beautiful daguerreotype" she had sent him. "It is very kind of you to send me this precious token of your regard," he added. "It is not only pleasing in itself, but as an accurate likeness of our dear little Regent, the leader of the great Mount Vernon enterprise, it will be doubly cherished by me. As a token of affection for your poor old grandpapa it is invaluable to him. I wish I could believe that the bloom which the pencil of the artist has bestowed upon the face had taken up its abode on the living cheeks of my dear little daughter, for whose health I feel so anxious."

There is a letter from Miss Cunningham, dated in August, thanking him for a likeness of himself sent in return, appealing in its characteristic stilted coquetry. She had been ill again, and although "overawed with surprise and gratitude, touched to the very heart," was still forced "to be content with what the strongest effort of will at present alone enables me to do—a few lines, not to express my indebtedness to Mr. Everett, for that would be impossible, but my warmest and most heartfelt thanks. Is it not Horace Walpole who speaks of the value of a feather from a friend we esteem? If a feather from Mr. Everett given as a token of his sympathy and regard would be more prized by me than the rarest gems from another, can he not realize the value of this gift, the one more to be prized coming from him than any other he could have chosen? May I ever be able to retain, nay, increase, the sympathy and regard which is now the source of so much pride and pleasure to your prostrated, but deeply grateful friend. . . ."

She was by then at Cape May with Christie Johnson, whose presumptuousness and inadequacies did not contribute to an improvement in the Regent's health. Both Mrs. Ritchie and Miss

Hamilton in their summer travels saw Mr. Everett at Boston, and were urging him to repeat the Washington oration in New York for what would be the third time. Mrs. Ritchie wrote affectionately to the Regent, giving news of the latest fashions, the balls she attended in New York, and the qualifications of the proposed Vice-Regents for obstinate vacancies.

She was becoming aware that her protégée was not giving satisfaction, and wrote advising Christie that she must learn to perform her secretarial duties efficiently, and keep copies of her letters, and try to induce the Regent to realize the value of a rest or change of occupation occasionally. "I was quite amused at the Regent's declaring that she has taken up 'fancy work' to stop thought," she wrote. "I should like to see her fairy fingers employed on a bit of 'fancy work.' A present, I presume, but for whom? Why, for her dear Papa, I hope!"

There is evidence that by the time they returned to Philadelphia in the autumn, and Mrs. Ritchie paid them a flying visit on her way back to Richmond, Miss Johnson was under the mistaken impression that she was capable of running the Association according to her own ideas behind the Regent's back—she had warned Mrs. Ritchie not to write anything to her in a letter that she could not show to the Regent—she was discussing a rise in salary independently with an embarrassed and non-committal Everett—and had somewhere acquired what Mrs. Ritchie lightly referred to as "an ancient and wealthy beau," while advising her to assure the Regent that age and wealth could never win her.

In the summer of 1858 the first issue of the *Mount Vernon Record* appeared—an eight-page quarto newspaper devoted to the Association, designed to keep the public informed as to the progress of the fund, to print the names of all contributors of $1, or more, to present interesting historical tidbits—recollections, old letters, anecdotes—as pertinent reading matter, and to introduce the Vice-Regents as they were appointed. It was a sort of periodical Mount Vernon scrap-book, published monthly by a Philadelphia

printing-house, and the proceeds, over and above the cost of production, were to go for the uses of the Association, the terms
being $1 per annum, "invariably in advance."

The *Record* has now become a literary curiosity. But by making
use of its yellowing pages as a guide to additional research we
can meet, sometimes all too briefly, the widely scattered ladies of
the first roster.

9

Mme. LeVert naturally became the Vice-Regent for Alabama, and with the aid of Senator Yancey of that State (another cousin of the Regent's) who followed Everett's example of stumping the countryside for contributions, they raised over $10,000 for the fund. Senator Yancey was a fire-eating Democrat, who had fought a duel—without bloodshed—in '45, and by '58 was an eloquent secessionist and opponent of the Republican candidate for the 1860 election—who was Abraham Lincoln. "But not content with inducing generosity in others," the *Mobile Daily Tribune* said of Mme. LeVert, "she wished to contribute something from the brain-sweat of her own fair brow, and for this purpose she contributed a part of the profits from the sale of her popular volume, *Souvenirs of Travel*."

Mrs. Isaac Morse, Vice-Regent for Louisiana, was of Maryland stock, with a Swedish grandfather, and was related to the Lloyds and Darnells of that State. When Margaretta Smith Wederstrandt was six years old her family moved to a luxurious sugar plantation in Louisiana, taking with them the Maryland slaves, some of these the fourth generation in the Darnell family. Like Mme. LeVert, she had met Lafayette during his 1824 tour of the country, when at the age of eight she was taken on board his ship when it arrived at New Orleans to present to him the first strawberries of the season, a laurel wreath, and a recitation of a poem composed by her mother. He was of course much amused, and at his insistence she was one of only two little girls who were present at the New Orleans ball given in his honor.

Her family were at that time the guests of the Morses at their fine house in Rampart Street, and her future husband would have been fourteen. Her mother died when she was thirteen, and one of the duties she then assumed was the administering of medicines to the colored folk on the plantation, and the Sunday hand-out to the colored children of gingerbread from a supply piled in a clothesbasket.

She and her sister were sent back to Maryland to school at Emmitsburg, and she married in Louisiana at eighteen. Isaac Morse had graduated from Harvard in '29 and then studied law in New Orleans and Paris, and became Attorney-General for Louisiana and Congressman in Washington. His wife was one of the few from the South or West who always accompanied her husband to the capital city—in the '50's it was a journey by river-packet and stage-coach which took several weeks—and she had, in the end, twelve children. At Bethel Cottage in C Street she entertained her husband's political friends, and hers was one of the first houses in Washington to be lit by gas.

To raise money for Mount Vernon, she visited every parish in her State, though transportation was primitive as soon as she left the river-banks, and she somehow induced the emotional city of New Orleans to devote to the fund the appropriation usually given to their July 4th banquet and ball, which featured the Old Continental Guards in their blue coats, perukes, and cocked hats —to forego the customary parade and festivities represented a real sacrifice in Creole society. There was also an item in the *New Orleans Picayune* about a schoolboy named Thomas Shute, whose grandfather was a Revolutionary soldier, and who collected in less than three weeks $855, mostly in sums from one to five dollars. The only time he had in which to accomplish this was an hour or two daily from his recess at school, and with the thermometer at 85°. The newspapers played it up, and the persuasive Master Shute was known as "the little knight of Mount Vernon," even after he was a tall white-haired Confederate veteran. Mrs. Morse's Certificate of Appointment, one of only two known to survive, is dated April 28th, 1858, and she remained an active—sometimes too active—member until 1870, when an incomprehensible animosity to the Regent would cause her, in effect, to be read out of meeting, the only instance of its kind among all the lifetime appointments.

Mrs. Catherine Anderson McWillie, Mississippi, was the wife of the recently elected Governor, who was originally a South Carolina man, having practiced law in Camden, where he was doubtless known to the Cunninghams. The appointment was apparently made at the suggestion of Mrs. Fogg, though the connection here is not clear, and Mrs. McWillie had relatives in Maryland. She worked in association with Mme. LeVert, Mrs. Morse, and Senator Yancey, and was frequently in Washington, where, like her friend Mrs. Morse, she was a popular hostess and, in a day when the phrase meant what it said, a queen of society.

A letter was addressed to the Regent by the ladies of Tallahassee, Florida, requesting that Mrs. Catherine Willis Murat should be appointed Vice-Regent for that State. The appointment was promptly tendered by telegraph from the Regent. Madame, the Princess Murat, was a grand-niece of Washington through his only sister Betty. She was the daughter of jolly Colonel Byrd Willis, of Fredericksburg, who said of himself, "I am remarkably fond of pleasure, but as remarkably averse to everything like business." She had married at seventeen Atcheson Grey, whose father owned Traveller's Rest on the Rappahannock and the remnants of the old Washington estate called Wakefield, where the General had been born. The Wakefield house had long since disappeared, and young Grey lived in a cottage while acting as his father's manager there. Catherine Daingerfield Willis Grey lost both husband and baby within a year of her wedding, and returned to her father's house in Fredericksburg, her gay spirit, which she doubtless came by honestly from him, remarkably unsubdued, it was observed, by her bereavement or the conventional mourning she wore.

It was the year of Lafayette's grand tour—1824—and she was not at all inclined to forego the festivities in his honor. She was therefore at the Fredericksburg home of her mother's uncle, Robert Lewis, who had been aide and secretary to General Wash-

ington during the war, the night that Colonel Lewis was host to
Lafayette, and a serenade to the hero was performed by the
Marine Band outside the house. Bowing to young Mrs. Grey and
her still younger cousin Betty Lewis III, Lafayette insisted that
they accompany him while he appeared on the piazza to make
his acknowledgments. Colonel Lewis caught up a pair of silver
candlesticks and placed one in each girl's hand. With their other
hands caught in Lafayette's elbows they thus appeared on either
side of him, lighting his face as he bowed and waved to the
cheering crowd. Must we question so charming a legend?

Soon after this picturesque episode, Colonel Willis's affairs became so involved that he decided to join other financially embarrassed Virginians in the new Territory of Florida. It has been
more or less forgotten that in the 1820's Florida was a favorite
new frontier, such as the Far West became some twenty years
later. To be sure, there were hostile Indians in it—Seminoles and
Creeks—and there was an abundance of alligators, snakes, and
mosquitoes. But the cotton and sugar were very fine, and corn,
rice, and pumpkins were easily raised in quantities, and cattle
and hogs could range. The fishing, too, was famous. And the
applejack.

The Willises settled down in a log house on Monroe Street in
Tallahassee—three sons and three daughters—and Colonel Willis
wrote his old friend ex-President Madison that it was "a rare
country." Miss Kate, so briefly Mrs. Grey, and still only twenty,
at once attracted admirers, with her dark eyes and long brown
curls, and the same criticism followed her from Fredericksburg
to Tallahassee—she was too merry for a widow. Dates have become a little blurred—but the world was smaller then, and it is
quite possible that the future Mme. LeVert and the future Mme.
Murat might at least have heard of each other as girls in Florida,
Octavia Walton being several years the younger.

Prince Achille Murat, son of the one-time King of Naples and
Napoleon's sister Caroline, was certainly heard of all over Florida's
northern counties. When his father had lost his throne—and his

life, in front of a firing squad—in 1815, Achille was fourteen
years old. After refuging with his mother in a castle near Trieste
for a time, he had arrived in America in 1821, bringing with
him a small fortune in bags of gold and silver. His uncle Joseph
Bonaparte, ex-King of Spain, had fled to America after Waterloo,
and was living in style at a fantastic house near Bordentown,
New Jersey, where his benevolent hospitality had made him very
popular. On his advice, young Achille applied at once for natural-
ization papers. There was some talk of a marriage between him
and one of Joseph's daughters, but she was shipped off to Europe
for a better match. During a tour of the country, Achille came
to Florida and fell in love with it. He settled first at St. Augustine,
bought a plantation, slaves, and cattle, and read Blackstone, with
the intention of becoming a lawyer. One of his neighbors there
was a man named Benét, left over from the Spanish régime, who
was to have descendants named William Rose and Stephen
Vincent.

The process of an American State in the making Murat found
fascinating to watch—the influx of speculators, squatters, and
politicians, the easily corrupted Indians peddling venison and
berries in the streets to buy ammunition and drink. A fourteen-
year-old mulatto slave girl bore him a child, and died. Murat
went up to Savannah to join the reception for Lafayette. At about
this time he decided on the move from St. Augustine to Tallahassee, which was pioneer country and suited him better, and
his mother in Austria had arranged an annuity for him—$1500
a year. He had ambitious plans to write—to interpret America,
which he loved and believed in, to the Old World he had left
behind. He sold out in St. Augustine and set out across the Peninsula, with his slaves and cattle and household goods, and a pet
owl, which presided over the log house he built on the new
plantation fifteen miles west of Tallahassee.

He has left voluminous letters and writings, wherein he says
that he first met Miss Kate at a picnic and drank from her slipper.
His courtship became a sensation. He was Napoleonic in appear-

ance, but untidy—he had reverted to the Corsican. It was said that he did not change his clothes often enough, and that he ate anything he could catch. He chewed tobacco and spat. But he loved Miss Kate so much that he vowed he could not live without her, although she had no dowry. Somehow he won her. Perhaps it was a challenge she could not resist—to tame a Bonaparte. Perhaps he improved himself, for her. They were married in July, 1826.

He built her a new log house, and called it Lipona. Other buildings sprang up, enclosing a garden in the center, arbors, and a riot of bloom. The household linen was marked with the coat of arms of the King of Naples. They served delicious food at their entertainments, which soon became famous—chocolate, tiny cakes, exotic preserves, Arabian coffee—from golden spoons bearing Napoleon's crest. She was young enough to find it all a great game.

In 1827 he took her North to show her off to Uncle Joseph at Bordentown. They embarked at St. Augustine for Charleston in March, and one of their fellow passengers was a young clergyman from New England named Ralph Waldo Emerson, who had been wintering in the South to recover from a bronchial ailment, and regarded St. Augustine as "the remote outskirts of civilization." It was such a dreadful passage that they were nine days at sea in a tempest, ran out of food, and nearly went to the bottom. But a strange thing happened. The gentle, reflective, unworldly Emerson, and the violent, godless, but intrepid Murat became fast friends, and Emerson described his unexpected shipmate as "a philosopher, a scholar, a man of the world; very skeptical, but very candid, and an ardent lover of truth. I blessed my stars for my fine companion, and we talked incessantly." Murat even urged Emerson to establish a Unitarian church at Tallahassee. The voyage ended at Charleston and they never met again, though for a time they corresponded. There was one lasting result—Murat wrote that whenever his language got too colorful thereafter, his wife reminded him of Emerson.

It was a turbulent but apparently happy life she lived with her Bonaparte, and it was certainly never dull. From Bordentown they visited Saratoga Springs for the sake of his health, which did not improve under the boredom he suffered there, so he returned home to Lipona and worked his own cure with "a simple diet" of whiskey and milk, augmented by juleps. He fought a duel—then a common practice in the Tallahassee neighborhood, where men went always armed as they were to do later in what is affectionately known as the Old West—with a political candidate who in Murat's opinion was a turncoat, and he said so. The Judge denied it, Murat called him a liar, and three days later they met to shoot it out. "He fired first and shot off half of the little finger of my right hand," Murat wrote. "That did not keep me from shooting, and my bullet went through his shirt and scared out the lice. He declared himself satisfied without asking either an explanation or a retraction. And he was not elected!"

He passed his bar examination and hung out his shingle—"Colonel Murat, Counselor at Law"—and thought a courtroom better than a theater, because the emotions there were genuine. He made a little money on the side as postmaster, which besides his commissions allowed him to frank his own letters.

Events in Europe in 1830 roused family ambitions again, and he took his wife to England, but Louis Philippe cannily barred Bonapartes from France. While in England they visited another Bonaparte exile—cousin Louis, whose father had been King of Holland, and who some twenty years hence would be known as Napoleon III. Murat's American wife made such an impression here that after his accession, which occurred after Murat's death in 1847, the new Emperor invited her to come to Paris as his guest and tactfully sent the money for her travelling expenses.

In the meantime, the Murats went through a bad patch, after their return to Florida, and had to give up Lipona for a smaller place called Econchatti. The death of his mother rescued them from actual penury, with a share of her estate, but Murat's spectacular course was run—he was frail and emotionally wrung out for two or three years before his death. His widow, by good management and good sense, made Econchatti pay, mainly by its fine sugar. Then, accompanied by her colored servant William, she accepted the invitation to Paris, where she was received at Court as a Princess of the Second Empire. The formalities and restrictions of Court life irked her, and her French was always more amusing than effective, according to her husband, whose fluent English had remained eccentric to the end. She declined the gift of a chateau, accepted a settlement of 125,000 francs instead, in token of the Emperor's friendship—she still called him Louis, and he was after all five years younger than she was—and returned to Tallahassee with a splendid cargo of gold plate, gold chairs, crested china, carved tables and mirrors, and royal linen, with which she furnished a modest house she called Bellevue—and from then on, black William as her butler wore the Bonaparte livery. Tongues wagged again—she was a widow again, and still only in her forties—she was too gay—she gave lavish little parties at which she served odd, exotic delicacies—there were apparently more gentleman than lady callers—but of course there were also her charities, and there was her title, which she was too democratic to use, although at the time of her appointment the Vice-Regent for Massachusetts was to take exception to the Bonaparte connection.

Mme. Murat's letter of thanks to Miss Cunningham for her credentials as Vice-Regent for Florida, written in a lacy script with the old-fashioned long *s,* is dated July 22nd, 1858—"You must not expect Florida to produce such grand results as her sister States, as she is one of the youngest daughters," she wrote. Florida had been admitted to the Union in 1845. It contributed some $3000 to the Mount Vernon fund.

There is a small item in the back pages of the *Record* for February, 1860:

"A Tallahassee (Florida) paper says that by a series of calamities the private fortunes of Mrs. Murat, the widow of the late

Achille Murat, has become much embarrassed," it read. "Her crop for the present year, as for the past, has proved a failure—this year nearly destroyed by unfavorable seasons. During the past year we regret to record the loss by fire of a roadside inn, established by the late Col. Achille Murat, for the accommodation of the public, which by the generosity of Mrs. Murat was tenanted by a colony of poor German emigrants. Add to this the loss of all the mules of her plantation by the crushing of a barn during a severe gale, and the subsequent loss of crops, and pecuniary embarrassment will readily be accounted for."

Mrs. Rosa Griffith Vertner Johnson, Vice-Regent for Kentucky, was born in Natchez, Mississippi. Her mother died a few months after Rosa's birth, and she was adopted by her maternal aunt, whose name she took, and who lived near Burlington. When Rosa was ten years old, her adopted parents moved to Lexington, Kentucky, where there was an excellent seminary for her education. At seventeen she married Claude Johnson—"a gentleman of fortune," who had a home in Lexington and a plantation in Louisiana, and after his death in the '60's she married a Scot named Jeffrey. She was distinguished for her beauty and social grace, and had considerable ability as a writer of novels and poems. A volume of her verse had been published in 1857, under the pseudonym "Rosa." She lived to be one of the last survivors of the original group, serving thirty-six years under two surnames, but resigned in 1885 without attending Council. A long poem, signed, was published in the Association's monthly newspaper for March, 1859, entitled simply *Washington,* which read in part:

> "Down the gory tide of battle,
>   When our foes were wrecked and lost,
> On Columbia's shield of freedom
>   One bright name her love embossed—
> Name of him who, when victorious,

Of his ransomed country thought,
And though hailed as 'Patriot,' 'Hero,'
    For *himself* no honor sought;
And with honors heaped upon him,
    Crowned with fame's undying crown,
Turning fondly to Mount Vernon,
    Lo! he laid them meekly down—
Glorying in his country's freedom,
    (Not that by himself 'twas won).
History with her countless heroes
    Has no peer for WASHINGTON! . . ."

The Vice-Regent for Ohio was the daughter of Francis Scott Key, who wrote other things besides the *Star-Spangled Banner,* and was for a time District Attorney for the District of Columbia. In 1846 Mary Alicia Lloyd Nevins Key had married George Pendleton, an Ohio politician who was known in the rough-and-tumble of Western politics as Gentleman George, for his unruffled dignity and the grand manner he inherited from his Virginia family. She resigned in 1863, having assumed the care of her elder brother's children, who a few years earlier had been orphaned as the consequence of a tragic scandal.

Philip Barton Key was called the "handsomest man in Washington society"—he was of course a Southerner from Baltimore, tall, with rather long hair and an overwhelming mustache, and he rode a big iron grey saddle-horse through the muddy streets of the unfinished capital. In 1858 he was thirty-eight, five years a widower, and father of two children. His sister's husband, George Pendleton, had become a member of Congress in 1857, and brought his wife to Washington. They took a house in C Street, where Barton Key, and presumably his children, lived with them. Mrs. Pendleton was a famous beauty, and once attended a fancy-dress ball appropriately gowned as the Star-Spangled Banner.

One of the New York Congressmen in Washington at that

time was the professional Tammany politician Dan Sickles, whose reputation with women was notorious—while a member of the New York Assembly he had had the bad taste to take his current fancy lady named Fanny White to Albany with him, where she appeared openly in the gallery and at his hotel. Sickles nevertheless acquired a young and lovely wife, whom he had known literally since her babyhood, when as a young man with his way to make he had lodged with her family in New York— her father was an Italian musician and her mother an American girl. When Teresa Bagioli was sixteen and Sickles was thirty-three, he married her, though his connection with Fanny White and others of her kind by no means ceased. Short, well-groomed, and possessed of a mysterious charm, Sickles had a way of getting on regardless. He went to London as secretary to the American Minister, Buchanan, in 1853, and Fanny White went with him instead of his wife, who was pregnant. By the time Teresa was able to join him there with the baby the following year, his philandering was common gossip, but her simplicity and child-like beauty won the hearts of the London hostesses. In 1858, when his friend Buchanan had become President, Sickles was riding high in Washington, with a fine house in Lafayette Square where the Pendletons came to dine, along with Philip Barton Key.

Teresa was resigned to her husband's open infidelities. She was petted, expensively dressed, and shown off as one of his posses-sions, but he pointedly preferred women of more experience— and she was lonely and hurt. Her connection with Key began harmlessly enough. He took her riding, escorted her to social functions her husband was too busy to attend—considered her, he said in reply to criticism, a mere child. (She was then twenty-two.) It ended in a singularly clumsy and indiscreet affair, when Key hired a house in a shady neighborhood near the Square, overlooked by curious neighbors, for their meetings, which were conducted in daylight and arranged by ridiculous signals which could hardly fail to attract notice. For a man of the world, with a reputation to maintain, Key's behavior seems utter madness. Everyone knew about it before Sickles, preoccupied with his career and his love affairs, caught on. The usual anonymous letter precipitated a dreadful scene in his house, during which he extorted a written confession from the weeping Teresa—which when the story broke was published on the front pages of newspapers from San Francisco to New York.

On the Sunday morning following the row, while Sickles, himself in floods of tears, was discussing with a friend the disgrace Teresa had brought upon him, Key with his usual recklessness was seen to be signalling with his handkerchief in the usual way from the opposite curb. Sickles simply snatched up a pistol—he was one of those men who sent and received challenges almost as a routine—and rushed into the street, where he overtook Key and shot him down in the gutter before several stunned witnesses. While Key was carried into the nearby National Club to die, Sickles gave himself up and insisted on going to the verminous common jail, refusing bail.

The press, of course, had a Roman holiday, the gist of the opinion being that as an "unmitigated blackguard" himself, Sickles had acted inexcusably in shooting an unarmed man without even the formality of a challenge, and that his so-called honor was anyway a joke. The *New York Post* mentioned his "notorious profligacy" and *Harper's Weekly* was perhaps more to the point when it remarked with conspicuous understatement: "It would appear that neither Mr. Key nor Mrs. Sickles acted with ordinary prudence."

The Pendletons were in Washington at the time, and had dined at the Sickles residence only a few days before, with Key among the other guests. They could hardly have been unaware of the situation—but their feelings at its outcome can be imagined. Sickles was brought to trial for murder, with eight top-rank lawyers to defend him. The prosecution was in the inexperienced hands of the dead District Attorney's assistant and one other lawyer hired by his friends. Sickles wept openly and often in the courtroom—he did not testify himself—evidence that would have demonstrated that Teresa had far more to condone than he did was for some reason never used by the prosecution—and he was acquitted. What's more, while he was still in jail an affectionate correspondence was carried on between himself and his repentant but incomprehensible wife—and after a period of exile with her parents in New York she was taken back under his roof, where except for Key things seem to have resumed much as they were before, although she was forever ostracized socially. For him to reinstate her after saving his neck by proclaiming her guilt was considered a little too much by most of his friends who had so far stood by him, but would not stand for forgiveness. He was thought to be finished, though he continued obstinately to occupy his seat in the House—young Mrs. Chesnut in her *Diary* remarked that he was "left to himself as though he had small-pox."

The war saved him. He plunged into it, raised a New York regiment of volunteers, established a surprising rapport with the Lincolns, who actually visited his camp outside Washington with their son Tad—and after many ups and downs with the in-and-out Northern command, Sickles, as a major-general, succeeded in losing a leg at Gettysburg, at which engagement he had exercised his own judgment against General Meade's and was not stationed where he was supposed to be. He survived, with a theatrically empty trouser-leg, to the age of ninety-five.

George Pendleton was appointed Minister to Germany in 1885, and his wife accompanied him abroad, where her beauty, even in middle age, was considered remarkable. The Keys were always stalked by tragedy. Barton's elder brother Daniel had been killed in a duel at the age of twenty some years earlier. In 1886, when Mrs. Pendleton's son lost his wife in childbirth she returned from Germany with his sister to sustain him in his grief—and died from injuries received in a carriage accident in Central Park in New York. The horse had bolted, dragging the driver from his seat, and both women tried to jump. Mrs. Pendleton struck her head and lived only a few minutes, on the grass at the roadside.

The daughter survived, but George Pendleton never recovered from the shock of his wife's death.

Mrs. Robert Walton, Vice-Regent for Missouri, had been called away from Miss Cunningham's bedside in Richmond in the spring of 1858 by the sudden death of her husband in Washington. Later that year she resigned, because of "severe domestic afflictions and illness," but she remained in close touch with the Association for many years, and even visited Mount Vernon during Council. Her successor was appointed in 1860—Mrs. Anne Lucas Hunt, a true daughter of the pioneers, who had come to St. Louis with her father when it was a log village in a wilderness full of Indians. Her first husband was Lieutenant Thomas Hunt of the U.S. Navy, who had been held prisoner at Tripoli till the Treaty released him. After his death she married his cousin, Wilson Hunt, a wealthy merchant of St. Louis, associated with the Astor family. One of the most elderly of the Vice-Regents, Mrs. Hunt nevertheless attended Council when the first meetings became possible after the war.

Michigan's Vice-Regent, Mrs. Elon Farnsworth, was born in New Hampshire, and married a Detroit lawyer with an extensive practice, who became Attorney-General and Republican Congressman. She raised $4300—and the Detroit postmaster gave her his personal check for $100. After the war Mr. Farnsworth practiced law in Washington, which enabled his wife to be in close touch with Mount Vernon affairs until her death in 1879, and she was one of the most beloved by the Regent. "Mild and lovely," she was known among her colleagues as "the wise woman of Michigan," and will become better known later in the story.

The letter of acceptance from Elizabethtown, New Jersey, was written in August, '58, by Miss Phebe Ogden, who except for Mrs. Chesnut was the eldest of the Vice-Regents. Her father had been a colonel in the New Jersey Continental Line, was present at Brandywine and Monmouth, accompanied Lafayette to Yorktown, was a founder of the Cincinnati Society, trustee of Prince-

ton University, Senator, and Governor of New Jersey. Miss Ogden
was a great lady of the old school, and at the age of seventy-five
in 1864 attended the first Council in Washington and made a
valiant journey to Mount Vernon, at which time she was said to
have had "the vivacity of sixteen." She died in 1865, and was succeeded by the energetic Mrs. Halsted, whose post-war activity did
more than any other to carry Mount Vernon through the difficult
transition period.

The Vice-Regent for Delaware was Mrs. Joseph Comegys—
probably the most influential and at the same time most elusive
figure among the Vice-Regents. Almost none of her letters have
survived—perhaps due to the fact that her daughter Harriet,
raised in the traditions of the Association, became its fourth
Regent in 1909, and may have exercised too much discretion
with the records. But everyone wrote to Mrs. Comegys—everyone. And those letters which remain express an affection, a confidence, and a trusting frankness which can only inspire wonder
about the woman who received them, and an increasing frustration that so little is known about her. Her advice and that of her
husband, Judge Joseph Comegys, was invaluable during the war,
when they gave comfort and support to the gallant little woman
who represented the Association at Mount Vernon in the Regent's
absence during those perilous years. Mrs. Comegys's zeal in the
early collections is revealed by a letter from Miss Cunningham's
secretary in 1859:

"Hearing that you had determined that your State should do
more in proportion to its population, 'if you had to sell your
house over your head,' Miss Cunningham—anxious to prevent
such a sacrifice on your part—thinks best to inform you of the
state of the case:

Rhode Island, population ...... 147,000 ...... $2,050.00
Delaware, population .... 91,555 ...... 2,150.00"

Close enough. But it served.

The first Vice-Regent for Iowa was Mrs. Jane Maria Yates Van Antwerp, Albany born, with Maryland connections which made her a cousin of Miss Emily Harper, who would become Vice-Regent for that State. General VerPlanck Van Antwerp was an authority on Indian affairs, and she had gone with him as a bride to Iowa, where they lived at Keokuk. By some mysterious chain of circumstances now undefinable, Mrs. Van Antwerp was also related to Mrs. Ritchie's mother, at whose suggestion the appointment was made, and the second surviving Certificate of Appointment is Mrs. Van Antwerp's, dated October 26th, 1858. Her first appeal was published in the *Fort Dodge Sentinel* in December, and one of the money-raising entertainments was a fancy-dress ball at Davenport, which earned $200. Travelling in the East in 1859, she met Miss Cunningham at Philadelphia, and was one of the small, faithful group who attended the first Council presided over by the Regent after the war in 1866.

Mrs. Alexander Mitchell, Vice-Regent for Wisconsin, was the daughter of a Milwaukee pioneer, and married a banker and railroad tycoon. This is not the same Mrs. Mitchell who had accompanied Miss Cunningham to Mount Vernon in June of '56, and who was a relative living in Philadelphia, signing herself "Becky." The Vice-Regent had lived in Milwaukee since it was a hamlet in a wilderness, and her appeal was remarkably successful for a thinly populated area. One of the last survivors of the original group—she was the only 1858 appointment to see the turn of the century—she contributed generously in effort, advice, and money, and was one of the mainstays of the difficult post-war years. She could hardly write a letter without revealing her deep love for her husband, and her plans were always prefaced by a qualifying "D.V."—God willing—which seems to have been as much humor as piety. When she offered her resignation after serving forty-four years, the Council voted instead of accepting it to confer on her an honorary membership for life.

Mrs. Ritchie wrote to congratulate the Regent on securing "the

glorious, young, and witching Vice-Regent for Pennsylvania"—
Miss Lily Macalester was a Philadelphia débutante, a close companion to her millionaire father, and well known to Mr. Everett,
who wrote, "She has energy, tact, enthusiasm, and unites the
vigor of a man with the delicacy of your sex. I prophesy the best
results to the cause from her accession, especially with the aid of
a charming secretary." This latter refers probably to Mary Mc-
Makin of Philadelphia, who had recently joined the Regent's
household as assistant to Christie Johnson, who was not, to say
the least, dependable.

In 1873, when the Regent was reluctantly preparing to resign,
it was Lily Macalester, then Mme. Berghmans, that she nominated
as her successor. Heiress to a large estate, she was a good business
woman and executive, and as wife of the Belgian Minister had
become an experienced diplomat. After the death of M. Berghmans in 1874 she married again, to become Mrs. Laughton, rendering eighteen years of service under three different names.

The wife of the Hon. Salma Hale of Keene, New Hampshire,
was Vice-Regent for that State, and considering its population
did very well with her contribution. Her term was one of the
shortest, owing to a mental breakdown, and she never, apparently, saw Mount Vernon, left any useful correspondence, nor
attended a Council. It was some years before a successor was
appointed.

Mrs. Josiah Little, for Maine, had been born a Vermonter. Her
husband was a prominent political and financial figure in New
England, a graduate of Bowdoin College, and a classmate there
of Longfellow and Franklin Pierce. She collected over $4000 for
the fund, and resigned in 1866 when a second marriage took her
out of Maine and into New Hampshire. She was immediately
succeeded by her capable friend and secretary, Mrs. Sweat, who
had worked at her side from the beginning—an attractive, highly
educated woman with a ready pen, who has left valuable correspondence and records of the early days. One of the late survivors of the original group, she often found herself, like Mrs.

Walker of North Carolina, delivering a eulogy on yet another departed colleague.

The close friendship existing between Everett and the Horatio Greenoughs was doubtless responsible for the appointment of the sculptor's widow as Vice-Regent for Massachusetts, and her Cambridge circle included Emerson, Longfellow, and the Harvard society. The Greenoughs lived in Italy till the political unrest in Florence forced them to return to America in '51, and Mr. Greenough died soon after. He had been bitterly disappointed in the reception of his colossal, half-draped marble statue of Washington, executed at his studio in Florence and delivered to the capital city in 1845. The classical treatment had caused much controversy and some derision—people preferred a general on horseback—but Everett, who was acquainted with its conception from its early days when he and his family lived as neighbors to the Greenoughs near Florence, went to its defence. An endearing sidelight on the sculptor is that instead of the usual Latin word *fecit* (has done it) following his signature on the statue, he wrote *faciebat* (tried to do it).

Mrs. Greenough's secretary, Mrs. Hopkinson, wrote to the Regent early in 1859 when Massachusetts contributions were lagging: "I wish you only had Mrs. Ritchie to talk it into them. With her little French graces of manner and quick sensibility, she has a power of imparting a vitality which she herself possesses in an unusual degree. If we could have got her to go the rounds as we desired to, to tell the story of the Association in her own simple bewitching way, we could have doubled the contributions." Mrs. Ritchie had given some readings in Massachusetts the previous summer, on Mrs. Greenough's invitation, her expenses paid by the Vice-Regent, with happy results.

The letters from Mrs. Greenough to the Regent are especially lively and well-written—as for instance her objection to Mme. Murat on the grounds of the title. "I shall publish the list of Vice-Regents with Mme. Murat's name as Mrs. Catherine Willis Murat, for the following reasons," she wrote in July, '58. "As a

titular princess and relative of royalty, she is out of place and
has no business among us. She enters the Association at the good
pleasure of our Regent, and in virtue of her birthright as an
American. And as an American she must be content to appear
among us. Besides all this, a title is not republican, not in accord-
ance with the spirit of the letter of the American Government,
and I am sure would tend to render the Association very unpopular. Now, 'them's my sentiments,' and if you scold me for
them I cannot help it, for with your leave I feel it my duty to
omit Madame la Princesse. I believe Mme. Murat is a very lady-
like and amenable person, but her connection with a man like
Louis Napoleon is a very great objection, and should be kept in
the background as much as possible." It does not appear that
poor Mme. Murat ever laid any stress on her right to a title, and
the Regent had already listed her in the *Record* as Mrs. Catherine
Willis Murat, so it is hard to see what set Mrs. Greenough off.

She was also a purist, as evidenced by a postscript to one of
her earliest letters. "Has it ever seemed to you," she wrote the
Regent's secretary, "that our title is wrong? It should be the
Ladies' Mount Vernon Association, and not the Mount Vernon
Ladies' Association. This is upon the same principle that in our
Northern newspapers we sometimes see advertised 'Black ladies'
gloves for sale.' Excuse the joke. But would it not be well to ask
the Regent if this mistake, for it is one, could not be altered? I
want everything about the Association to be *right!*" But the Regent took no action. And they are still Mount Vernon ladies.

During the search for a representative for Rhode Island, Mrs.
Greenough was not backward in expressing her opinion of any
lady proposed. "Mrs. Ives I am not acquainted with," she wrote,
"and Mrs. Burns I know and like. Since writing you, sundry
objections to the last named lady have occurred to me. She is
not a native of Rhode Island, but only an exotic transplanted
there. She has no roots, among the people or soil. She has lived
mostly in Paris, and belongs exclusively to the fashionable class,
the upper *ton*. When she likes people she is very cordial, but

although she has many friends she has some enemies and these are very spiteful and pull her to pieces. Nothing can be said against the perfect propriety of her conduct, but she is rich, good-looking, and when people are disagreeable to her she takes no pains to conciliate them. As you may imagine, there is considerable picking and finding fault with the poor lady. I think the Regent wise to pause."

Either she was unacquainted with Mrs. George Chace, who finally got the Rhode Island appointment, or her estimate of that choice has not been preserved. Mrs. Chace was the wife of the distinguished Professor of Chemistry and Physiology at Brown University, and her home at Providence brought many eminent people into the cause. She too was one of the late survivors, but little of her correspondence remains. She made many substantial contributions, such as the replacement of the sundial, until her death in 1893.

The irresistible Mrs. Greenough also had her say in favor of Mrs. Samuel Goodrich for Connecticut, at whom Everett and Mrs. Ritchie appear to have looked a little askance in the beginning, for reasons now unknown. Mrs. Goodrich's husband had published a number of books for young readers, of an instructive nature, which he signed with the pseudonym *Peter Parley*. A somewhat wordy man of intense convictions, he also wrote two volumes of *Reminiscences,* published in 1856, and contrived never to mention in them either one of his two wives, of whom our Mary Boott Goodrich was the second. After some years abroad—they were in Paris during the stirring events of 1848—they had returned to America in '55 and bought a house on Ninth Street in New York and a summer home at Southbury, Connecticut.

Having some misgivings about his wife's eligibility on only a six months a year residence in the State, Mr. Goodrich decided to make Southbury his official residence by voting there, in order that she might be considered a true Connecticut lady. "I have just returned from a visit to Southbury where I matronized a young niece," wrote Mrs. Greenough to the Regent, "more than ever struck with Mrs. Goodrich's energy and practical good sense. Everything in her large family and household goes like clockwork, but you never see the machinery. Mr. Goodrich was for many years Consul-general in Paris, and many of his best articles in *Peter Parley* are from Mrs. Goodrich's pen. This is said, however, confidentially, and I am sure you will so consider it. During my visit I never even hinted at the appointment, and have no idea whether her manifold duties would allow Mrs. Goodrich to accept it, though I am sure she would feel honored and flattered by the request, and will do so if within the range of possibility."

Mrs. Greenough returned to Italy in the winter of 1858-9, and remained there throughout the war, resigning in 1865 from abroad. It was a great loss to the Association that even after she came home again she refused to resume her office. She was eventually succeeded in 1879 by one of Longfellow's daughters— "grave Alice," the eldest—as the second Vice-Regent for Massachusetts.

In Connecticut Mrs. Goodrich flung herself into the work with enthusiasm, and her early letters are brimming with suggestions for other appointments, and for more ways to raise money. In the spring of 1859 the Goodriches visited Miss Cunningham at Philadelphia, and a warm friendship was established. Thereafter Mrs. Goodrich was distressed if she did not hear often enough from the Regent, and her affection sometimes overflowed. "Am I not your priestess," she wrote in July of that year, "and may I not hear of the well-being of my saint?" And again in September: "Dear Regent— May I call you Pamela? And will you call me Mary?"

During the Philadelphia visit the Goodriches learned of Miss Cunningham's search for a permanent private secretary who would be more congenial as a daily companion than the erratic Christie Johnson, whose co-worker, Mary McMakin, was not able to cope with the correspondence alone, though she was to remain as a stand-by assistant for many years. The business of the Association would soon require a woman of experience, judgment, and background as a resident representative after the estate was taken over. It was through the Goodriches and their New York friends that the invaluable Sarah Tracy, who will appear in due course, was secured for the post. And it was Mrs. Goodrich who in November of '59 wrote to Miss Cunningham the rather startling query: "Have you heard the rumor that Miss Hamilton is engaged to Mr. Everett?" This would have been shortly after the death of his invalid wife, and nothing more is heard of it, though there is evidence of a lasting friendship between him and the Vice-Regent for New York. In 1869, several years after Everett's death, Miss Hamilton at fifty-one was to make a surprising marriage with her elder sister's widower, George Lee Schuyler, who was fifty-eight.

Mrs. Goodrich had as an ardent assistant the poetess-author Lydia Sigourney. One of the more touching money-raising efforts was conducted in the village of Southbury, where a festival was held at the Goodrich summer home, called Maple Hill, and those who felt unable to give a dollar to the fund made an offering of the produce of their farms and dairies from which their scanty living was derived—the little community added all of $66 to the Connecticut total.

Mr. Goodrich died in 1860, and a few years later his widow went into a mental breakdown which forced her resignation. She was succeeded by her friend Mrs. Susan E. Johnson Hudson, after the end of the war. Mrs. Hudson proved to be one of the most active, not to say aggressive, women in the Association, and has her own particular mystery—it has been impossible to discover anything about her husband, even his Christian name.

Mrs. Fitch of Indiana emerges in her letters—some of which we shall read when the time comes—as a forceful and amusing personality, a good friend to the Regent in the early days, with an astringent quality which must have been a healthy influence in the Association. Her husband was a doctor of medicine and surgery who became a Senator, though he had practiced in

Chicago and always maintained a house in Logansport. When the war came he raised some Indiana volunteers and took them into battle at Fort Pillow, and was compelled to resign from the Army because of injuries received there. His political activities kept them in Washington much of the time, from where the Vice-Regent was an interested observer of Mount Vernon ups and downs, about which she wrote delightfully indiscreet letters to Mrs. Comegys. As has been noted, everyone wrote recklessly to Mrs. Comegys, including the Regent, and even the circumspect Miss Tracy. She must have been a singularly magnetic and sympathetic woman.

The remaining appointments before the war, which interrupted everything but the dogged occupation of Mount Vernon by representatives of the Association, were: Mrs. Elizabeth Willard Barry for Illinois, whose elaborate hand-wrought memorial volume carried the name of Abraham Lincoln on the list of her Gentlemen's Advisory Committee, and who served till 1883; Mrs. Sarah Sibley for Minnesota, who died in 1869; Mrs. Mary Pepperell Jarvis Cutts for Vermont, who resigned in 1878; Mrs. Sarah H. Johnson for Arkansas, who died in 1866; Mrs. Magdalen G. Blanding for California, one of whose contributions was a solid gold bar, valued at $3302.74, the result of one month's collections, which arrived by express; and Mrs. George Washington Riggs, for the District of Columbia, who resigned in 1867.

Oregon was admitted to statehood in 1859, and Mrs. Ritchie wrote the Regent in February of that year: "Pray don't forget, while Oregon is glorying in her new honors, to awaken her patriotism and secure her gold through a popular Vice-Regent. I wrote to you of Mrs. Judge Williams, Mrs. Van Antwerp's daughter, who is all that could be desired. Did you not think well of the suggestion?" But Oregon did not achieve a Vice-Regent until the appointment of Miss Mary Failing in 1907.

The original roster of Vice-Regents at the end of 1858 showed twenty-three appointments out of a possible thirty-two. Seven more were added in 1859, and one replacement. Some of these

remarkable women served only a year or two, resigning because
of family reasons, or poor health. One of them survived on active
duty till 1908.

Before leaving the *Record,* which published its final number
in June, 1860, with the purchase of Mount Vernon all but accomplished in half the time allowed by Mr. Washington, a glance
at some of the contributions will show the nationwide, up and
down, whole-hearted response aroused by Mount Vernon's plight,
which brought in such a stupendous sum in such a short time, in
spontaneous proof of the adage that "many a mickle makes a
muckle."

The Express Companies, led by Adams, tendered their services
to the Association to any point on their routes free of expense.
This was a great help in transporting the heavy bundles of circulars, subscription books, and prints and portrait copies suitable
for framing which were sold for the one dollar which entitled
the purchaser to have his name printed in the *Record,* with the
amount of his contribution. In the later numbers the pages increased to sixteen to accommodate the lengthening list—the onus
of seeing one's name in print having been transformed into
pride.

The Independent Odd Fellows of Richmond gave $41.22.

In Alabama the Montgomery True Blues (Light Infantry
Corps) contributed $212. Proceeds from a Ladies' Strawberry
Feast came to $334.50.

Mrs. McWillie, Vice-Regent for Mississippi, reported from
thirteen small counties, thinly populated, $2291.47.

Without waiting for the appointment of a Vice-Regent for
California, San Francisco sent $46.50 through *Godey's Lady's
Book,* which had published articles and pictures in support of
the cause.

President Buchanan sent his check for $50 with a courtly letter
to Mrs. Ritchie.

Miss Laura Keene, who had recently opened her own theater,
famous for its elegant white and gold and damask interior, in

New York, sent her check for $500 to Miss Hamilton, and offered a benefit performance of *Our American Cousin,* which was given on December 29th, 1858. It was this durable play, with the same star, which Abraham Lincoln went to see at Ford's Theater in Washington on the night of April 14th, 1865.

Miss Cunningham's home district of Laurens, South Carolina, where her mother acted as Lady Manager, sent $537.25.

The Hartford Public High School sent $30.25.

The American Legation at Honolulu, in what was then called the Sandwich Islands, sent $141.00, and the ladies at Fort Randall in Nebraska Territory sent $268.25, both of them through Mr. Everett.

The crew of the U.S. sloop of war, *St. Mary's,* then off Acapulco, Mexico, raised $130.

The famous Seventh Regiment of New York contributed $2000, at the rate of $1.50 per man.

Pennsylvania turned up with its own "little knight," ten years old, who raised $146.

The Sons of Malta in Wheeling, Virginia, gave $48.

The twenty-three conductors and employees of the Delaware Railway, in one and two dollar donations, sent what they could to Mrs. Comegys.

At a "handsome collation" at the house of the American Consul-General at Havana on July 4th the Mount Vernon Ladies' Association was toasted, and $150 collected from the guests.

The manufacturers of Mount Vernon Fine-cut Chewing Tobacco enclosed to Miss Hamilton $100 as a percentage of the sales for the year.

The newsboys of New York City sent their pennies to Miss Hamilton through the Superintendent of their lodging-house on West 36th Street, amounting to $4.18. "It is a mite from their hard earnings cheerfully given," he wrote. "Could their means correspond with their wishes, the donation would be large indeed. They are familiar with the eventful life of the Father of His Country, having often heard with much enjoyment pleasant readings from such works in their little library as treat of the glorious struggle for independence, of which he was the life and soul."

Mr. Morphy, world chess champion, gave a public exhibition of his skill at the Philadelphia Academy of Music, playing four blindfold games simultaneously with four local volunteers, and winning them all. Receipts for the fund, $300.

The West Point Cadets gave $2.00 each, and the Midshipmen at Annapolis, $2.50 each.

Everett's Certificate Number 34 was issued to Charlotte Wise, and duly signed by him, dated December 25th, 1858, for 50¢. She was his granddaughter, and had given her Christmas money.

From Fort Defiance, New Mexico, which was not yet a State, Miss Cunningham received the following letter:

"Madam

"I have the honor to transmit herewith Major Cary Fry's (Paymaster, U.S. Army) Draft No. 510, payable to your order, for one hundred and eleven dollars and fifty cents. ($111.50.) being the amount contributed by a portion of the officers, non-commissioned officers, and privates, now serving at this post, in aid of the Mount Vernon Ladies' Association.

"We are aware, Madam, that this amount is but a mere trifle, but we feel assured that it will be received by you in the kindest spirit, as an expression of the desire of this portion of the army to rescue the tomb and home of the Father of our Country. Be pleased, Madam, also to accept it as a slight token of the pride we feel, when we reflect that George Washington was the first commander-in-chief of the army to which we have the honor to belong.

"Assuring you of the heartfelt sympathy of my comrades and myself—and in all our names bidding you God speed in the noble work so generously undertaken by the ladies of America, I have the honor to remain, Madam, in behalf of his command, With great respect, Your most ob'dt serv't, W. DICKINSON, 2d Lieutenant, 3d Infantry, Post Adjutant."

These were the people who saved Mount Vernon, under God and Miss Cunningham—children, soldiers, sailors, housewives, professionals, workmen, ex-patriates, politicians, business men, backwoods country folk, ladies of wealth and leisure, newsboys, the President. And it worked.

In a place of honor on the middle page of the *Record* for December, 1858, set out in special type, there appeared a copy of a telegraphic despatch dated Washington, December 2d, to Miss A. P. Cunningham, which read: "I have paid Mr. Washington the bond and interest. GEO. W. RIGGS."

Anticipating the due date in February, 1859, they had paid the first installment of $57,000 with interest on the fifth anniversary of the first "Southern Matron" letter. The premium would not be forfeit.

IO

Early in 1859 Miss Cunningham at Philadelphia
received a disturbing letter from Mrs. Ritchie, who was continuing
her work as Vice-Regent in Richmond.

"My dearest Pamela (it read)
". . . I enclose scraps, and among them a splendid, a sublime
letter from Mrs. Eve. She clearly proves that the first association
was started in Georgia, and the credit should be Georgia's forever!
and forever! Do you know, that I was not aware of this before
and feel strongly inclined to *chide*—nay, positively *scold* you for
leaving me in ignorance! Here you have allowed me to think, and
to state *over and over again*, that the first association was started
in Richmond. In the very first letter that you wrote to me this
was the impression that you gave me.—Our taking out our charter
in Virginia probably *legalized* the first association here—but the
movement was actually started in Georgia under the auspices of
Mrs. Eve. . . .

"I wish I had time to scold you more. Indeed, I am quite vexed
with you for not correcting my error. Why, you let me put forth
an appeal saying that 'the first ladies' Mount Vernon Association
of the Union was formed in 1854 in Virginia,' and I believed I
was writing the strictest truth. It's too bad. I can't tell you what
I feel like doing, for I hold it to be one of the meanest things
imaginable to rob any individual of one *particle* of the credit due
to them for their exertions. But no more at present. I could not
sleep without venting my vexation in these few lines. . . ."

This teapot tempest was somehow resolved by the Regent—
Mrs. Eve had a certain amount of right on her side, in that she

had been at work with Miss Cunningham from the beginning, but it is odd that she should have seen fit to call Mrs. Ritchie to account at this late date—and Mrs. Ritchie's nerves were rasped by her domestic affairs, so that she fled North again to her father's house early in the summer. She was not an abolitionist, and had accepted slavery as a part of Southern life. But she was always outspoken, and abhorred prejudice, and her position as a Northerner in the steadily increasing sectional tension was making an already difficult situation worse in her Richmond home. On her way back there, she stopped at Philadelphia, and the misunderstanding was smoothed away in the warmth of the mutual affection between herself and the Regent, so that Mr. Everett wrote to Miss Cunningham from Boston: "I had a letter from Cora the other day speaking with great satisfaction of her interviews with you in Philadelphia. I myself am truly rejoiced that you met as in former times. Any coldness between friends so dearly cherished would have been a great grief to me, and its injury to the cause would have been incalculable." The next time Mrs. Ritchie went North, for the wedding of a sister the following summer, she was never to return to Virginia.

In February of '59 Mrs. Robert E. Lee wrote to Mr. Washington from Arlington to inquire if he would give "a resting place" to the old harpsichord which General Washington had given to Nelly Custis before her marriage, and which had been at Arlington since she left Woodlawn to live at Audley in the '40's. Nelly's widowed daughter-in-law, Mrs. Lorenzo Lewis of Audley, wished to present it to the Association. Mr. Washington notified Miss Cunningham of the gift, the first of all Mount Vernon's scattered treasures to return to its former home.

They paid as an installment of the second bond $41,666.66 plus interest on February 22, 1859, a year before it was due. Miss Cunningham had hoped for the whole sum by that date, but for once had failed to do the impossible.

The condition of the house meanwhile had worsened so rapidly in the five years since she had first approached Mr. Washington

that when Mr. Everett was in Philadelphia in January it had been
decided to request permission to begin repairs at once, on the
grounds and outbuildings where it would cause the least inconvenience to the family still in residence. Aware that it was now
only a matter of time—less time than he had thought possible—
till Mount Vernon was actually paid for, Mr. Washington was
disposed to agree, was even disposed to be helpful, on his own
terms. It would be necessary, of course, to provide close supervision of the work of reclamation, as it progressed, a responsibility
he had no wish to assume, but fortunately he knew of some one
suitable who might undertake it.

"If you have not already fixed upon a person (besides a mere
gardener) to reside here when I vacate the place," he addressed
Miss Cunningham early in 1859, "to look after its repairs, preservation and improvement, to receive visitors (both the 'great un-
washed' and the politer mob) give such information as they require, and repress their destructive plundering propensities, and
in short to act as general managing and business agent on the
premises, I have it in my power to call your attention to a gentleman, a friend of mine and a connection of yours, who I think
would be admirably adapted for the position. He and his family
for generations have been upon intimate terms of association and
friendship with the successive generations of my family who have
resided at Mount Vernon, and he is probably as familiar with
everything of interest here as any other person now living. His
intelligence, information, courteous bearing, and kind manner
will render him acceptable to those who come here, while his
unflinching courage, steadiness of purpose, and pure integrity will
make him an invaluable agent for the Association. And in short
he is in birth, character, habits, manner, and education a high-
toned gentleman, and I imagine you will find a person of this
sort almost a necessity in your future management of Mount
Vernon."

This was indeed a recommendation to live up to, but Mr. Upton Herbert did just that, supremely, for the next ten years. The "connection" with Miss Cunningham referred to was one of the tenuous Southern cousinships which doubtless lay in her mother's Alexandria background, for his mother was a Dulany of that city, and his great-grandmother was a Fairfax of Belvoir, whose elder sister Anne had married General Washington's elder half-brother Lawrence of Mount Vernon. Mr. Herbert was by some miracle still a bachelor, nearing forty, with a military carriage left over from his service in the Mexican War.

Miss Cunningham was anxious for a personal interview with Mr. Washington on this and other matters, and her letters became urgent. She wanted him to come to Philadelphia and himself collect the February payment at a meeting which Mr. Riggs would attend, and possibly Mr. Everett, and whatever Vice-Regents were available. "Please do not order me to repair to Philadelphia on the 22d unless it is absolutely necessary," wrote Mr. Washington, who obviously was feeling badgered. "Should it be, then write to me at Charlestown, Jefferson County, as well as at this place. I expect to leave here on the 16th for Norfolk, and if no accident occurs to leave there on the morning of the 18th to be at Charlestown or at my brother's residence near there the following day."

But she did not get him to Philadelphia until May, when he wrote with his characteristic lack of enthusiasm: "I will have the pleasure of waiting upon you Wednesday morning, and hope that the business on which you wish to confer with me will be in such condition as to enable me to leave Philadelphia Wednesday night, on my return home." Everett, also commanded to be present, took a somewhat different tone: "I leave Boston tomorrow morning and pass the night at New York. Wednesday morning I start for Philadelphia, where I hope to stay until the beginning of next week. This will leave me ample time to confer with my dear little daughter, which I am very desirous of doing. I am delighted to hear that your health is somewhat improved, and that your Carolina papa does not expect your return at present." It was during this conference that Mr. Herbert was approved and secured, though whether at this time he was interviewed by the Regent does not appear.

As at Richmond the previous spring, Everett's time was again cut short by his anxiety about his wife, and he returned to Boston, from where he wrote at some length his reflections on the recent discussions, and the proposed procedure for the coming months —pointing out that when the necessary sum for labor and materials for immediate repairs had been deducted, up to $20,000, from the funds in hand, it was doubtful if they would be able also to pay the final installment on the purchase price in time to take possession the following February (1860), which was after all two years before it was due. He also suggested that so long as the final payment had not been made, Mr. Washington would continue to occupy the place and be responsible for it, which was to some degree an advantage. And it was now for the first time that he ventured the advice that they should apply to Congress for a permanent maintenance fund and Government protection of the property, now that they had gone so far alone. It met with no approval, but no immediate argument, from the Regent. A few years hence, this conviction of his went further, into a recommendation to turn the whole thing over to the Federal Government to support and to superintend—a pusillanimous surrender of all the Association's accomplishment which was supported by Miss Hamilton, and which was to make considerable trouble and schism within the Association.

At the end of May Miss Cunningham wrote to Mrs. Comegys of Delaware, that universal confidante, asking her to pay a visit to Philadelphia at the same time that Miss Hamilton, who was travelling with friends, would be there. "Of course the meeting I propose is only a gathering of patriotic friends," she hastened to explain, "not an annual or extra meeting of the Grand Council. But after all, it will be a very important gathering between Miss

Hamilton, Miss Macalester, Mrs. Comegys, and the Regent, for
at it we will decide or arrange matters for our future course in
reference to payments and calling of Council." She thought they
would need a lawyer, and David Paul Brown, who had acted for
her in that capacity on some other matters, seemed to her dis-
gracefully young in appearance, and therefore not suitable. "Is
not Mr. Comegys an elderly, fatherly-looking gentleman?" she
inquired with her rare playfulness. "I trust so. If so, please make
a Mount Vernon *victim* of him and bring him to my bedside!
This writing is execrable, but my nervous fingers will not behave
any better. Pray keep your visit a profound secret! The public are
on the *qui vive* at any move, and as Mr. Washington has been on
to see me, if *that* gets out, and it is known I have held a meeting,
no matter how informal, some sensation writer will announce that
Mount Vernon is paid for, which it is not, and cannot be for
some time, from motives of prudence—more of this when we
meet. . . ."

Therefore in May of 1859 the first meeting of the Regent with
anything like a Council, however much she might disclaim it,
took place in Philadelphia. It must have been an occasion—the
frail, resolute invalid of forty-two; the worldly New Yorker, only
two years younger, but vigorous and stimulating; the Philadelphia
heiress, now in full bloom; and Mrs. Comegys—what was Mrs.
Comegys like?

They decided over the tea-cups that some one ought to go to
Mount Vernon and make a report to the Regent, who was unable
to do so. Washington City was on the way, and Mr. Riggs was
there, and he was the Treasurer, and he should go too. Miss
Cunningham wrote to break the news to him that Miss Hamilton
was travelling to Richmond with friends and would be in Washington over the week-end, and begged that he would accompany
her on an inspection tour to Mount Vernon, and supply a master-
builder who would make a professional survey and give estimates
and advice. Mr. Herbert was already there, as Mr. Washington's
guest, and work was beginning. Miss Hamilton's address in Wash-

ington was so and so, and she could explain their intentions in detail, and desired it to be quite clear that she made the visit as a private individual only, and not in any official capacity. Miss Hamilton's discretion and caution were to become increasingly formidable.

It was short notice, but Mr. Riggs complied, master-builder and all. The boat ran only on Tuesdays and Fridays, so he must also provide a carriage from Alexandria.

They found the Washingtons conspicuously absent from Mount Vernon on the excuse that they had expected to visit the day before. This total lack of cooperation at least left Miss Hamilton's party free to go over things very carefully, and they were distressed at what they saw, from the disintegrating wharf to the raw timbers propping up the piazza. "There should be a universal desire that the Association should take the place, as everything is so neglected and so shockingly careless," she wrote in her Report to the Regent. "The old tomb is being carried away piecemeal, we want a railing around it and a guard who will permit no further pillage. The Tomb is a dreadful sight. A few days work would make the inside at least decent. It seems to me a much more simple thing to do the necessary work there than I had thought before, and that was a great relief. Indeed, I seem to long to have some lady of taste on the spot with command of labor, to begin what would be so pleasing and delightful a task. Mr. Herbert was most gentlemanly and sensible, and Mr. Riggs is a host in himself."

After a second visit in July, Mr. Riggs wrote of substantial progress visible after only a month's work under Mr. Herbert's supervision. As the family remained in residence, nothing could be done about the interior of the house itself, but the walks and seed-houses and garden walls were receiving attention—which Mr. Riggs thought would show visitors from now on that the Association had already begun the work of restoration. "The portico in front of the house will have to be entirely renewed," he wrote. "The timbers supporting the roof are almost entirely gone. Mr.

Washington might consent to have repairs on the portico commenced at once. If it be your wish, I will get Herbert to ask him. A severe storm might blow it down in its present condition." The wharf also, he emphasized, was "in *very bad* condition, hardly safe for the passengers who land at it. I would suggest that you authorize at once a new wharf and the making of a road which would lead to the Mansion, and serve for the transportation of materials for repairs and afterwards be kept as a walk for visitors to the house. By doing this the earth required for the wharf could be taken from the road to be opened. It will cost money, but it is necessary." He was being inundated with applications from landscape gardeners and busybodies who wanted jobs laying out the grounds according to their own ideas. "No doubt many of them could furnish plans for making the most of the grounds and woods," he wrote, "by introducing terraces, walks, and parterres of flowers, but is it not best to put the place in the condition in which General Washington had it? His gardens are there, the ruins of his brick walls can be traced all round the lawns—the walks can be found and restored, without the aid of a professional man. Is it not best to do this, and after all is done, see whether anything else is required?"

Miss Cunningham agreed, and they found an old Negro man on the place whose memory guided them along the original walks which were to be cleared and gravelled and brought back to their proper condition. The income from the boat visitors who were landed at the decrepit wharf had been worth over $1200 a year to Mr. Washington. This amount he was able to turn over to the Association in the autumn of '59, having by then received some $170,000 of the whole purchase price. An army engineer, Captain Meigs, at that time employed at the still unfinished Capitol Building in Washington, gave an estimate of $2800 as the cost of an adequate new wharf.

It was now painfully clear that the $200,000 purchase price was only the beginning. Miss Hamilton, always practical, pointed out that they would have to raise another $100,000 beyond their original goal, just to save the house they had bought, and to restore a semblance of order and decency in the grounds and outbuildings. Fences were an important item. Labor costs would mount up. Building materials must be bought and transported. It was decided to withhold the last payment and use that money for the most urgent repairs, trusting to an increased number of admission fees and more donations to make up the difference in time. They were, after all, well ahead of schedule. The final payment of less than $7000 was not due for another two years.

At the same time they were impatient to possess the place and have it to themselves, without being confronted at every turn by the Washingtons, who seemed to have become accustomed to dwelling in a state of progressive decay. The supposition had been that the family would leave Mount Vernon early in 1860, as the Association could have been paid up by then. Now they seemed apprehensive that they would be forced to vacate before their new home was ready—though it is hard to see how they could have been worse housed at Waveland in any case.

The time was approaching for Miss Cunningham to escape the humid summer heat of Philadelphia in her annual retreat to the New Jersey shore at Cape May, but she was now involved in the unhappy business of Christie Johnson's dismissal, in which she was supported by Mary McMakin, the Philadelphia girl who had for some time overlapped Miss Johnson in the secretarial duties, which were too much for one person to handle. Some years later, when Miss Harper finally had been secured for the Vice-Regency for Maryland, Miss Cunningham recalled in a letter the incidents which led her to the realization that Christie Johnson simply would not do, and blamed her "intolerable presumption" for putting Miss Harper off the whole idea in the first place—Miss Johnson having volunteered to "persuade" Miss Harper to take the appointment by going to see her at Baltimore. Miss Cunningham at that time had not been fully aware of Miss Johnson's peculiar character, but soon discovered (among other things) that she was in the habit of opening the mail and removing from it anything she wanted to before showing it to the Regent. This was done, Miss Cunningham believed, to cover letters received from a lover—perhaps the "ancient wealthy beau" referred to by Mrs. Ritchie the summer before.

Altogether, the position seems to have gone quite to Miss Johnson's head, so that she "spent a good part of her time due to the Association visiting and playing the 'fine lady,' until I was asked," wrote Miss Cunningham with pardonable indignation, "if she was not a lady of fortune travelling at her own expense, and doing what I was—serving the Association gratis." This was hardly acceptable in view of the fact that when Miss Johnson got the post on Mrs. Ritchie's recommendation she was in such straits that it was necessary for the Regent to provide her with suitable clothing, and she was glad to have board and lodging, leaving the matter of salary to be decided whenever the first Council should meet. Also, her health had proved unreliable, and she took a good many days off with that as an excuse, which was not convenient to an invalid employer.

When Miss Cunningham nerved herself to "a serious, kind talk," and told her that she must look out for another situation, she was treated to an exhibition of amateur theatrics in which Miss Johnson "threw herself on her knees before me, clung to me, told me she was a poor orphan, no way to gain a foothold in society necessary to secure her good situations, and it was everything to her future to remain long enough with the Association to familiarize her name to a large circle of correspondents, promised better behavior, and insisted on my retaining her as an act of charity, simply for her clothes and food, during the next winter. If the Association gave her any more she would be thankful, but she would be satisfied if I would accept her own proffer, and regard herself as well paid by the 'fame' she would have a chance to acquire, and the situations 'fame' would open to her! I hesitated," Miss Cunningham recalled, "for I knew the result to my health would be dreadful, but with a silent prayer to God to accept the sacrifice for the sake of the orphan I finally consented."

Unfortunately she neglected to get Miss Johnson's proffer in writing, and early in '59 while Mr. Everett was in Philadelphia the secretary's self-confidence had returned to such an extent that she had had the effrontery to write to Miss Cunningham demanding a new arrangement for her compensation and detailing her requirements, which were quite staggering in the circumstances. "I am willing to give nine hours a day industriously and conscientiously to the duties of my office," she stipulated, "but the remainder of the day must be at my own disposal, and I must be left in perfect freedom to accept or refuse invitations and attentions offered me. The salary is also an important and indispensable consideration, and I cannot think $500 a year, independent of board, washing, and travelling expenses, to commence from 14th of July, 1858, is more than should be given for my services, even before the meeting of the Grand Council. . . . If these arrangements can be made," she continued after further financial details, "I see no reason, my dear Miss Cunningham, why we should not live happily together, you as a kind and useful friend to me, and I as a faithful assistant to you. But if on consultation with Mr. Everett you think you cannot subscribe to them, I must kindly and respectfully say that I shall feel it a duty to myself, though with many regrets, to seek other occupation, and give you the opportunity to obtain another private secretary."

She was apparently counting on the threat of resignation to paralyze Miss Cunningham, but the whole tone of the letter was such as to make any continuance of the relationship embarrassing, if not impossible, and she seems to have discounted Mary McMakin as a substitute. There was a flurry of correspondence, some of it through Miss McMakin, between the Regent and her advisors, including lawyer Brown, as to the customary salary for private secretaries and what Christie Johnson was entitled to in

the normal circumstances which in this case had not existed—
Everett submitted his opinion that it would be kinder to allow her
to resign than to insist upon dismissal—but Miss McMakin on the
Regent's behalf returned a letter of resignation with a curt note
to the effect that the circumstances would not admit of a letter of
that nature—$400 was settled on as sufficient compensation, and
Miss Johnson found, doubtless to her astonishment, that she was
not indispensable.

"A few months after she left me," Miss Cunningham concluded
her recital, "a cousin of hers was killed by accident and she heired
all he had—enough to keep her in comfort, I understood."

To add to Miss Cunningham's afflictions, news had come from
Rosemonte of her father's failing health, and she felt that before
she could make the long journey home to see him she must meet
and confer with some one of the Vice-Regents whose responsibility it would be to watch over Mount Vernon in her absence.
She turned first of all, as everyone always did, to Mrs. Comegys,
who was occupied with a family wedding and could not get away.
The Goodriches, however, arrived from New York for that visit
which was to have such fortunate results, and after their return
home, charged with the search for a private secretary, Mary Mc-
Makin wrote them a letter describing the qualifications of the
ideal candidate in a way which made the whole thing sound
rather like going into a nunnery, and might account for the
egotistical Miss Johnson's rebellion. In the somewhat glaucous
and serpentine style in which Miss McMakin always embalmed
the Regent's dictation, one passage runs like this:

"To be a successful and faithful private secretary, there must
be a capability of laying aside pro tem all individuality, that his
or her mind may be but as a glass to reflect the mind of the
employer. To natural qualities must be added a thorough education, with that facility of composition which will enable her to
perform the necessary duties of secretary to the Regent. Situated

as the Regent is, anyone who took the office would have to give up their whole time, their family, and themselves, to her, while it is absolutely necessary the person should be a lady in feeling and manners. . . ."

The strange thing was, that before the summer was out this paragon appeared, in the person of Sarah Tracy.

Meanwhile the death of Colonel Cunningham at Rosemonte in July caused a complete prostration of the Regent's strength, and Miss McMakin wrote to Miss Hamilton from Cape May where she had accompanied the Regent, along with the maid Grace— "In this nervous and dispirited state, Miss Cunningham shrinks from making the necessary effort to secure at once a secretary, whose services will be so indispensable in the fall, and who should now be learning the duties of her office, which instruction Miss C. feels at present so incapable of imparting."

Miss Tracy's letter of application was dated August 3d, from a place called Mount Savage in the Maryland mountains, where she was spending the summer in the household of John Graham, perhaps employed as a governess, certainly a beloved friend of the family. Prolonged and patient research has failed to solve Miss Tracy and the Grahams, who also maintained a house in New York City. There are two Grahams in the *Appleton Cyclopedia* whose names and dates are nearly right, and who share the same middle name of Lorimer, though apparently unrelated unless coincidentally through their mothers, who are not named there. James was a charming dilettante, though something more than that, a collector of fine books and autographs, a member of the Century Club, a famous host who served his guests champagne and oysters, and who said that "a man should know everything about something, and something about everything." The residence of John at Mount Savage, which might have been a summer home, would be unaccountable, unless again through some connection on the distaff side—he was a criminal lawyer with a large

New York practice, who after the war began received an appointment in the Treasury Department which would have taken him
to Washington just at the time when a "Mr. Graham" figures in
Miss Tracy's correspondence as one of her advisors there. When
we have hopefully progressed this far, the familiar research
monkey-wrench is thrown into the works, and a small photograph
turns up in the Mount Vernon files with writing on the back
which says that the middle initial of Miss Tracy's "devoted friend"
Mr. John Graham was A. and not L. This leaves us nowhere.

Her name had first been mentioned to the Goodriches by their
friend Charles Gould of Madison Square, about whom nothing
further seems to be discoverable. He had written to them in July:
"In every sense she would be just the person, and would, we
think, accept the plan. Lady-like, well educated and bright, agreeable, ready with her pen and her tongue. Every needed requisite.
You will do a good thing for your friend, Miss Cunningham, and
for our friend, Miss Tracy, if you can secure the service for one
and the place for the other."

And a good thing for Mount Vernon. After some correspondence she came for an interview and was promptly engaged. She
was then nearing forty, but most attractive—small and slight, with
humor and self-possession—"a lovely woman," Miss Cunningham
wrote of her that winter. She was born at Troy, New York, one
of a large family, and was educated at the ladies' seminary there
which still functions as the Emma Willard School. She had spent
some time as a governess in New Orleans, where she learned to
speak excellent French and to dress cleverly on very little expenditure. Otherwise, she came out of the blue—a godsend and a mainstay for years.

In any case, by September of 1859 she was installed at the
Regent's side in Philadelphia, working in accord with Miss Mc-
Makin, who was probably only too pleased with her new companion after Christie Johnson. And thus the summer of '59 had
introduced two significant names into Mount Vernon's destiny—

Upton Herbert and Sarah Tracy. The Regent had acquired a
resident superintendent capable of directing the immediate work
with as little friction as possible while the family was still in
possession—and a permanent secretary with tact, charm, and
courage. Both were to demonstrate a lasting devotion to the house
and its traditions without which its future would be inconceivable.

II

There is no doubt that Miss Cunningham felt the increase of national tension as 1859 came into its autumn—if the worst happened, and secession began, the city of Washington stood on the border between North and South, where actual fighting might occur, and Mount Vernon was only a dozen miles South of that line—it might be overrun by one or both armies, it might be shot to pieces, or burned down. And certainly the funds to complete its reclamation would dry up in a nationwide crisis of such magnitude. Neck and neck with disaster, the Association pressed on.

In mid-October John Brown with his twenty-six men raided the arsenal at Harper's Ferry, only fifty-five miles from Washington. Colonel Robert E. Lee, with a company of marines, was sent to take him—and with two sons already dead in the futile fight, Brown surrendered. He was hanged at Charlestown, Virginia, on December 2d. It was a grisly shock to both North and South, and gave cause for additional differences of opinion, which often became violent. The Democrats in Congress said the Republicans were instigators of lawlessness and murder. The Republicans began to wear revolvers under their coats.

About the middle of December the *Mount Vernon Record* got out an Extra—not about John Brown, who was ignored, but to announce that Mount Vernon was now "virtually the property of the nation." With a balance of only $6,666.66 due, the Association had in hand upwards of $20,000 with which to clear itself and begin the long, expensive program of repair and restoration. Miss Cunningham had prepared for the *Record* her final published statement:

131

"In the deep gloom now overspreading our political horizon," it read, "this noble sisterhood of the Mount Vernon Association stands as the chief beacon light looming through the darkness which can cheer the eye or encourage the heart of patriots. Radiating from the tomb of Washington—himself the beacon light of the world, whose life, with all his virtues, toils and sacrifices, cannot have been in vain—its fire will never be extinguished until his memory ceases to be revered on earth!

"By raising the means to effect the purchase, we have redeemed *one* pledge. Mount Vernon is now no longer *in danger from any contingencies* incidental to *private* possession. It remains now for us to consider what is included in the other obligation, in order to prevent contingencies incidental to public possession, viz., to provide for Annual Maintenance, Constant Security, Constant Repair, after we have transformed Mount Vernon *from what it is* to *what it was* under the watchful care of the great Chief, who, though he lived for his country, never forgot nor neglected his much loved home. . . ."

The question of calling a Grand Council, thus interrupting the Vice-Regents in their work of collecting funds, was decided in the negative, until the ceremony of taking possession could be given a date—Miss Cunningham longed to make this in February of 1860, but was reminded of the bad weather at that time of year, the travel conditions for the Western Vice-Regents, and the immediate need for expenditure at Mount Vernon—so the 4th of July, 1860, became by a sort of tacit consent the general goal. Mr. Herbert wrote from Mount Vernon that the road from the boat landing was under construction, and that he had sent to Susquehanna for new pickets for the fence, as there were none suitable in Alexandria. A newspaper account, signed only by initials, describing a visit to the house, complained that boat passengers were in actual danger of losing themselves through the crevices of the wharf, which "oscillated" under their weight, and urged its immediate reconstruction.

Everett's wife had died during the past summer, in the same month that Miss Cunningham had lost her father—and persistent eye trouble shortened his letters to her, though he was now likely to write an enclosure—one which began "My dear friend," and was designed to be shown as his official opinion, being accompanied by a briefer personal message to "Dearest Pam." In this November the rumor of his engagement to Miss Hamilton was current in New York, as reported to the Regent by Mrs. Goodrich —an old acquaintance having been quickened by mutual interest in the Association was probably the foundation, but nothing came of it, and it was never referred to between himself and the little Regent on her sofa—so far as remains.

When Miss Tracy went up to New York to spend Christmas, '59, with her sister and friends, the Regent wrote to Miss Hamilton of her "secretary and friend—a treasure to the Association and myself," and Miss Tracy was expected to make contact with her and with the Goodriches. On December 30th the first of Miss Tracy's beautifully penned, gay, and affectionate letters was sent back to the Regent—"I am not certain that you really expect to hear from me, but as I like to be *civil*, if nothing else, I conclude to announce my whereabouts," it began. It was full of news and chat, and quite without the formal involutions of the McMakin style. Her friends had met her at Jersey City—her sister was in "an ecstasy of delight" at their reunion—they had all gone to Christmas service and heard one of Dr. Hawks's choicest sermons —they had made an expedition through bitter cold to Brooklyn on a visit—she had called on Mrs. Goodrich, found her out, left a card, and returned home *"congealed."* "Does Miss McMakin coax you out of bed?" it inquired, revealing that Miss Tracy habitually tried to do so. "I know of nothing to prevent my returning as I promised on Tuesday. Will you be glad to see me? I can see no difference in the sleeves worn here. The most universal is like my *blue merino*—tight sleeves are the latest, but few persons fancy them. Small flowing, like my *green silk*, are also worn. . . ."

On January 3d, she wrote that she had had a "pleasant interview" with Miss Hamilton, and had caught a terrible cold—"I have not been able to utter a loud word since Tuesday"—and Miss Hamilton urged her to remain a day or two longer until she got rid of the hoarseness. She had nevertheless packed her trunk "in opposition to my body," but might not after all be able to come as she had hoped, and if she waited might still be able to see Mrs. Goodrich—"God bless you, and grant you all the happiness consistent with His justice, and renewed strength for every trial. . . ."

New life, new light, new warmth and energy, had entered the Association—along with a sense of humor, which it had hitherto been lacking.

A depressing report from Mr. Herbert in mid-January said that a third of the wharf had fallen in, and if the break-up of the ice should be accompanied by a strong wind, he would not answer for the remainder. The road leading to it was in such a state that a pair of horses could hardly pull an empty wagon up. He had sent the estimates to Captain Meigs, who made no objections to them, and Herbert was now anxious to close the contract with a man named Bradshaw to begin the job.

A few days later he wrote indignantly about a story in the Philadelphia press which the Regent had enclosed to him—to say that its statements that visitors to Mount Vernon had been subjected to rudeness and unfriendly supervision were false. There had been a day, he recalled, "when some one called my attention to a person descending the hill on his way to the boat with a large piece of holly partially concealed under his shawl. I took that occasion to express my disapprobation of such conduct to such persons as were near me, in strong language. I did not know the man, nor was I near enough for him to hear me, though it was not my intention to conceal from him my feelings regarding such conduct. I did not know whether he was from North, South, East, or West, nor is it necessary for me to know anyone's place of birth or residence in order to treat him with politeness. The attempt to give the vigilance necessary for the protection of the grounds and buildings a sectional turn is simply absurd, as it is simply impossible for myself or for the hands in the employment of the Association to know from what portion of the Union the numerous visitors come. . . ."

The strange, unrelenting hostility of certain elements of the press toward the Association and Miss Cunningham herself was to continue for years without any reasonable foundation.

It was about this time that she confided to Mrs. Comegys her intention to go to Washington and establish a headquarters there, where she would be much nearer to Mount Vernon, and to the several Vice-Regents whose husbands' affairs brought them to the nation's capital. She hoped, wrote Miss McMakin, to "build a Council fire, and have a great talk over matters and things pertaining to the cause." And she begged Mrs. Comegys to join her there for a private conference first.

Contributions had slowed down, and the vast sum needed to salvage their treasure and maintain it—forever—was nowhere in sight. Miss Cunningham had at last made up her mind to ask help from Congress, now that she had done all the spade-work and Mount Vernon was about to come into the hands of its saviors. Everett in Boston assured her that there should be no difficulty with Congress now—and advised her not to be "too humble" about the amount she proposed to ask for.

Mr. Washington still resided at Mount Vernon with his family —the final payment had not been made, because that money must be devoted instead to the wharf and the portico and a general tidying up of the grounds. But some time, surely by the 4th of July, there must be some kind of flourish, as the Washingtons departed and the Association took formal possession of its prize. This too required discussion by all the Vice-Regents available short of a Grand Council.

Miss Tracy and the maid Grace were to accompany Miss Cunningham to Washington. Miss McMakin would remain in Philadelphia as a sort of home office until the Regent's return in a few weeks' time. What seems not to have occurred to them was that it was an election year and Congress had a few other things on its mind.

Settled in at Willard's Hotel, the Regent lost no time in her attempt, in her own rather surprising phrase, "to raise the wind" for the maintenance fund. The *National Intelligencer*, run by old Colonel Seaton ever since 1812, was one newspaper which was kindly disposed towards them. Seaton was a Virginian himself, and had been born fourteen years before Washington's death. A friendly article which appeared in its pages was widely circulated by the Association, and did something to arouse new interest in the public mind, now much diverted by politics. Along with Colonel Seaton, Mr. Riggs was of course a powerful Washington influence in their favor, though his wife, who was the Vice-Regent for the District of Columbia, was a very retiring woman absorbed in her family duties, and inclined to leave her other obligations to her friend Mrs. Merrick.

But the Vice-Regent for Indiana proved to be an unexpected reinforcement. Mrs. Harriet Satterlee Fitch was the wife of the Honorable Graham Fitch, the distinguished doctor of medicine and surgery from Logansport who had become Senator from Indiana. Mrs. Fitch's lively letters make the record of this anxious period both vivid and, in spite of everything, amusing. As the wife of a Senator she was of course well acquainted in Washington society, though there was a sharp distinction between the political set and the regular citizens, to both of whom Miss Cunningham came as a stranger. With Mrs. Fitch's aid she began to organize entertainments and benefit performances by well-disposed professionals, carrying on her campaign in the preoccupied and excitable atmosphere of the imminent Presidential Conventions which would precede the election in November.

Among their several projects was one to bring Mr. Everett back to Washington to act as a sort of figurehead—they contemplated among other things an excursion to Mount Vernon for the members of Congress, with him as one of its sponsors and guest speaker

—but he was correcting proof-sheets on both his memoir of Washington for the *Britannica* and the volume which contained his *Mount Vernon Papers*, and wrote that much as it grieved him he would be compelled to refuse.

Mrs. Comegys had come to Washington only to be called home by the illness of her husband, which proved to be so serious that she was unable to return. Miss Cunningham and Mrs. Fitch wrote despairing letters to her, in the firm belief that her continued presence there would have somehow solved all their problems, as her acquaintance in the city was apparently wide. Plans for the excursion went forward, with the Rev. Dr. Hawks, the New York clergyman, author, and late editor of the *New York Review*, invited to appear in Mr. Everett's place. Miss Cunningham hoped that if she could show the members of Congress and some distinguished citizens of Washington the state of the Mansion and the work now going forward there under Mr. Herbert's direction. they would respond to the need for money for all that was still to be done.

"The die is cast!" she wrote to Mrs. Comegys on April 11th. "Our invitations are out. Every member of Congress with his family has been formally invited to an excursion on Saturday at 2 o'clock. Mrs. Riggs issued the cards in her name. Of course this forces her into a very public connection with it, and in consequence she will not attend herself. I have never seen or heard of Mrs. Johnson [Kentucky] since my note urging her especially to visit Mount Vernon in company with Mrs. Fitch and myself on a former occasion. Mrs. Pendleton [Ohio] is in seclusion, Miss Macalester [Pennsylvania] is here. The President's and Miss Lane's reception day is Saturday—we asked her to postpone it but the city is full of strangers, and the President, I suppose. objected on their account. So poor sister Fitch stands alone, and hopes that sister Comegys can arrange to take part in this grand demonstration!

"Jesting aside, dear friend, it is an *important event* in our history, and one you will no doubt wish to behold and to take part in. Come, then, and try to aid in carrying it out well, can't you? Mr. Saunders says it is Easter holidays for the children, but run away for all that, if Mr. Comegys is well, nay, can he not come too, and hear the plea for help issued from that tottering piazza at the door of that decaying Mansion we are trying to save!

"I leave here next week, feeling I have done all my feeble hands can do to overcome the apathy existing over this whole country. If this last effort fails, why, I had better shut shop, dismiss secretaries, and go to my own home. If we collect no money, we must not spend any. Of course I keep up a show before the uninitiated, but even that can't last much longer, if things continue as they are. *Truly, this is our Valley Forge!* A season which tries me far more than all the difficulties encountered before, because of all the trying responsibilities it forces upon me. Much more could be done through Washington City, were I in a situation to do it, not a stranger shut up in a sick room with access to but a few, and those not of the kind to carry out our plans—this being the case, it is useless for me to remain, only until I see the result here of my present device to create an interest.

"The Rev. Dr. Hawks, who has been invited to repeat his address on the character of Washington at Mount Vernon has not replied yet, so you may imagine my anxiety, for our success depends on his coming. . . ."

Dr. Hawks, for some now unknown reason, cruelly disappointed them. Miss Cunningham's account of the expedition, written to Mrs. Comegys, is nevertheless quite a happy one, though a severe reaction on her own nervous system followed the unusual exertion. After a wet morning, which may have deterred the timid from starting, the sun shone, the marine band on board the boat played, and there was never a dearth of orators in a gathering of that kind. The Vice-Regent for Delaware had been unable to leave her husband, Georgia was detained and did not arrive in time, and Ohio failed to appear as promised. But Mr.

and Mrs. Riggs deferred their intended journey to New York to attend, which was considered a victory, and Mrs. Eve was expected the next day, which would be a comfort.

Mrs. Fitch, whom one longs to know better, took a slightly oblique view of the occasion, in her report to Mrs. Comegys:

"Well, our excursion went off pretty well," she wrote, "much better than I feared at a time when politics absorbs the minds and bodies of all the 'lords.' Dr. Hawks you know did not come, and Miss Cunningham was in despair at the disappointment, and feared that the proper speeches would not be made. She ordered me up to the Capitol to see John Cochran, and make him promise that he would go, and if necessary speak. I went and saw and 'conquered.' My husband had the promise of Mr. Keitt that he would go and speak. He did neither. Mr. Crittenden promised Miss Cunningham that he would go at all events, which promise he did not keep. (I think the lady is the opposing power in that case.)

"There were some two or three hundred persons. Mr. Herbert had a platform erected before the piazza facing the Potomac, and seats prepared for the audience. Mr. Thomson of Indiana was persuaded to speak, which he did in a very appropriate manner. He did not allude to the important object of the excursion, but left that begging part to be done by Cochran after he finished. Cochran was loudly called, but echo answered *Where?* Dr. Fitch was called, he had vanished. We did not think it well for the husband of one of the Vice-Regents to be begging. It might be called 'interested motive.' At last Mr. Doolittle mounted the rostrum and bawled about union and disunion, a regular political speech. I was in despair.

"I went to Mr. Riggs and to Mr. Herbert and told them that man would ruin all. Some one *must* speak who would say what ought to be said. I at last went up the back part of the platform and spoke to Colonel Seaton, who presided, to ask *what* could be done, I would not dare to go back, Miss Cunningham would die outright. He said Cochran must be found. Mrs. Merrick started in one direction and I in another, after him. She found him, with some others, 'wetting their whistles'! As he came out, he said to me, 'Mrs. Fitch, *what* do you want me to say?' I said—'*Dilapidation, decay, money, Association*—point to those old posts propping up the piazza! Tell them to listen to that rattling window—! etc. etc.' Mr. Riggs thought it would not do to say much about the desolation and decay on account of the Washington family, who were listening. I told him I didn't think they were very sensitive on the subject!

"Cochran at last began, and said all *beautifully*. One of the young ladies (?) of the family stood on the piazza immediately behind Mr. Cochran and talked and laughed with some young man so loud that it disturbed everyone. It must have been to show her indifference to the subject, I presume.

"How very much I wished you had been there. Miss Cunningham wished and wished for Mrs. Comegys, but not as much as I have. You have no idea what a time I have had since you left! It would be impossible to describe all I have experienced, on paper at least. Mrs. Saunders looked shocked when I said to her the other day that I was 'tired of Mount Vernon,' but I defy the greatest patriot living to have my experiences for two months and not feel tired of the subject *sometimes!* I would not for the world say such a thing before anyone but those who I *know* to be true. Mrs. Saunders had just heard that Miss Macalester had made such a remark to some persons here, which I do not think was at all proper. She said so to me, but I did not suppose she would speak in that way to those not interested.

"Miss Cunningham has now strong hopes that Congress will make an appropriation, which as you probably know was the object in inviting them to this excursion. If they do we can take possession of the estate on the Fourth. I cannot think they *will* do anything so sensible! *Now*, of course, it would be folly to attempt to call it up, when half of them will go to Charleston, even if they do not adjourn, and after the Convention they will have forgotten that they went to Mount Vernon.

"Miss Tracy has had a better offer for her services, and talks of leaving the cause, but may conclude to remain. Miss Cunningham does not know what to do about remaining here until Congress decides what they will do. I do not see that she can further it by remaining, do you?

"I have scribbled on here and can't tell what I have said, but I must stop, it is after twelve. The house is full of Hoosiers going to the Charleston Convention. Our rooms have been full all evening. All are now in bed but me, and I am almost asleep, so excuse all errors and write soon how your dear husband is. . . ."

Everett wrote to his "dear little Regent" that he had begun to hope that now Congress might be willing "notwithstanding the engrossing business of President-making, to make a handsome appropriation" for Mount Vernon, in consideration of what had already been raised—if the grant were stated to be for the necessary repairs, the enclosure of the grounds, and their restoration to the condition in which they were left by Washington. He spoke of $100,000. Meanwhile, he had delivered his Washington oration in New Hampshire for proceeds amounting to $225, and was off the next day to Maine where he did not expect to pick up more than $150.

Mrs. Fitch's low opinion of Congress was entirely justified. Not a penny. But Miss Tracy did not desert the ship.

12

In April of 1860 the Democratic Presidential Convention in Charleston split in two and half of it walked out, to reassemble at Baltimore and nominate Senator Stephen A. Douglas as their candidate. The rump decided on Vice-President Breckinridge, a Mexican War veteran and lawyer of Kentucky, who had been in Congress since 1851.

In May the Republican Convention in Chicago nominated the "Black Republican" candidate, Abraham Lincoln, over his chief competitor, Senator William Seward of New York State, and South Carolina let it be known that if Lincoln was elected the State would secede.

Miss Cunningham and Miss Tracy returned to Philadelphia in June, having watched these ominous developments with deep thankfulness that at least Mount Vernon had been secured against time—for who could tell what the situation might be by February of 1862, which would have been their final deadline on the purchase, and which they had beaten by a comfortable margin? But the idea of taking full possession with July 4th ceremonies (1860) had been reluctantly abandoned, and the last payment was still withheld in Mr. Riggs's bank, while funds for the immediate work going forward under Mr. Herbert were being doled out from there. The contract for the wharf and road had been closed, for a sum not to exceed $4000, and a lumber bill of $1700 had been paid.

By the evidence of letters written long after the event, it appears that Miss Tracy had recoiled fastidiously from the repercussions of the Christie Johnson affair, into which she had stepped unawares, when she first entered upon her service with Miss Cunningham. She thought David Paul Brown, who appears to have taken Miss Johnson's part against the Regent, a vulgar man the like of whom she had never encountered before, and she experienced an almost overwhelming impulse to retreat at once to the more attractive offer which would have taken her back to former associations in Louisiana. Moreover, she had soon found the position of secretary to the Regent too exacting, in the long hours of writing it entailed, and the hours themselves often extended beyond a normal working day.

The Regent somehow persuaded her of the necessity of remaining until the organization could be got on a more stable footing. Miss Tracy saw it as her duty not to desert the frail, overwrought woman she had come to regard as a friend. With much inward reluctance still, she resigned herself, and in July signed a contract as private secretary, on the understanding that she could return to the Grahams at Mount Savage for the summer, while Mary McMakin again accompanied the Regent to Cape May. In September she would rejoin them at Philadelphia and they would go down to Mount Vernon together, with the intention of residing there and making it the headquarters of the Association during the work of reclamation. Mr. Herbert wrote to inquire whether it would not be advisable to have two or three rooms newly plastered, painted, and papered, with a view to their proper accommodation.

With Miss McMakin as the Regent's companion at Cape May, letters went out from there to all the Vice-Regents, regarding the proposed meeting of the first Grand Council, which would signalize the formal possession of the estate and transact the necessary business for its maintenance and restoration during the year to come. Two dates were offered—the anniversary of Washington's death, which was December 14th, or his birthday, which would be February 22d, 1861. Both were in the winter time, when travel was more difficult, but writing for the Regent Miss McMakin added that Miss Cunningham hoped that no Vice-Regent would allow "a light obstacle" to prevent her attending. At least, the

Regent's temporary mood of despondency had passed again, and there was no more talk of shutting shop.

Miss Tracy's letters from Mount Savage that summer were a cheerful chronicle of welcoming festivities in her honor, carriage picnics, and church goings with old friends—besides an endless discussion of candidates for the still vacant Vice-Regency of Maryland. Returning via Baltimore and Philadelphia in September as agreed, she made arrangements for their lodging in Philadelphia until they would be ready to move to Mount Vernon, and continuing her holiday in New York she called on Mme. LeVert, who was at the Fifth Avenue Hotel after a Northern tour during which she had visited Mr. Everett at Boston.

The Washington family had finally removed themselves, bag and baggage, to their new home near Warrenton, sometime in June, although John A. was still likely to turn up unexpectedly at Mount Vernon, where he had kept a room for his own use during visits to his farms roundabout—which must have made rather a jumpy state of affairs for Mr. Herbert. Early in September, at about the time the Regent left Cape May for Philadelphia, a visitor to Mount Vernon wrote an unhappy account of its condition:

"The work of restoration is going on slowly, and from what I could see and judge, correctly. The house presents a dreary aspect enough. Every room is thoroughly sacked of its contents. Pictures, statuary, and furniture are all thoroughly cleaned out, and nothing but the naked walls remain. In the [cut out] one table and three old knapsacks remain. In the first room on the left hand side of the hall [west parlor] one old sofa is all that is left. The rear room is stripped of everything. The old Bastille key is all that remains in the hall. The Library contains a single table and chair only; books and everything else have been removed. These were the only rooms to which we could obtain access, for the reason, as assigned to us by one of the Washingtons who was there, that 'the ladies still owe Mr. Washington $6000, and till that is paid visitors could not have access to the *whole* house;' though he assured us that the other rooms were entirely empty. He also said that the remaining furniture would soon be removed. This was a surprise to us all, because we had supposed that the *old* furniture of Washington was included in the purchase of Mount Vernon. If it was not so included, a great mistake has been made; 'the home of Washington loses more than half its interest without these old relics,' was the universal remark yesterday by the unusually large number of visitors."

It seems unlikely that it was Mr. Herbert, noted for his courtesy, who was quoted by the writer. And as practically all of Washington's own furniture had been long since dispersed, the removal of the recent contents of the house was probably no great loss, except to those who were soon to inhabit it, and must begin with naked walls—though Mr. Herbert was of course roosting in one of the upstairs bedrooms with a few articles of his own furniture brought from his home called Bleak House near Fairfax Courthouse.

Another visitor to Mount Vernon, one of considerably more importance, arriving in October, found only Mr. Herbert to receive him as the Regent was still in Philadelphia. Accompanied by Mrs. Riggs as hostess for the Association, England's Prince of Wales, the future Edward VII, and a distinguished party which included President Buchanan, sailed down the Potomac in a revenue cutter.

"The day was lovely, and the run of twenty-five miles down the River was enjoyed by all," one of the Prince's suite recorded in his journal. "As the President and the Prince left the vessel for the shore in the first boat, the latter with the tiller ropes in his hands, no one could fail to be struck with the singular circumstances of a President of the United States being steered by a Prince of Wales, great-grandson of George III, to visit the tomb of Washington! As they both stood together before his tomb, how much was suggested by interest in the past, of hope in the future!

"The house is sadly dilapidated. It has been recently purchased by an association of ladies for a large sum, and presented by them to the nation. Mrs. Riggs, the lady secretary, was with us and did the honors of the place. It commands beautiful views of the River from the rocky and wooded eminence on which it stands. . . ."

Writing on October 20th to Miss Cunningham, Mr. Herbert said that the old portico had been pulled down and the new one was being put up, so Mount Vernon must indeed have made a sorry appearance for the royal guest.

The political situation that autumn made it unlikely that anyone would bestow much attention on Mount Vernon, to say nothing of cash money for the collections, until after the new President was elected, and even a February Council would be overhung by the dislocation in Washington City of an impending inauguration. The immediate problem was to make the old house habitable for the invalid Regent and Miss Tracy. "I would like to know if you intend to have grates put up in the dining-room and library," Mr. Herbert wrote. "If you do, what kind of coal would you prefer, so that I can get the grates and have them put up in anticipation of your coming to Mount Vernon. I have been looking out for servants. . . ." Mr. Herbert's communications to the Regent always began: "Dear Madam—I have had the honor of receiving your letter—" and his handwriting was exquisitely beautiful and very hard to read.

The death of Miss Cunningham's father a year ago had made her presence at Rosemonte an obligation, though why she was needed to run the plantation where her mother still lived, while her brother was close by, is unanswerable, except that Ann Pamela Cunningham seems always to have been the one, frail as she was, on whom responsibility fell. After a short stay at Mount Vernon she now intended a visit home during the winter and a return early in '61, when she would settle down to supervise the repair and restoration of the Mansion—and would then presumably release Miss Tracy, at the end of her year's contract term in the summer, providing a suitable substitute could be found and trained.

Meanwhile it was Miss Tracy's fearful joy to be sent to New York to shop for Mount Vernon—everything from kitchen utensils to window-curtains—to supplement the bleak bachelor arrangements of Mr. Herbert. A continuous documented record of the early days of the Association is impossible to accomplish, despite the hundreds of letters and press cuttings which are now in the possession of the library at Mount Vernon—hundreds more were burned at the Regent's desire and by some of the Vice-Regents for a variety of reasons. But occasionally one comes upon a run of letters which are a delight, and this occurs during Miss Tracy's sojourn in New York that autumn. It is another mystery why they did not procure their supplies in Philadelphia, unless they had reason to suppose that things would be much cheaper in New York, and that the advice of Miss Hamilton and the faithful Mr. Graham would make the journey worth while.

However it came about, Miss Tracy wrote back to the Regent her oddly gay, yet meticulous letters, revealing at once the humor and the resolution which were to sustain her and Mount Vernon in the perilous years so soon to come. The weather was against her, and the people she wanted to see were elusive. But Miss Tracy was enjoying herself, and knew very well what she was about.

"It can rain in Gotham, equal to any other place!" she wrote on October 30th. "It has poured incessantly all day! I have lost this twenty-four hours entirely, not a line from either Mrs. Goodrich or Miss Hamilton. Mrs. LeVert leaves town tomorrow, if she did not go today. All the advancement I have made has been to talk with Mr. Graham and make him think where our articles can be bought. He will have to work the harder when he begins. If I hear nothing from Miss Hamilton I will go to the house at which I saw her last summer and enquire about her. If she is not in town I will go to Dobbs Ferry, a not very agreeable alternative, but it will save time." On Wednesday morning it was still raining, and she added a postscript. "The moment it lessens a little I am off to see who I can find. The enclosed note has this moment arrived, and I have written to Miss Hamilton that I will see her this evening. And now I am off to look up Mrs. Goodrich. I think it will clear, the clouds look brighter, and anyway I can *paddle,* for it will be little else in these frightful streets. I hope you are feeling well and 'patriotic.' Love to Miss McMakin . . ."

On the 1st of November she could report progress, and the details, considering that the house was Washington's, and the occupant would be the woman who saved it, make fascinating reading.

"I am so tired that I can scarcely guide my pen," Miss Tracy wrote, "but nevertheless if you will put on your *patient* spectacles and remember that you often receive extraordinary *looking* documents from me, I will try to tell you all the news I can of my doings and Miss Hamilton's sayings. In the first place, I saw Mrs. Frank Goodrich who informed me that Mrs. Mary Goodrich had left early Tuesday morning for Connecticut, so my advisors were reduced to *Miss Hamilton,* but as you rely so much on her judgment I kept my appointment with her last evening—I was with her two or three hours, and she talked not only like a *business* woman, but very sweetly of you. She had just received a letter from Mrs. Ritchie about your going to Mount Vernon; she understands your feelings on the subject, there was no question but it would be best for the Association, but you ought not to pay *anything* towards the furniture unless to please some fancy, your room ought to be *nicely* furnished by the Association. I told her you preferred not at present, but were anxious to be as economical as possible for the Association. She said she understood that, and approved of an economical and careful disposal of the

money, but you must be comfortable, and live in a proper manner
for the dignity of your office. She said I must buy a Brussels
carpet for the sitting-room, and a set of furniture (Mr. Graham
came in at the last, after I had talked over the confidential part
with her.) She and Mr. Graham decided that a nice set could be
bought for $75. In this she enumerated sofa, chairs, center-table,
small side-table, and table-cover; these she said were no more
than she and every lady would think *essential*—she said that I
must buy *good* carpets, and oil-cloth by all means.

"I inquired about the spoons and forks; she said I ought to
get a *dozen* of everything for the table, that there would be no
place to buy more if they were needed, and they must be marked
Mt. V.L.A. I told her if I did as she said it would, I feared, cost
$400 or $500, if not more, and she said she knew that, and it was
not too much. I then said that if she said so I would do it, but
it was too great a responsibility for me, and *you* told me to do as
she said. She replied, 'I do say it, and you had better get everything here, even crockery.' She said she was very sorry she could
not aid me personally, but she was to be occupied with the artist
until Saturday evening, and her sister was to be married on the
8th. I told her if I was troubled I would see her again in the
evening. She thanked Mr. Graham very handsomely for being
willing to aid me. She thought you did right to send me on, but
you ought not to pay my expenses. She thinks it right to defer
the meeting till spring. I will tell you the rest when I see you. I
have been all day buying. I bought the carpets at *cost,* the Brussels
at $1 [per square yard?] and the ingrain at 75¢. They are very
nice. I was frightened at the idea of *daring* to choose *carpets* and
oil-cloth for Mount Vernon—but did the best I could.

"Miss Hamilton advised me to buy all that was to be bought
for the other rooms first, and leave the sitting-room until the
last, then try at some of the *auctions,* and if I could find none,
buy it at a store. I want you to please send me word which color
you prefer, crimson or drab? The parlor carpet is crimson and
wood color. It is almost impossible to find the hair-cloth nice,

and it is as expensive as the colored coverings, and shall I get a striped table-cover, they are fashionable, or is it of no consequence? I shall be able to let you know tomorrow how much more money I shall want, they could not send me the bill in time for the mail. . . .

"Mr. Graham said I must buy a *soup tureen* and plates. I told him you had said nothing about it and I would not venture without asking. The crockery is to be packed on Saturday, so please send me word. They will cost, tureen and soup plates, $4.00— and he says Mr. Everett cannot eat soup out of *cups,* and they cannot be bought so cheaply again, as I have bought everything at *cost.*

"Of course I cannot get away before Monday afternoon or Tuesday morning, but am just as busy as I can be, too busy to think of politics, though most of the world is excited on the subject, and the Democrats say if Mr. Lincoln is elected it will be the fault of the South, for they have by their course sent *thousands* of votes to him!

"The freight all goes in a schooner on the 10th by sea, at low rates, and I have had it *insured,* as it cost but little and the Association could not afford to lose it. Mr. Graham thinks at a rough calculation that $100 or $150 more will pay our bills, but you had better wait till I receive the bills. Shall I buy a large-sized kerosene lamp and have it packed with the crockery? A *very* nice one can be bought for $5.

"I believe I have said my say—if I was not so tired I would be all in a *bumble,* at my temerity, but I am too weary to be frightened! I *hope* I have done right and that you will be pleased with my purchases—

"Love to Mary McMakin—adieu—yours truly,

SARAH C. TRACY

"I hope you will not be obliged to keep this till I come to decipher it—if you lose patience, try to read one of Mrs. Fogg's by way of recreation!"

Mrs. Fogg of Tennessee, who was then in her sixties, wrote a large, unconventional scrawl, four or five words to the line, possibly with a quill pen, which had apparently caused some anguish at Philadelphia. The artist with whom Miss Hamilton was engaged at that time was the English miniaturist, Richard Staigg, who did an exquisite likeness, set in pearls, which is now the property of the New-York Historical Society.

On the 2d, Miss Tracy wrote that she had nothing to say, and hence wrote to say so. Miss Hamilton had left town, as had Mme. LeVert, and she supposed the Regent had by now seen the latter. She expressed concern because Miss Cunningham's maid, a Philadelphian, was threatening to leave her rather than be separated from her accustomed surroundings—but again Miss Cunningham's persuasion prevailed, and Grace accompanied her back to South Carolina, where she died of typhoid fever during the war, still in the Regent's service. "I am going about three miles to attend an auction," Miss Tracy wrote, "and if I was certain I had not done the best I could, would offer myself to the highest bidder, provided he bid high enough. What is the use of being *downhearted*," she demanded briskly of the mournful Regent, "I think if you were to undertake to wade through this mud and drizzle your heart would sink if your feet did not! I never saw anything like it! And then the fear and trembling lest all should not be right! I am told the weather is not to change till after the election. . . ."

The next day she had received two letters from the Regent written by Miss McMakin, which restored her confidence to some degree—"There is some comfort in the consciousness of trying to do right, but it is exceedingly agreeable to be approved of in one's course," she remarked with her wry humor. "I have done nothing in the way of purchases that Miss Hamilton did not advise, in the presence of Mr. Graham. The merchants not only sold us the linen and crockery at cost, but when the bills were made out the crockery merchant took off five per cent of the

whole, and the linen merchant took off ten per cent! Today it
has poured every moment. I went out, but found the storm so
violent that the auction sales were postponed, and I was wet
through and was obliged to return, and it has not ceased raining
for one second, but is, I believe, the commencement of the second
deluge! You will be shocked to hear that Mr. Graham will not
reach home in season to vote! But there are many Democrats, I
am told, who will not vote who are at home. I expect you will
have to resign yourself to Mr. Lincoln as the next President of
the United States! Suppose you object to permitting him to visit
Mount Vernon—he can get the rails split by other hands. . . ."

Jibes at Lincoln by even the most enlightened and gentle folk
were common at that time. He was a stranger to the East in
general, he was an unknown quantity, he had been widely and
wilfully misquoted, and in many minds he had assumed the
proportions of a monster. And the jest about his visiting Mount
Vernon was to prove not so far-fetched as Miss Tracy thought at
this time.

She got back to Philadelphia to find Miss Cunningham "completely overcome at the political prospect," but looking forward
to what was for her an ambitious project—a visit to Mrs. Comegys
at Dover. Judge Comegys was not yet sufficiently recovered for
his wife to leave him, much less to attempt the journey to Philadelphia himself, and they all felt the advisability of a conference
before Miss Cunningham departed South for the winter.

It is surprising that neither secretary accompanied her to Dover,
but Miss Tracy was required at Mount Vernon to supervise the
disposal of her purchases before the Regent's arrival there, and
Miss McMakin was left as usual to hold the fort at Philadelphia.
They saw her off with only Grace to attend her, on the afternoon
train, in a state of fatigue after "being tortured by a dentist,"
and what was probably almost as bad, having her likeness taken.

Miss Tracy wrote to her on the 23rd of November from Washington, where she was staying with her friends the Hills—her

acquaintance was amazingly wide, and in Washington included the Varnums and a friend of Mr. Graham's who was—with an exclamation point—a *widower!* Mr. Herbert and the captain of the Mount Vernon boat, Bryan, had come at once to see her, to report that the furniture and so forth, sent by boat from New York, had not yet arrived. A violent rainstorm had prevented her from going down to Mount Vernon to see what was already there, in the way of accommodation—Mr. Herbert had thoughtfully arranged that a friend of his, Mrs. Hyde, should accompany her as soon as the freight arrived. He was to let them know when the vessel reached Alexandria, and "if not a boat day, he can get us down," she assured the Regent.

Mr. Herbert had in the house four bedsteads, but there was a shortage of mattresses. "If our own purchases will only come, I am sure we can be made very comfortable," wrote Miss Tracy hopefully, and indeed for both of them it was a doubtful adventure. In spite of the election and the coming inauguration of Mr. Lincoln, Washington was still very quiet, and most of the hotels were closed. The Mount Vernon boat had been running twice a week, with only eight or ten passengers, but Captain Bryan promised her that "if it would pay, he would be glad to run every day!" It was thought that by December Washington would begin to fill up, and justify more frequent trips.

There was now an additional worry in the formation of a commercial company to build and operate a railroad from Alexandria to Mount Vernon, just for tourists, with a terminus at the boundary of the estate. They had even taken the Association's name in vain, and published that it would buy stock up to $20,-000, whereas the Regent felt only dismay at the prospect of crowds of "promiscuous visitors" being dumped there at all hours of the day at cheap rates, which would make the protection of the property by the employees of the Association almost impossible. Mr. Herbert was quoted by Miss Tracy as saying they were "a pack of swindlers," and Mr. Varnum thought it would be a good idea to insert a notice in the Washington papers to the effect that such an enterprise was against the interests of the Association, and that its name had been used without its consent.

The letter ended with the news of Mrs. Washington's sudden death from apoplexy, leaving seven children motherless, the eldest, Louisa, only sixteen, the youngest, George, not yet three.

The next letter from Miss Tracy at Washington found the Regent back at Philadelphia, confined to bed with a severe cold, although she had been so stimulated by her Dover adventure as to brave the dentist again on a damp afternoon. Miss McMakin wrote the bread-and-butter letter for her to Mrs. Comegys, and provided an affecting glimpse into the loneliness and bleakness of Miss Cunningham's accustomed existence: "She feels most sensibly the return to her old life, after the oasis of domestic happiness she has been permitted to touch at in her visit to you," she wrote. "It seemed almost like a new world to her, and she will not soon forget your affectionate entertainment of her. The brief sunshine of her visit already exists only in the past, and the shadows of anxiety and apprehension have settled once more upon her path." A few days later she wrote again, with reference to the railway company, and added that the visit still seemed "like a dream." Poor little Regent, so soon to set out, with only Grace as a companion, on the long winter journey to her remote up-country home, to a widowed, ailing mother, and the cares of a mismanaged, masterless plantation.

Miss Tracy's November 28th letter from Washington was full of bustle and confidence. The furniture had come, and was being sent on to Mount Vernon, and she was to follow it down with Mrs. Hyde for company. Captain Bryan was ready to make any arrangement desired for the Regent's convenience, including a revision of his schedule to spare her the necessity of an overnight stay at Alexandria on her way. Miss Tracy had inquired and learned that there was a very comfortable Ladies' Room at the depot where the Regent could rest, and get breakfast.

On December 1st she wrote an account of her first visit to

the house which was to play such an enormous part in her as yet
unsuspected destiny, and whose existence as it is today she herself probably preserved. She had had to go down and return in
the same day, as Mrs. Hyde failed to receive Mr. Herbert's message in time, and Miss Tracy could not, of course, remain overnight at Mount Vernon without her.

"The house looks better than I anticipated," Miss Tracy wrote,
"though some rooms are shabby enough—still, we can make it
very comfortable. I will have to make some purchases in Alexandria. There are hardly any kitchen utensils at all, and an *absolute necessity* is window shades for the library, or curtains, for
the windows open to the floor and 'the people' all feel privileged
to look in the windows; if you will answer this by the five o'clock
mail, directing to Mr. Varnum's care, he will send me the letter
by Tuesday's boat, and then you can tell me which to buy, *shades
or curtains,* and if the latter of what material. Miss Hill has just
informed me that there are very pretty worsted materials cheaper
than chintz, that I can buy, and I will run out to see and add
the prices in a P.S. She says she will buy it for me and send it
down.

"The servants Mr. Herbert has engaged seem *very* nice, there
is a man, a fine Negro, who is jack of all trades. He made and
put down Mr. Herbert's carpet, is an excellent waiter, and has
quite *an air*—and will be of value to us; a good cook, and a
young mulatto for a housemaid for us, she *looks* civil and useful.

"I enclose the sample of the *cheapest* thing I can find for
curtains, it is one yard and a half wide, one dollar per yard.
Perhaps it would be well to have turkey red for the library and
something better than this for the sitting-room. I think it will
require at least eight yards for the library windows, this material
is so wide that one breadth will suffice for each side of the window, so after all, it is not so very dear. Please write me what you
think, something is very necessary, and you will not be obliged
to buy any other furniture for the dining-room, unless you pur-

chase of Mr. Washington the tables now in the room; they are part of the large ones that were in the banqueting-room; the chairs are *good enough.*

"Mrs. Hyde will go down with me on Monday unless it rains, which it does most of the time. I hope you are better, and are not out of patience at these many but unavoidable delays. We have done all we could to conquer adverse circumstances, but they cannot always be overcome. Much love to all my friends, and tell Miss Smith [the landlady at their Philadelphia boarding-house] that I did not see a single *rat* or *mouse*—but I did see a *cat!* Yours affectionately—"

It was December of 1860, and the country was poised on the brink of what many still hoped and prayed could by some miracle be avoided—civil war. Miss Cunningham, firm of purpose, high of spirit, however frail in body, accomplished one more tremendous step—she arrived at Mount Vernon. This time she came not as an intruder on its rightful owner, nor as an anxious visitor or a mere inspector of work done by a deputy—she came with personal luggage and with business records and correspondence files which would constitute a headquarters, and a room had been prepared for her reception which was to be recognized henceforth as hers. In effect, she came home to Mount Vernon.

To avoid climbing stairs, she apparently occupied from the beginning the room still furnished as a downstairs bedroom, opening into the library, which was used by the Washingtons and the Association as a dining-room, and the old dining-room was then furnished as her sitting-room. There were five bedrooms opening off the hall at the top of the staircase, besides General Washington's room over the library. The four corner rooms were almost of a size, two of them shaded by the roof of the piazza from the glare of the morning sun on the River, two looking westward down the bowling-green. The middle one, over the west entrance, was smaller and by tradition had belonged to Martha's son, Jacky Custis. Mr. Herbert had been established in one of these five as a guest of the family—the one always known as the Lafayette Room for its most distinguished occupant in the old days—and he remained there after the departure of the family, having brought his own bedstead, bureaus, and wash-stand from Bleak House. Miss Tracy and Mrs. Hyde probably shared one of the others, which would remain the secretary's room, and Grace probably had a cot downstairs in the sitting-room or the Regent's own room, to be within call night and day. At least one of the upstairs bedrooms was still unfurnished the following spring, and the third floor rooms would have been impossible in winter.

It is interesting to contemplate the Regent's emotions, as she sank thankfully into bed that night, after the long, cold journey in December weather—and Miss Tracy's too, as they said good-night and she carried her candle away to her own chamber upstairs. They must have exchanged a look of triumph and exhaustion, mixed. They had actually done it. They were here. Mount Vernon was actually theirs, by virtue of the Association, of course —but they held possession now, it was in their very hands at last. They were both sensitive, highly strung, deeply religious women. There would have been no nonsense about a Washington ghost, but perhaps they could feel with due reverence that wherever he was, however far removed from this imperfect world into everlasting glory, he would know in some way what they had done, and be pleased. Tired as she was, it could not have been easy for Ann Pamela Cunningham to drop off to sleep that night under Washington's roof, which was now to shelter her for a time, and would be forever preserved by the machinery she had set in motion.

Her unconquerable nervous energy would have roused her next morning to an exhaustive tour of the house and its wintry grounds, guided by Mr. Herbert with some pride of achievement since she was last there during the previous spring—the piazza restored, the outbuildings carpentered to house the remaining workmen, the garden walks opening up to reveal the remnants of Washington's old brick walls.

Inside the house, the sitting-room must have looked fairly comfortable, with the crimson carpet and the "set" of furniture insisted upon by Miss Hamilton as due the Regent's dignity, and the fire in its new coal grate giving at least the appearance of warmth—the walls still needed refinishing. The dining-room furniture was miscellaneous, the tables purchased from Mr. Washington—who had not the grace to present them—and chairs which were "good enough" but did not match, the windows framed by the cheap new Turkey red curtains. And it was doubtless here that Miss Tracy would do the endless writing in the endless correspondence of the Association, which it would soon be her responsibility to deal with alone during the Regent's absence—an interval which she expected to spend with the Grahams at Mount Savage.

From Mount Vernon on December 17th, 1860, the Regent wrote to Mrs. Comegys:

"My dear friend—Your most welcome letter of the 7th was forwarded to me from Philadelphia and received on Saturday in the midst of one of the severest snowstorms I ever witnessed! A thousand thanks for its loving words—they stirred the chilled blood in my veins, and helped to warm up the other ice-bound prisoners in this isolated spot, so dear to *us* and *history*.

"I have not been able to write you before, and can only send a line now, for I have been and still am under highest steam pressure—almost bewildered—by the multiplicity of cares and rapidity of events pushing me on in advance of energy to meet demand. I was ill for some days after my sweet visit to Dover—which did my heart good, and helped me to nerve myself to meet the future with more courage. But between my severe cold and the exactions of and sufferings from the dentist, my business was greatly interrupted and delayed, giving me neither time nor strength to communicate with my friends.

"I bore my journey to W. City far better than expected—was

met by Mr. and Mrs. Riggs (as well as the faithful Mr. Herbert) the latter of whom took us in her carriage to the boat. The new road was used for the *first time* on the day of my arrival—so that I had the pleasure of being the first person driven over it! Miss Tracy had done all she could to make us comfortable—but this is like all old houses—every door and window (and their name is legion) provides ample space for the entrance of cold and wind, and as we have had the severest kind of weather we have suffered seriously.

"Nothing but a residence here could make known *all* the difficulties which have attended and *must attend* all arrangements to protect the place. Even I could not enumerate them on paper, even if I had the time. Suffice it to say that we have a *treasure* in Mr. Herbert, and that he has done wonders under the circumstances, and that his life has been and must be one of self-sacrifice—for Mount Vernon is removed from conveniences to business as well as all *society*, which makes his strict confinement here a severe tax. He will feel this not a little on my return!

"Everything looks well—a great change in all out-buildings. The portico is up & being painted. New sills put to the Mansion, etc. To protect ourselves & treasury against visitors by land some arrangement will be made to close the gateway to Alexandria & prevent the entrance of visitors except by payment of the 25¢ received on the River side. I have not done anything in reference to the railroad yet, because the financial crisis now felt everywhere precludes the *possibility of collections at present,* & will enable us to delay action—prudence will suggest this—as act when we may, we provoke controversy and make enemies.

"The whole earth is covered with snow!—the prospect is magnificent! I wish some fairy could transport your household to the cupola of this 'sacred mansion'—you would revel in the *coup d'eil* —but alas! for the poetical things of life. This beauty is bestowed greatly at our expense, for we must if possible leave here tomorrow, & as the land side is 'snowed up' it is very alarming to behold the immense sheet of ice which the River presents at the moment. To be blockaded *now* will be distressing, for I desire to reach my gallant State *ere the storm breaks!* . . .

"I can give you no definite idea as to my plans. I had determined to go first to Columbia—Capital of my State—but the small-pox has broken out there, and I must now await my arrival in Charleston ere I can tell how long I may be absent, as I am the slave of circumstances and must not return until I have concluded my own necessary *private* arrangements.

"If you do not get posted, dear friend, from time to time, it will be because I am incapacitated by journeyings, and being without a secretary I shall be powerless. There is an extra chance to mail this letter by private hand, and I have only a moment allowed me to enclose this little lock of hair cut from my head some years ago, as a token of love borne to your kind and highly prized family. . . . Ever your most attached friend, A. P. Cunningham."

They were none of them aware that Mr. Herbert's ordeal at Mount Vernon had only begun, nor had they any idea of what lay before the secretary, who had given up the opportunity to return to a comfortable situation in New Orleans to stand by the Association and its hard-pressed Regent.

This letter to Mrs. Comegys makes no mention, oddly enough, of a meeting with Mr. Washington which had taken place a few days before. Miss Cunningham had written him from Philadelphia to express condolence on the death of Mrs. Washington, her deep concern over South Carolina's threat to secede as a result of Lincoln's election, and her obligation to go home and set her affairs in order there before the worst happened—which would not be, they thought, before the inauguration in March, by which time she hoped to have returned and established herself at Mount Vernon with Miss Tracy until its reclamation was completed. She asked him to come to Mount Vernon now during her present stay there, and he complied. In a somewhat hurried interview— owing to the pressing affairs he always pleaded when she required an audience with him—they had discussed the dire possibility that Virginia might also secede, and he reassured her that his will protected the interests of the Association in the event of his death, although the deed to the estate had not yet been delivered to her by his executor. She in turn urged him to feel welcome there whenever he chose to make it his home during a visit to his adjacent farm, and they parted on the best of terms.

She and Miss Tracy worked very hard on the correspondence, sending out long letters to the Vice-Regents, of which those received by Mrs. Little and Mrs. Morse have survived, and duplicate each other—long hours of patient copying by the secretary being involved. It was explained therein how the public impression that the Mount Vernon work was accomplished with the payment of the purchase price, together with the political agitation of the public mind, had caused contributions almost to cease, so that the necessary repairs had absorbed a large part of the remaining capital, and left the final payment still to be made. The Regent had therefore spent a wearisome time in Washington City to very little effect, and had then decided that the only possibility of reawakening interest was to call a meeting of the Council for the formal assumption of the title, with appropriate ceremonies including an address by Mr. Everett before a distinguished audience at Mount Vernon, and the 22d of February, 1861, had been unanimously chosen.

However, the letters continued, recent events—meaning Lincoln—had now produced an emergency which made it necessary again to postpone such an occasion until the country was calmer. The Regent had accordingly taken what steps she could for Mount Vernon's safety, for while the workmen employed on the repairs also acted as its protectors, most of their immediate work was done, and their number would be reduced. She had therefore thought best to remove the effects of the Association from Philadelphia, its files and records, to the Mansion, with the intention of residing there herself for a time, as by so doing she could make her private resources available for its maintenance.

That is, by living at the Mansion and eliminating her Philadelphia expenses, the Regent could herself support and guard Mount Vernon until a meeting of the Council could devise some better arrangement. But first, she must make a visit to Rosemonte, leaving her private secretary in charge of all correspondence, from the address at Mount Savage where she would await the Regent's return.

It was the best they could do pro tem. They left Mount Vernon by the snowy road a few days before Christmas, and said goodbye to each other at Washington—in sufficient anxiety, heaven knows, but still mercifully ignorant of all that would take place before they met again. Another of those unanswerable questions arises here—if the Regent had known that it would be six years before she could return to Mount Vernon, would she ever have left it at all?

13

She had a frightful journey home in inclement weather, and sent back an account of it to Mrs. Comegys. She had found Charleston in an uproar. South Carolina had passed the ordinance of secession on the 20th of December. Major Anderson, a Federal officer from Kentucky, in command at Charleston Harbor, had for some time been begging for an increased garrison at Fort Moultrie, believing that the State would attempt to seize it if and when secession occurred. On the night of December 26th he slipped out of Moultrie, leaving spiked guns behind him, and arrived with his small force of some seventy men including a band at Fort Sumter, on an island in the Harbor —thereby making it necessary for the Federal Government to reinforce and supply him, or order him to surrender to secession. His motive was to avoid bloodshed, he said in his report, for his men were certain to fight if South Carolina had tried to take possession of Fort Moultrie while he occupied it. His action of course infuriated Charleston, and even at Washington was thought hasty and ill-advised.

Miss Cunningham left Charleston soon after Christmas, and pressed on to Augusta, where she arrived at Mrs. Eve's home at 11 P.M. in a state of exhaustion. She remained there for a few days' rest, and between there and Rosemonte, travelling by railroad and carriage, she encountered freezing rain, which caused further delay in the hospitality of her "second mother," a onetime teacher.

At home she stepped into another hornet's nest, for Mrs. Cunningham was a "violent secessionist," and urged her to resign from the Association altogether and devote herself to the management of the plantation in the absence of her brother, who had rushed off to Charleston. "She calls me a Northerner because I mourn over the past and present," Miss Cunningham wrote sadly to Mrs. Comegys in February, "but above all she takes it hard as a neglect of her for me not to give up, come and attend to her interest and mine." Later in the month she wrote again, as though still in full expectation of her certain return to Mount Vernon as planned:

"I have been ill ever since I reached home, and am just beginning to feel better. Shall be overwhelmed with business until I leave. Not only has our estate to be settled but a division made of everything. But I, who know nothing of such business have to instruct myself how a plantation should be managed, in order that I may keep an overseer in the path of duty, and keep our darkies from seeking property—which is about all that has been done for some years past. Between Mount Vernon on one side and my own perplexing cares on the other, I am truly beneath the upper and nether millstones.

"I am greatly distressed at the situation of my mother; her life of solitude, harassed with business cares of a nature entirely new to her, has proved too much for her age and infirmities. She needs some one to lean upon, though it be but such a frail prop as myself. She is bitterly opposed to my going to Mount Vernon, she thinks it unkind to retain my office if it takes me from her and causes, as it must do, the sacrifice of my own interests—so you see how it is. Yet should I resign, the election of another officer in the present distracted and embittered state of the public mind would be opening our pandora's box and perhaps lead in the end to the destruction of the Association from dissension, etc. It is not, therefore, to be thought of, but how can I bear the load which is nearly crushing me? I expected to have returned by the 4th of March! I cannot say now when I can go. Buchanan has not the firmness to meet the exigencies of this crisis, Congress seems destitute both of reason to comprehend and of will to try to do so. . . ."

She did not, of course, hope for anything constructive from the new administration which would take over in March. Whereas Buchanan, old and tired and confused, was only waiting to dump the whole thing into Lincoln's lap.

There ensued at Rosemonte a lop-sided compromise, which found Miss Cunningham attempting to cope with both responsibilities at once, and by a much interrupted correspondence to keep in touch with her representatives in the North. Her hands were crippled with rheumatism. Her eyes troubled her, and she feared blindness. She had the assistance of some devoted nieces, from her brother's home twelve miles distant, which made it possible for her to dictate her letters. The maid Grace, who had accompanied her reluctantly from Philadelphia, on the promise that she would not have to continue in service at Mount Vernon after their return, was unhappy and uprooted, and the girl whom Miss Cunningham had hoped to take back with her from Rosemonte to fill Grace's place was expecting an increase in her family and could not go. Her mother, infirmities or not, was to live on in whatever state of resentment until 1873.

Writing reminiscently some years later to her friend and physician Dr. Dickson, who had gone from Charleston to Philadelphia, she gave an account of the disastrous situation she found at Rosemonte even before the war began: "Negroes are an expense under the most energetic and economical managment. I had neither friend, relative, nor capable neighbor to look to; and overseers are proverbially unreliable, even under the constant surveillance of a competent master. From ill health and old age my father had been, for years before his death, incapable of managing his plantation; his overseer proved faithless, his Negroes careless and wasteful; consequently at his death the plantation had gone to rack and ruin, and needed more than it produced to restore it and to support the Negroes and make a living. I received nothing for a year after his death, and was compelled to incur debts. When I returned home I found my affairs and my prospects depressing indeed. Additional debts had to be incurred in order to carry on farming at all." And yet, in an undated scrap of a letter written some time during the war, she would advise Miss Tracy to draw on the deposit in Mr. Riggs's bank for the day-to-day maintenance of Mount Vernon, and add, "I will replace it as soon as I sell my cotton; at present, what little money I can command from any other source is more than needed to buy mules."

Miss Tracy went back to the Grahams at Mount Savage in time for Christmas, 1860. After seeing Miss Cunningham to the boat for Charleston, she had paused in Washington for a last consultation with Mr. Riggs, who thought that the final payment of the purchase money should now be made out of the funds in his hands, to provide against any emergency—but for some reason this was not carried through.

Her first letter which followed Miss Cunningham South contained a characteristic passage of her glancing humor: "Mr. Riggs wishes to be particularly remembered to you, and said I must be certain to tell you that he said now that you had gone to South Carolina, which would be full of heroes, he hoped you would marry one of them; that there was a certain Captain Quattlebaum who was quite distinguished, that he would recommend. If you should do such a wonderful thing, please make him change his name. It is not half as nice to write as *yours*! I shall be very anxious to hear from you. Try to keep quiet, lest you exhaust yourself. A happy New Year. . . ."

She immediately caught a heavy cold at Mount Savage from the severe weather, and was confined to the house except for going to church, when she had to "bundle up like a mummy." But she wrote to the Regent nearly every day, giving news of the state of opinion in the North, and reporting on the letters she received on behalf of the Association.

She was in frequent correspondence with Mr. Herbert at Mount Vernon, and there was another flurry of anxiety in January over the proposed railroad, which as planned by its directors would be an outright eyesore, requiring a third entrance and a gravel walk to be made where none had ever been before. "I think those railroad people are very annoying and excessively stupid," wrote Miss Tracy, "for they have surveyed the ground and I only walked over it once. How they could imagine you would permit such a gash to be made in the grounds solely for their benefit I do not understand. I think when you return you will have to have a personal interview with the whole company, to convince them that if you *are* a woman, you are not to be imposed upon!"

The railroad died of the hard times and a proposed turnpike, and did not arrive till 1893, when it proved to be a mixed blessing, as it subtracted passengers from the boat, from which the Association derived a percentage.

Miss McMakin had been left at Philadelphia without a job, but in reply to a kind inquiry from the Regent she wrote that she had got a sort of temporary employment with something called the Publications Society, as "the School Institute folks can do nothing for nobody just now." The long suspense and wild rumors preceding the inauguration of so controversial a figure as Abraham Lincoln was killing business, and poverty was increasing everywhere. "I don't see what you are going to do down there with the political question," she wrote, "or what any of us are going to do, in fact. You are no stronger a Union woman than when you left, I perceive. Are you going to stand by the Association notwithstanding its Northern elements? I presume so, and I hope no distractions may agitate it." Miss Macalester had married a Belgian diplomat, M. Berghmans, in an impressive ceremony. "They had seven bridesmaids," Miss McMakin reported, "headed by Miss Lane. The groomsmen were all members of the Corps Diplomatique. The richness and beauty of the toilettes was very remarkable. The diplomatic ceremony came first, involving the reading of the Belgian laws on matrimony, and the signature of some papers by the bride's brother and others. Then followed the Catholic ceremony, and finally the Presbyterian, when the knot was considered firmly tied." So henceforth the Vice-Regent for Pennsylvania would be Mme. Berghmans.

Miss McMakin was not the only person, friendly and otherwise, who wondered how the Regent's inevitable Southern sympathies would affect Mount Vernon, and Miss Tracy was the natural target for many awkward innuendoes, some of which were bound to find their way into the newspapers. "There is one thing that troubles me very much," she wrote from Mount Savage as early as the end of January. "I am constantly asked by people from every direction whether it is true that Miss Cunningham is a secessionist, and that with not the most agreeable prefaces to the remark! I do not know half the time what to say, particularly when told, as I was the other day, that it would break up the Association; for how could they have at their head a woman who, after proclaiming through the country her love for Washington and the Union publicly sides with the disunionists? I asked him his authority. He said from a friend with whom you had discussed politics. I told him there must have been some misunderstanding, but I could not move him, and as I did not know him very well was obliged to let the matter drop. But I was very much worried. On Saturday a gentleman living three miles from here sent me the Alexandria *Gazette* with the enclosed marked. It is taken as you perceive from a South Carolina paper, and this closes my mouth until you give me a decided answer. I fear this will do great injury as it will be copied everywhere. . . ."

It was only one of several vicious rumor campaigns against Mount Vernon and the Regent, with more to follow—a form of political and partisan malice which it is hard to comprehend.

When letters from South Carolina were delayed, either by illness, or interference with the mails, Miss Tracy's anxiety did not overcome her sense of proportion—"I begin to think it is time to advertise for you," she began her January 31st letter, when she felt she should by then have received word of Miss Cunning-

ham's safe arrival at Rosemonte. A week later she had heard of
so many letters being opened and read along the way that she
was convinced theirs had been interrupted in this way. "I intend
in future to seal them, for while there is not much treason in
what I write, yet I do not quite like the idea of my property
being meddled with," she wrote.

Her almost daily bulletins must have been eagerly awaited by
the Regent, isolated as she was from the beloved spot on the
Potomac where her every thought had dwelt so long—Mme.
LeVert's mother had died of heart disease, and the Vice-Regent
was prostrated with grief, Miss Tracy wrote; Mr. Riggs had lost
his young daughter Jessie from diphtheria at her convent school
in New York, arriving there only five minutes after she died;
Mr. Herbert's place in the military company which as a Mexican
War veteran he was expected to join had been filled, and he refused to join any other, somewhat to the surprise of his friends.
(Virginia was still in the Union at this time, though by February 1st, 1861, Mississippi, Florida, Alabama, Louisiana, and
Texas had all followed South Carolina in dissolving the bond
which had linked all the States to the central government over
which the first President had presided.)

Mr. Herbert wrote Miss Tracy that he feared he had too small
a force at Mount Vernon for the protection of the place, let alone
in any emergency. There was trouble about the boat which plied
between Alexandria and Mount Vernon—the company having
decided to lay it up for repairs after February 5th, just as Washington would fill up with visitors for the inauguration, and a
substantial increase in the number of admission fees might be
expected. Mr. Herbert wanted the Regent's authority to run the
boat himself for the Association, or to buy the charter, but Mr.
Riggs advised against it. As it turned out, Mr. Herbert was more
than right, but this was discovered too late.

The Grahams intended leaving Mount Savage for their home
in New York, which did not appeal to Miss Tracy for a variety
of reasons—"climate, high board, etc."—and she had arranged

to stay with her friends the Hills in Washington for a time. She
wrote from there on February 19th:

"I am very glad I came down when I did. I came a week
sooner than the family, but it was instinct brought me. I was
uneasy at not hearing from you, and when I reflected upon what
Mr. Herbert wrote about the *Collyer* being laid up for repairs, I
concluded to come and see about it, and glad I did. I stirred them
all up. I found from friends who are staying at Willard's and
the National that there was a good deal of grumbling because
there was no boat for Mount Vernon. I sent for Bryan [the boat
captain] and scolded. He has been so stupid. During all the bad
weather of January, because the River did not freeze, they continued to run at a loss, carrying from 5 to 40 people. And now
when Washington is literally crammed, and so many want to go,
they have laid up the boat!

"I saw Mr. Bryan on Friday and told him to do something
The Peace Congress want to go down in a body on the 22d or
before, and he said he would see. He came yesterday and said
he *hoped* to have a boat by Thursday. I told him there was no
such thing as Hope or Perhaps, *it must be done* He owned he
had made a mistake and now he must repair the mischief, and
that the public would be down on the Association, and the Association upon his company. He said he would do his best and
let me know this evening. I told him that in the meantime I
would see Mr. Riggs and consult with him. Mr. B. replied, 'You
need not see Mr. Riggs, I will make some arrangement, and run
every day after till the 4th of March.' I saw he was more afraid
of Mr. Riggs than of me, so up I went to see Mr. Riggs. I told
him the story, he knew nothing of it, but said he would see Mr.
Bryan, for a boat must be had. So I consider that thing done."

It is doubtful if the genial Mr. Riggs was half as terrifying to
any male culprit as little Miss Tracy with her deceptive fragility
and the sharp edge to her tongue.

Her February 22d letter to Miss Cunningham said that after wet, miserable weather that day was perfect—and if only the Council could have met at Mount Vernon "would it not have been grand?" After some uncertainty as to where it would be best for her to live, pending the still hoped-for return of the Regent for their anticipated residence at Mount Vernon, she had settled in the Clarendon Hotel at Washington, where her friends the Middletons were staying and wished to keep an eye on her. It was more expensive than the rather dreary lodgings she had contemplated at Alexandria for reasons of economy, but Alexandria now was really no place for a lady to be alone, and all the single rooms in the small lodging-houses in Washington were long since taken. Besides the Riggs family, Mr. Graham was in Washington, Mr. Everett had been there, and Mrs. Comegys was apparently a frequent visitor to the capital. Mrs. Fitch was at home seriously ill, and the Doctor meant to go to her. It is pleasant to be able to record that she recovered, and exercised for years her valuable astringent influence in the Association. Mrs. Barry of Illinois wrote of her intention to come to Washington, and hoped to see the Regent then—adding her approval of Miss Cunningham's proposed sojourn at Mount Vernon, as a pledge of its "wise care," no matter what happened.

The inauguration of Lincoln took place in an atmosphere of tension and gloom. The weather that day was raw, the parade was brief because it was not thought tactful to make a display of military force in a city which was on the borderline of secession, and there was little applause for the man who could scarcely be seen riding with Buchanan in a carriage closely surrounded by a protective screen of cavalry. It had been publicly threatened that he would not live to be inaugurated, and that the day would not pass without an outbreak of sedition. Nothing happened.

Anderson had now been immured at Fort Sumter for two months and his supplies were running low, so that he could soon be starved into surrender. The foremost of many hideous problems confronting the new President was whether to reinforce and

supply Sumter, or order it evacuated, which amounted to surrender. His Cabinet was divided, suspicious, and unhelpful. There
continued to be threats of assassination and kidnaping against
Lincoln, and the Commander-in-Chief's mail also was full of
menace by cranks. General Winfield Scott, who held the position
Washington had once filled with dignity and wisdom, was toler-
antly known as Old Fuss and Feathers, from the plume in the
old-fashioned cocked hat which surmounted his six-foot-four
bulk. His career went back to 1812, and he had distinguished
himself at Chapultepec in 1848. An aging, ailing, overweight
wreck of former glory, he had first advised Buchanan to
strengthen the Southern garrisons, and now was all for evac-
uating them to avoid bloodshed. A Virginian, he was still a
Union man, and showed no disposition to resign his post and
place his allegiance with the South, as Beauregard, Johnston,
Magruder, and eventually Lee were to do.

Miss Tracy made no comment on the inauguration, and doubtless took no notice of it, though the streets of Washington were
filled with unwelcome strangers—Western place-seekers, Baltimore plug-uglies looking for a fight, uneasy militia men called
up to keep order, and the gilded society crowd come to inspect
and possibly patronize or ridicule the household from Illinois.

14

Early in March, Miss Tracy went down to Mount Vernon by the restored boat, on a lovely day.

"The place looked very sweet," she reported to the Regent, "though nothing more has been done about the Mansion than painting the portico and one side of the house. They are now at work on the other side. The windows have been washed, and a great deal of cleaning done—but there is plenty yet to be done. I could not see the half I wanted to, there were so many people about. But Mr. Herbert informed me he had about $200 more than when we were there.

"He wants permission to put General Washington's room in perfect order, that is, *plaster, paper, and paint*. He says if the room had been in order, he could have paid a man to guard it, and made money besides. One of the Lewises is about breaking up housekeeping, and Mr. Herbert says he can get some chairs on deposit, and I am on the track of a dressing-table used by General Washington, which I think I can get on deposit. In this way the room can be furnished and will pay. Mr. Herbert says the sills will last three or four years longer, but the *roof* can no longer be delayed, it leaks badly and will injure the house. He wants permission to *shingle*.

"The little porch by the library windows is coming down on itself. Would you like a plain narrow balcony, or platform-like, without a roof, or steps placed there temporarily until the rest of the house is finished, just for our accommodation? It would not be expensive. . . ."

On the next boat day, when she was going down again, she encountered on the pier the Vice-Regent for Pennsylvania, Mme.

Berghmans, with her husband and a friend, and made the trip in their company. The former Lily Macalester was glad to hear news of the Regent, which she was seeking, and went over the Mansion with Miss Tracy and Herbert, agreeing with them that it would be a good thing to furnish and exhibit the General's bedroom as an additional attraction. Hitherto apparently only the ground-floor rooms had been shown. She then presented Miss Tracy with a proposition which it was perhaps as well that Miss Cunningham was not there to rule upon.

Mme. Berghmans, it developed, had seen Mrs. Lincoln several times—she was "rather stout, dresses in admirable taste, and receives like a lady," Miss Tracy reported. "Nothing coarse, or unladylike in her manners or conversation. All the slang and bad grammar attributed to her was false." Mrs. Lincoln—who came of a good Kentucky family—having passed muster with the Vice-Regent, Mme. Berghmans had felt obliged by various queries and hints received in the course of her conversations with the President's wife, to suggest to Miss Tracy that the Association should offer the use of the boat to Mrs. Lincoln for a visit to Mount Vernon with a party of her friends. Miss Tracy was sufficiently horrified.

"I told her the proposition had been made to me, but I had declined, saying I had not time to hear from you, and I never did anything that looked like assuming authority, and I would tell her what I did not like to say out loud—that I did not care if they never went! She said she thought I was mistaken, and if the offer was made in the name of the Association to Mrs. Lincoln and party, it would have an excellent effect. The city is as full as before the inauguration, and if we cannot get other money we may be thankful in our poverty to get Republican gold!"

Miss Tracy therefore conceded, on condition that Mme. Berghmans would go down with the Lincoln party, and take the re-

sponsibility—and agreed to write out the invitation as Secretary
to the Association. Mme. Berghmans—Corps Diplomatique—
suggested that refreshments should be provided at Mount Vernon.
Miss Tracy thought not, and Mr. Riggs, who was "always against
excursions," backed her up. It was enough that the party from
the White House should be welcomed at all, and "the thing is
to be kept quiet and not published. Mrs. Lincoln has accepted
this morning, and they go down on Friday," the letter concluded.
"I hope you approve. I think if you were here, you would as
Regent. As woman, I do not, but have been overpersuaded by
unanswerable arguments. All the Republican town will go down
afterwards, and we must make money. The rumor is this morning
that the troops are to be withdrawn from all the forts in the
seceding States. If they do that, they deserve to go to Mount
Vernon!"

But complications arose. On Friday it rained, and Mrs. Lincoln
asked for another day. Then the young Lincolns came down with
the measles, and it was again deferred. Mme. Berghmans went
off to Philadelphia on a visit, and Miss Tracy considered the
matter at an end, until she received an agitated message from
Mrs. Merrick, Mrs. Riggs's friend, begging her to make arrangements for the Lincoln party to go *tomorrow,* which was a public
day.

Miss Tracy collected the indispensable Mr. Graham as escort
and hastened to Mrs. Merrick, who—because of the secrecy maintained—had first heard of the affair from Mrs. Riggs that day.
"Of course it would not do at that late hour to take the boat off
a regular day for Mrs. Lincoln," wrote Miss Tracy to the Regent,
so she and Mr. Graham had driven on to the White House to
explain that Mrs. Lincoln could not be given the boat on any but
an intervening day, that the Association could do nothing that
would excite unpleasant feeling or look like taking part with
any public policy, that the Regent was absent, and also the Vice-
Regent for Pennsylvania, who had requested the invitation for a

day named some time ago—but if the party wanted to go as
ordinary passengers on the regular trip they were quite welcome
to do so. . . .

They were received at the Presidential mansion by Mrs. Lincoln's brother-in-law, Mr. Kellogg, who was "very much of a
gentleman," and perfectly comprehended the situation once it
was explained to him. He said he would inform Mrs. Lincoln
that if she chose to go on that particular day she must take her
chances with the crowd, and he promised to send Miss Tracy
word of the decision that evening. "That is the last I have heard,"
she wound up the letter. "It is raining, so I presume they did not
go. But I am tired of them, and wish they were in Joppa!"

She soon learned that the weather notwithstanding, Mrs. Lincoln and her friends had gone by the regular boat, "like anybody
else," and, added Miss Tracy for the Regent's consolation, "they
did keep it quiet, and Mr. Lincoln was not invited, and could
not go, and there has never been any notice in the papers, I see
them all, of his going, for he has been over-run with office-
seekers." Nevertheless on the following day a brief paragraph
about Mrs. Lincoln's trip did appear in the *Washington Star,*
which Miss Tracy enclosed to the Regent, with a conscientious
addenda: "Mr. Herbert was very polite to them, took them in
the Banqueting hall and General Washington's bedroom, and
the gardens. His dinner was just ready, and he gave them a little
lunch, of bread and butter and *ham!* On the whole, they had a
very pleasant time, and particularly Mrs. Merrick. She has been
shut up all winter with a very bad sprained foot. She sprained it
last November, and has been a great sufferer. She walks with
difficulty even now, but was so anxious that some one should go
that would do the honors properly that she went notwithstanding
—and notwithstanding it was a private party to which she was
not invited!"

So thanks to Mr. Herbert's Virginian good manners, refreshments were served to the Lincoln party after all.

Having reassured Miss Cunningham against the dreadful possibility that Abraham Lincoln had set foot at Mount Vernon, Miss Tracy passed on to more important matters, unaware that the time was coming when she would think more kindly of him.

"I think my letters must be bewitched," she wrote, of inexplicable delays. "I received yesterday yours of the 19th, saying my last was dated the 3d of March. Why, I have written a dozen letters in that time, sometimes every day, and when there was nothing to write about, I have written a few hasty lines to say there was nothing to say!" The roof continued to cause concern, and without waiting for the Regent to authorize its repair she had told Mr. Herbert to have the shingles cut ready. A post office depot exclusively for Mount Vernon had been established, with Mr. Herbert as postmaster. They were still awaiting the Regent's opinion about furnishing the General's room with bedstead, dressing-table, and chairs, and showing it at an additional fee. The wind had carried away the covered passage from the house to the kitchen, and one side of Judge Washington's rickety little porch. Some of the details are illuminating:

"Mr. Graham went with me to Alexandria to inquire about the furniture there, and he thinks you could not get the same any cheaper in New York, or Philadelphia. The man will make a single bedstead, a kind of French bedstead, simple but rich, for $14, a tufted, haircloth mahogany chair, low, such as I think you would like, for $13, and like the one you saw in the hotel parlor, a kind of rocking-chair without rockers, for $30.

"I could find but one place to inquire about curtains, etc., and the prices were absurd, but I have heard of another to which I will go, and write you the answers to all your other inquiries. I could not get a pillow-case that pleased me, and wrote to my sister for the latest. The weather is very Marchy and disagreeable. I have a wretched cold in my head, and have not been out since Monday, but if I had received your letter yesterday I would have gone down to Mount Vernon today. I forgot to say that I asked Mr. Herbert the price of one coat of paint on the sitting-room. He said, Not much; but I said that would not do, you must have a definite answer and he said he would tell me the next time.

"What are you going to do about another carpet?"

These furnishings were of course further to the expected occupancy of Mount Vernon by the Regent and Miss Tracy during the coming summer, for neither of them was willing to recognize the difficulties which were so soon to become insuperable as the fatal April of 1861 slipped away. A Mrs. Matthews, who had accompanied the Regent on her homeward journey the past December and was apparently counted on to return North with her, besides the maid Grace, does not emerge from obscurity in the correspondence, but was to be provided with at least temporary lodging at the Mansion. After another visit to Mount Vernon on April 5th Miss Tracy made a further report:

"I found the house in good order, all the rooms have been swept and cleaned. There was no trouble about the garret. The rooms look quite tidy, and some of them are habitable. I could not cut the carpet, for the men were sanding the paint on that side of the house, and have closed the windows so tightly with their scaffolding that I could not run the risk of doing it in the dark.

"The vegetable garden is in fine order, green pease six inches high, strawberries in blossom. We had plenty of lettuce. The men have not quite finished the road yet, but in a week it must be done. They have been delayed by so much wet weather. It seems the contract only requires them to finish the road to its connection with the path leading to the old tomb. All that bad place from that point to the entrance to the lawn is to be left.

"Mr. Herbert says he has a black walnut extension dining-table which you can borrow if you will. It will shut up so as to be just a good size for four persons. Do you think you would prefer that to buying a new one? I am sending you the enclosed notice to see if you would like me to get some one to buy half a dozen dining-room chairs. You know there are but four in all, and they are not alike, and would be useful elsewhere.

"As for a room for Mrs. Matthews, I think the room next to Mr. Herbert can be easily arranged, if you can decide what you want to do about a carpet. If you are going to keep the one down that is in your room, then I could buy matting for that room. If you intend sending on a carpet, it would reach here before you if you sent it to Columbia, and directly on here as soon as you leave home. In the meantime, I could have the one now in your room fitted to the guest-room.

"Mr. Herbert has two wash-stands in his room, and an old-fashioned kind of bureau that I am sure he would lend temporarily, and if you buy a new bedstead and mattress yours can be put up there, and the only things to be bought would be a looking-glass and a toilet seat. If you will decide about these things I can go down again, and have the room in order when you arrive and make Mrs. Matthews perfectly comfortable.

"I do not see how you can come on alive. Shall you go direct to Mount Vernon? If so, the captain of the boat from Aquia Creek would leave you there and you need not have the additional fatigue of coming either to Washington or Alexandria.

"What did you decide about the one coat of paint on the sitting-room? It does need it, and now the painters are there can easily be done, and ought to be, if done at all before we go there. . . ."

Miss Tracy's letters at this time have an odd echo in them of letters which passed between the master of Mount Vernon and his resident managers while the war and the Presidency kept him from home and everything had to be done at long range, by endless, painstaking correspondence. Miss Cunningham, nearly a hundred years later, was experiencing the same frustration of finding herself in exile, while the beloved house was being painted and carpentered and held together by deputies who, however devoted, were not mind readers, and were sure not to do exactly what she would have done if she could have met the daily problems personally as they arose.

"The Wood part of the New Room may be painted of any tolerably fashionable color," Washington had written from Philadelphia during the 1787 Convention, *"so as to serve present purposes, and this might be buff. 'Tis more than probable it will receive a finishing color hereafter. The buff should be of the lightest kind, inclining to white. . . ."*

THE SURVIVAL
1861–1865

I

Miss Tracy was still at the Clarendon Hotel in Washington when the headlines of Saturday, April 13th, announced that Fort Sumter was being bombarded by Beauregard's batteries in Charleston, and later that evening the dispatch was posted that the fort had surrendered. She wrote to Miss Cunningham during the day, a letter determinedly sane and undeviating from the course they had set—to furnish, occupy, and restore Mount Vernon. She gave Fort Sumter barely a dozen lines:

"I am writing without the least idea that you will receive my letter, for I suppose the mails will be completely stopped," she began. "This war news has completely unnerved me. May God forgive the ring-leaders and provokers of such an evil, both sides. Heaven only can see the end. It cuts into my heart whichever way I look. But I cannot write of this.

"Of course, if you wish the roof of that porch propped it must be done, but it will prevent the painting of that end of the house, which looks very shabby in contrast with the other two sides, and while the roof is bare Mr. Herbert says it cannot be done. There is no repairing the colonnade, for the wind left not a vestige of it, but levelled it to the ground.

"I feel sorry about Grace, I do not believe she will come to Mount Vernon with you. I am afraid that by depending on her you will be disagreeably situated. You ought to have some one to rely on, and I do not see how you are going to get anyone if you wait till you reach Alexandria, for you cannot be twenty-four hours without a servant. I should think at this season you might hire some one to come on with you just as well and better than to wait, for you are among your friends, and they ought to help you. I hope Mrs. Matthews will come with you, and she would be grand with a new servant, but I do not know, I only fear to have you dependent on Grace, for I am sure higher wages will not tempt her. I wrote Mrs. Matthews some days ago, but presume she will never get the letter. . . ."

Contrary to expectations, the mails continued to function fairly well for a while, though the firing at Fort Sumter brought about Virginia's secession, which was followed within a few weeks time by Arkansas, North Carolina, and Tennessee.

The controversial little porch, which was never there in Washington's time, but was an excrescence devised by Judge Bushrod, somehow survived till 1932, when it was at last removed by the third superintendent, and the library and bedroom windows behind it were restored to their original proportions.

One of the many tragic aspects of that dreadful spring was the inevitable disillusion or alienation of Everett's many friends in the South. A Bostonian, he naturally viewed secession with horror, though he also differed from the Republican policy and considered Abraham Lincoln "wholly unequal to the crisis." Once the catastrophe he had dreaded and prophesied for years came to pass, he devoted himself to the Union cause with the same energy he had once expended for Mount Vernon, and delivered an address called *The Causes and Conduct of the War* some sixty times, from Boston to Dubuque, and eventually came into close touch with Lincoln and the Cabinet. He was now nearing seventy, and his health had for years been unpredictable, but he could always rise to the occasion before an audience, and was in great demand on the public platform.

Miss Cunningham must have written him urging that he preserve a personal neutrality, as she fancied she herself could do,
and he replied on May 30th, courteously and at some length, that
his position in the community where he lived, if not the whole
country, and his known views heretofore forbade such a course
—and he added that he regarded the war as entirely defensive
on the part of the North, as the seizure of Washington City was
known to be a part of the Confederate plan. She wrote again,
deploring his speechmaking—her own neutrality was from the
first a figment of her imagination—and he replied with marked
and determined patience to "My dear and valued friend—" expressing gratification for her assurances that her personal feelings
toward him remained unaffected by their differences of political
opinion, "as I pray you to believe that mine do toward you. What
you have in mind, my dear friend, in saying that my speech on
the 8th of July contained some of the harshest terms in the language applied not only to your section but to yourself, I am at an
entire loss to conclude. I remain, my dear little friend, with un-
diminished attachment, Sincerely yours. . . ."

With the growing difficulties of communication, this may have
been the last word between them. By the time she returned
North in 1866, he was dead.

Miss Tracy's letters of April 17th and 18th took little notice
of the tension in Washington during that eventful week, when
the city existed in an atmosphere very similar to the early days
of a still remembered war. The capital was in a unique position
of alarm and uncertainty. The seat of the Federal Government,
it now stood on what, with Virginia's secession, amounted to
enemy soil. There were wild rumors of an impending all-out
attack by the rebel forces from Virginia, now that Sumter no
longer occupied their attention, and Lincoln himself was heard
to remark that if he were Beauregard he would try to take Washington. Maryland was still a borderline case, with sedition rampant in Baltimore, through which the only railways ran from the

North, so that Union troops sent to defend Washington must run the gauntlet on the way.

Miss Tracy expected to hear daily that the mails had been stopped, and supposed she might still be able to communicate with the Regent in South Carolina by way of the Adams Express Company. With many others, both North and South, she condemned Lincoln's action in calling for Northern volunteers, believing he had wilfully worsened a situation which might still have been temporized if properly handled. If Miss Cunningham were to be prevented now by unimaginable events from returning to Mount Vernon, Miss Tracy intended to rejoin the Grahams, either at New York or Mount Savage. In the next sentence she reverted obstinately to the furnishing of the Regent's room at Mount Vernon. "You spoke of sending on your carpet, but you did not say whether you wished me to take up the one now in your room before you come or not. Will you wait and buy your own chamber set, or did you mean me to? I think you had better select it, or say what colors, and what price, and have it bought in New York. . . ."

Mr. Herbert came up to Washington to see her, bringing a letter to be sent on to the Regent, and an estimate of the cost of repairing the General's room. He was "disappointed" to hear that the Regent wanted the little porch propped up instead of torn down, and said it would be very difficult to do, and would interfere with painting that end of the house. "They say we are not to have war," added Miss Tracy. "That is the rumor this morning, but I do not see on what it is founded. But a fortnight will decide everything, I hope. This variation from hope to fear is very exhausting. I think if you can carry out your plans you will make yourself very comfortable at Mount Vernon. . . ."

One is impressed by how little wars change, in their essence, in the human nervous system. Later generations well know the alternating confidence and despair which inhabit the days of waiting. The fortnight which intervened before the next letter which has survived contained the grim day when the Sixth

Massachusetts men on their way to duty at the capital were stoned and fired upon by, and fired back at, a civilian mob at Baltimore. They arrived at the Washington depot in the late afternoon, haggard and hungry, with stretcher cases of wounded, and four dead, and they camped that night on the carpeted floor of the Senate Chamber, overflowing into the tiled corridor, and cooked their rations on the furnaces in the basement. Two days later Baltimore rioters burned the railway bridge north of the town, and seized the telegraph office, which left Washington isolated and afraid, without newspapers or communications.

In a state of incredulous shock, which has become only too familiar a sensation in the twentieth century, the civilian population of the city found itself preparing for a siege—sentries were posted around the public buildings and at the bridges, barricades were going up, shops were closing, women and children were being sent away, hotels were emptying, vehicles were at a premium and there began the dreary, inevitable march of the humbler refugees—the word was used even then—with their few necessities loaded into wheel-barrows and baby-carriages, bound for anywhere away from the scene of the anticipated conflict.

Aware that Washington "would soon be no place for ladies or unprotected females," Miss Tracy went to send a telegram to her friends to ask what she should do, and found the Washington telegraph office in the possession of the administration, with no private messages permitted. This shook her. "All communication with anyone north of Baltimore is cut off," she wrote. "There had been no mails through from New York City since Friday, and no prospect of any. The ladies will all leave the hotel within a few days. Mount Vernon seemed the only place. I went to consult Mr. Riggs and wife; they both advised my going there by all means, at least until matters here are better or worse. Mr. Riggs told me not to wait to see Mr. Herbert, there was no chance of communicating with him. 'They' have seized both the Alexandria boat and the Mount Vernon boat, and he urged my leaving immediately with my baggage. I did not like the idea. I told

Mrs. Riggs I did not know whether Mr. Herbert's cousin could go with me or not. She said she promised she would in a few days, and these were no times to hesitate."

Another mysterious cavalier, "Dr. Young," drove Miss Tracy down to Mount Vernon in his carriage. She had now worried herself into a sick headache, and had additional anxiety for a nephew and cousins in the New York Seventh, which was on its way to Washington. On the following day—perhaps only out of a prudent spinster regard for the proprieties—she returned to Alexandria and went to a hotel there. Mr. Herbert had meantime hurried back to Washington, where he had business to attend to, for there was a probability that soon people from Virginia would be prohibited from going to and from the capital. His cousin was not ready or was not willing to accompany Miss Tracy to Mount Vernon as companion, and so she lingered in Alexandria "in the most uncomfortable excitement, the hotel filled with soldiers and refugees from Washington, arriving every hour. As much as I had at first disliked the idea of going to Mount Vernon, I become impatient to get away from here."

But Mr. Herbert had chosen this time to dismiss two of the servants, Dandridge and Emily, and she decided to stay on in Alexandria a day or two longer till he could make other arrangements. Mr. Riggs advised dismissing all the workmen but two, for reasons of economy, and they, with the man to be hired in Dandridge's place, would be charged with the protection of the house against intruders. With the boat stopped, there would be few visitors—and few admission fees. Mr. Herbert had formed a home guard in the neighborhood. "I can scarcely hope you will come on for a long time to come," wrote Miss Tracy to the Regent, "and yet perhaps there is no place where you would be more quiet and safe than at Mount Vernon, if you could get there!" She remembered that Miss Cunningham would want her summer clothes, which had been left partly in Miss McMakin's care at Philadelphia, and partly at Mount Vernon, and promised that she would get them ready to send as soon as she heard where they were to go—the Express Company advertised its ability to deliver parcels in the South at a moderate charge.

The April 30th letter, written at Alexandria, struck a final note of stout-hearted determination. "I know you must be exceedingly distressed," she wrote. "Events have succeeded each other with such a rapidity that I feel as if I had lived months in the past weeks. I have written to a friend who is in Virginia not far from here to come and stay with me, and I am sure she will, and if Mr. Herbert is obliged to fight, and he may be, *we* will take care of Mount Vernon!"

Let no one smile. For that, in effect, though without losing Mr. Herbert, is exactly what Miss Tracy did, throughout the war.

The exodus from Washington of Southern Army, Navy, and Government men was under way, but General Scott stood firm, though he lost the man he most wanted and needed to run the war for him. It was said that at an interview on April 18th with Lee—who had been recalled from the Mexican frontier to be offered the Northern command, and had refused it—the old Commander-in-Chief told him sadly that he had made a great mistake. It is worth a pause to consider the possible course of events if Robert E. Lee had been able to put the uniform and the flag before his loyalty to the State of Virginia, as Scott did. Instead, he went home across the Long Bridge to Arlington, where his family waited. Two days later Virginia seceded. Lee sent in his resignation to Scott, and was soon in the train bound for Richmond—by request of Virginia's Governor. He wore civilian dress. He never saw Arlington again. The rest is history.

Miss Tracy's concern was of course with General Scott. Miss Cunningham had at once foreseen that troops of either side might be posted at Mount Vernon on the pretext of protecting it, and that as a consequence it might even become a battleground. She wrote to Miss Tracy to say that the absolute neutrality of the place must be preserved, with no sentries or outposts within its boundaries. The same thing had occurred to Miss Tracy and Mr. Herbert, and they had even discussed trying to get a pledge from

General Scott that no arms of any kind should be permitted at Mount Vernon, which should be kept above all sectional feeling.

Miss Tracy was, however, about to leave Alexandria for Mount Vernon when the Regent's letter arrived. Twenty minutes later she was in the omnibus for Washington—the only mode of travel possible then. She was not quite sure how she was going to do it, she later confessed, but some of her friends were still in town, and she decided to go first to the Varnums. There, in the fortuitous way things happened for Miss Tracy, now that she belonged to Mount Vernon, she found the faithful Mr. Graham, who had supposed her already gone to her post on the Potomac.

"I told him what I wanted, and that he was just the person to go with me," she wrote Miss Cunningham, and Mr. Graham was in for it again. "He first said Edward Mansfield who acts under General Scott was the person to see. He knew him very well, and we went up to the War Department, but Colonel Mansfield was away. I then insisted upon seeing General Scott.

"We went to his office. One of his aides, Colonel Townsend, an old acquaintance of mine, came and said it was impossible to see the General even for a moment. I told him what I wanted, and that I would not detain him. Mr. Townsend said that he would see to it. He went into the next room, where the General was, and told my errand. I could hear through the door the old General exclaim, 'God bless the ladies!' and something he added in a lower tone which I didn't hear. But then Colonel Townsend and another officer came out. They were all laughing.

"Colonel Townsend then said that General Scott assured us that no one should under any plea be sent there. He wanted to know if I could be equally sure of Virginia. I told him Yes. And then Colonel Townsend added that if by any combination of unforeseen circumstances such a thing should be thought of, the ladies should be informed before it was done. I told him I would admit of no such possibility, but relied upon him as a friend in case anything of the kind was attempted, to remind General

Scott of his promise. This I conjured him not only in the name
of the Association, but demanded it of him as a personal act of
friendship. He said I could rely on him, and that there need be
not the least uneasiness felt by the ladies; it was a place too sacred
to be tampered with, and not in a position to serve any military
purpose."

How the Assistant Adjutant-General to the Commander-in-
Chief, who was Colonel Townsend, happened to be "an old
acquaintance" of Sarah Tracy does not appear. It must have been
a fearful and wonderful thing to be counted among her friends.
From the War Department they went to Mr. Riggs about finances. The insurance carried by Mr. Washington on the Mansion
would expire in June—Mr. Riggs promised to renew it. There
was some doubt about checks and the transfer of funds between
the Regent in South Carolina and her representatives in Union
territory under the present conditions—Mr. Riggs would let them
know. Mr. Graham was urging her to get a female companion
to go with her and stay at Mount Vernon, at least for a time.
"He said," reported the intrepid Miss Tracy, "the presence of
ladies there would be its greatest protection, even from the un-
ruly." It seems a Spartan viewpoint on Mr. Graham's part, but it
was still a gentleman's world, where ladies could expect consideration even from intruders, even in a war. A maid called
Priscilla and her sister were still at Mount Vernon, to look after
its tenants, and they would get an extra woman to come in every
week and do the washing. The only problem Miss Tracy recognized as such was the companion. Very sensibly, she decided to
go without one, though the presence there of the bachelor Mr.
Herbert would have raised a few eyebrows in normal times.
In the following September, she would be writing to Miss
Cunningham from Mount Vernon that there was not a white
woman within three miles of her, and that she had never had
one to speak to in the four months she had lived there, except
during her few brief trips to Washington on business. It was not

until October that she succeeded in getting Mary McMakin to join her, Mary's arrival being delayed by her own misgivings and the fearful warnings of her friends, who had not Mr. Graham's sublime confidence in the civilizing effect of a lady's presence at the seat of war.

The obvious hazards of their residence at the isolated house between the lines was doubtless a factor in Mr. Herbert's decision to forego the military service his friends expected of him, and which he must have desired, to remain instead as some protection at Mount Vernon. The three of them were to sit out the war there together, and as it is interesting to contemplate their experience in the light of its dénouement, it should be stated here, at the sacrifice of future surprise and suspense, that in 1868, after the Regent had returned to take full charge, Miss Tracy resigned her post, exhausted in body and spirit—and that five whole years later, at the age of fifty-three, she married Mr. Herbert, who was the same age. Which one of them held back, what they were waiting for, why they were so long about it, remains their secret.

2

We are, however, still in the eventful spring of 1861. When Miss Tracy left Alexandria for Mount Vernon the city was "frightened almost to death" of an attack by the Northern troops gathering in Washington. Mr. Graham, apparently acting as a resident of Maryland, was in the capital "on a mission to the Government" on behalf of that State, which had the spirit to resist the passage of Federal troops southward, but lacked arms and ammunition, and would eventually be obliged to submit. On May 11th she wrote from Mount Vernon to the Regent:

"I wish you were here, everything is so beautiful and peaceful one cannot realize that at so short a distance from us men's passions are driving them to all that is wicked and horrible. Mother Earth promises bountiful supplies from her storehouse to keep us from want, even if the foreign luxuries are cut off. We are eating delicious asparagus, the strawberry vines and fruit trees are laden; on the trees the fruit seems thicker than the leaves. But sugar and tea and coffee we must do without! *That will be pleasant!*

"There seems just now a lull in the intense excitement that prevailed in Washington a few days since. It may be a lull before a storm, for in their madness no one knows what they will do. . . .

"I have your box of summer clothes ready to send as soon as I hear from Miss McMakin. I wrote to her that I was waiting for her, but we all of us have our patience wonderfully taxed nowadays. I feel sometimes as if I had entirely reached the end of *mine!* But I renew the supply, and remembering that 'to whom much is given, of them much shall be required,' I take up my

burden and try again. I received a few days since a box of preserves and orange syrup from New Orleans, it proves very acceptable, I assure you.

"We had a great rain yesterday, and oh! *how the roof leaked!*
Mr. Herbert is in great distress about it. Mr. Riggs told him
there was no money and everything must be stopped, and Mr.
Herbert felt it was right, but he frets over the evil, for he says
he can only mend one or two of the worst places, and the injury
to the house, he fears, will be great, long before there can be
money enough to repair it. But it would take over $100 to shingle
the roof, and that is now a large sum. Mr. Herbert drew from
Burke & Herbert the money he had deposited there, and I put it
in the safe. There is now in the safe $493.50. . . .

"I am writing this hoping to have a chance to send it to town
by one of the men, there are two here now, but am by no means
certain he will go. I have now very faint hope of seeing you this
summer. If you and Mrs. Matthews should come, and your carpet
does not arrive till too late, how would it do to spread down in
Mrs. Matthews' room the linen drugget I bought for the dining-
room? It would almost cover the floor, and would look better
than bare boards."

There were persistent rumors that the Government would send
troops to take possession of Alexandria in order to include it in
the District territory under Federal control—which would put
the town out of bounds for Mr. Herbert as a Virginian. So far
he was free to come and go by road, to visit his brother's bank
and do the necessary shopping. During a trip to town on the
20th of May he had heard disturbing news, as reported to the
Regent by Miss Tracy:

"Mr. Herbert came home on Thursday and said there was a
story in the *Herald* that caused great excitement in Alexandria,
saying that General Washington's body had been removed to the
mountains of Virginia. He could not get a paper, but told the

editor of the *Sentinel* to contradict it. When I read the infamous
story my blood boiled, and will not get cool. I was furious at the
baseness of the insinuation. The more I thought about it, the
more indignant I became. I saw it would go like wildfire and if
people in this part of the world were excited, what would they
be farther off? I knew it must be contradicted decidedly and
without delay. I wrote the enclosed, which I sent today to Colonel
Seaton and requested him to oblige you by publishing it. If I had
the author I think I should use the woman's weapon on his eyes.
My nails are always long! Oh, the *wretch!*

"I will send your clothes as soon as I hear from Mary. Part of
them have been ready for some time. I hope I can find them all
for you must need them. Mr. Herbert told the captain of a company of soldiers stationed near here your wishes with regard to
their not coming here in uniforms or armed, and they have behaved well about it. Many of them come from a great distance
and have never been here, and have no other clothes *but* their
uniforms, but they borrow shawls and cover up their buttons,
and leave their arms outside the enclosure, and never come but
two or three at a time! This is as much as can be asked of them.
Since the story of the removal of the remains, several persons,
evidently Northerners, have been here, we suppose to see the
truth of the story. On Saturday we made $5.75 out of them. They
behave perfectly well, and are quiet and gentlemanlike. . . .

"Mr. Riggs told Mr. Herbert he must send off every workman.
Mr. Herbert felt it would be very wrong not to have any white
man on the place but himself. He says the plan you speak of, of
making this a sort of place of refuge for those out of work is
impracticable, because every man out of employment who could
be trusted has enlisted. Those who are left are not persons who
ought to be trusted with Mount Vernon. He says he thinks he
can get the men to work for half wages now, paying the remainder bye and bye, but it is very difficult for him, he says, to
work in the dark. If he can know anything about the amount
of money the Association can afford a month he can then make

the best arrangements possible. He says if he can be allowed $80 a month, even, he can then he thinks make such arrangements as will keep the grounds in passable order, and have a little work, small things that ought not to be neglected, slowly accomplished and the place protected. For the five months from now to the middle of November would require but $400, a small portion of the $10,000 a year decided on as necessary.

"Mr. Herbert has resisted every tempting offer to join the Army. He has had several, both his brothers and every friend he has have done so, and they wonder much that he has refused the command of every company offered. He says very little about it, but has, I know, made a sacrifice for Mount Vernon.

"I am distressed for you. Why are your eyes so painful? I am so sorry you have to remain on the plantation, you will be so lonely. It is lonely and quiet here, but I can see, and walk about, and busy myself. Alas, how sad all this makes us, and what a change has come over the spirit of our dream!

"I am going to put the sitting-room carpet away in tobacco, there is no use in having it down. Good-bye, and God bless and comfort you. . . ."

They hoped that when Congress was again in session the boat would be restored to them, along with the income from the visitors it brought. As troops from the North poured into Washington the city had come out of its trancelike suspense and begun to enjoy the parades and the uniforms and the bustle of trade. And as Washington's confidence returned, the fears of Alexandria, a Virginia town flying the Confederate flag, increased.

Early in May, Colonel Ellsworth's tough New York Zouaves in their spectacular dress arrived, spoiling for a fight and complaining of having been transported via Annapolis instead of Baltimore, which might have obliged them. One of them bragged to a reporter that they "would have gone through Baltimore like a dose of salts." They wore their hair shorn under a rakish red cap, and carried big bowie knives, and in contrast to the disci-

plined New York Seventh behaved like wild schoolboys, clown-
ing round their quarters in the Hall of Representatives. Unlike
the short-term militia, they were enlisted for three years. Soon
after their arrival Washington's mood changed to resentment
against the Yankee soldiers who persecuted secessionists wherever
found, got drunk in the streets, insulted ladies, and worst of all,
were ignorant or careless of sanitary conditions in a city none too
well provided in that department at the best of times. Fears of
pestilence grew as the hot weather fell due.

It was Mr. Graham's friend Colonel Mansfield, commanding
in the Department of Washington, who was finally responsible
for the seizure of Alexandria. A West Point engineer and Mexican War veteran, he appreciated the value of Arlington Heights,
which stood within artillery fire of the Government buildings,
and the old port town of Alexandria which commanded the
Potomac below the capital. Both the orderly New York Seventh
and the hoodlum Zouaves took part in the operation, which began
with a midnight drum in the Seventh encampment under a
white moon on May 22d. The Zouaves were sent by water direct
to Alexandria, arriving at about the same time as the main body
which marched across the Long Bridge. The firing of the Confederate pickets spread the alarm, and many Virginians were able
to escape southward by rail and carriage.

Colonel Ellsworth and his fire-eating Zouaves arrived in the
main street of Alexandria to find a Confederate flag flying over
the Marshall House, a hotel owned by a secessionist named Jackson. Without hesitation, Ellsworth climbed to the roof and tore it
from the pole. Descending the staircase with his trophy, he was
shot dead by the proprietor, who was then brutally killed with
gun and bayonet by one of Ellsworth's men. There had been a
few other casualties before then, but when the popular young
soldier's body was carried into Washington on a litter of muskets,
the war had really begun. A personal friend of Lincoln's, he was
buried from the White House after his body had lain in state in
the East Room.

The seizure of Alexandria could not but have a profound effect
on life at Mount Vernon. It lay now between the Federal pickets
at Arlington and Alexandria, and the Confederate mustering
point at Manassas Junction. Lee's deserted home, which his invalid wife had left in haste and in tears only a few days before
the Government troops crossed the River, became the headquarters of General McDowell, commander of the Union Army of
the Potomac. Roads were cut through, trees were felled, and
earthworks were dug around the serene white-pillared house.

Conditions in Washington worsened, as the idle soldiers drank
and rampaged in the streets, and the police force there was
notoriously inadequate. Miss Tracy had indeed done well to go
to Mount Vernon when she did. Mails, however, were now to
become a problem, for nothing came beyond Alexandria, and
while Occoquan to the south was to have a little post office, it
was not yet established. Miss Cunningham's box of summer
clothes seemed stranded before it started, unless Mr. Herbert
could send it by wagon all the way to Manassas, which was
eventually done. Miss Tracy sent out a few letters by people going
into Alexandria or to Manassas—and remarked that what letters
she did receive were not as fresh as when they started.

At the end of May a Federal flotilla attacked the batteries at
Aquia Creek on the Potomac, designed to interrupt the arrival
of supplies by water to Washington, and the guns could be heard
for several hours on two succeeding days at Mount Vernon, up
the River.

On June 1st, Miss Tracy wrote to the Regent "hurriedly, merely
to save you all the anxiety I can." She had been to Alexandria
and had had an interview with the Federal Colonel Stone, who
commanded there. "He is very gentlemanlike and courteous, says
not a soldier shall come here. He gives passes to the servants at
our request, and Mount Vernon and the Association are talis-
manic words. As there are always persons who hope to benefit
themselves by injuring others, and the 'test oath' is being administered in Alexandria, Mr. Herbert thinks he would rather avoid

any disagreeable examination by not going into town. But he must have communication there for letters, etc. He has concluded to hire a boy whose expenses to the Association would be less than those of Dandridge or any man, and when not otherwise employed he can clean walks, which have been entirely neglected on account of the expense. I shall continue to have Priscilla do the housework and I shall pay her wages myself. This is the best arrangement we can make. I cannot write you anything about politics, but could tell you many strange things of the times in which we live. But people must not talk, much less write. . . ."

A week later she had heard nothing from South Carolina, and wrote to say that Mount Vernon was very quiet and undisturbed, with now and then one or two visitors by the road, but not many. She had gone up to Washington—unlike Mr. Herbert, she did not fear the test oath—and spent the night with Mr. and Mrs. Riggs. Miss Hamilton had been in Washington, having come expressly to visit Mount Vernon, but her brother "feared to have her venture, I do not know why," observed Miss Tracy sensibly, "for surely she need not have feared their own troops, and would easily get a pass to Mount Vernon." Nevertheless, Miss Hamilton had retreated to New York before Miss Tracy had herself crossed the lines into the capital. She also missed seeing Mme. Berghmans, whose husband had lost a relative in Belgium and they were sailing for Europe the next day. "We are in despair about the roof," she added. "Mr. Herbert had it mended as he and the carpenter thought perfectly. We have now had a two days steady rain and it leaks terribly, and they think can never be mended. I have just had word sent me that the Post Office at Occoquan is now open. Mr. Herbert desires his respects, begs me to tell you that everything is safe and quiet here, and the best that can be done in these times without you. . . ."

In the eternal game of pussy-wants-a-corner which was the Northern command in the early days of the war, the "gentleman-like" Colonel Stone was recalled to his former post at Washington, and his place at Alexandria was filled by Colonel Heintzelman, a gruff and profane old Regular Army man from the Mexican War, who succeeded in putting Miss Tracy's back up at once. "One day that I went to Alexandria I had to go to the office of the Commander to get *passes*, not only for myself but for the servants, so that they might be sent to the Post Office, to market, etc.—then to ask the Commander the same thing that had been asked of the others, that was to prevent the soldiers coming here *armed*, or rather to give the order that they should obey the Superintendent and leave their arms without the enclosure. He was not very courteous, and I was obliged to *insist*, and then tell him what General Scott promised you. He asked through whom you had obtained the promise. I replied, 'Miss Cunningham sent me to General Scott.' This silenced him and he gave the order. Several soldiers have been here, but *not as soldiers*. The other good is that *I* am known as a *Northerner*, and Mr. Herbert is a Virginian, so they consider that a 'resident lady manager' who is a *Northerner* will prevent a *Virginian* Superintendent from running away with the bones!"

The man Dandridge whom Mr. Herbert had dismissed was in Alexandria in bad company, trying to stir up trouble by sending threatening messages to the men still in Mount Vernon's employ, hoping to scare them into leaving. There was only one of these who could be trusted to go to town, and when he was sent in with a wagon-load of cabbages to sell, with a pass procured for him by Miss Tracy, he was stopped by the pickets and his wagon searched. Miss Tracy was incensed. "I am going to Washington to see Colonel Townsend and see if something cannot be done to prevent what I call insults to the Association," she wrote the Regent, "though they are not intended as such, for they have all, with the exception of that one Colonel with a Dutch name, been perfectly courteous and civil the moment the name of the Association is mentioned, and I am certain that when I see Colonel Townsend I can get some orders or pass or something from General Scott that will save us further annoyance from that source, at least. And when another arises, we must meet that too!"

She added a postscript the following day to say that she had
been again to Washington, and that from Alexandria to the outskirts of the capital was one vast camp-ground. Failing Mr. Graham, she had looked up one of her several cousins in the Federal
Army and made him go with her to General Scott's headquarters.

"After telling my story to Colonel Townsend, he gave me a
beautiful note to Colonel Heintzelman, urging him to afford
every protection to all persons connected with Mount Vernon,"
she reported. "Colonel Heintzelman received me with great kindness, all his roughness of the former occasion now entirely
smoothed down, and he was ready to do *anything*; was very much
provoked that the man had been interfered with, etc. He gave
me a pass that would cover any emergency, and begged me in
case of any further difficulty to write him a note. . . .
"Mr. and Mrs. Riggs desired their love to you. Mr. Riggs says
I must be very careful about sending letters. I am, and it will be
at intervals only that I can send them." The box of summer clothes
was still on their hands, as the road to Manassas was full of recruiting parties and Mr. Herbert did not want to risk the wagon.
"I want him to go part of the way with it, and he wants to, but
dislikes to leave here," she explained. "But he would not be gone
long, and I am not afraid, as we have one old white man here,
and for days sometimes there is not a single visitor."

She was not afraid, however prudent Miss Hamilton was. And
Colonel Heintzelman had been put in his place. Her next opponent would be the cocky McClellan in his new command later
that year, and it would take Lincoln himself to settle that. "I like
to go to the fountainhead," she had said of Colonel Townsend
when he held that position. Something Antaean in the soil of
Mount Vernon must have entered into little Miss Tracy. "It seems
so strange that within the limits of these grounds all should be so
quiet, and yet from time to time the booming of cannon announces
in stern tones the strife of evil passions," she wrote in June. "There

are rumors of every kind afloat. When I was in Alexandria on
Thursday no one thought it worth while to attempt to get out, as
there were stories of a meditated attack on the place, but as I never
believe anything but *facts*, and nothing that I see in the papers,
I persevered, and came out without trouble."

Trouble had not yet really started, for the war was young. But
before the guns at Manassas began, another attack was made upon
the Regent and Mount Vernon.

3

Miss Cunningham had named the Vice-Regent for Delaware as her nearest deputy if Miss Tracy were ever in doubt, and on July 1st, '61, Miss Tracy did turn to Mrs. Comegys for advice. Now that several weeks had gone by without a letter from the Regent, she had begun to feel a little stranded, and thought it was time to bring Mrs. Comegys up-to-date.

"Soon after the Baltimore difficulties, at her request I came down here, she expecting to join me soon, and feeling anxious about Mount Vernon, thought with others that the presence of ladies here would tend to the *security* of the place in these doubtful days, and serve to preserve what she was so anxious for, its perfect neutrality," she explained, reverting to that ingenuous assumption that a lady was Mount Vernon's best guardian against pillage or violence in wartime. "One thing and another, principally sickness and suffering from her eyes, kept her South until too late for her in her feeble state to pass through country filled with armed soldiers! She has written me full instructions in case anything occurred to stop intercourse. I have not heard from her in some weeks, but have written her. I shall now remain here as long as it may seem best. For the sake of Mount Vernon, I am glad I have remained, though for my *own*, I have a thousand times wished I was in *China!*

"I was about to write you in reference to the extraordinary circular Miss Johnson has sent to the Vice-Regents, one of which being sent here I forwarded to Miss Cunningham. I wrote to several of the ladies, urging them to wait till they could hear from Miss Cunningham before replying, as I knew she wished above all things that *everybody* connected with the Association should remain *perfectly neutral*. I was so occupied that I did not write you, for I felt you would pursue the right course anyway, but Saturday night I was horrified beyond measure at the receipt of letters from my friends enclosing extracts from papers speaking of a Washington-Secessionists correspondence with General Beauregard *via Mount Vernon!* Then this enclosed article by Colonel Forney, for he wrote it, he is the editor of his own paper. Such an outrageous inference to tack upon a lady I never read!

"The only correspondence from Mount Vernon South are letters to Miss Cunningham, and a very *neutral place* it would be indeed, if the Regent cannot be permitted to hear what is going on here! I enclose a copy of the contradiction inserted immediately by a friend of mine, which so far as I am concerned is sufficient, but I am anxious for Miss Cunningham's sake that a reply to the whole article should be written by one of the Vice-Regents. It will come with better grace than from *me*, more authoritative, and from none better than *yourself*. You are the nearest Vice-Regent. And you know how to lash him, and are not afraid to do it under your signature as Vice-Regent, if not under your own name. Can his object be to make the only sacred spot in the country an apple of discord? Do scourge him, call him by name, he does not hesitate to use a woman's freely! You perceive I am indignant. If you had gone through with all the Mount Vernon annoyance you would excuse me. I hear all the guns fired at the different engagements around us, but nothing has *unnerved* me like this article. . . ."

The article in question had appeared in a Philadelphia paper, and apparently had been concocted as a letter to the editor by the man Forney, who had had a colorful career as a journalist of the Republican press. It depicted Miss Cunningham as "residing at Mount Vernon and entertaining her friends there like a princess." It said that Mount Vernon had been paid for by Northern capitalists, but that Miss Cunningham now made frequent trips from there to Washington to "damage the free States and assist the armed traitors at the South." It is difficult to see how an invalid lady of limited acquaintance was supposed to have accomplished all this treason, but commonsense plays little part in such tactics at any time.

Miss Tracy was of course upset, and conceived that a prompt denial by the Northern Vice-Regents might have an effect. Writing to Mrs. Mitchell, Wisconsin, at the same time as to Mrs. Comegys, she expressed again their conviction that a lady's presence at Mount Vernon would act as "a double protection," and would give assurance to the neighborhood that the Association did not intend to neglect the house—the story of the removal of General Washington's remains having been "easily silenced when it was known that some responsible person was here," Miss Tracy wrote Mrs. Mitchell. "I have been twice to Washington since I came here, both times on business for the Association, at the office of General Scott, once at Miss Cunningham's request to obtain the assurance from General Scott that no troops would be stationed here, and once to make some arrangements for unmolested intercourse with Alexandria, both of which errands were successful. Mr. Forney's letter, you will therefore perceive, is a tissue of unvarnished, unfounded falsehoods; his attack on Miss Cunningham is of such a nature that I fear it will do much injury. Another of Mr. Forney's insinuations, not assertions, is that slave labor is employed here. All the Negroes employed here have been freed, and as much as possible those descended from the old stock, who have been free for generations. I hope you will be able to procure a copy of this infamous letter. If you decide to reply to it, please do not mention me by name, and please send me two copies to the care of G. W. Riggs, Washington City. . . ."

Regarding the Christie Johnson circular, in which she presumed to take the name of the Association as though she was still an accredited member of the organization and it endorsed her views on the subject of neutrality, peace movements, and other matters

from which it endeavored to remain aloof, Miss Tracy wrote again
to Mrs. Mitchell at the end of July:

"You will be very glad to know that I received quite a package
of letters from Miss Cunningham a few days since, dates as late
as the 6th. She is much better than she has been for some months,
and would come on if she could reach here, and will, as soon as
possible. She had heard of Miss Johnson's circular, but had not
seen it, had written me by way of Kentucky, giving me instructions as to the course to pursue. These letters I never received.
She now wishes me to state that Miss Johnson is 'a very peculiar
character, reared without the usual method of education and discipline, very ignorant of the world as it is, and laboring under a
mania that she is a *genius*, and that it was to her mind that the
Mount Vernon Association owes its success and good management! She was with Miss Cunningham but twelve months, who
after much forbearance in consequence of her orphaned condition
was obliged to dismiss her peremptorily, because of a course of
conduct in keeping with the presumption exhibited by the issue
of such a circular, and such an absurd proposition. I regard it as
the offering of a diseased vanity and ambition, and I trust the
ladies will unite with me in dismissing the subject with the contempt it deserves. Although I consider Miss Johnson as deserving
of no forbearance at my hands, yet in consideration of her being
an orphan I desire my communication to be private.'

"She adds her earnest hope that the women of our country will
prove themselves worthy of the tribute contemplated to the great
Washington, by being above all 'sectional and party feeling' where
his home and grave are concerned, 'that we may one and all resolve, *come what may*, to be of one mind and heart on the subject,
with the hope that an overruling Providence will permit us the
noble privilege of smoothing hereafter the asperities which have
always resulted from civil war!'

"Thus you perceive, dear madam, that Miss Cunningham is
earnest for perfect unity in the Association, and it is to be hoped

that her continued efforts to preserve Mount Vernon as a neutral and rallying point for the future, when God shall have sent peace on the earth, may prove successful. She urges my remaining here through all difficulties, and I shall do so."

Meanwhile the war lumbered on towards its first disastrous battle. Richmond had become the Confederate capital, and President Davis was there, as was Robert E. Lee. The Army of Virginia was now a part of the Southern force, which was deploying under Beauregard roundabout Manassas Junction, only thirty miles from Washington. General Joseph Johnston and the man who would be known as Stonewall Jackson were in the Valley to the West. Generals Huger and Magruder were in the Peninsula, below Fort Monroe.

In Washington, General Irvin McDowell had been given command of the Army of the Potomac under Scott, who was unable to take the field—a robust, reserved, impressive man, McDowell had been chosen by Scott to draw up a plan of campaign, and about the middle of July he began to move his supply wagons and troops out into Virginia, via Fairfax Courthouse and Centreville, to confront the Confederate concentration at Manassas. Secrecy was of course impossible, and the maneuver soon assumed the general aspect of a picnic, as civilian Washington drove out in its carriages, provided with refreshments and opera glasses, expectant to "see the rebels run."

A few miles nearer to Beauregard than Washington City, as the crow flies, Mount Vernon spread its greening lawns and reviving gardens, and there Miss Tracy on the 16th of July had received the overdue packet of letters from the Regent, after an anxious interval of nearly a month, and sat down to write her reply. The letters brought the news of the maid Grace's death from typhoid, which left Miss Cunningham without the practiced care she had relied on for years. Miss Tracy was deeply concerned about who was to take Grace's place, especially when the Regent came to travel North again; what had become of Mrs. Matthews, she wanted to know. Mr. Graham had been in Washington a week, and could not get a pass to come to Mount Vernon—she confessed she had shirked going to him, dreading the journey through the lines, but she intended to summon her courage when he returned in ten days. Her own unchaperoned position at Mount Vernon troubled her more, it would seem, than McDowell and Beauregard put together, for she never mentioned them.

"Your kind letters have given me great encouragement," she wrote to the Regent on July 16th. "A week ago I felt as if I could not brave it out any longer, but when I reflected upon the importance of my being here, I determined to *stand to my post*. The only difficulty is in getting anyone to stay here with me. Among so many other vexations I should not trouble you with this. Everybody has a home, or in these days ties elsewhere—they were *afraid* to stay at Mount Vernon, or some other *private* reason. I talked with Mrs. Riggs and Mr. Graham. They said 'Under the circumstances and *in these times* you must be there, and no one *can* say anything.'

"Mary McMakin wrote me of her troubles, and I urged her coming here. I knew she wanted a place to go, and I did not believe she had the money to go to St. Louis, but if she must go I offered to lend her the means. She declined coming here, and mentioned several other offers she had received from friends for a summer home. I will try and find her! I have now a scheme of trying to *hire* somebody to come and stay with me. I am well, except the occasional nervous excitement caused by these newspaper writers. I shall now remain here. I feel myself that it is best. And while my position is not that of my own choosing, I try to accept it as I do all other things, as a dispensation of One wiser to judge than I.

"We occasionally have visits from troops, but do not make much money. Today eight officers were here, and gave us $6.50. Every little helps. We have money enough here, I think, for the summer. . . . I am afraid you cannot have your box, for the trees are so cut down as to make the road dangerous at one time, and now there is no express north of Raleigh. Later it is possible, and only possible, I may be able to send it. If the Federal troops go to Occoquan I shall be puzzled *how* to write to you, but will try. The cook does not know much about preserves, but the secretary made some currant jelly and means to try other things.

"I am glad you say the roof may be shingled, for it is very necessary. Everything is very sweet about here, and I have enough scrubbing and window-washing done to keep the house in order. I avoid the night air, and have no symptoms of fever. Perhaps I shall escape it as it is the first summer. You speak of your arm suffering from writing. Mine does frequently, and my right thumb is sometimes perfectly numb for days after writing. I have tried placing my pen in a *quill*, and find it does not hurt me at all. Try it. I will do all I can to keep you advised of everything, but if you do not hear regularly or frequently try not to be *over-anxious*. You must take a great deal on faith and trust nowadays. Mr. Herbert desires his remembrances. He is *faithful*, and as a Virginian is sorely tried in spirit. Good night. Yours with love—"

A postscript written crosswise of the page refers to a proposed visit from Brady the photograher to take pictures of the interior of the house, and which rooms did Miss Cunningham wish to have taken? "The only objection I can see is that it will be difficult not to have the pictures common," she remarked, "but precautions can be taken."

Mr. Brady would shortly have his time occupied with less tranquil subjects, on a battlefield.

The opening skirmish at Blackburn's Ford on the creek known as Bull's Run occurred two days later, on Thursday the 18th, and the Federals fell back in confusion, badly mauled, with the first advantage going to the South. It was a reconnaissance only, which developed into some sharp fighting, and the gunfire could be heard at Mount Vernon, where Miss Tracy wrote to Mrs. Comegys that "it was so constant and rapid for hours that I could hardly control my tears."

McDowell re-formed at Centreville, and for the next two days made his preparations for another attack. He had something less than thirty thousand men, and all of forty-nine cannon. Beauregard, well informed by spies and traitors, at the same time was organizing to attack the position at Centreville, and advance from there on Fairfax Courthouse. McDowell remained unaware that Johnston was on the way to Manassas, where his arrival would give Beauregard a small advantage in numbers.

On the night of the 20th the Federal Army moved south from Centreville under the hot moon, with Miss Tracy's old adversary Colonel Heintzelman commanding on the right flank, but the sun was up on Sunday morning when the first gun spoke.

"Before this letter reaches you, you will have the news of the terrible fight of Bull's Run," wrote Miss Tracy to Mrs. Comegys on the Monday. "I have considerable strength of nerve, but it was tried to the utmost yesterday. The wind was south on Thursday, and we did not hear much of the firing until late in the afternoon, when for two hours it was very distinct, and again on Saturday. But yesterday we will none of us ever forget. At six o'clock in the morning I was roused by the cannon, and from then till one o'clock there was not three, no, hardly one minute between each fire. Then for half an hour it ceased, recommenced, and continued till dark. The sun rose upon their fury, and went down upon their unquenched wrath. We have as yet only flying rumors, but fearful must have been the destruction of life. I never imagined anything so terrible. I could not think, could not read, could hardly pray, every sense and faculty seemed concentrated in my hearing! I tremble at the idea of those who saw their last sunrise yesterday morning. It has come—the climax of this war! God forgive the instigators!"

A generation tragically inured to slaughter on the battlefield should reflect that except for the local skirmishes of 1812 the longest memory in America could not recall the sort of thing which was about to take place in this country, and even European conflict was then remote and often unreported. The shock was truly unimaginable, when husbands, brothers, sons, and fathers were dying on their own ground in a quarrel so unthinkable as to be still unrealized even by the well-informed.

The dreadful chorus of the guns at Manassas could be plainly heard in the streets of Washington on Sunday, as well as on the green lawn above the River at Mount Vernon. By nightfall President Lincoln and his Cabinet had gathered at Scott's headquarters, along with the old retired generals and the spruce young staff officers. There they listened with white-faced incredulity while Miss Tracy's friend Colonel Townsend read aloud the dispatches which arrived one by one from the War Department across the street, in the hands of perspiring orderlies on the run. In this way, Secretary of War Cameron learned that his brother had been killed.

Sight-seers returning from the hill at Centreville, which had once looked rather like a grandstand, were demoralized and frantic, frightening each other and bystanders further by exchanging excited stories of their experiences—carriages wrecked, commandeered, or abandoned in the surge of the Federal retreat —wounded with bloodstained bandages collapsing underfoot—a horde of yelling, victorious rebels headed for Washington City. The weary men at Headquarters had tried for a while to discount these unofficial reports of debacle. Then they got it from McDowell. The broken Federal troops would not re-form. It was defeat—total and terrifying. Johnston and Jackson from the Valley had turned the tide for the South.

By morning it was raining in Washington, and the main body of the routed army reached the capital—a smoke-stained, muddy, exhausted, hang-dog rabble, with only here and there a group of men who still carried their arms and behaved like soldiers, even beaten ones. The Long Bridge was choked all day with wagons, ambulances, sutlers' vans, walking wounded, and men who groaned in the jolting wagons. There were even some prisoners.

But Beauregard's army, while they held the field, were in no shape to follow up their advantage. They sat down to lick their own wounds, and Washington was not taken.

4

They blamed McDowell, of course, in Washington, though it was not so much his fault as that of the inexperienced officer who had failed to prevent Johnston's army from joining Beauregard in time. Even Scott was blamed. There was a young fellow named McClellan who had actually won an engagement at a place in Western Virginia called Rich Mountain, though he had for a time retired from the Army after service in the Mexican War to become a surveyor and then president of a railroad at Cincinnati. He was barely thirty-five, sturdy, magnetic, confident, with an attractive wife and a new baby. They brought McClellan to Washington, and told him to make an army. And for a time the new broom was busy.

First he cleaned up Washington—rounded up the stragglers, ousted the beggars, set up a provost guard of regulars with an experienced provost marshal to run it, and clamped down on passes and permits to go in and out of the city. He also established his own secret service system under his friend Pinkerton from Chicago. Smuggling, especially of liquor, was effectively dealt with, and spying, in which even the Southern ladies who remained in Washington had participated—"galloping in with the exact number of the enemy done up in their hair," wrote the lively Mrs. Chesnut in her *Diary*—was materially reduced.

"Little Mac" enjoyed wearing out his aides, and appeared to spend his life in the saddle, visiting the encampments round the city, winning the admiration of his troops. New volunteers poured into Washington—enlisted now for three years instead of three months—and the hardened West Pointers went to work on them. Among the new brigadiers were names soon to be familiar—Sherman, Burnside, Meade, Hooker, and Miss Tracy's Dutchman,

Heintzelman. Fortifications went up around the capital—earth-works which were ruinous to orchards and gardens and meadows —McClellan was an engineer. Two French princes of the house of Bourbon—exiled by Napoleon III—were members of his showy staff. When Lincoln ventured to suggest that the duties of General-in-Chief added to McClellan's other responsibilities might be too much for one man, Little Mac replied, "I can do it all." His self-confidence soon became conceit. He believed that he was a man with a mission, capable of dictatorship. Lincoln deferred to him, as an old acquaintance from their mutual Western days, and Mc-Clellan actually patronized the President.

Scott was ruthlessly eclipsed by the arrogant young general who considered the Commander-in-Chief obsolete, but to Miss Tracy he was still the highest authority. Her next letter to Mrs. Comegys was written on August 1st from Washington City, where she was always a welcome guest in the hospitable Riggs household.

"I am here on another visit to General Scott," she wrote, "but perhaps it had better not be spoken of. Some time since, a volunteer company came to Mount Vernon, about 150. They had some hesitation about stacking their arms, but finally consented, and behaved very well. We were annoyed at so many being on the grounds, but hoping it would not occur again, said nothing about it. A few days before the battle of Bull's Run another large body of men came down, and *refused* to stack their arms, but for over an hour were straggling all over the place, without any order, with their guns in their hands. The Colonel said if the men were to lay down their arms we must have an order to that effect from General Scott.

"I wrote a letter to Colonel Townsend, but before I sent it heard of the first attack on Bull's Run, and concluded that it would be better to wait until that excitement was over, and my letter would be more likely to receive proper attention. Then followed the second battle. I decided to wait till all was quiet, and come myself, as I found it necessary to have a pass signed by General Scott himself. I saw Colonel Townsend on Tuesday, and he said I should have all I wanted.

"Yesterday I received a pass, and a paper, the wording of which I did not like, being certain that it would make trouble, particularly as it was in the form of a military order and would be published. I therefore went with Mr. Riggs to Colonel Townsend, and from him to General Scott. The Order is to be changed, and they told me the publication would be suppressed, but I see it in the *Intelligencer* this morning. I suppose it had been sent to the paper and was printed before the counter-order was signed. I am worried to death, am writing an article contradicting to be published in the *Intelligencer* tomorrow, unless General Scott will *himself* send a counter-order. I will send a copy to Colonel Townsend for decision. I am glad I came up, and will settle the matter before I leave.

"I thank you most sincerely for all your kindness, I have no desire to be a heroine, but *do* wish to do my duty, and since I have made up my mind to stay, will fight for Mount Vernon *inch by inch!* Excuse this, I have no time for more. Must attend to *General Scott!*"

They had yet to be convinced at Headquarters that Miss Tracy's requests were better heeded than forgotten. General Scott did not alter his Order as he had promised, and her contradiction therefore was duly published, a copy being sent to the *New York Times*, where it must have smarted, for it laid the blame where it was due: "The officers of the Ladies' Mount Vernon Association have been much pained," it read, "to see in your issue today an Order from General Scott containing a statement which they fear will lead to a great deal of trouble and misunderstanding, General Scott having been misinformed in regard to the facts. The statement referred to is that Mount Vernon has been overrun by bands of rebels. Since the occupation of Alexandria by the Federal troops not a single soldier from the Southern Army has visited Mount Vernon. It is but justice to say that the intruders who refused to accede to the regulations of the Association heretofore willingly followed by soldiers from both armies, were a company of New York volunteers, headed by their colonel and officers. . . .''

There.

The next letter from Miss Tracy to Mrs. Comegys can only be transcribed here as she wrote it, without futile comment, so that no charge of romancing can be brought against this book. With her happy faculty of classic understatement, the intrepid little woman who had no desire to be a heroine reduces her experience to the word "odd."

"I had a curious adventure the night I left Washington," she wrote. "I have a pass from General Scott permitting me to pass the lines 'at all times,' and recommending me to the courtesy of the troops. When I reached Alexandria, I found the man had come for me as I requested, the day previous, but not finding me had left the horse and buggy and returned. I wanted to hire someone to drive me, but a friend persuaded me to take his nephew, a lad of fourteen. The orders were to let no one leave town after five; but armed with my pass, I was not the least annoyed to find it a quarter after before we left.

"We passed the camps without the least difficulty, and were three miles on our road when we found the crossing *barricaded*; we came back the three miles and took another road. After going a short distance we met a large body of troops at a turn in the road where there had never been any before. Instead of a sentinel an officer came forward and said he 'was sorry' but I could go no further that night. I showed him my pass; he pointed in another direction and said that after going a short distance I would find the road barricaded but by crossing a field I would come to a road through the woods which would eventually bring me on the right road. It seemed literally 'going round Robin Hood's barn'—but we went on.

"Before quite reaching the barricade, we were stopped by more troops. The captain said it was *impossible* I could go on; I told him what the other officer had said. He did not believe there was such a road; but would I allow him to see my pass? He read it and said that would take me anywhere it was possible to go, but he had not heard of such a road. A little sergeant who was standing by asked if he 'might go and see.' The captain said Yes, and I waited.

"Presently my friend returned and said there was a road, but a bad one. I said I would try it. My little sergeant acted as a guide through a field, took down the bars, and let us into the woods. It was a pretty little road, narrow, and the trees lowering their branches to greet us as we passed, we two, without the most distant idea exactly where the road would take us; but we continued until we found ourselves at the back entrance to a gentleman's farm. We passed through till, reaching the house, I sent John in to inquire if we might pass through to the road. The gentleman was very kind; said he feared our troubles were not over, but if we could not get through he would be happy to accommodate us for the night.

"Another short drive; another body of troops, and another officer, more decided than the rest. He would not let us go by. I showed him my pass. He said, 'This is all right; but if I allowed you to go by here some of my men are further on, with positive orders to let no one go by, not to look at any pass, and shoot anyone who resists.'

"They were Poles, and I did not believe they would shoot a woman, but I asked him to send a soldier with me. He did so, and we passed them without a word! We turned into the Mount Vernon road, and I felt safe;—when lo! another barricade, more formidable than the rest. The road was narrow, and so situated that there seemed no outlet but over a high fence, or over the tops of the trees! This latter I knew the horse would object to, for he was already showing signs of mistrust in the apparent vagaries of one who generally allowed him to trot along home on a regular road. The former mode I could not try alone; so John went back to ask the lieutenant to allow a couple of his men to come and open the fence. He came himself—with five men; examined the fence, and said it was so strongly made that it could not be taken down without cutting, and *that* they were forbidden to do.

"The men walked all around to see, and finally said there was a little gate they could lead the horse through, and would *lift the buggy over the fence*, if they found I could get out on the other side. I told them I *must* go on, and if once around this barricade, I could reach a blacksmith's house, whose children worked at Mount Vernon, and I could leave the horse and buggy with him till morning and could walk the rest of the way, the blacksmith knowing so many paths through the woods.

"One of the soldiers came to me and said I had better not attempt it with only that lad. I asked him if there were more troops in the road. He said there were some of their own men further on, and some of another regiment that they could not be answerable for. The others returned and said there was no chance of getting out that way, but if I would stay all night at a gentleman's house near by they would help me in the morning.

"The gathering darkness was an unanswerable argument for the propriety, so I did what I disliked—turned my horse's head and begged a night's lodging at a house before whose gate three soldiers were stationed. While waiting to gain entrance, the lieutenant told me they had received information which made them expect an attack every minute, and he was glad I was not on the road. They had been cutting trees for two days to stop the cavalry from passing. I did not tell him what nonsense I thought it, and how little I believed in the danger. I was very comfortably lodged, and slept soundly; though when I saw their arms glistening through the trees I thought *if* there should be an attack it would be pleasanter to be *somewhere else!*

"In the morning the captain came to say his men had found a way for me to get around; and we once more commenced our 'winding way.' We went to another farm, where there were two

soldiers waiting to show us. We came into the road, and they said
a little farther on we would find the *last* barricade, and some
soldiers there would show us the way around. This we reached in
safety, and found three soldiers, who took down a fence, and led
us through bush and brier down a hill, over a ditch, through the
fence—and congratulated me on being in a clear road! I assure
you I was thankful! These soldiers were so kind (Poles of the
New York Thirty-first) that they relieved me of half my trouble.
But was it not odd?"

Her sense of proportion—alone in the unfamiliar world of war,
with a no doubt frightened and useless fourteen-year-old lad as
her escort, at night, with Mr. Herbert only a few miles away but
unaware of her predicament—is staggering. The road, she observed, was pretty—the horse would object to a route over the tree-
tops—if there was shooting it might have been pleasanter to be
somewhere else—but she slept soundly. One can only wonder
about her pulse rate at the barricades.

The imminent attack was only another scare, she wrote the next
day, and they soon opened the road to Alexandria again. "Since
which all is quiet, for how long, God only knows," she added.

Again, her letter of August 14th to Miss Cunningham defies
paraphrase or elision. Miss Tracy wrote without flourishes, from
a gay, brave, troubled heart outward, and her pages are still warm
with life and courage. To edit, to curtail, to meddle, is wrong.
"I often wish you were here," she wrote. "I feel so often my own
inefficiency. Then again, I am glad you are spared so much of
these war incidents. How could your nerves bear the sound of
those cannon, or the thousand rumors we are startled with every
day!" And then, in four short, blinding sentences, she expressed
that basic sensation of bewilderment, incredulity, and fatalism
with which everyone in the world has since then faced up to
another war. "I feel myself as if I was somebody else," wrote
Miss Tracy. "I feel like some one *acting*. I cannot believe all this

is *real*, and yet how fearfully real it is. And instead of acting, in
the sense of imitating the part, how sternly, promptly, unfalter-
ingly, we must *act!*"

She did not often falter, even for four sentences. And always
mindful not to disturb the Regent's nerves more than was unavoidable, she at once passed on to reassurance and anecdote.

"Since my return from Washington there have been several
groups of soldiers here, but all unarmed and perfectly respectful,"
she added. "I hope it will continue. If not, well, I will try again!
If any exertion of mine can keep this place neutral, it shall be
made.

"But I must tell you of the visit of Prince Napoleon. When I
left Washington, he was expected there that evening, and I asked
Mrs. Riggs if she would come down and help me to receive him
if he came here. She said she would. Monday I sent to town for
some groceries I had purchased, and some claret wine that had
just arrived from New York, as I was ordered to drink it. Thinking that the party might come at any time, I had given directions
to have the house put in order, I had been gone, and many things
had been neglected.

"Tuesday morning I was in the second story when I heard a
loud rapping at the door. Priscilla came and said there was a party
of soldiers in citizens' dress at the door. I heard them walking
about with Mr. Herbert, but took no notice until happening to be
by a window as they passed I heard them conversing in *French*.
I looked out and heard enough to satisfy me who they were. I
waited till they had, as I supposed, all gone to the Tomb, then
rushed down-stairs to make some lemonade, open a box of claret
(so *thankful* it had arrived, for you know to a Frenchman it is
essential.) Priscilla had just arranged the waiter, and I was in the
pantry making my lemonade. I wanted something from the side-
board and came into the dining-room, to find myself face to face
with two gentlemen!

"I started and bowed, and they likewise. I made some remark about the heat, they looked blank, bowed, and shook their heads. I repeated my remark in French, asking them if they would have something. This opened their eyes and hearts, and loosened their tongues. I soon found by the questions they asked about a near village hotel, etc., that there was some cause of embarrassment. I then asked one of them to please tell me frankly their trouble, and if I could relieve them I would.

"It seems there was a party of seven, the Prince and five of his suite and Count Mercier, the French Minister at Washington. They had left Washington at six o'clock (it was ten when they arrived) without any breakfast, thinking they could get some on the road. They had a driver who did not know the road, probably because of the changes—they had been provided with such miserable horses that they knew they could not return with them, and they were anxious to have them cared for, and to find others.

"I told them how we were situated, and how simply we were living, but if I might be permitted, I would order the best breakfast we could give them, trusting they would excuse anything that was wanting. They were full of thanks, feared the Prince would be annoyed, but also feared he might suffer, they had no idea of imposing on me, etc. I immediately set everybody to work and ordered *everything we had to be cooked*, and when the party returned from the Tomb, breakfast, or rather lunch, was fairly under way. The Prince told me the President had offered him a steamboat, which he declined; then, if he would come by land, a bodyguard of *a hundred men*. This he also declined, preferring to come without parade.

"They ate like hungry men and seemed to enjoy the freedom from restraint and ceremony. I will make you laugh some day at some inconsistencies which agonized me at the time. They remained till *four* o'clock. We sent a man with them to show them a road, and in fifteen minutes he came back to get the *mules*— one pair of horses had given out. They were sent, and *Prince*

Napoleon rode to Alexandria in a carriage drawn by the Association *mules!* At Alexandria they procured fresh horses to Washington.

"The Prince is a man of pleasant features, slightly Napoleonic —mild expression, quiet, gentlemanlike manners, soft low voice, rather grave in its tone, but a merry laugh that sounds honest. He speaks English exceedingly well. The gentlemen of his suite were all very pleasant, varying enough to make the party agreeable. After lunch, I saw it was entirely too hot for them to think of leaving, and after much persuasion, the Prince, who was evidently very weary, consented to try for a little sleep *on your bed.* He slept for half an hour, and was another man.

"They were all very much interested in the place, and the Association, made many inquiries about you, seemed perfectly familiar with Washington's history. The Prince was deeply impressed with the peculiarity of the position of Mount Vernon at this time, removed from the scenes of conflict, yet surrounded by them—so quiet itself that it seemed impossible that the spirit of war could be hovering so near, yet within the sound of every gun—almost equidistant from the camps of the two armies, yet this little corner of earth was kept *sacred, neutral ground!* He said it was a fact by itself in the history of the world, and the wars of the world, and he sincerely hoped we would be able to keep it so to the end! And I am sure all will echo that prayer."

His Imperial Highness, known to his intimates as Plon-Plon, was Jerome Bonaparte's son by Catherine of Württemberg, whom he had married in 1807 after his unauthorized connection with the Baltimore belle, Elizabeth Patterson, was liquidated by his brother the Emperor. Nearing forty now, the Prince was himself the recent husband of a young Italian princess, who had accompanied him to America, but chose to remain in New York—the first real princess to set foot there—while the gentlemen of the party continued their tour. Included in the suite was the son of the eccentric novelist George Sand, by her early marriage to Casimir Dudevant.

The liberal-minded Prince Plon-Plon was not popular at the starchy Court of his cousin Napoleon III, and was quite free to indulge his passion for travel, more or less incognito. He had dined with the President at the White House—Mr. Lincoln committed the social error of assigning to him the wrong Bonaparte father, which created an awkward silence—and having visited the Federal encampments roundabout Washington, he was now anxious for a view of the other side. This he eventually accomplished by flag of truce, exchanging McDowell's hospitality at Arlington for that of Jeb Stuart at Fairfax Courthouse, escorted from there to Beauregard's headquarters at Manassas—only a matter of weeks after the battle.

Meanwhile the expedition to Mount Vernon occurred. An account of this extraordinary visitation was written by the Prince's aide in a letter to his superior officer, who had been obliged to remain in France. Ferri-Pisani wrote that they left Mercier's house at Georgetown at dawn, in two carriages, armed with a pass signed by General Scott. At the last Federal outpost they found two large trees felled across the road, and were much amused by what was apparently standard Army procedure at such road-blocks—the carriages were lifted "like feathers" to the other side, while the horses were led around the barrier. The Northern commandant accompanied them into enemy territory, risking capture, until he could point out the white spot above the River which was Washington's home, and waved them forward. The road was poorly marked, and they lost themselves in the marshes and woods and detours, until they came to a handwritten sign-post which said "Mount Vernon Alley." It was another half hour to the house, which they thought very small and "without any definite architecture." Behind it were eight little cabins for the use of the colored servants. They asked a girl sitting in front of one of them if the house was opened to visitors, and she nodded.

"The sight of this poor, silent, deserted house in the midst of
this wood, which daily encircles it more completely until it will
choke it—of this artless work, this common landscape—over-
came us with an indescribable emotion, quite deeper than anything else we had felt so far, despite the many magnificent spectacles scattered throughout the country by Nature and American
genius," Ferri-Pisani wrote. "The rooms we entered first were
dilapidated and empty, which was to be expected after long aban-
donment. Yet the noise of a door, and the ruffling of a white
curtain at a window warned us that the house was inhabited by
a woman, and that our bold entrance might have been somewhat
indiscreet. We were rather embarrassed by this apparent silence,
which we knew was alive and quite close to us. . . ."

The observant Frenchman detected and recorded some interesting details which Miss Tracy omitted to mention to the Regent.
They were of course delighted with her when "in the best possible French" she welcomed the Prince and "extended to him
the Nation's hospitality in Washington's house." She then explained to them how the estate had recently been purchased by
public subscription and was administered by a group of American ladies, of whom she was the representative. She showed
them over the house, pointing out the rooms occupied as Washington's guests by Lafayette and the Duke of Orléans (during
the latter's 1797 exile before he became King Louis Philippe),
and of course the key to the Bastille. Miss Tracy made quite an
impression.

"Mrs. Tracy (sic) who has lived so long with Washington's
memory, seems to have lived with Washington himself," Ferri-
Pisani wrote. "She knows the slightest details of his public and
private life, his most insignificant habits, as if she had witnessed
them. Her memory was as boundless as the Prince's curiosity was
unquenchable . . . by making us forget the hour, [she] not
only displayed her charm, but again acted as a clever admin-

istrator. She had to measure her stories by the time required to prepare lunch. The preparations, I believe, were quite long and difficult. The time has passed when the gracious hospitality of Mount Vernon—always ready and never failing—seemed to be forever expecting some illustrious personage, even a Prince! Today our hostess, both austere and charming, thinks she would cheat Washington's memory if she took anything for herself beyond strict necessity. I suspect unheard-of efforts were required to re-create for the Prince a vague likeness of the ancient receptions. . . .

"Anyway, we did not wait in vain! Lunch was excellent. Two beautiful colored girls served while Mrs. Tracy presided in an exquisite manner. As for us, we responded with a formidable appetite. At dessert, the small colored colony was introduced to the Prince. They are the children of Washington's slaves, freed at his death through a special clause in his will. These good people are very proud of their origin. The silent old Negro woman has known and served the father of the land; a six-year-old Negro boy questioned by the Prince answered that he was General Washington's servant. . . .

"As we left, Mrs. Tracy, with attentive delicacy, placed in the Prince's carriage a small box filled with the soil of Mount Vernon, and a rare plant growing near the tomb. It was a present for the Princess Clotilde. Such, Colonel, was our journey to Mount Vernon! As you can see, we did not encounter a single Confederate soldier. Yet I believe, and I think you will agree, that we did not waste our time."

Mount Vernon had worked its accustomed magic on Ferri-Pisani.

5

McClellan's strict security measures soon inconvenienced Miss Tracy. Her letters to Miss Cunningham were now carried to the Occoquan Post Office by a man who had worked as a carpenter at Mount Vernon. He made the nine-mile journey, sometimes on foot, once a week, "for love, declining any compensation," safeguarded by a letter from Miss Tracy to the soldiers he might encounter en route, requesting that he be allowed to pass, on her responsibility. But communication in the opposite direction, to Alexandria, was a different matter. On the 23rd of August she wrote to Miss Cunningham to say that she was going to Washington again tomorrow, to procure more passes.

"Since General McClellan has taken command, there are new regulations," she explained, "and all passes must issue from his office or General Scott's. None of the servants can get to Alexandria, and we have had a mail but once in ten days! I dislike so much to make this journey, that I have tried every means I could devise, but must either go to Washington and get proper passes, or go myself three times a week to Alexandria, or go *without the mails*. This last I cannot think of, for how could I stay down here without either letters or papers? Then too I must keep watch lest anything concerning Mount Vernon appears. So I have concluded to take up my courage once more and walk into the lion's den. It is very pleasant while at Mr. Riggs's, they are *so* kind. But from two miles this side of Alexandria until I reach Mr. Riggs's it is nothing but *soldiers*—in the street, on the boat, and then all the camps to pass through. I shall for the rest of my life have a dislike to a gun or a drum or a military uni-

form. Martial music, that I used to love above all other, is now
like a dirge, without its soothing effect. I anticipate no trouble,
only the disagreeableness, and at that I ought not to murmur,
when so many have so much that is sad and terrible to encounter.

"I feel troubled at not hearing from you, because your last
was so sad, and you referred to some new cause of grief which
I fear may be serious in its effect. Alas, how many heavy burdens
are laid upon us by God, which require the strength of an Al-
mighty arm to lift! How do you get along without Grace? Who
supplies, not fills, her place to you? I have not heard from Miss
McMakin yet. Poor girl, she has a hard struggle between the
unselfishness of her own heart and the intense selfishness of
others. I may have a letter in town now from her.

"I have been preserving a few pears and peaches this week,
the latter it was difficult to find good enough for the purpose,
but I selected the best I could. The soldiers all behave very well
now, and I do not believe we will have any more trouble. We
have had very disagreeable rainy weather for a week, fine weather
for chills. Mr. Herbert has had one or two little touches, not to
be really ill, but I have escaped entirely so far. I try to be very
prudent, and am very well. I seem to be Providentially granted
health and strength, for all the requirements of my position. I
hope to hear that you are better than I fear. Strive to keep up.
You do not know how much strength you may require for the
future. Trust in God. Yours sincerely. . . ."

Autumn, 1861, came and went in Washington with nothing
but drilling and recruiting from McClellan. The capital was
grumbling again, full of foreign adventurers and cranks pro-
moting some form of graft, ladies of no reputation, and quacks.
The blockade of the Potomac by the Southern batteries down the
River continued. There was a dreadful possibility that England
might enter the war on the side of the Confederacy. Lincoln
looked weary and depressed, and people complained that, like
McClellan, he did nothing. It seemed to rain all the time.

"I have been in a state of expectation and disappointment about Mary McMakin," Miss Tracy had written the Regent in September. "She wrote me more than a fortnight since that she would come, intimating that it was her *last* resort. She wrote me more plainly and sadly than ever before. I wrote to know *when* she could come, and received a letter saying after all her friends had frightened her with stories of the impossibility of her coming without taking the oath of allegiance to the Southern Confederacy, and the danger of her being arrested, etc. I wrote her there is no danger for *women,* that there were many annoyances, but they all fell upon me, and so far they had not quite overcome me, and I did not intend that they should. She then wrote she would try to be here by the 20th or 21st, so I am in hopes of seeing her in about ten days.

"I shall be much relieved, I do assure you, for come what will, there is not a white woman within three miles of me, and I have never had one to speak to in all the four months I have been here, except when I have been to Washington, but I have kept cheerful, and thank God perfectly well, and it seems as if a kind Providence had given me strength for what I had to accomplish. I am very glad you are pleased with all I do.

"Since that order of General Scott's we have had not the least trouble with the soldiers, and I do not now believe we will have. They behave with much more respect than the visitors who came by boat used to. They never offer to touch or carry away anything, and this we have often remarked even when they refuse to lay down their arms. We have the Southern soldiers quite near us, both pickets are about three miles from us, each way. The battleground [Manassas] was about sixteen or eighteen miles from us on an air line, so while we heard the whole firing we are too far away to be affected by any infection. The woods that General McClellan has caused to be burned are beyond Georgetown. There would not be the same reason for burning in this neighborhood, and I am sure it will not be done.

"I wrote you some time ago about photographing these rooms, inquiring which you wished taken, and whether you were willing to run the risk of the artist making copies of them common. This letter you could not have received. *Now* it would be impossible to have it done, for no one but myself has or can get a pass to come outside the Federal lines. . . .

"You frighten me when you write so much of your feelings on the war question. If your letters were opened they would make trouble. No one says anything on *that* subject. If you write Mrs. Comegys do not say a word about it, for the correspondence of every prominent person, I am told, is watched, and aside from the injury to the Association, it might seriously affect *her*. Excuse this suggestion, but you have no idea of the extreme caution necessary. . . .

"Mr. Herbert has had one or two rather sharp attacks of fever but is well now. When I was in Washington I made partial arrangements for a man to roof the Mansion and when the equinoxial storm is over, he will begin. We have had such constant rain that it would not do to uncover the house, and yet it leaks so badly! The mosquitoes are *dreadful,* night and day. I am afraid Mary will be eaten up entirely. Mr. Herbert desires his regards and inquires when you may be expected. Good night, and God bless you and comfort you—"

It must have been a strange, beleaguered life at Mount Vernon as the days drew in towards the first winter of the war—two white people only, in the echoing, half-furnished Mansion, ruffled curtains at some of the windows, and the sitting-room carpet put away in tobacco for safe keeping. They must have shared a lamp, with books and accounts and the all-important newspapers, needlework, and conversation, in the long evenings. She was too sensible to withdraw behind a primly closed door, especially when he was ailing. They would have had a great deal to talk about, regarding Mount Vernon's problems of survival—they had a common endeavor, the same dedication. Their very meals, served by the maid Priscilla, would have brought them together in a sort of domesticity. He must have been to some extent mothered or dragooned, and certainly entertained, after lifelong bachelorhood. When did the tardy attachment begin to set in, on either side?

6

General Lee had remained in Richmond during the battle at Manassas, at the wish of President Davis, while Beauregard and Johnston became the Southern heroes. In what amounted to exile, he was then sent, the latter part of July, on an inspection tour of the forces in Western Virginia, against which McClellan's success had taken place—the mountain passes and railway lines to the West were at stake there. And with Lee as a member of his personal Staff went his friend and kinsman, John A. Washington.

They found confusion and bad weather in the mountains—there was a saying that it rained *thirty-two* days that August. On September 13th, while on a routine reconnaissance with Lee's son Rooney, John A. was killed in a little skirmish with Federal pickets at Cheat Mountain. Lee himself wrote from camp to the eldest Washington daughter, Miss Louisa, who was seventeen: "With a heart filled with grief, I have to communicate the saddest tidings you have ever heard. . . . He is now safely in Heaven, I trust with her he loved so much on earth. We ought not to wish him back. . . ."

The news reached Mount Vernon via the *National Intelligencer.* "Poor Mr. Washington's family!" Miss Tracy wrote to Mrs. Comegys in October. "Is it not dreadful, six children, in one short year to lose both father and mother! This is grief indeed. There need not be the slightest anxiety about Mount Vernon in consequence of his death. When he came here last fall, Miss Cunningham sent for him, and everything was arranged, and he assured her that his death would alter nothing. His *will* was explicit, and his heirs would never molest Mount Vernon. The title is in Mr. Riggs's hands."

In this October letter to Mrs. Comegys she gave an account of her late August visit to Washington, necessitated by Mc-Clellan's high-handed ruling about passes. And by the time this letter was written she had made yet another eventful journey through the lines, to carry her case to the President himself— another odd experience, which she reduces to a single paragraph:

"We are still safe and unmolested," she wrote, "the grand difficulties have been for the present surmounted, but I have 'had a time of it!' I believe I wrote you that after the issuing of the new orders by McClellan, a month ago, the passes granted the servants were valueless, and I went up to Washington to procure them from General McClellan himself. He *declined* giving them, saying no servant could be trusted, etc. I came back disappointed, but as I had a pass from General Scott, resigned to be *market woman* and *mail carrier* myself. But to my consternation, my pass was disputed by the outside pickets, and it was not until I insisted upon seeing the officer that I could get by. They said they had received orders from General McClellan.

"I resolved to return to Washington to learn the cause, but the day before I intended to leave, word was brought that the Federal pickets had moved down to within three miles of Mount Vernon and had *barricaded the road!* This was a contingency we never thought of, for there seemed no reason for it, but that made no difference, the *fact* was there, and for ten days the 'outer world' was unapproachable. Finally I became desperate. *Candles* and *Oil* disappeared entirely, and many other small things, considered the necessaries of life, were not to be had. All of this amused me. I laughed until there was *no meat* for the servants! This looked serious, for laborers must be fed, and on something more substantial than would satisfy *me*. I announced my determination to 'run the blockade.' There were several ways, and I intended to try each until I succeeded.

"I heard of a farmer living some three or four miles west of us whose road had also been blockaded, and who had made himself a way through the woods. From here to his farm the road was open; so I decided to 'take to the woods.' I started early one morning ten days since, not knowing what was before me, but that obstacles *must* be overcome. Such a ride! My attendant, a Negro of admirable *sang-froid,* old enough to be reliable; my horses, *a pair of mules.*

"With a trembling heart, I confess, I began this wild ride! We found the woods, after many discouraging directions from the farmer. The sky was bright and sunny, and that always gives one courage. We entered the woods and found that where the underbrush was not so thick as to be impassable, the grass was too high to leave any trace of previous wagon-tracks. We were constantly being *lost.* I feared that we would be forced into what my nature revolts against, *turning back.* For two hours we wandered around, but finally saw a fence, then 'the bars,' and were ready to shout, for we were 'out of the woods.'

"I went direct to Washington, resolved to find *the* man, whoever he might be, who could help me. Some said Mr. Cameron, some said Mrs. Lincoln, but with a woman's instinct and faith in those who have *proved* kind, I went to Headquarters. General Scott was sick, but my friend Colonel Townsend, a noble, true-hearted man, listened to my story, and requested me to write it all down and send it to him. I did so, and received a reply, saying General Scott advised me to see Mr. Lincoln—if his pass was disputed, there was 'no power but the President who could help me.'

"So to Mr. Lincoln I went. He received me very kindly, and wrote a note to General McClellan requesting him to see me and arrange the matter in the best way possible. I carried this to General McClellan, who said it was a grand mistake, he had *never* given an order revoking one of General Scott's passes, he knew his position too well! It was over-zeal on the part of the volunteer officers. He offered to do anything he could for me, would send a steam-tug with provisions from time to time, as I might desire, etc. In fact, *everybody* was kind. General Scott gave me a new

pass, rather more positive than the first, and also one for Miss
McMakin, that I might not be obliged to come and go alone.
Did I write you that I had sent for Miss McMakin from Philadelphia? She is now in Washington, and I am going up for her
tomorrow.

"Thus you see me once more quiet, I have climbed the 'Hill
Difficulty' once more. I may find myself at the bottom again
tomorrow, but I never anticipate. I have found the troubles of
today so absorbing as to annihilate those of yesterday, and those
of tomorrow too far off to command attention. I have so much
to be thankful for. I have found that as the path of duty has been
made plain to me, God, who is the strength of the weak and the
confiding, has gone beside me, smoothing the rough places; and
where the help of human friend was needed, placing the kind
and willing in my way, and I am glad to feel it will be so till
the end. The kind approval of yourself and husband, of our good
Regent, and the other ladies, is an admirable stimulant.

"I have been perfectly well, having had to play *doctress* not
only to nearly everyone here, but also to some still left on Mr.
Washington's farm. I myself have escaped all ailments. I would
love to come and see you, but my presence here was never so
necessary. We have a great many soldiers visiting here, sometimes
all day long they are coming, in companies of four or five, and
it requires two of us always. They behave perfectly well
now. . . ."

One of the many unexpected pictures which the history of the
Association presents to the mind's eye is that of the towering
Lincoln confronted by spunky little Miss Tracy, in an interview
which must have enlivened the weary man's day, however briefly.
McClellan having been obliged to back down, did so handsomely,
and within a few days a small official boat carrying provisions
docked at the Mount Vernon wharf, and was promptly acknowledged by a polite note from Miss Tracy to General McClellan.

Her plea for discretion on the Regent's part was received too late to influence a letter written to Mrs. Comegys early in September and sent via Mount Vernon to be forwarded—which left to Miss Tracy's own discretion was probably not done, at that time. One of the few war-time letters of Miss Cunningham's which have survived, it was written with great difficulty in reply to one from Mrs. Comegys enclosed by Miss Tracy to the Regent —written "under such pain that I have to stop every few moments, close and wash my eyes, and when I do write the eyelids have to be opened but partly, so that I fear you can scarcely decipher what my trembling fingers are trying to trace. Mine has been a sad life since you received my last letter. The death of Grace was a fearful shock to me. I had never watched by a sick bed before, never seen death. From the hour she became dangerously ill I never left her, night nor day, unless compelled by exhaustion, and she was so much better the afternoon and night she died that the doctor had high hopes for her. I had therefore only one half hour's warning. It nearly killed me when all was over. For three days I knew nothing. Hers was a glorious death, one I now feel it was a privilege to witness. But I rue her loss every day. No severer affliction nor one entrenching more upon my daily comfort could have befallen me. She was beginning to read to me, to write for me, and alas, I have no one to do this now, and I am in danger of becoming blind in consequence. I am surrounded by affectionate family servants, but it is different here from your region. You hire only those suited to you. We have our house servants by families. Thus my maid has an infant two months old. You can judge by that what a chain is around me. I could not get white servants where I am now. I am spending the summer in a sort of rural village, some twelve miles from my home, very quiet, and so very peaceful that it would be impossible to realize the horrors of civil war are being enacted in this country, but for the fact that each family has some loved one gone to defend their country. Thus in this peaceful looking place we have aching hearts too. . . ."

This long letter, which cost her so much to write that the

postscripts extended it several days, alternated between pious references to a merciful God and unreconciled lamentation for the innocent victims of "corrupt ambition"; and between a caution which reduced names to blanks, and an amazing amount of detailed misinformation about military affairs, even to the battle-field at Manassas, showing the power and scope of the flying rumors which penetrated as far as the remote mountains of South Carolina, where some few newspapers also found their way. She had heard "on good authority" that forty rifles were indented by the balls of the enemy while the holders were unharmed, demon-strating divine interposition for the Southern cause—for which another company of soldiers in an exposed position with bullets raining round them, having escaped all casualties knelt on the spot and rendered thanks. She had heard that one of General Johnston's regiments arrived late on the field because the Federals had bribed the railroad conductor to delay the train—for which he was hanged when detected. She had heard of atrocities "never surpassed in barbarism" committed on the soil of Virginia—the Federal Army, she had heard, carried with it 30,000 handcuffs (rumor failed to say where, and from what source of supply they had been assembled) and quantities of halters—(the latter, considering the number of horses which went to war, were needed for more practical purposes than stringing up the rebels); and there were official Federal plans, she had been assured, for a victory ball-supper at Richmond on Monday night, the 22d of July, when the city was supposed to have been captured—etc., etc.

But the Regent was alone and ill, and saw her great dream shattered on the very eve of its fulfillment, and even she could not foresee Mount Vernon's power of endurance—had not yet realized the forces of tenacity and fortitude which she herself had engendered. "We all owe a debt to Miss T——," she wrote in this letter to Mrs. Comegys. "Nothing could have prevented mischief or kept that spot as it is still kept, but for her firmness and courage and presence. I am so glad you urged her to stay. I have implored it. She has promised she will not fail. God bless her."

Miss McMakin at length arrived at Mount Vernon, in what state of mind and nerves no one recorded, and Miss Tracy continued to fight her own little war.

"When your letter arrived it found me in a *new* position— *nursing a sick lieutenant* of the Mich. 5th named Pomeroy!" she wrote to Mrs. Comegys on November 30th. "The poor fellow had been very ill of congestive fever, and was discharged from the hospital with the injunction to be *very prudent;* the next day some of his friends were coming down here, and he joined them, insisting he was entirely able. Soon after reaching the house he was taken ill, and Mr. Herbert found him under a tree wild with delirium. He had him brought into the house, and he and the young man's friends did what they could.

"Miss McMakin and myself were in town; when we returned we found two or three messengers had been sent for a doctor and an ambulance. The poor fellow was on blankets on the floor, in a raging fever and perfectly unconscious of anything, and the men were frightened that he would die, notwithstanding which they wanted to *move* him back to *camp!* I insisted that if forty ambulances came he should not be moved, had him put to bed, mustard footbath, mustard behind his head, and all those remedies—his captain and an ambulance came, but I would not let them move him. He was not quiet until eleven o'clock, when his friends left him with a corporal to take care of him. His groans were fearful, and his calls upon his wife heartrending—he had been married but one month when he came here!

"The next day he had a return of the bad symptoms, but we fought them off. He was with us four days, and we sent him back to camp feeling well, without a doctor having seen him. He was a *very* agreeable, gentlemanlike young fellow, and seemed so grateful for what we had done for him, we were much interested in him. I shall long remember his tone and manner in reply to me when he said it was useless for him to attempt to thank me

for he had no words. I told him we had only done as we would
wish others to do for those we loved, who were separated from
us, and all I asked was that if he found any poor fellow sick or
suffering he would think of me and do what he could for him;
he replied, with full eyes, 'So help me God, I will!' I stopped at
camp a few days after, and found he was still well. That is another of our little episodes I write for the amusement of your
invalid daughter; tell her our Lieutenant was *very* handsome!
Tell her also I have unbounded faith in codliver oil. I believe it
once saved my life.

"I am sorry to dispel your romantic visions of Miss McMakin
and myself and donkey—in my loneliness last summer I followed
behind the trottings of a not very vigorous *horse,* in an open
buggy with a small Negro beside me, but when the picket guards
began to move down the road, and such journeys became frequent and *public,* my friends began to remonstrate. Finally the
small boy ran away, and it became necessary for me to do all the
errands. I could not take a *field servant* beside me, the style was
not proper. My friends insisted I should hire a carriage. I found
it would cost a fortune. Then I must buy a second-hand rockaway. I found a very nice strong little affair that was made to
order for a lady who was willing to dispose of it for $100—less
than cost. I consulted Mr. Riggs, and had some gentlemen au
fait in such matters examine it. They all said it would sell in a
year for what I gave for it, and advised me to purchase. I finally
concluded to do so, and if the Association did not approve when
it came time to sell, I would pay the difference myself, if there
should be any. The mules were put in requisition, and Mary and
I go in comfort and in a quiet way, if not very *stylishly!* I have
had reason to be thankful that I yielded to the wise counsels of
my friends, for now that we drive through *three miles* of camps,
it would not be proper. You can form no idea of the country we
go through. Alexandria itself is a *camp.*

"I see some one has started the idea of running a steamboat to

Mount Vernon, and I must go to Headquarters to remonstrate. I was there on Wednesday, to request an order to be given to the commander of this division, General Heintzelman, forbidding *large* bodies of troops coming on the place. After General Scott's Order the soldiers were very particular, and came few at a time, but since his resignation they have been less particular, and within a week twice several *hundred* have come at once; they trample over everything, and it is impossible to watch them.

"Long since, Mr. Herbert and myself decided there was no way in which we could save the Association so much as by acting as *police ourselves.* As there was no special work for him to super-intend, he would receive the visitors, show them the house, etc. I take my post in the sitting-room, from the windows of which I can command a view of the *garden walls,* and General Wash-ington's magnolia and holly trees, the leaves of which are objects of particular desire. In this way we save three or four dollars a day.

"When there is a succession of visitors and Mr. Herbert is in one place, I show the *privates* the house. I will not the officers, except the most elevated in rank, they are not polite enough. This takes of course all our time, but that is what we are *paid* for. We have some annoyances, but have so far succeeded in our plan, but if they come by hundreds in at the gate, and boat-loads at the wharf, *fifty* police could not protect the place.

"So I posted to Headquarters on Wednesday, was, as I have always been, received with the utmost kindness. Col. Key, one of the Staff of General McClellan, said, 'Miss Tracy, General Mc-Clellan will do anything you wish, only say what you wish.' I said what I wished, and he said, 'It shall be done.' Now I must go up on Monday or Tuesday and protest against this boat specu-lation. You know the Association received 25¢ on every passenger by the boat when it was running regularly. Well, I found there was some reluctance to subscribe, and have had notices put up, requiring an entrance fee of 25¢ from *land* visitors. We have collected a little, but of course the soldiers plead poverty, and many with truth. We are trying to keep these contributions to pay the laborers necessary.

"After weeks and weeks without any news of Miss Cunningham, I received a letter from her a few days ago dated November 5th. It was written by her niece, at her dictation—her eyes are still a source of great suffering to her. She says it will be utterly impossible for her to come North, for many reasons of a private nature, even if she could pass through the country—urges my remaining, etc. Her letters had been opened and read, and sealed up. She is much safer where she is than anywhere else—their plantation is so far in the northwestern part of the State as to be more remote from the seat of war than any other place I know of now. Oh, how sad all this is, six months in the midst of camps and in sound of cannon have not in the least reconciled me to seeing my beautiful country so destroyed. I dare not think. . . .

"Please accept the thanks of Miss McMakin and myself for your Christmas invitation, but we must decline all such indulgences. In my estimation Mount Vernon never needed so much watching as now. I do not like to be absent for a single night. I wish you could come to see us.

"I have not read *Lucile,* but will try to get it, for readable matter is scarce. If you will you can send the bulbs direct to the Association by Adams Express to Alexandria—they continue to bring small packages *free. Anything* crosses the Potomac, but as letters are sometimes examined Mr. Riggs thought it was best my private letters should come to Alexandria. Give my best to your husband and daughter—Miss McMakin and Mr. Herbert desire to be remembered—yours with love—SARAH C. TRACY.

"*Wednesday morn.* All right at Headquarters. They are very kind, will do anything *or* nothing, as I say."

Doubtless Headquarters found it more peaceful that way.

The rockaway carriage, named for the New Jersey town which manufactured it, was a light four-wheeled vehicle with a top, open at the sides. Washington himself had driven mules to his coach, and thought them as good as horses for that purpose, and better on bad roads.

Like certain other wars since then which were supposed to be all over by Christmas, this one had barely begun. Presumably the odd little household at Mount Vernon made its own Spartan observance of the day, with home-made gifts and a little something extra for dinner, and perhaps a toast in Miss Tracy's claret wine to the absent Regent, whose situation was surely recognized as far drearier than theirs.

7

For some reason, perhaps only the uncertain mails, almost no correspondence has survived for 1862. This was the year of the nasty little fight outside Williamsburg, Virginia, in May, when Johnston withdrew strategically before McClellan at Yorktown,—of Fair Oaks, and the tragic Seven Days, when McClellan failed to take Richmond—of the second battle at Bull's Run near Manassas, which ended pretty much as the first one had done a year before, in disaster for the Federal troops and an indecisive victory for the South, though Lee was in the field now, and in a position to move on Washington.

As before, the capital was full of wild rumors, and the wounded, and the demoralized volunteer male nurses who had partaken too freely of the stimulants intended for the wounded. Cannon had been heard again in the streets of the city—and at Mount Vernon.

The new Secretary of War, Mr. Stanton, always an hysterical man, was organizing to evacuate the President and Cabinet to some unspecified place of greater safety, though Lincoln was taking no notice of that. McClellan, who had been in eclipse since his failure on the James, was hastily recalled to repair the damage his successors Pope and Halleck had wrought at Manassas, and he rode up towards the gunfire along roads choked with loaded ambulances and the troops of bewildered officers whose men would not stand and fight. The Alexandria road was bright at night with the campfires of an exhausted, drunken, hungry army, dropping in its tracks. And always the panicky rumor ran—Lee was coming.

McClellan brought some kind of order out of the chaos, made another army out of the remnants, and marched them into western Maryland to defend Washington. Lee took Harper's Ferry. In September the armies met at Sharpsburg, or Antietam, and fought to a terrible draw, with twenty thousand dead. Lee fell back into Virginia, without taking Washington. McClellan sat down in Maryland. The command passed to Burnside, who was already convinced of his own incapacity.

During the summer of '62 small-pox was rampant in Washington, and the Sanitary Commission was organized under the direction of Dr. Bellows of New York—he who had coined for Mme. LeVert that happy phrase, "presence of heart." Miss Hamilton, doubtless already known to him, became one of the volunteer workers at the Washington office of the Commission, as everywhere women began to emerge as capable assistants and executives in a time of such dire need. Surgeon-General Finley of the old school—whose spinster niece was writing the *Elsie Dinsmore* books—was replaced on the demand of the Commission and the medics by the powerful, bearded, authoritative Dr. Hammond, who promptly clashed with Stanton. And beginning with Antietam, a shy, valiant little maiden lady named Clara Barton, now in her early thirties, was following the cannon and administering to their victims. Alexandria was known as Camp Misery, having become a horrifying catchall for sick and wounded, stragglers and incompetents, until the Sanitary Commission moved in with tents and warm clothing. The Federal base of supplies was at Aquia Creek, on the Potomac some twenty miles below Mount Vernon.

Miss Tracy's comment on this disastrous year of 1862 is scarcely to be found, but her life must have been even more eventful than during '61, so far as getting to and from Washington, and procuring passes and supplies went. In March, about the time McClellan moved his army down to the Peninsula, she wrote again to Heintzelman's adjutant-general to request that the soldiers would come to Mount Vernon in smaller groups, and not on Sunday. For a while in the spring and summer the Mount Vernon boat had been permitted to run again, but after the

second Manassas battle it was stopped by order of Secretary
Stanton for the remainder of the war—on the grounds that it
afforded opportunity for espionage and treason, linking as it did
Federal territory to Virginia soil. Stanton was to hear from her,
more than once.

In November, '62, Lee was at Fredericksburg, entrenched on
the heights around the city, and Burnside was sent down to confront him—passing so close to Mount Vernon on the way that his
dust was visible in the western sky. On December 16th, the dreadful freight of the ambulances and transports began to return up
the River to Georgetown, where Miss Louisa May Alcott had just
arrived—without any training—to be an army nurse at the hospital set up in the old Union Hotel. Miss Barton had actually
been at Fredericksburg, and under fire.

Burnside had bungled it. The Army of the Potomac was staggering back again, across the Rappahannock, with over twelve
thousand killed and wounded in repeated futile attacks. The
Christmas of 1862 found the whole country appalled and discouraged. Grant had failed at Vicksburg, and Lee was digging in
along the Rappahannock and setting up cavalry outposts. Burnside resigned, and Hooker, one of his severest critics, was given
the command—big, blond, vain, and ambitious, Hooker rode a
white horse. Lincoln took his family on a winter boat ride down
the River to visit the Aquia Creek base.

The change of commanders, and the appearance of a spectacular, confident man like Hooker, somewhat restored morale
in the Union Army. For replacements to their casualties, Congress passed an act for conscription, which could still be avoided
by paying $300 or supplying a substitute—who usually required
the same sum. By April of 1863 the armies had refitted and re-
couped themselves for a summer campaign, though food was
becoming a problem, and not least at Mount Vernon, where in
May Miss Tracy was writing Mrs. Comegys a letter which now
has the opening paragraph cut away with scissors. "You may well

ask what we live on," the remainder begins. "But though money is scarce, and for some unaccountable reason our boat is not permitted to run, yet we do live, simply, but even comfortably. I wish everybody had as much. And now fresh vegetables and fruit will come, we will luxuriate. We make a little all the time from entrance fees, 25¢ on each visitor, some days not a dime, then again three or four dollars. Last summer when the boat was running we not only paid expenses, except salaries, but shingled the roof, and did some small but essential repairs. But since the last of August it has been stopped."

Here again some later censorship interrupts the text with x'd out lines, and it resumes with a reference to the Regent and the long hiatus in their correspondence. "I had a long letter from Miss Cunningham some three weeks ago, the first I have had from her in *eighteen months.* She had not heard from me in eighteen. I have written her two or three times by the flag of truce, but she has received none. I went to Mr. Stanton and told him I must write, and a longer letter than was permitted generally. I asked if I might write such a letter and have it examined by a friend of mine in one of the departments, and thus secure its passage. He said Yes. I wrote a volume, which my friend kindly waded through and endorsed as examined, as being simply on the affairs of Mount Vernon from the secretary to the Regent. This he enclosed, open, to Col. Ludlow, who has control of the flag of truce. This I hope will reach her. If not, I know of no other way, and I know how intensely anxious she must feel, though she kindly expresses great confidence in us. She is living far away from any disturbance, and says if it were not for the newspapers she would not know there was a war. I can hardly realize anyone so situated."

More sentences are here x'd out by a much later pen in very black ink, and a letter from Miss Tracy to Mrs. Mitchell, who had sent a friendly inquiry from Wisconsin, fills in some of the intervening months:

"I do not know of anything in particular that you could do for us, or of any special necessity for your visiting Mount Vernon, yet we all like very much now and then a word of encouragement, and if you should come East during the spring or summer we would be delighted to welcome you here. Last year when you were in New York I heard of you, through my sister, Mrs. Keith, who teaches at Mrs. Macauley's. I immediately wrote to you, begging you to come and see us, telling you I would meet you in Washington and bring you down, assuring you that the talked-of danger existed only in the fears of the ignorant, unless you might fear chills and fever! Neither Miss McMakin nor myself have ever had any, but everyone else on the place has; from the last of July to November ['62] there was never a time when I had not some one ill, sometimes quite so, but although entirely without the advice of a physician, except when I went to Washington to consult with one, yet we have had no fatal sickness—even when all the surrounding country was filled with small-pox, measles, typhoid fever, and so forth. Of course we have very little money, and the loss of the passengers by boat for the last seven months has been a great trial. . . .

"I have gone through so much, have known so much of war, that I am in despair. I seem to feel that a cessation of war is farther off than at the commencement. I am weary of it, and wish that I could escape to some peaceful clime, I care not how far off. We are beginning to enjoy spring violets and hyacinth, and green things are abundant. I shall be very glad to hear from you, and we will all be very glad to see you. . . ."

Some time during the past year there had been another fire at the greenhouse which had been sheltering the old plants, some of which were believed to go back to General Washington's time, and in June, '63, in another letter to Mrs. Mitchell, Miss Tracy wrote that in order to rebuild it Mr. Riggs thought of selling one of the Virginia bonds he held for the Association. They had the planks and the bricks, and Mr. Herbert thought $800 would be

GEORGE WASHINGTON RIGGS. First treasurer of the Mount Vernon Ladies' Association.

MISS TRACY'S MYSTERIOUS MR. GRAHAM.

Right: MME. ACHILLE MU-RAT. First vice-regent for Florida. *Below:* MRS. FRANCIS FOGG. First vice-regent for Tennessee.

Mrs. Joseph Comegys. First vice-regent for Delaware.

"Dear Mrs. Farnsworth." First vice-regent for Michigan.

Mrs. Graham Newell Fitch.
First vice-regent for Indiana.

Mrs. Horatio Greenough. First
vice-regent for Massachusetts.

Mrs. Isaac Morse. First vice-regent for Louisiana.

Mrs. Nathaniel Norris Halsted. Second vice-regent for New Jersey.

Mrs. Alexander Mitchell.
First vice-regent for Wisconsin.

Mrs. Susan E. Johnson Hudson. Second vice-regent for Connecticut.

"PRETTY MRS. SWEAT." Second vice-regent for Maine.

MRS. LEWIS WILLIAM WASHINGTON. First vice-regent for West Virginia.

THE MAINE ROOM, as furnished by Mrs. Sweat.

THE 1870 COUNCIL. *Left to right, standing:* Mrs. Barry, Mrs. Walker, Mrs. Washington, Mrs. Halsted, Mrs. Emory, Mrs. Chace. *Seated:* Mrs. Mitchell, Mrs. Brooks, Mrs. Sweat, Miss Cunningham, Mrs. Comegys, Mrs. Eve.

sufficient, but they had not been able to raise any money. "Mr. Stanton has very politely but positively refused to allow our boat to run, which places us very disagreeably in many respects," she explained. "I feel the hothouse is of such importance that it would be better to make some sacrifice than to lose these plants, whose place can never be supplied, but I cannot authorize Mr. Riggs to sell until I have the approbation of five of the Vice-Regents. Will you please write me what you think?"

Mrs. Mitchell replied that she agreed to the sale of the bond as it was impossible to raise any money at that time by contribution. "I regret exceedingly that you cannot run the boat," she wrote. "Perhaps just now it would not be safe, but ordinarily as the boat might be made distinctive, and as being neutral, I should think the favor might be granted, if we take the risk. I have a little influence at Washington. Would you recommend our petitioning for the privilege? I leave for the East next week, and shall be at Saratoga until the middle of August, afterwards at Newport.

"I do trust this dreadful war is coming to an end. I have suffered so much anxiety it has added twenty years to my age. If all things are quiet when I am in New York, if I can secure an escort I will go to Mount Vernon. My husband is engaged in active business and can give very little time to pleasure, and my only son and nephew on whom I formerly depended are still in the army. Trusting we shall soon see better days. . . ."

It is noticeable, however, that in spite of aging anxieties the Saratoga and Newport social routine was maintained. And Mrs. Mitchell's proposed visit to Mount Vernon was apparently not made till the autumn of the following year.

Miss Hamilton also, consenting to the sale of the bond, wrote that she was using all her influence in Washington for the resumption of the boat. Her letters to Miss Tracy on that subject indicate that her position with the Sanitary Commission and consequent contact with official red tape had gone a little to her head: "I am making what efforts I can to obtain the running of the boat," she wrote. "Have you any proof that no mail, or spies, or secessionists have ever been conveyed by the agency of the boat or Mount Vernon to the enemy? If so, please let me know what they are. In case I wish to ask a sum equivalent to that we are losing by the absence of the boat, please make out for me an average fair sum for what will be the ordinary time of running for the year—take the year or half year since the war began, and please let me know what proof you have for your figures. . . ."

Mr. Everett, doubtless at her behest, wrote to a Washington lawyer for advice which he required to be gratuitous patriotism, regarding the application for indemnity at the rate of $500 a month, "for the pleasant season of the year," and was referred to the Court of Claims. It was later apparent that Mrs. Mitchell might have been a more effective advocate than the officious Miss Hamilton.

Writing to Miss Cunningham three years from now, in 1866, in reply to the Regent's expressed fear that Mount Vernon would be deserted by its exhausted care-takers before it would be possible for her to return and take charge herself, Miss Tracy recounted an incident which took place in this spring of '63.

"You know very well that while neither Mary nor I are given to much palaver or many protestations, we will go as far as we consistently can to serve a friend," she wrote in her matter-of-fact way. "Mary has always been very devoted to me, and she has had some hard struggles with her mother, I will tell you a long story some day. But Mary fancies she owes her life to me. Three years ago, when money was scarce and we had few visitors, Mary and I went every afternoon to the wharf and caught enough fish for breakfast. Sometimes Mr. Herbert went, but often we went alone. One day we went and Mary made a mis-step and fell into the River. We were alone, and the tide was high. I took off an overskirt I had on to protect my dress and threw it to her, holding one end, and thus she got back unhurt, only both of us dreadfully scared. I have never been fishing since. Mary insists that but for me she would have been drowned."

Meanwhile the usual summer holocaust was in the making roundabout Chancellorsville, and early in May the loaded ambulances streamed back again to the streets of Washington, where the citizens in the freak prosperity of a war were becoming callous to the sight—and the ladies who were not yet wearing black sported dresses in a new shade of red called magenta, which was named for a different battlefield.

By mid-June the capital had sobered up. Lee was in Pennsylvania. Jeb Stuart's cavalry was fanning out—Hagerstown, Chambersburg, Harrisburg, spread the alarm. Rather abruptly, Hooker was relieved of the command, which passed to a little known general named Meade.

On the 29th of June, '63, Miss Tracy, who had never heard of Gettysburg, Pennsylvania, was writing to Mrs. Comegys:

"I must take a few minutes to acknowledge your very kind note, and your very kind authority to Mr. Herbert and myself for building the greenhouse. Just now we can do nothing. We are outside the Federal lines once more, and no passes are given to anyone to come to us. Miss McMakin has a friend, a teacher, who was to pass a week of her vacation with us. She came into Washington, and on Friday Mary went for her, but could get no pass to bring her down. She went to Headquarters. Mr. Stanton's orders were decided, and Major-General Heintzelman, commanding the forts and defences, was not allowed discretionary power of giving a single pass! Miss Reese was obliged to return to Philadelphia.

"We are told that if we go into town tomorrow we cannot return, but we *must*. I am going up for provisions, and *must* return. We are in the midst of excitement. This is the third repetition of the same act in this drama. Were it not that some intervening events have been seared into our hearts and brains we might almost think we had been asleep for two years. The only comfort is three times and out. Perhaps we are nearing the end. Oh, how I pray it may be. I am in such haste, will write again—if the communication is open, for you have the Confederates in your distant neighborhood, and yesterday they were within three miles of us. It may therefore be some time before we have regular communication again.

"P.S. Mary and I passed the day at the picket post. Orders had been given to admit no one into the lines, but I was sure when the officer of the day came his rounds he would pass me through to Headquarters. But he did not come, and we waited till night, then returned here to begin again in the morning.

"We have had old West Ford brought here. Mr. Herbert and myself went to see him Sunday and found him very feeble, and fearing all this excitement might hurt him, we have had him brought here, where we could take better care of him. I felt it was our duty to see that he should want for nothing in his old age.

"I will let you know the result of our expedition tomorrow.

"*Washington*. Thanks to Major Smith, Mrs. Goodrich's son-in-law, I am here. Shall have no trouble in our passes. Am sending provisions down by a tug."

There is a marked difference in the ink in this letter. Only the few lines written in Washington, at Mr. Riggs's house, are easily decipherable. The rest looks as though it had been written in a watered down, or home-made ink.

Old West Ford was an exceptional Negro who had been one of Judge Bushrod's household, and could remember the stories told in his somewhat boozy old age by Billy Lee, who was General Washington's body servant. Benson Lossing, that amiable historian who was a friend of George Washington Parke Custis and as a welcome visitor at Arlington and Mount Vernon wrote the first history of the Mansion not long after it passed into the possession of the Association, left a touching description of this fine old

Negro as he was in 1858, when Lossing talked with him at Mount Vernon and sketched his portrait. He had found Ford at the blacksmith shop near the conservatory, engaged in making a plough, but very ready to reminisce about the old days which Billy Lee had so vividly described to him. It was agreed between them that Ford would sit to Lossing for his portrait the following day before breakfast, when he appeared in his best, "having on a black satin vest," Lossing recorded, "a silk cravat, and his curly grey hair arranged in the best possible manner, 'for,' he said, 'the artists make colored folks look bad enough anyhow.' When my sketch was finished, he wrote his name under it with my pencil."

And this signature, as it appears in Lossing's book, should settle the general uncertainty about the spelling of the old servant's name. He wrote it with the *t*, West · ford, as two words.

The battle at Gettysburg lasted three days, before Lee's army fell back, outnumbered, mauled, and beaten, but leaving a total of twenty-three thousand Federal casualties. The celebrations in Washington of what was nevertheless considered a Federal victory coincided with the fire-crackers and ceremonies of July 4th. The next day word arrived that Grant had now taken Vicksburg, and the double triumph brought out all the bands in the capital. But Meade had the universal disease of the Federal command. With the advantage in his hands, he hesitated. Lee crossed the Potomac southward, taking his big guns with him, and got away into Virginia. Meade then offered to resign, but there was no one else —so far—who seemed capable of doing any better.

When the soldiers' national cemetery at Gettysburg was to be dedicated that November, with solemn ceremonies in the presence of several State Governors, the President and members of his Cabinet, and an enormous crowd, Edward Everett was the unanimous choice as chief orator, and the occasion was postponed in order to give him more time to prepare his speech. Of almost secondary importance was the fact that Mr. Lincoln had been asked to say "a few appropriate words," following "the oration."

Everett spoke for his customary two hours, his well-set-up body erect and graceful, his white hair shining, his magnificent voice rolling out his rounded sentences. When it was Lincoln's turn his thin, untrained voice and awkward carriage suffered by contrast, and he had finished speaking almost before he began. The audience did applaud, however, and though the press comment was brutal, many people left the field aware that they had heard something worth remembering.

Everett was among the first to recognize that he had been outdone by an innate power and sincerity which would become immortal. "I should be glad if I could flatter myself that I came as near the central idea of the occasion in two hours as you did in two minutes," he wrote the President the next day, in a letter thanking him for finding a seat on the platform for his daughter Charlotte. To which Lincoln with his infinite courtesy replied: "In our respective parts yesterday you could not have been excused to make a short speech, nor I a long one. I am pleased to know that, in your judgment, the little I did say was not entirely a failure."

By the end of 1863 there was a general feeling in Washington that now the tide of war had turned—that the Confederates could not win. Even the cavalry skirmishes along the Rappahannock as the winter inactivity set in went against them. Behind its fortifications, and the army still under Meade's command, the capital began a season of feverish gaiety and high living, playgoing, weddings, dinner parties, and dances—with an undercurrent of serious labor unrest; while out in Tennessee the man named Grant went on winning battles.

8

By a letter from Miss Tracy to Mrs. Comegys in January of '64, it is apparent that she was absent from Mount Vernon in the autumn of '63, on a valiant mission to North Carolina, where the only son of her widowed sister was in critical condition with concussion as a consequence of being thrown from his horse. The boy was in the signal corps at an outpost somewhere beyond New Berne, and Miss Tracy hastened South to join her sister there. They found him by some miracle still alive and recovering, though the surgeons had all given him up and predicted paralysis if not death. She was a week on the road each way, but considered the trials of the journey as nothing "when we reflect how much we owe to God in preserving our darling to us."

She returned before Christmas, to find Mount Vernon much the same, "only more so." Nothing seems to have come of the projected greenhouse at this time, for the financial situation became acute in other ways. "So strict are the injunctions against giving passes that the few land visitors who come from day to day leaving a small fee to eke out our small expenditures have ceased entirely, and we have not ten visitors a month!" she wrote Mrs. Comegys on January 6th. "I do not believe there is any remedy for this until the war is over—or a change in the Cabinet! I am sure there is a motive, but I cannot see through it. If the spies of the Government are no more truthful in their representation of other points than in regard to Mount Vernon, I think they are indeed a useless lot! This state of things leaves us of course entirely without funds. Mr. Riggs is very anxious to sell the Virginia Bonds, he has been supplying us with money for more than a year, and I have urged him to sell enough to refund himself. But he says that he ought to have enough to pay Mr. Herbert too, that because Mr. Herbert does not ask for the money is no reason it should be any longer withheld, and there must be at least $2500 due him. Mr. Riggs therefore begs permission to sell all the bonds. He says it is nonsense to hold on to them any longer under the present circumstances. I promised to write to several of the ladies for authority for him to sell them."

Probably as a result of this second request for ready funds, a bombshell arrived in Miss Tracy's hands in mid-January, in the shape of a letter from Miss Hamilton, reminding her of the annual meeting on February 22d of the officers of the Association which was required by their Constitution, and which had so far always been deferred for one reason or another. With her usual juggernaut efficiency, Miss Hamilton enclosed a draft of the notice she requested Miss Tracy to mail out to the Vice-Regents, and to the Regent, with a Washington postmark, if you please, and further announced that she had arranged for the meeting to take place in one of the rooms at the Sanitary Commission in Washington City. "You of course will be there with the Minutes and prepared to give all the information in your power," she informed Miss Tracy. "Perhaps Mr. Herbert will also come up to the meeting, there are so many things we would like to have him tell us about. I would be glad to have you send these notices without delay, as the time is short. As soon as I receive mine I shall correspond with the different ladies, so as to be sure if possible to obtain a quorum for the transaction of business."

Miss Tracy was floored, and flew to her pen to beg Mrs. Comegys's advice and support, enclosing Miss Hamilton's letter and a copy of her own reply. Ice blocked the River and the boats were not running above Alexandria, while travel in the omnibus was considered a risk because of small-pox in the city, and the roads were too bad for any Mount Vernon vehicle, which cut her off, temporarily, from the Riggses as well as Mrs. Comegys, but her letter suggested a conference in Washington before the proposed meeting of the Vice-Regents could take place.

Her protest to Miss Hamilton was a model of tact and diplomacy, pointing out that no Southern Vice-Regent could possibly attend a February meeting, and that the Western ones would almost certainly be prevented by conditions of winter travel in war time, and by the shortness of notice, so that the meeting could probably consist only of Miss Hamilton, Mrs. Comegys, and Mme. Berghmans—which was perhaps just what Miss Hamilton intended. Miss Tracy forbore even to mention that Miss Hamilton must be perfectly aware that Mr. Herbert as a Virginian could not set foot in the Federal capital, and that the presence of the Regent would be, to say the least, appropriate.

Her objections were ridden down by Miss Hamilton, who "insisted" upon a February meeting, and Miss Tracy sent off another troubled letter to Mrs. Comegys. "I do not think it en règle, but could not contest the point," she confessed unhappily. "I am sure there has been a mistake about this meeting, which will worry our little Regent, but I did all I could. Now we must only make the best of it. I enclose you Miss Hamilton's reply, which of course did not please me. I tried to curb my rebellious spirit and answer as would please Miss Cunningham, I do not know the effect, but I do know that I think I am right! I think I understand the whole of this last move. How much more dignified and kind it would have been to have pursued your plan of procuring passes for the Southern Vice-Regents. Mrs. Eve and Mrs. LeVert I know would have come. Well, I hope no harm is done except to try my temper because that won't hurt me, it is good discipline. . . ."

She wrote of course to Miss Cunningham, but as she could never be sure if the letters reached her, she wrote at the same time to Mrs. Ritchie in Italy, giving an account of the situation at Mount Vernon to be forwarded from there to the Regent. "All things considered, we have got along very comfortably," she told Mrs. Ritchie. "We have been the greater part of the time between the Federal and Confederate lines, but no depredations have been committed. Since the first May of the war no Confederates have been in the place. A very large number of Federal soldiers have visited here, but after the first month in a respectful and orderly manner. During the second summer of the war the boat was permitted to run regularly from Washington here, but after the second battle of Bull's Run the Secretary of War would no longer permit passengers to land on the Virginia side. This has been a serious loss to us. No attempt has been made to do anything more than keep the place in neat order and repair the occasional breakages. But even this requires some money. Consequently we have been obliged to draw upon Mr. Riggs to advance upon securities in his hands. Now the ladies think something must be done towards selling these bonds, etc. Mr. Herbert has never drawn his full salary, simply taking what was absolutely necessary. In view of all these points a meeting has become urgent. I am sorry you cannot be present. As it is quite impossible for Miss Cunningham to come on, it would be well if all those who particularly understand her views and opinions could be present. I do not know whether you ever hear from her. I do occasionally, at long intervals. She seems to be about the same—very sad and very lonely, on her plantation with her mother. She says nothing of her brother, and I am not even sure he is alive. If you can write her, tell her what I have written you, tell her we will all be faithful to Mount Vernon and her till the war shall end. Beg her to write to me as often as she can, if only short letters. Tell her it is very important I should be able to say I have heard from her. Please entreat of her not to mention the war. She does not know how excited the subject makes her, and the two things must not be connected in the slightest way."

In view of the unhappy misunderstandings which were to surround Miss Tracy after the Regent's return to Mount Vernon when the war had ended, her attitude towards her own financial position should be expressly followed in her letters at this time. She worried about other people's reimbursement, even to the affluent Mr. Riggs, but was quietly drawing on her own resources, whatever they were. In reply to some query from Mrs. Comegys on this matter, she wrote on January 30th from Washington, where she was always a welcome guest at the spacious Riggs home in I Street which she called her "hotel"—"You are very kind, but I am not in the least troubled about my compensation. If I have done right about the expenses on the place and have managed matters prudently and satisfactorily I am content. But I do want an addition given to Mary's salary. When Miss Cunningham wrote to me to send for her she also asked me to make the best arrangement I could. Mary agreed to come for her expenses and $100 for clothing the first year! It was soon apparent to me that she could not do with that, but she never uttered a murmur or asked for more. On my own responsibility I told her last year I would give her $12 a month, and I have done so, but this is not enough at present prices to half clothe her. If in consideration of the present poverty of the Association they could give her one good round hundred in addition to what she has received for the past, and vote her in future $18 from the first of this month, I think it would be only justice and even generous. Then I would like the ladies to decide upon the exact amount a year they are willing for the present to devote to household and outdoor expenses, and Mr. Herbert and myself will *make* everything come into that sum, sometimes doing without one thing, sometimes another. Heretofore I have acted blindly, everything was new to me, never having provided for anyone but myself, and never caring where my money went to, as it was mine and I was not in debt, which I never was for a dollar in my life, and the Association is not. I have tried to manage rightly, but know it is impossible in every instance. I only write this now that you and Mr. Comegys may think about it, and I can give you particulars and show you my accounts and ask you a thousand things I never can write. I have had today a very pleasant interview with Mrs. Berghmans. She says you and she could have secured the boat. She is quite intimate with the President's wife, and will try with you and is sure it can be accomplished! Wishes she had been written to instead of Miss Hamilton. I wish so too, but never mind. . . ."

The letter closed with an invitation from Mrs. Riggs to the

Comegyses to stay with them as house-guests during their visit to Washington for the February 22d meeting, and suggested that they arrive a few days early to allow time for consultation.

Miss Hamilton, acting according to Hoyle, notified Mrs. Comegys that she had sent telegrams to all the Vice-Regents, including the Southern ones, and would herself be at Willard's Hotel on February 20th, which was a Saturday. The response to her peremptory summons may have surprised her.

Mrs. Farnsworth of Michigan was already in Washington for the winter, as her husband was a congressman.

Mrs. Little of Maine was accompanied by her friend and co-worker Mrs. Lorenzo Sweat, whose husband was also in Congress, and who was by way of being an authoress, having contributed to the *North American Review* since 1856, and published *Highways of Travel*, the result of a summer in Europe in 1859, and a novel called *Ethel's Love-Life*. Just turning forty, and one of the youngest ladies present, "pretty Mrs. Sweat," who rhymed with *sweet*, would shortly succeed Mrs. Little as Vice-Regent, and for many years fill the post of permanent secretary to the Association.

Mrs. Fitch of Indiana, who had been such a joy during the spring of 1860 when the Regent was in Washington organizing the Congressional excursion, wrote to Mrs. Comegys that it seemed a long journey to undertake, but if nothing prevented she would attempt it, and rejoice to see her friends again, though she dreaded Washington as it must now appear.

Mrs. Van Antwerp of Iowa made the journey simply to attend, and in a charming letter to Mrs. Comegys after reaching home again said that in making the acquaintance of the ladies of the Association she felt amply repaid for the inconvenience. She had paid a visit to an elderly friend in Philadelphia on the way. "Persons of the olden time interest me much more than persons of the new régime," she added. "Probably it is because I am a little passée myself!"

Lily Macalester Berghmans as the wife of a Belgian diplomat

was residing in Washington, and Mrs. Comegys of course made
nothing of coming up from Dover. Mrs. Riggs, whose hospitality
embraced Miss Tracy, the Comegyses, and Mrs. Fitch, represented
the District of Columbia, and Mr. Riggs, as Treasurer, was also
present. The eldest of them all, from Elizabethtown, New Jersey,
was the indomitable Miss Phebe Ogden, aged seventy-five.

The Minutes of this momentous session, as kept by Miss Tracy,
who was appointed Secretary at this time, are veiled in discretion,
and it is from later correspondence that most of the facts must be
gleaned. Mr. Everett had regretted, in a letter to Miss Hamilton,
his inability to be present in an advisory capacity, but at the same
time he acceded to an apparent proposal by Miss Hamilton that
the Association should now and forthwith turn over the estate of
Mount Vernon to the United States Government—or as he said
"cede" it—"on condition that it should be ever faithfully kept by
them as a national treasure."

The effect on Miss Tracy of this cold-blooded heresy, sprung
without warning at a meeting called without precedent, at only
Miss Hamilton's wish, and as it were behind the Regent's back,
can be imagined. Without doubt she turned instinctively to Mrs.
Comegys and found there a surprise and horror equal to her
own. Miss Hamilton's contention was that the Association had no
funds to speak of, was even behind with its salary payments, and
in the middle of a war could no longer expect contributions from
the public. Behind this lay her still unspoken private dread that
the members of the Association would be held liable for its debts,
and could be sued by its employees—i.e., Tracy, Herbert, Mc-
Makin and lesser folk—for the amounts due, which should therefore at once be prevented from increasing.

Mr. Riggs's masculine tones joined the spontaneous protest,
which came to order under his assurance that he would meet
whatever financial requirements arose. The resolution to cede
Mount Vernon was voted down, and a financial survey was made,
with the result that Mr. Herbert was to have his salary paid in
full, Miss McMakin got the additional $18 monthly, and a house-

hold expenses fund of $150 monthly was to pay Miss Tracy, the servants' wages, and meet the bills. It was not enough, and Miss Tracy said so privately to Mrs. Comegys, who asked Mr. Riggs to add $25.

Whatever Miss Hamilton had had in mind, her trial balloon was speedily punctured, though no one seems then to have brought forward the obvious objection that the United States Government had demonstrated over and over again that it wanted nothing to do with Mount Vernon, and that if the Association ever found itself unable to maintain the place it was legally bound to forfeit to the State of Virginia.

The following day, February 23d, was devoted to an excursion to Mount Vernon in a Government steamer provided by the quartermaster-general—courtesy of Mr. Stanton, by request of Miss Tracy—with a lavish luncheon at the Mansion also provided by the War Department. There was enough on the table, Miss Tracy later recalled, for twenty, and the party numbered fourteen. Mrs. Sweat, to whose professional pen we owe valuable sidelights, described the day which she enjoyed as the guest of the Vice-Regent for Maine, little aware of the long service to the Association which lay just ahead of her.

"The sail down the Potomac was delightful, and the tokens of war around us added interest to the excursion," she would write some years later. "The corrals along the riverbanks were full of horses. The white tents of the camps, the roll of the drums, and the soldiers scattered about made the scene very striking. But we had become so accustomed to these features of daily life that some of us took them as matters of course. We approached Mount Vernon almost with feelings of awe, and as we gazed upon the venerable mansion crowning the cliff it seemed to frown upon the evidence of fraternal strife, and to stand as a central ground of neutrality where brother could still meet brother, even if one wore the blue of the Union soldier and the other the grey of the Confederates.

"The tugboat transferred us to the shore and we clambered over the dilapidated wharf. We were welcomed most courteously by Mr. Herbert, who was in charge of Mount Vernon as resident superintendent. He was a very handsome man, with the somewhat sedate manner of the olden times, though cordial and ready of speech. Miss Tracy was always an agreeable person in my estimation, sensible, active, clear-headed, and of much cheerful courage. She had as her companion in this then lonely spot Miss McMakin, afterward private secretary to Miss Cunningham. We climbed to the house, pausing of course at the tomb, which at that time was adorned with small and graceful shrubs and trees. They made the spot very lovely, but stern necessity decreed that they must all be removed, for their embrace was fatal, and would soon have destroyed the vault and disintegrated the brickwork. The air was so chill that we were glad to enter the hospitable house, which even in those pinched and evil days wore an air of welcome. And the cheerful fire in the so-called morning parlor drew us round its blaze for a long talk over the prospects of the Mount Vernon Association.

"We afterwards took a long stroll over the grounds under the guidance of Mr. Herbert, who gave a most interesting account of the various experiences of the place since the war broke out. It was also delightful to wander over the old house, with a person as familiar with all its traditions as Miss Tracy. Only a portion of the rooms had been made fit for occupancy, but to those an appearance of comfort and cheer had been given by womanly taste and skill.

"We dined in the library upon fare as attractive to our sharpened appetites as the conversation was to our eager ears. One seldom hears better table talk than made that meal something to remember. I give the bill of fare, because it smacks of a now bygone Virginia life. Oyster soup, roast beef, roast ham, homemade bread and butter, vegetables and fruits grown on the place, wonderful pickles and rich sweetmeats, and to finish, coffee with cream from the most patriotic of cows. We all put our names down in the big register, and left our dollar apiece, it was a satisfaction to do. Mr. Herbert presented to us a bouquet of evergreens, and at four o'clock we bade farewell to the dear old place and returned to Washington."

The death of an aged aunt of Mr. Herbert's detained Miss Tracy at Alexandria and before returning to Mount Vernon she saw Miss Hamilton again in Washington and on March 3rd gave Mrs. Comegys a straight-faced account of the interview. Miss Hamilton must have been feeling some chagrin. "I told her she need feel no anxiety about being sued," Miss Tracy reported. "I certainly should never lose my self-respect enough to sue anyone for so small a sum, and was sure I could answer for the rest; that Mr. Riggs had said he would be responsible for the year, which greatly relieved her mind—but I believed the money would be raised, whether the boat was running or not. She said several of the ladies had been to see her to say what a delightful excursion they had had, and how pleased they were with everything. She had a great horror of increasing debt, that was her only trouble. She then sent a message of sympathy to Mr. Herbert, and added that she went away with so much satisfaction at leaving him in charge here. I said I was glad to hear her say so, for we all thought that perhaps she would like us all to leave, and that some one else might be placed here who would manage better. She said, Oh, no, I did not understand her, she did not want any changes, only she felt it was very unwise to increase debt. I told her she fancied my salary was raised, but it was lowered—it would be impossible for me to save much out of that allowance at present prices. Well, so we talked, and she finally said she went away perfectly satisfied on every point. . . ."

It didn't last. Early in March Miss Hamilton was writing to Mrs. Comegys to reiterate her fear that the committee lately met in Washington would find itself liable for the payment of future salaries, and that she for one could not place herself in that position —adding that it should be made clear to the present staff at Mount

Vernon (as though it was not already clear enough) that they continued there only with the understanding that they took the chance that the resources of the Association would enable it to pay them, and were at liberty to leave whenever they considered that probability no longer justified their remaining. Such an attitude, in the face of the loyal and uncomplaining service already rendered, seems a little obtuse.

Mr. Herbert had a quantity of first-rate bricks, made on the place, which he thought could be sold in Alexandria so that he could have perhaps $200 for phosphates, seeds, and other outdoor supplies. They would injure by keeping, and the Association was not in a position to make use of them in the proposed repairs. Miss Tracy's slanting humor emerged again, as well as her affection for Mr. Herbert, in her March 16th letter to Mrs. Comegys:

"Mr. Herbert is much obliged for the power to sell the bricks but he cannot do so now, as he has an elephant to take care of. Mrs. Farnsworth did as she promised and secured permission from Secretary Stanton for General Rucker to send to Mount Vernon the much desired manure. It came in such quantities that the wharf was more than full, and having but one cart and one wagon it could be removed but slowly. Mr. Herbert was both enchanted and in despair. I had to write the General and beg him to send no more at present, and now everything is to be fertilized! I tell Mary I am afraid she and I will grow a foot! I hope we will make our fortune. We have laughed much at Mr. Herbert, but now he is using the manure, so he can afford to be laughed at a little."

Miss Hamilton, having received a set-down, was not amused. In a letter to Mrs. Comegys enclosing Mrs. Pendleton's resignation, which had been sent in response to her summons to the meeting, she remarked: "Those bricks are valuable. I only wonder they were not reported at our meeting. And Miss Tracy writes that they have been getting as much manure as they could receive. *Entre nous*, was there no way they could manage to receive as much as they could get? But as I do not fully understand the thing, this cavilling is for your ear and for my satisfaction."

She added that Mrs. Pendleton was a lovely woman and fulfilling well her part in life, but "as she says, with her brother's children and her own, she has no time for public service." Ohio's contribution to the fund had been small, owing to Mrs. Pendleton's preoccupation with family matters. And the vacancies must be filled next year, said Miss Hamilton, "if Miss Cunningham is not with us."

Another hiatus in the letters occurs for the summer and autumn of 1864, when the war passed into its grimmest days so far. Grant had been given the command, and was told to take Richmond, which lay between two Federal armies, with young Custis Lee, great-grandson of Martha Washington and a brigadier at thirty-two, directing its northern defences. The city was determinedly social, giving starvation parties and amateur theatricals. Tripe and liver sold for $1 a pound, chickens were $35 a pair—Lee himself was living on cabbage and cornbread.

Early in May Grant crossed the Rapidan and confronted Lee in the Virginia Wilderness—where in six days carnage he was outfought and narrowly missed a crushing defeat by an army whose bravest and best were so many of them already dead. This was the battle where the Confederate cry, "Lee to the rear!" was raised to preserve the beloved leader from his own reckless gallantry, and Grant said, "I propose to fight it out on this line if it takes all summer." Lee forced him to move, by withdrawing. Longstreet was wounded, Stuart was killed. The tocsin sounded again in the streets of Richmond, along with the guns. Butler struck at the back door, at Drewry's Bluff. Beauregard drove him off. Grant crossed the Pamunkey, taking forty thousand casualties in one week. Cold Harbor was fought in June, with little result but the terrible losses, and Grant swung round to come at Richmond from the Petersburg side. Sherman's artillery was now parked in front of Atlanta.

Richmond, on a diet of Indian peas, rice, and salt bacon and cornbread, still regarded itself as invulnerable, and a letter from Mrs. Pellet to the Regent in August said it was the safest place in the Confederacy and would never be taken. The cavalry was living on watermelons, which brought $20 apiece inside the city, where the cannon could be heard all day long.

Atlanta went in September—Mobile was gone—and in November Sherman began his march to the sea. On the 25th he reached Augusta, where Mrs. Eve's mansion stood, and arrived at Savannah in time to ruin Christmas, when the war moved into the winter lull.

9

The autumn of 1864 was a low water mark for the beleaguered little household at Mount Vernon. Writing to Miss Cunningham in 1865, Miss Tracy reveals in her untheatrical way to what they were reduced:

"Last fall when the prices of everything increased so fearfully, and our corn crop proved a total failure in consequence of the drought," she explained, "I saw I could not possibly make both ends meet, with the allowance given, and yet I did not want to own to a deficit. One of my resources had been the making of bracelets out of Kentucky coffee beans. I had them drilled in Washington and strung them on elastic cord. I sold one year over $30, and was sure I could do more in the same way. I therefore thought I was perfectly safe in borrowing of a friend $250, telling him I might be long in paying him, for I must do so out of bracelet sales. He agreed to wait any length of time, and I bought the bacon, sugar, coffee, etc. necessary. But when I came to have more beans drilled I could not have that done. The man who had done them before said he had too much to do. I could not find anyone else who would undertake it. I tried to buy a drill that we could work ourselves, but could not. I was annoyed, but could not help myself and must wait till something else suggested itself."

Miss Cunningham, in a letter to a Philadelphia friend early in 1866, said that "a lady who came South in December, 1864, by flag of truce, had had a conference with Miss Tracy before coming, and said they had been nearly starved out at Mount Vernon, but they would hold on, and not to be alarmed if I saw a motion

264

to transfer the place to the Government. I never received any explanation, as she was afraid to risk anything she would object to seeing published."

The letter file begins again with January, 1865, when Miss Tracy wrote Mrs. Comegys to say that she had at last heard from the Regent, roundabout through Dr. Hodge, who had forwarded a letter written to himself as well. Out of all the Mount Vernon correspondence entrusted to the erratic mails in the past two years, Miss Cunningham had received only the important letter regarding the February meeting at Washington, which had somehow gone straight through, arriving before the same news sent through Mrs. Ritchie. Her attempts to reply had been less successful, and almost another year had passed before Miss Tracy heard from her. As she had anticipated, the Regent was like a disappointed child that they had proceeded without her. "You will perceive I was right when I opposed to the extent of my power the meeting last year," Miss Tracy lamented to Mrs. Comegys, "and my distress at any proposition which changed the management of Mount Vernon. I was so fearful that she might hear of the meeting through some paper and be troubled and anxious that I wrote her by private opportunity telling her it was to be." Not trusting the Dover Post Office with the original, she copied most of Miss Cunningham's letter in hers to Mrs. Comegys:

"This is the third letter I have written in reply to yours of January 12th, received a few days before the 'Meeting' was to have taken place!" the Regent had written. "My retirement and isolation is an almost insurmountable obstacle to any communication with you. I was rejoiced to hear of you all, and that Mary was with you. I had hoped so, but was not certain that all were well, getting on well, so faithful through all the trials to the responsible and precious charge committed to you. My faith in Mr. Herbert and yourself was so strong that I had learned to be passive after the first year of distressing anxiety. The rest of your letter pained me beyond expression, so certain had I been that the boat would not be interrupted, and that surrounding circumstances would make the trip so profitable *at all seasons* as to go far towards covering expenses, needing in addition to income from securities but little aid to ward off what I dreaded, viz., a meeting *until better times.*

"No words can express my regret! You know how much I looked forward to the *first* meeting. So much depended on its tone, and to have it take place under present circumstances depresses me not a little. I know that each met from high purposes, and your letter came in time for me to be present in spirit and to add my ardent wish that wisdom would preside. Our paper copied a short notice of the meeting from the Baltimore paper, giving the names of some of the parties present. I was gratified to see some from such a distance.

"Your letter to Mrs. Ritchie gives me the information I desired to hear, about your situation, management, etc. Thank you for your assurance of all being faithful to Mount Vernon and *me.* I felt on my first acquaintance with the members of your present household that each was sent to me as an especial mercy. My judgment and feelings were prophetic. May the All-powerful shorten these days of trial and let us meet ere too long.

"My health is and has been very wretched. I have been at death's door many times. Give my love to my dear friends in Dover and tell them I am often with them in spirit. Edwina Marks and her mother passed the last winter within ten miles of me, and visited me often. Edwina wrote you for me by flag of truce. Mrs. Matthews passed two and a half months with me last spring, so if my bodily afflictions were severe, my loneliness has not been so constant. They all send great love to you. My cares are very great, much greater than any invalid ought to have. My servants are uncommonly good and faithful, and I manage all things through them, and my plantation is more successfully managed than those around me, while I never leave the house and am almost entirely confined to bed. I can give you no advice, situated as you are, you can best judge. . . ."

Poor Miss Cunningham, wrote Miss Tracy at the end of this long quotation, how sad her life was. And where would her senses have been if the place had been given up?

Mrs. Matthews was the friend who had accompanied Miss Cunningham southward in December of 1860 and was expected to make the return journey in the spring which became impossible. This is the first mention of Edwina Marks, whose father had founded and maintained the South Carolina Female Institute at Barhamville which both Miss Cunningham and Mrs. Eve had attended, and where Edwina was doubtless a fellow pupil. When Miss Cunningham returned to Mount Vernon after the war, the Marks family would for a time reside there with her, Edwina acting as secretary.

Miss Tracy copied again that portion of the Regent's letter referring to the February meeting and sent it to Miss Hamilton. "I did not know," she wrote Mrs. Comegys, "but after she saw Miss Cunningham's feeling about the meeting she would think it just as well not to call another meeting, and I wished her to perceive that even if I yielded last year it was not because I did not know I was in the right, but because I could not help myself. If this weather continues, we will have a jolly meeting on the 22d! The River has been twice closed within ten days, the roads so bad we could not go even to Alexandria. Could not your committee people decide there need be none? Suppose you write and ask Miss Hamilton. It is even dreadful business travelling in the cold and snow."

Miss Hamilton wrote to Mrs. Comegys, referring coolly to the extract from the Regent's letter as "interesting," and "showing that she not only still lives but that her interest in Mount Vernon is as strong as ever." She left the decision about the next meeting up to Mrs. Comegys, as in any case it would not be in her power to attend, but she could not resist once more stating her case. "I wish, dear Mrs. Comegys, you could bring about something by which we shall be relieved of our pecuniary obligations without the means of discharging them. You know that my preference is, if practicable, to place the property in the hands of the U.S. Government, but I shall be thankful to sustain you in any plan which is equally good or better. There seems to be no prospect of our being permitted to run a boat between Washington and Mount Vernon while the war lasts, and until then it seems unnecessary to keep so expensive an establishment there, when no visitors can possibly get there. If it could be any object for Mr. Herbert and the ladies now there to make Mount Vernon their home for the present, *without salary,* of course, we should be too glad to have them do so. But if they decline, is it not a question whether we ought to put some respectable man and his family upon the place, giving it to him rent free on condition of his taking care of the house and outbuildings? I suggest this as a matter of sheer necessity. If any money can be raised to pay as we go, no arrangement is as good as the present one."

The nature and scope of the devotion already shown by the residents of Mount Vernon seems to have been entirely beyond Miss Hamilton's comprehension, as well as the difference between their care of the place and that of some indigent family allowed to live there in return for unspecified duties, and naturally without the moral courage demanded of its protectors in the past as well as in the uncertain future. Miss Tracy's suspicion that she wanted them all to go seems to have been justified.

Mr. Everett's death in Boston only a few days after Miss Hamilton's letter was written complicated the situation, as the funds still in his hands and tacitly assigned to the final payment due the Washington family would now be involved in his estate. Mrs. Riggs wrote Mrs. Comegys that she could not imagine Mount Vernon being taken proper care of in any other way than under its present administration, and that what was needed now was some small sum to pay the expenses for the coming year at least, and she could not help hoping that ways and means might be designed in a meeting to raise this amount. Mrs. Mitchell of Wisconsin, who had not been present at the 1864 meeting, was in Washington in the autumn of that year and paid her promised visit to Mount Vernon, greatly heartening Miss Tracy from that time on. She spoke to Mrs. Riggs as though she was prepared to help, "out of her own pocket, if nothing else could be done," Mrs. Riggs wrote Mrs. Comegys. "Perhaps some of the others may feel they can do something of the same kind." And indeed, at this distance one cannot but wonder that Mount Vernon was allowed to beg and borrow so long when any one of several Vice-Regents was quite able to relieve their anxieties with a substantial check at little personal sacrifice.

A second meeting was therefore decided upon, to take place in Mr. Riggs's library on February 22d, 1865—which found Mrs. Comegys laid up with a broken ankle and unable to travel at all. "I wonder if you did it to escape the meeting!" wrote Miss Tracy in one of her reckless little jokes which sometimes fell on barren ground, and then continued: "As for giving up Mount Vernon —that seems to be a ghost that vanishes at the first touch of determination. So far from any majority in its favor, Miss Hamilton and Mr. Everett stood *alone* in the idea. I agree with Mrs. Mitchell, who writes in regard to it—'To think of our making such a fuss and working so hard, to give it up at the first difficulty! So womanlike!' But Mr. Riggs says no use in talking about it, or thinking of it, it cannot be done. It would be a violation of charter and contract. He thinks it best now to think how to keep it, not give it up! If the ladies will fix their attention on it, and make a little exertion, it will not be necessary to borrow. There is more than one way out of the difficulty, but it requires something besides folding the hands. If they all do that, and say to Miss Hamilton in spirit if not in words, *You can do as you like*—of course we know the result! And if it does end so, they will have but themselves to blame, for I cannot believe *three* would be found today who would agree with her if they dared disagree! But I have little to say about it. I have long made up my mind to my course, and so have each of us who have more to do than say in the matter."

It was in this atmosphere that the 1865 meeting assembled

under Mr. Riggs's hospitable roof. Besides Mrs. Comegys's ankle, the indestructible Miss Tracy was another casualty, having caught a terrible cold running up to Alexandria to see Mr. Herbert's surviving aunt—rheumatism settled in her right arm, rendering it almost useless, and she was compelled to remain at home. Perhaps owing to her absence, the Minutes for this year are unilluminating. Not so, a letter from Mrs. Riggs to Mrs. Comegys on February 24th:

"Notwithstanding your discouraging letter, I kept hoping your Mount Vernon spirit would get the better of you and bring you to the meeting. Mrs. Mitchell of Milwaukee, Mrs. Chace of Rhode Island, and Mrs. Berghmans were present. Mrs. Barry of Illinois was in the city, but sent word she was too ill to drive up from her lodgings, so there was no quorum. Miss McMakin was on the ground here, while Miss Tracy was on her bed at Mount Vernon, laid up with rheumatism, so the meeting was adjourned till tomorrow. Meanwhile we hope that Miss Tracy can come to us, and have brought Mrs. Barry to your room, where she seems to have recovered herself wonderfully. Miss Hamilton wrote a short note regretting her inability to attend, and enclosed a sealed letter to Mrs. Barry, in which I expect she expressed the same views with which you have had to combat during the year. She worships Mr. Everett and his memory, and would quickly hand over Mount Vernon and all the Southern people have contributed thereto, and imagine she was conscientious to the letter. What would the U.S. Government do with the elephant? With such a persistent woman as Miss Hamilton you must have had a very trying correspondence. If Miss Tracy and Mr. Herbert are not retained, I fancy the Treasurer will relieve himself of the responsibility, and the Vice-Regent for the District ditto. At present Mr. Riggs is very hopeful of our being able to go on without being involved in any danger, but Miss Hamilton's economical plan of a man and wife living off the sacred soil I know would never do.

They would be feckless people who would take such a place, I am sure, not fit for the solemn charge."

Miss Tracy recovered sufficiently to reach Washington before the ladies dispersed for another year, as her admiration for Mrs. Chace appears to date from here. The Minutes as finally assembled record a Resolution of appreciation "to the faithful service, self-denying devotion, and prudent management of the officers of the Association appointed as the resident guardians of Mount Vernon during the long period of exposure and peril to which it has been subjected"—voted the monthly allowance and salaries to be continued another year—and exhorted the Vice-Regents to aid in raising during the coming year a small sum for the continuance and support of Mount Vernon. There was also a Resolution to "enshrine in the annals of the Association the name of Edward Everett, their wise counsellor and to the end their unfailing friend," and to procure a portrait of him to be placed at Mount Vernon.

This latter seemed a bit excessive to Mrs. Comegys, for in a later letter to her, of which the whole first page has been cut away with scissors, Mrs. Riggs wrote: "At the meeting I felt much as you write, but I knew considering previous events it would not do for me to object, especially as I saw that Mrs. Barry, who has been staying here, was a little insane on the topic of Mr. Everett, Cambridge, etc. However, she was not moved by Miss Hamilton's suggestion, any more than Mrs. Mitchell, who is *a mighty nice person*. On the whole, I thought it would be best to let it be set forth, otherwise we might be considered ungrateful. As to the portrait, it will be some time before the Association will be rich enough to invest in that sort of thing."

Miss Hamilton never came to a meeting again, and never again saw the Regent. She resigned later this year, in a letter to Mrs. Comegys, announcing her intention of going abroad for a year, with the remark that all her suggestions had met with disapproval. Mr. Everett's death may have been a severe blow to her. It was four years later, in 1869, that she married her sister's widower, whose chief claim to fame seems to have been as a yachting referee and donor of cups.

The war was warming up again, like the weather. In February, 1865, Sherman started northward from captured Savannah to join Grant at Richmond. He flanked Charleston and forced its evacuation—but had nothing to do with the fire which engulfed it from the explosion of a powder depot. Columbia had believed itself off the line of march, and safe from invasion, and it was full of refugees, with food and shelter very scarce. On February 16th Sherman lobbed in a few shells and the mayor rode out to surrender the city. Sherman set up his headquarters in Gervais Street and promised that order would prevail. According to Lossing, who toured the South for his history immediately after the war, the fire which devastated Columbia the next night was due to an order by General Wade Hampton, commanding the rear guard of the Confederates, to burn the cotton in the streets so that it would not fall into Federal hands. A high wind was blowing, and the destruction of eighty-four city blocks resulted.

There are no letters to show that Miss Tracy was aware of the events in South Carolina as they took place, but she was in any case able to see on a map that Rosemonte in Laurens County lay well to the west of Sherman's route. Lincoln was inaugurated in March, '65, for the second time, and Mrs. Mitchell in Washington referred to the "disgraceful proceedings"—Vice-President Andy Johnson was undeniably drunk that day, and his attempt to make a speech which preceded his taking the oath of office was embarrassing to a petrified audience.

Lincoln had been persuaded to submit to a bodyguard now, as cranks and crackpots multiplied in Washington. Seated on the inaugural platform, by a ticket secured for him by the infatuated daughter of a Senator from New Hampshire, who considered herself his fiancée, was John Wilkes Booth, then a popular figure around the bars and hotel lobbies and theaters in Washington.

Lincoln always enjoyed going to a play, and had more than once attended Booth's performances at Ford's Theater, though Forrest was considered a far better actor, as was Booth's elder brother Edwin. Booth was even then involved in an elaborate abduction plot against the President, and other abortive schemes against his life and safety had been detected or had come to nothing. The inauguration ball, with a catered supper, was held in the Patent Office Building, and ended in a wild destructive stampede on the refreshments.

The final crucial battle was now in the making, and Lincoln paid one of several visits to the Federal lines outside Richmond. On April 2d the telegraph keys in Washington ticked out the news—*Richmond has fallen.* Jubilant workers, clerks, colored people, and private citizens spilled into the streets to celebrate. Courts ceased, schools let out. Stanton made a speech to the crowd outside the War Department. Bands turned out, bunting bloomed, and there was an impromptu parade. By nightfall illuminations were rigged on the public buildings.

At daybreak on April 10th Washington was awakened by its own guns firing a salute to the surrender at Appomattox, and a further uproar of bells, cheering crowds, and speeches began, and people gathered outside the White House in the rain to cheer the President, who appeared briefly but would not speak. He looked grave, but less ill and old. Ahead of him was the heavy responsibility of rebuilding the Union. Grant's terms to Lee were considered generous. In the evening from a lamplighted window Lincoln read a prepared sober speech, mainly on reconstruction and Negro suffrage, which did not suit the gala mood of the exultant crowd, who dispersed to the strains of *The Battle-Hymn of the Republic.*

The fourth anniversary of Fort Sumter's surrender was on April 14th, which was Good Friday, and Thursday night was set for a grand illumination of the capital, with fireworks. Lincoln's friend, Colonel Lamon, the District Marshal, had been haunted for days by rumors and fears of an attempt on the President's life, and Lincoln himself had had a dream that a corpse lay on a catafalque in the East Room of the White House, where young Captain Ellsworth's had lain in the spring of '61—but now it was his own—and Lincoln was visibly shaken.

Although the White House carriage did not drive out to see the celebrations Thursday night, Mrs. Lincoln had arranged a theater party at Ford's for Friday, to see Miss Laura Keene's closing performance of *Our American Cousin*. General Grant and his wife were invited, and declined because of their anxiety to rejoin their children at home. The reservation of the Presidential box had been announced as though the Grants would also be present, and the theater was decorated for the event.

Early the next morning, after a night of wild rumor, hysteria, and stunned realization, the bright bunting all over Washington, hung to celebrate the end of the war, was swiftly eclipsed by lengths of black mourning cloth, and the murdered President's portrait in the shop windows was draped in crape. On the Tuesday after Easter, Lincoln's body lay in state in the East Room, in awesome fulfillment of his dream, while an endless procession of mourners, both white and colored, filed past it. On Wednesday, while the minute guns boomed, it was carried to the rotunda at the Capitol, where all the pictures and statues were covered, with one exception—the bronze figure of General Washington, around which some one had tied a black sash.

10

Miss Tracy's letters for the spring of 1865 have not survived, so her immediate comment on the surrender and the assassination is lost. There is one from Mrs. Mitchell in New York on April 25th, to say that she must give up coming back to Mount Vernon as she was returning home—"D.V."—in a few days. She recommended the immediate presentation to the Johnson administration of the Association's claim for remuneration for the loss of the boat during the war—a previous effort in this direction at the time of the last Council having been unsuccessful. "I shall try hard to raise some little money during the coming year," she wrote, "but my spirits are so low that I think I must give the work into younger people's hands as soon as the Regent returns." Fortunately her spirits recovered, for another forty years.

Hope and urgency for the Regent's return to Mount Vernon began as soon as General Johnston's surrender to Sherman in North Carolina was completed, late in April, though the countryside along her usual route of travel northward had been devastated by the war. "I am constantly asked now when you will come," Miss Tracy wrote on May 9th. "I presume you could hardly attempt it before fall, as it would be so very difficult for you to travel until the country is quiet. I must not write of the one subject which I know fills your heart and bows your very soul. I comprehend the whole. Do not be tempted to write about it quite yet, though I don't apprehend any opening of letters, but it might be done. We are beginning to make a little money, and soon regular communication will be re-established, and then our severe trials begin."

Mary McMakin's father had paid a visit to Mount Vernon, and

she went home with him for a short holiday, the first in eighteen months, and had since returned. Mr. Herbert's sister was with them for a fortnight, the first time they had met in four years. "I hope these last catastrophes have not made you ill," Miss Tracy's letter ended. "Do write us and say if you have been disturbed or lost much. As I have traced the course of the armies, I fancied you had escaped."

This letter went through, and Miss Cunningham's reply to it was written on July 10th at Rosemonte, on rough blue paper in her usual crowded, uneven, sometimes illegible hand. She had seized an opportunity to send it by the doctor who had been called in last year "when I was expected to die"—her servant would have to swim his horse across the river to take it to him before he started North, as the war had destroyed their ferry.

Listing the few letters she had received, in order that Miss Tracy might be able to fill in the story, with the long gap running from just after Prince Napoleon's visit in the summer of '61 to the first meeting of the Vice-Regents in early '64, she mentioned one from Mrs. Comegys recently received, the contents of which "amazed" her. "It intimated that you were mainly supported by Mrs. Riggs, that there was a movement originating with Papa E. to pass the place to the U.S. Government, but you felt assured that would be baffled, that the latter was playing into the design by refusing to allow boats to run. Mrs. Comegys felt that there was some opposition to you, advised me not to attempt to address you through the blockade as your reception of any letter other than by flag of truce might be used as a handle to oust you. I was so astonished I wrote and asked many questions. I omitted to state just now, her saying that one Vice-Regent gave trouble. She replied by opening my eyes to a state of society existing in the North which should prevent my astonishment at such a breach of faith being contemplated as that of passing the place over to the Govt. Now, dear Miss Tracy, you have the amount of knowledge which reached me prior to the receipt of yours of the 9th [of May]."

The letter broke off there while she wrote again to Mrs. Comegys and to her cousin Mrs. Mitchell in Philadelphia. When it resumed the next day, she had taken laudanum in order to finish a letter to Dr. Hodge, and mentioned other heroic measures for doctoring herself to build up her strength prior to attempting the journey back to the Potomac. "I keep my spine irritated with croton oil, I use calomel to act on my torpid liver, I bathe daily when I can, but these remedies, while they keep me living, recruit me but very little. I need change of scene, cold climate, sea bathing, relief from the trials and anxieties which are crushing in their weight." She asked about Mrs. Ritchie, who was constantly in her thoughts, asked the extent of Mount Vernon's indebtedness, made suggestions which might aid in making the place self-sustaining, such as the introduction of goats and pigeons. "You say persons ask when I will come, and you suggest I could not travel till all is quiet. My answer is that the moment I am able I will go. The roads can be rebuilt in a few months, but as my journeys would have to be short ones I would not dare start until there were places for me to stop at. At present the burnt city of Columbia has no hotel, few private houses crammed with homeless people, and what horses and mules our army left the conquerors took. I doubt if I could find a carriage to convey me to a hotel if there was a hotel left. Richmond and Petersburg are in the same condition. All along the route plantations have had everything burnt, so there would be next to no stopping places for one who could not travel night and day."

Disregarding Miss Tracy's entreaty not to write about the war, she alluded to the destruction of the railroad to Columbia, and the fire during Sherman's occupation, which she of course laid at his door. Cut off from the outside world, with only such newspapers as an occasional traveller brought, she was a prey to the wildest rumors and unrelieved anxiety, and had been seized with what she believed to be heart trouble, which left her prostrated, though Rosemonte was so far spared the "insulting despotism" meted out by the conquerors. "No mind has yet been gifted with the power to solve the riddle of emancipation," she wrote, "be it ever so gradual. This sudden upheaving of the social status of the whole country is so fearful in its present and future results that none but demons could have devised it. When it is too late I see the folly of disregarding the advice of Dr. Hodge and Mr. Petigru to sell out land and Negroes at the time I came here."

The letter rambled on at great length, written in spurts and dabs, recounting past misfortune and the present harrowing prospect, reiterating that the Mount Vernon effort must triumph, sending messages to her friends, and making inquiries about Mr. Herbert's relatives and the Washington children. Miss Tracy's reply may never have reached her and there is no way of knowing now what it was, but she wrote to Mrs. Eve at Augusta in August, hoping to reach Miss Cunningham that way:

"I will only mention a few facts which you can communicate to her either by writing yourself or sending this," she explained. "First and most important, the boat has been running since the first of June. For a month before that we had a rush of visitors every day and all day long by land. We have since April made this year's expenses. After this, all is clear except what is owing Mr. Herbert. He left what was due him a year ago to carry on the establishment, up to the first of January last. There is no other debt. During the war Mr. Herbert has been manuring and preparing the ground for raising such crops as could feed the stock, and the people here. He has this summer harvested sufficient wheat for the year's consumption, or nearly so. He will have an abundance of corn, his crop is the finest around here. Last year the drought killed everything. He has a little rye. Of course he has cabbages, potatoes, etc. in abundance.

"I think the greatest trial on the place after its publicity is its unhealthfulness. We are hardly ever free from chills and fever or some billious attacks, except for two or three winter months. Miss McMakin had them all the month of May. Mr. Herbert was quite ill in June. I have never had them, but have this summer had two attacks of low fever that has been very uncomfortable. Since May there has never been a time when there was not some one on the place ill, and often two or three. This season has been particularly unhealthy all around us.

"Tell Miss Cunningham she need have no apprehension about any particular trouble here. Now that the public have free access they abuse us heartily for not having accomplished impossibilities. A meeting of the Vice-Regents with herself as head this fall is a necessity. At their last meeting they resolved never to meet again in February. The weather at that season is so bad that it makes travelling for those who come either from the East or West not only uncomfortable but dangerous. They resolved to meet either in the fall or spring. The meetings were not Grand Councils, but regular annual meetings.

"Please tell Miss Cunningham that I do not answer her questions, for the friend who enclosed my letter before told me not to write anything I was unwilling should be made public. If I can send through you it would be very much more comfortable. Poor Miss Cunningham, I feel intensely for her. Dr. Hodge has received her letter and will write as soon as possible. Mrs. Pendleton of Ohio resigned peremptorily and positively two years ago. Mrs. Goodrich of Connecticut is in a lunatic asylum. Also Mrs. Hale of New Hampshire. Mrs. Little of Maine is married and has moved to New Hampshire. Mrs. Berghmans of Pennsylvania has gone or is going to Europe. All this requires official attention."

In September Miss Cunningham wrote distractedly that she had heard nothing for weeks and doubted the security of the messenger by whom she had sent the long, confidential July letter, which had reached its destination safely. She was again taking calomel for a bilious attack, and her maid was down with bilious fever. Drought was burning up crops and gardens. One of their stray newspapers had said there had never been so many visitors to Mount Vernon, and she hoped they had had a "golden harvest."

On the 9th of the same month Miss Tracy wrote to the Regent a valuable account of life at Mount Vernon in 1865.

"During the winter and after the [second] meeting we about made up our minds that the war would never end, and we would have no boat and must manage as best we could, for no one dared in any State to mention the Association or try to raise money," she recorded. "Give it up we would not, but to hold on was hard work, and debt we would not incur. Williams, whom you remember was gardener, was in miserable health, could only do half work, yet wanted increase of wages. Mr. Herbert let him go the first of January. I had a servant man whom I was paying myself, for he was a necessity to me, I made constant expeditions to town when we had to buy and bring out with us everything used on the place, and drive over bad roads, through camps, pickets, etc., often late at night. A sober, faithful, and reliable man was a necessity. The Association had given me no authority to hire such. I therefore found him, a freeman mulatto, and hired him. When I did not want him he worked in the garden. Toward spring I let Mr. Herbert have him all the time in the garden. They two made hot-beds and planted the vegetable garden."

Deprived of the income from her coffee-bean bracelets now that she could not get the beans drilled, she devised another means of earning a few extra dollars, as the men from the Federal Army streamed homeward. It should be noticed that in her account of this summer's finances the money she took in for her flowers, grown and sold by her own hard work, she still considered Mount Vernon money, with no thought of putting it to her own use beyond repaying the debt she had already incurred by borrowing on her own credit for daily expenses. It is here placed unreservedly at Miss Cunningham's disposal:

"I was determined I would not live here without flowers," the letter continued. "You know I will not live anywhere without. We had some roses, some of my own and some Mr. Herbert had bought for the place. I expended about $8, not more, in seeds and plants for my own comfort. We—Robert [her servant], Mr. Herbert, and myself—planted, transplanted, and trimmed the plants ourselves. We had just got things in fine condition when came a rush of visits from the soldiers. They were crazy for flowers. We had no gardener. Robert had to aid Mr. Herbert with the visitors, he was the only help he had. So Mary and I gathered the flowers, made bouquets, and sold them. With these flowers I have paid my debt of $250 and have now some $50 in hand.

"I have written to Mrs. Comegys for her approval of hiring another man to help in the garden, as at this season there is much work to do, and with it I also want permission for Mr. Herbert to repair some fences. I intended to keep the remainder we should make until you came on, for as the garden has not since the first of January cost the Association a dollar extra for labor or plants, every cent made was clear gain. Therefore I thought you would be justified in appropriating the money to replenish the furnishings in the house.

"You know there were but three common table-cloths, one dozen napkins and one dozen towels. Of course these wore out. I had no right to replenish, so Mr. Herbert and I have for the past two years used our own. Mr. Herbert has always used his own linen and towels. I had some linen sheets and pillow-cases, and when we have our friends here we have always used our own linen, and paid all that was necessary for any extras. Mary did not like linen sheets. Mr. Herbert had some cotton, which have been on Mary's bed all the time. Some other little comforts that we fancy we have provided for ourselves. But when you come there are things you will find necessary, I presume, for the Association, and the flower money I thought to keep for that purpose. Of course after October that resource will fail. But then we will have another."

Even before the Regent went South there had been a project to sell photographic views of Mount Vernon to visitors, but her insistence that they should be sold only on the place, and that the photographer must work only on commission without the right to dispose of copies himself, had at that time blocked any business arrangement. It had come up again at the second meeting, as a possible source of income, and Miss Tracy's extraordinary circle of acquaintance again provided the answer. She knew an "amateur photographer and scientific man" who sent her a young man named Bell, who stayed five days at Mount Vernon taking pictures in all lights, with beautiful results, and he was willing to hold the negatives for the exclusive use of the Association. Prints would be sent to the ladies for their approval, and the Regent would have the whole thing under her control.

"I think if the sale of them is confined to this place it will fill a vacancy which is very much needed," wrote Miss Tracy. "I am satisfied from all I hear that for one or two years to come these are the only means for raising money that you can depend on, besides the boat receipts. You have been so isolated that you cannot form the slightest idea, not only of the opposition but of the violent animosity the very idea of a request for money excites. There are a few people who individually are inclined to aid, but they must be allowed to do it their own way or they will do nothing. There are no Masons or any other organization that singly or as a body will give anything now. When everything is settled and the bitter, violent feeling which prevails has died out, then and not till then can something be done, and any attempt to force the matter will not only not produce any result now, but would prevent anything for the future.

"You ask for the Washington children. They are now at their home with their uncle. He has suffered much, and they have lost some, not all. But all we see who have lost everything and have to begin life anew are cheerful and go to work like men and women. Alas, it is very hard for some. Mr. Herbert's brothers are alive and well. His cousins are in the main alive. He has lost some favorites. The pecuniary losses are great. If I were rich I would go to you for a couple of weeks in November, I could not be absent longer. There are so many things to be talked over that I cannot write. Mrs. Fitch makes kind inquiries for you.

"If you are receiving newspapers you will perhaps see some bitter articles against us. Some terribly insulting things have been written, some too low to care for. Some of them my friends have answered, much to my regret, for it is always detestable to me to be dragged before the public, and I thanked no one who prolonged the contest by replying.

"Mary's father and mother have moved to New York, have been there since June, '62. They have a confectionery and restaurant and are doing well. Mary's mother fights hard with her for staying here, and will I presume insist upon her going home at Christmas. Mary had another chill day before yesterday and is feeling very badly today, but I escaped. She has an only brother about thirteen years old who is unfortunately malformed and weak. Her mother wants Mary to go home and keep house for him. I am not sure he will live.

"I think I have given you enough for one dose! I will write again soon, but it is rather uncomfortable work when I do not know whether they will ever reach you. I am anxious for you to receive some of my letters, for they will relieve some of your anxiety. Do not direct in Mr. Herbert's care—he has not been in Alexandria since May, 1861!"

A letter from Mrs. Mitchell expressed the expectation that Miss Tracy would soon be relieved of her lonely responsibilities by the imminent return of the Regent, though she thought the next meeting might be a sad one, overcast by recent events. But by Miss Tracy's wish to go South it can be seen that she had now given up the conviction entertained in her August letter to Mrs. Eve that before the year was out a meeting headed by the Regent was a necessity.

It is at this point that the strange misunderstanding, misinter-
pretation, misjudgment—it is difficult to find a word—began
which was later to embitter the Regent's return to Mount Vernon.
In order to comprehend so far as is possible the bewildering
dénouement of 1867, the letters from now on must be scrutinized
bilaterally with that still cloudy event in mind. The most thorough search of surviving correspondence, and a careful evalua-
tion of what remains, provides no very helpful clue to what
seems a wholly unexpected and inexplicable crisis which developed in December of 1867, during the second meeting over which
the Regent presided, so that she felt compelled the following
month to write several long, rambling letters, of which only unfinished draft copies remain—to justify her own action in Council
and to try to prove by extracts copied from Miss Tracy's letters
to her that the secretary's loyalty and even her honesty were
questionable.

Quotations out of context can be the most dangerous and
damning evidence conceivable, for the very next sentence (which
has been eliminated) may throw an entirely different light on the
whole page. And it is already apparent that Miss Tracy's habit
of straight-faced humor was a risky one, especially as the Regent
seems to have had almost no humor at all.

In January, 1868, the Regent by quoting from Miss Tracy's
letters wanted to demonstrate two seemingly irreconcilable assertions—that Miss Tracy in 1865 was expressing disgust with her
job at Mount Vernon and threatening to desert her post—and
that in 1867 Miss Tracy considered that she had established some
sort of claim on the Association which entitled her to remain
there indefinitely. Neither contention stands up very well under
close examination of the available correspondence, but whole
pages have been cut away, and whole paragraphs obliterated with
black ink by a later hand, and whole letters are missing, on both
sides. In the attempt to square her two discordant hypotheses,
Miss Cunningham professed to believe she had deceived herself
regarding Miss Tracy from the beginning, which was of course

nonsense—but it must be remembered that the victims of nervous disorders often turn against the very people to whom they owe the most affection.

Certainly it will be agreed that so far, which is the autumn of '65, Miss Tracy had shown nothing but the most scrupulous concern for her duties as custodian, with an outstanding courage and fortitude in very trying circumstances. By December, 1867, both women were emotionally exhausted by a six years' ordeal, especially in Miss Cunningham's case, worsened by the turmoil and uncertainties which followed the surrender at Appomattox, when the South was in the grip of carpet-bag government and seething with the chaos which emancipation could not fail to produce. The Regent's already shattered nervous system had become increasingly dependent on a steadily increasing dosage of the opiate called laudanum—there was nothing so safe and simple as aspirin then, and pain, from the original spinal injury, from a recurrent neuralgia, and from countless nervous repercussions, was her constant companion, demanding any form of relief available. She was taking laudanum as early as 1855, by a letter from Mrs. Ritchie warning her against it, even before they had got on first-name terms. "I am so glad that you are not annoyed at what I said about laudanum," she wrote. "The doses you mention are 'baby doses' indeed, to what my physician once gave me during a period of terrible suffering. But you know what wrong impressions people take up over using stimulants—with what horror they regard the use of laudanum—" The bottom of the page is cut off.

After ten years the doses were necessarily larger, which undoubtedly made her unstable and unreasonable, through no fault of her own, and her temperament was always imperious. Debilitating as Miss Tracy's life at Mount Vernon had been, it was ameliorated by good health in the early years, congenial companionship in Mary McMakin and Mr. Herbert, and a regular correspondence with nearby friends like Mrs. Comegys for moral support. The Regent at Rosemonte was at the same time con-

fined to a dreary household consisting of her unhappy mother
and an aged aunt, isolated most of the time even from newspapers as well as letters, always in wretched health, with nothing
to mitigate a growing hypochondria.

Even so, the effort to trace the inception and growth of what
must be called no worse than a tragic error precludes anything
like taking sides. Whatever went wrong later on, this September
9th letter of Miss Tracy's is the first one cited by the Regent in
her 1868 rationale, and the lines she quoted there under this date
do not appear in the letter now, though the first page or pages
of it are missing. Moreover, the tone of the extract does not seem
to conflict with the dogged endurance of the remaining text.
"Four years in one place with all the cares and anxieties we have
had is a tax on anyone's health," the extract runs. "Friends are
becoming irritated about it. I had a letter yesterday which said
'Mount Vernon is a dreadful place for anyone to live, and I fear
that your constitution will be impaired for the rest of your days.'"
That is all.

Miss Cunningham replied to this letter on October 9th, without any rancor at that time—another of her enormous crowded
letters in very small writing on large foolscap paper, written on
several successive days, a little at a time. She began with a bitter
account of conditions in the South as emancipation proceeded
under the Federal administration at Charleston. Her brother had
made her a visit and stated his belief that they were living over
a volcano, and that preparations for a general Negro insurrection
in their neighborhood had been discovered. "The Yankees have
left nothing undone to make them think they are not only as
good but better than the Southern white men, and to convince
them they think so too," she wrote, "while they have used every
species of petty tyranny over our own race. They have done everything to sink themselves to the level of the blacks by association.
Our own plantation has been called a model plantation, so perfectly have our Negroes behaved so far, everything going on as
formerly. But thus far in all insurrection those most trusted have

joined or led it. We are conscious that latterly the leaven of demoralization is showing daily, it is true in little and trifling ways, but they are seen as straws to show the wind."

She still had no hope of regular mails, until the railroad and bridges were rebuilt, but wagon trains went to Augusta by which she could send and receive letters through Mrs. Eve. The agonizing neuralgia which Dr. Hodge had warned her would always return when she lived in the damp climate of Rosemonte had begun again—before she went to him, about 1850, she recalled, she had passed the winters with her head wrapped in flannel, masks on her face at night, and "often would lie for days with the pillow over my head in dumb torture."

Instead of resenting Miss Tracy's references to the unhealthiness of Mount Vernon, as she seemed later to have convinced herself that she did, the Regent at this time showed nothing but sympathy. "Before the purchase Mr. Washington assured me that he did not regard the place as unhealthy, that his family enjoyed good health, and they looked as though they did," she wrote. "Prudence in avoiding the night air was all he thought requisite. From what you state after five years' trial, it is evident that it will undermine anyone's health to live there long. I am concerned about Mr. Herbert. I feel it would destroy his health. I do not see how he can get a chance to absent himself, but for you and Mary it is different. You must both go away. You have borne the strain for four years and coute que coute it must stop. I would never have accepted such sacrifices, I felt you would stay while there was a necessity for it but never expected you would have that necessity after the tide of battle had rolled away and the armies were permanently removed, anticipating that so far as this place was concerned business would roll in former channels."

But the one thing which would release Miss Tracy the Regent did not contemplate—her own return to Mount Vernon she postponed until '66, if she survived the coming winter and felt stronger in the spring, and she stressed the necessity for Miss Tracy's presence then till Miss Tracy must have felt the Regent's dependence on her like a stranglehold. "I am broken down," wrote the Regent. "I can never labor with my hands or eyes again. I will need some one then thoroughly au fait in the work, especially in the past. You will be needed. I have no idea now of ever seeing my first grand plans carried out, in reference to adorning the place, with a first rate horticulturalist to attend to certain kinds of improvements. All I expect now is to secure a fund sufficient at interest to maintain a superintendent and the requisite number of laborers to guard and keep all in order. When that time comes no one but the superintendent will live there. Now that peace has come, Mr. Herbert can go into Washington and provide as formerly, can he not?"

Faintness overtook her, and cramp, and she laid the letter aside to spend most of the day in a dark room, until between mustard plasters and manipulating the rigidity at her temples, and dosage of laudanum, she was able to resume. She was worried about the vacancies in the Vice-Regents' ranks and yet did not intend to fill them till work could be resumed under her direction. She was worried about Miss Tracy's health, and offered to pay her expenses to go to Philadelphia to consult a physician. "You speak of having had to purchase and bring out all supplies, often riding late through camps and pickets, etc.," she wrote, having only now come to a realization of these conditions because so many of Miss Tracy's earlier letters had gone astray. "My poor dear friend, did you have to do this in Mr. Herbert's open buggy? If so, you were very brave, and have had to encounter everything trying to the feelings, and it is time indeed that you had a rest and change of scene. Mr. Graham must help me to make you take care of yourself. Remember too that henceforth till the work is closed I must lean upon you, and you must get strong, for I am dead weight now. As to those terrible chills, you must be worn out with them. Mother insists that people so far North don't know how to break them, or they would not linger so long or return so often. Quinine, quinine, and care to watch and prevent their return at the right time, she says. The sunflower plant is said to be a great absorbant of malaria. It is planted largely on the Potomac at the end of the grounds of the Presidential mansion. We must try their efficiency on the descending cliffs towards the River. We are beginning to have chills and fever here now. My maid is sick again."

It is quite evident by this letter that the corroding suspicion which may in the end have amounted to hallucination had not yet begun, but was all drummed up after the trouble had started.

In the Minutes for 1893, nearly thirty years later, the answer to Mount Vernon's deadly health hazard is noted down: "The Regent informed Council that the Vice-Regent for California [who was then Mrs. George Hearst, mother of William Randolph] offers to defray all expenses incident to the drainage of the piece of swamp land donated to the Association by Mr. Heurich, from which emanates the main cause of the malaria troubles on this estate."

II

In the meantime, in September of 1865 the toll of sickness at Mount Vernon rose till Miss Tracy and Miss Mc-Makin had to do the housemaid's work of preparing for the boat, at the same time nursing seven cases of what she termed a severe "billious fever," always with two *l*'s. "We are both pretty well," she wrote Mrs. Comegys. "I give way utterly to fatigue but rally again after a few hours rest. Mr. Herbert has not been ill since late in July, and it is two weeks since Miss McMakin has had a chill. Dearly as I love the warm weather, I am longing for frost. We have had more or less of this since May, and the whole countryside is the same this year, I do not think there is a house between us and Alexandria that has not more sick than well persons in it."

The photographs taken by young Mr. Bell were approved and went on sale in three sizes—carte de visite, stereoscopic, and cabinet, at a small profit which Mr. Riggs thought quite suitable. In October Miss McMakin wrote Mrs. Comegys that Miss Tracy had "succumbed at last to the combined influence of fatigue from nursing and the poison of the atmosphere. She begs me to tell you that still another letter has reached her from the Regent, who up to that time had received none of the letters by varied channels with which Miss Tracy has tried to reach her. She was better, but wild for news." And she had then received it, which resulted in her October 9th reply already considered.

It may have been the "dead weight" entreaty in that reply which caused Miss Tracy to write the second letter to be quoted by the Regent in 1868 in support of her conviction that Mount Vernon had become hateful to Miss Tracy and that she complained outrageously against her continued incarceration there.

In fact, Miss Tracy had complained very little, and had also shown considerable philosophy, but in the November 8th extract, which is all that remains of that letter now, she had been goaded into an apparent attempt to force the Regent to face facts, pull herself together, and do something about taking up her share of the burden which others had borne for her throughout the war. The copy begins abruptly in the middle of an account of the continuing illness and fatigue at Mount Vernon, and is certainly plain speaking, even for the downright Miss Tracy. It would seem that in a mood of exasperation at what was becoming an endless obligation with no respite in sight, when her own hitherto remarkable health seemed to have deserted her at last, Miss Tracy sat down and wrote the Regent a piece of her mind. The mood certainly passed again, and before the Regent had had time to reply Miss Tracy's letters resumed their normal tone, as though she had intended no lasting breach and had probably forgotten how hard she had hit out. The extract from this missing letter, copied in a hand not Miss Cunningham's, runs as follows:

"This year has been worse than any other, and chills may be had at almost any time on this River, and if anyone remains here they must be always watchful and prudent. We are all tired of it, and feel as if there was no claim on us equal to that of our own health and strength, and we have each sacrificed enough of that. It is now time for some one else to take their turn. I am very sorry that you have made up your mind that you cannot get on without me, for you will be obliged to do so. I shall never forgive myself for the weakness which led me to yield to your persuasion to continue my position when both duty and inclination loudly urged the contrary. Of course when I agreed to remain and aid you it was with the certainty almost that you would return in the spring, but your plans and mine, like thousands of others, were thwarted. The war had come on, and the steps we took were imperatively demanded by the circumstances. I feel that I have more than fulfilled my promise.

"I have no ambition and detest being known beyond my private circle. I have had to endure the opposite of this. I have not always done it amiably, but it was done. Even now, nothing would induce me to return to the position I occupied before the war. I would not go back over the old history again for the world, and you know the constant writing was too much for me then. Now I could not bear it. Pardon my frankness, but there is no good mincing matters under the circumstances. The sooner you know the whole truth, the sooner you will learn to face it. I have not vanity enough to presume for one moment I am the only woman fitted to be yours or the Association's secretary, and now in these sad days there must be many who would be thankful for even such a small salary.

"I had hoped that you would have come back and I would have placed the charge I received back in your hands before leaving it, and that I should not be obliged to write this. Therefore I have delayed, but your last letter convinced me that disagreeable as was the task you ought to know the situation of each of us. Mr. Herbert has not the slightest idea of wearing out his life here, but as we none of us have fixed a limit to the period we will remain, we are very desirous to give it back into your hands, and if your coming is not delayed beyond reason we, at least I, will remain. Mr. Herbert has been a close prisoner long enough not to be made one any longer—four years and a half, except for one week this summer, he has not been off the place, either for private business or to see his relatives, from whom he has been so long separated. Chills have not been the most disagreeable of his encounters. He dismissed everybody that was not absolutely necessary here and until this spring he has been door-keeping as well as other things, taking the 25¢ from the visitors and showing them through the house and gardens, saving a servant's wages and doing a servant's work. One of the newspaper attacks this summer speaks of him as being descended from three noble Virginia families and yet he has come down to be door-keeper, fee-taker, and guide at Mount Vernon. He never saw this as we did not show it to him. With all that, he is entitled to some consideration. His losses during the war have not been trifling.

"Do not think me unkind, I have done more for you than for anyone else. But for you I would not have remained, and but for you I would have resigned the first meeting we had. There was a little trouble then, but it blew over. Mr. Riggs and I were on the eve of resigning, and but for you I would have resigned. But I too have some duties for myself, and they are not to die for this place."

Miss Cunningham replied to this letter on December 3d, reasonably and with affection, which only deepens the mystery surrounding the final flare-up two years later. "I know not what we are to do because of this drawback to a residence there," she wrote, "but it will be the duty of the Association to make such arrangements as will make the situation of a superintendent compatible with the feelings of a gentleman, as well as with his health, and Mr. Herbert may be assured of this, the moment means can be come-at-able, and I have any authority or influence to encompass it. Your full salary too must be made to suffer no losses because of your magnanimity in the past. I would like to reply to the one main object of your letter, but words fail me, my heart is too full, even if I were not too sick to trust myself to touch on what would unnerve me now. Let me assure you that I could never think you unkind, you who have acted so nobly, so disinterestedly, for four long sad years. Personally as well as officially I owe you a debt of love and gratitude. My heart does and ever will pay it to you. Mount Vernon has within its walls a noble trio and their like will not be there again, if you all desert it. As for me, I felt as though my last props were being taken from under me, I could not undertake to carry on the work with one wholly strange to its operation, ignorant of the past which she would be compelled to refer to. The resignation seems to me a necessity after winding up business necessary for a call of Council. Of course, my friend, you must consult your health and happiness. Neither myself nor the country has any claim. You have more than done your duty. God bless you, and those with you who hold on with the kind desire not to yield up till you put all into my hands."

Meanwhile she had sent a pathetic wail to Dr. Hodge, deploring the disillusionment the war had brought to her love of country, and the consequent change in herself towards the enterprise for which she had once labored so confidently. "Where is the enthusiasm to come from needed to rekindle extinguished fires?" she asked him. "I succeeded before because I *felt*, and I warmed other hearts from the fire of my own. I have become a brokenspirited woman whose inspiration is gone because the fountain from which I drew it is dried up forever."

The "model plantation" of Rosemonte, whose servants had always been indulged—Mrs. Cunningham thought too much so— was now becoming infected with the general unrest among the Negroes, and the Regent was shocked and hurt when her Negro manager came to her with what seemed impossible demands, under the threat of no more work. "I had no idea of retaining those who had behaved ill," she wrote, "but they compose all the young and able-bodied men and most of the women. Do you not see that I have my hands full here? I am confined to my room, shivering at every blast, my head feeling as I have no words to describe. I would gladly leave the country but I am powerless to move. Winter has come and neuralgia is beginning to lay hold. I have on a cotton flannel cap under my cap now while I am writing to you, and yet my head is so cold and rigid I can write but a few lines at a time."

She alternated between a conviction that she must live and die in poverty at Rosemonte, and an inextinguishable hope that she could sell her cotton to sufficient advantage to come back to Mount Vernon and go on to Cape May to recuperate. She wrote with "pepper plasters to my forehead and mustard to my neck," and feared she was prolix. Accusations had appeared in the Northern papers that Mount Vernon was dominated by a Southerner, a secessionist, and a rebel, which roused her indignation.

"So far from wishing secession, I would rather have died than lived to see it," she assured Miss Tracy. "My letters to Mrs. Marks, she afterwards told me, made her suppose I had become a Northerner, and lost all sympathy with the South. I was taunted as a Yankee because of my lamentations after I returned home. It took months after the war commenced, months of atrocious conduct by the US in conducting it, for me to be aroused enough to be resigned."

She knew she was overdue at Mount Vernon, and she sent another conciliatory letter to Miss Tracy as a consequence of mulling over the contents of the outspoken November 8th letter, and in writing it cast some belated illumination over the original arrangement between them. Mrs. Fitch had been aware in the spring of 1860 when they were all at Washington that Miss Tracy had had another offer which she was inclined to accept, and the Regent now alluded to what had been for her at that time a bad scare:

"I do remember the evening after we returned from Washington City, when you told me of the proposals of your friends from Louisiana, their claims upon you, and of your desire to leave your position then to respond to them. I remember well, for it was like an electric shock to me. I recollect too how I walked up and down my parlor, as I placed before you the almost certain consequence to me of throwing the entire burden upon me in my then condition, which the resignation of one familiar with the duties must do. To initiate a stranger, no matter how capable, was to assume and perform pro tem the whole work myself. And your reply to me after seeing and consulting Mr. Graham was to this effect: viz., that you could not assume the responsibility of the evil which might result to me. In reply to my query as to the effect of delay on the feelings of your friends, who were so urgent for your going to them immediately, you stated that you must do what seemed to be your duty, and leave the rest to God. You do not really know me if you think I could ever ungratefully forget this act of yours! And as long as we remained together you never made me feel as far as I can recollect by word or deed the sacrifice of feeling you had made, for which I felt thankful then and send you thanks now.

"The approaching storm in politics soon made it apparent after you returned to me [in October, 1860] that our labors could not be successfully carried out during the autumn and winter as we had expected, that collections would be suspended everywhere, and that no Council would probably meet in February, '61, as you and I had anticipated when our contract was made out in July. I determined then to remove to Mount Vernon, afterwards to come South and arrange my own affairs, and return by the first week in March, you to join me and remain till our preparations were completed for the Grand Council, after which I knew I was to lose you.

"You may ask, then, How could you in the face of this, now write as if you confidently anticipated my remaining not only to wind up the affairs of the past as I had promised but also to carry on the work to its completion without reference to time? My answer is that I cannot account for myself, except that my suffering life here had removed me from remembrance of life as it was when with you, that it had escaped me as dreams escape. Your letter on the subject was like a strong, shaking grasp needed to arouse a sleeper from the deepest slumber."

Which was exactly Miss Tracy's intention, for it is obvious that she had sacrificed herself twice over for the Regent and Mount Vernon—though as the war went in Louisiana, she may have escaped some very unpleasant experiences there, by being at Mount Vernon. Miss Cunningham continued in her customary verbal involutions to underline the harassments of her own situation, and to apologize for seeming to assume too much regarding Miss Tracy's future intentions, when she had "concluded that if you needed to continue a remunerative occupation you would prefer it in a position amongst familiar duties and appreciative friends—duties which had widely extended your mental sphere, had developed your uncommon capacity for business and brought you into contact with many congenial friends, which of course extended your heart circle."

She maintained (with some justice) that Miss Tracy's own letters had led her to suppose that she had come to identify herself with Mount Vernon too, and that in effect it was no longer to her just a duty, but a labor of love similar to the Regent's self-dedication. This Miss Tracy was to deny, for she seemed perversely to resist the magic of the place for herself, and preferred to lay her service merely to duty, as promised to an employer. Again the Regent paid generous tribute to the faithful endurance of the secretary—but only in order to plead for still more time on what had begun to seem to Miss Tracy a life sentence. "Let me add that you have done in the past four years far more than the duties of a secretary," wrote Miss Cunningham, weaving the coil, "you have done as much as the originator ever could have done under the enthusiasm which might be supposed to animate her. For all this I feel that neither the Association nor myself had any claim, and although your original promise included the labor of closing up accounts and history yet to be closed, yet after all that you have done since we parted I am bound in generosity, no matter how distressing my own situation, to absolve you. Should your health and inclination permit and decide you to finish that particular work, I would be grateful, of course, but I could not now ask it. Or should you assist pro tem in initiating another secretary when obtained to do it, it would be a good deed to be numbered with all that have preceded it. Whether I resign or not, all business of the past must be systematically arranged first, and just before Council, and until it is done resignation would be impossible. The harassments and anxieties of my situation, even as to my private affairs alone, is telling on me. I have suffered more from dyspepsia in three weeks past than in thrice as many months. Nothing can be eaten in comfort, and I have again to resort to Dr. Hodge's remedy used fifteen years ago—doses of hot water and ginger perpetually. Some more sacrifice is needed from both of us," Miss Tracy read, with what must have been a mounting resolution somehow to be free. "A reliable assistant can and must be found. I suppose I must not expect to see Mary when I go on, unless she comes to pay a visit. She has my thanks for her long, faithful vigil, my every wish for her health and happiness, my every wish that we may meet once more. I am not surprised that her parents think it hard that she is detained for a year after the war is over. It is hard, and it troubles me as much as it does them. Neither you nor she can be more troubled than I am, for I feel that I am the cause, and that I cannot help it for a time does not lessen my worry. As for my mother, I fear that her reason will go entirely. She has altered for the worse in the last four months more than in five years. At times I feel that I too will give way. . . ."

Mrs. Ritchie wrote from London that winter, sending in her resignation as she feared her health would never again permit a sea voyage home—but she was entreated to reconsider. Mrs. Eve in Augusta was trying to rent her house there for enough to pay her lodging elsewhere, and might have to find some kind of work. Barhamville, the handsome school which she and the Regent had attended in Columbia, was advertised for sale, which meant that the Marks family had lost their fortune. "If I had a balloon, and could bear the current of air," wrote the Regent, "I would join you in the middle of January to remain there, for annoying and uncomfortable as you have found your residence there it would be a desirable change to me now and do me good, returning here every now and then to see how things get on."

If she had been able to do that in '65, instead of '67, the end of the story might have been different, for her and for Miss Tracy.

12

Miss McMakin went home for Christmas, 1865, to placate her family as prophesied by Miss Tracy, and Mr. Herbert's sister arrived at Mount Vernon to keep Miss Tracy company in her absence. The question of chaperonage, which had been summarily dismissed with Mrs. Riggs's sanction in the spring emergency of '61, arose now that things were more normal.

In March, probably off her own bat in an attempt to jog the Regent into action, Miss McMakin wrote to her from Mount Vernon. The first page is missing, and another page from the middle, but the strategy is obvious.

"We are all looking forward with intense interest to the time of your coming among us," wrote Miss McMakin, "which I hope you will be permitted safely to accomplish. My expectation is not unmingled with sadness, for your arrival if it is not seriously delayed must be the signal for the dissolution of the association which has been of the pleasantest character to me during five years. And such years! Could any of us have foreseen all that has befallen, who would have had the courage for a single week!

"From the fall of 1862 I have been parrying the demands of my parents and friends to return to them. Indeed, they never consented to my coming at all. But I put them off, hoping from month to month the war would end and some other arrangements be effected for the place. Dear friends have cast off my friendship, believing me indifferent to their wishes, and my mother, sick and needing me greatly both on her own account and that of my young brother, has been deeply offended. But I could not bring myself to leave Sarah to bear the burden alone. Mine have been comparatively light trials, it is true, but no one

can escape making some sacrifice to this Moloch of a place, it
would seem. Sarah could not and would not remain here without a female companion, in our peculiarly constituted household,
though Mr. Herbert is one man in a thousand, I think, for purity
of character and strength of principles; and I knew too well all
her presence was to the place, as well as her executive ability in
managing the very delicate arrangements of the Association's
external affairs, to dare to take the responsibility of withdrawing
her prematurely from its immediate guardianship. I firmly believe had any other than just such persons as she and Mr. Herbert
been here the place would have been lost utterly. Her Northern
birth was taken by most as some guarantee of her loyalty, and
that the place would not be whisked off to the Confederacy—
while Mr. Herbert's nativity assured his compatriots that their
interests would be cared for, although the most abominable stories of treason and disloyalty have been freely circulated about all
of us. We know we have been closely watched, and the results
proved, the authorities confessed, that we were honest at least in
our neutrality. No one who entertained the faintest sympathy for
even individual Southerners escaped distrust and contempt, even
silence was accepted as tacit admission of unfriendliness to the
powers that were, and laid one open to coldness and reproaches,
if not worse.

"So you see, devotion to the Union did not count for much
in those excited times, nor does it yet, unaccompanied by the
endorsement of all the attendant ideas of the dominant party.
Well, the appeal to power settled the question, and a cheerful
acquiescence in the manifest will of God, however embittered by
the medium of second causes, is the wisest and best course left
to all concerned. . . ."

Here the text is interrupted, to resume again with evidence
that the "Moloch of a place" had nevertheless endeared itself to
one of its captives.

"This lovely spot is just rousing itself for its spring adorning, and although a bleak northwester is sifting through the many cracks today, the grass is growing green and the daffodils peep quite fearlessly out of the ground. If one could be secure from the dear public, and have plenty of money, I don't know a more charming residence, in spite of chills, of which I have had my share. On Wednesday we expect the floodgates to be opened by the beginning of the boat's trips, which is highly desirable for the Association's exchequer but very unpleasant for the residents. I am afraid these same 'boat days' will be a trial to you. . . ."

Miss Tracy wrote in March, '66, from Washington where she had gone to attend church and do some shopping. She had been compelled to spend some of her 'bouquet money' to replace worn-out kitchen utensils and buy linen for pillow-cases, but had done without new table-cloths and sheets until the Regent arrived, though they kept her busy mending. Miss Cunningham had begun to replenish her wardrobe in preparation for her departure from Rosemonte, and Miss Tracy replied to a query about chemises that she did not think there was any special fashion in those. "Yokes if you like them, pointed on the shoulders and in front, embroidered as much as you like, or very narrow frills. I hope you are better, and collecting courage for your journey."

Washington was full and prosperous and interest in Mount Vernon had quickened, though the roads were infested with the riffraff left over from the war. "It has been dangerous to ride alone in lonely places, and even in Alexandria it was not at one time safe to go out alone in the evenings," Miss Tracy wrote. "I have had more fear in returning home late than in the whole war, and during the past winter have always hastened home earlier than ever before."

Boat-day was always busy now, and in April the trips began to be made tri-weekly. "Of course we personally dread it," she wrote Miss Cunningham. "Every day will be 'boat day' or the day before. We are no longer anything but servants to the public. I have cleared since the boat began its trips $50 by photographs. Today we made our first bouquet of violets and hyacinths. We are always good for nothing the evening after the boat has been here—tired and worried, so—"

The rest of the letter has been cut off with scissors. To the resigned regret of the present Mount Vernon staff, this recurrent ruthless censorship of apparently harmless material, whatever the reason, cannot now be traced to any specific person or time, but dates back beyond this generation, probably to one of the many abortive attempts to write the history of the Association—a thing which Miss Cunningham always desired to see done—long before the present filing system (still unfinished) was begun.

In mid-April Miss Cunningham was blaming her increasing listlessness on a Dr. N., who was apparently overdoing a sedative in the effort to quiet her nerves in preparation for her proposed journey northward in the summer. "I don't improve, I am strangely weak, this afternoon my feet failed under me on getting up to have my bed made," she wrote. A carriage accident had left the vehicle unfit for use, so that she could not get out for an airing, and her tendency to consider herself bedridden was certainly a drawback to regaining strength. Meanwhile she occupied her mind endlessly with the vacancies to be filled, proposing a friend of Mrs. Ritchie's, now abroad, for New Jersey—Miss Ogden having died—and doubting the propriety of attempting to fill Mrs. Goodrich's place until they were sure her malady was incurable, and as for New York—

"Now, about Miss Hamilton," wrote the Regent. "In the *strictest confidence,* I must tell you that *that State* has given *more trouble* than all the others put together! A spirit of *dictation* and captiousness has been exhibited from the first, and *few* in my place would have borne it without ever letting the parties see I was aware of it. Once it went so *far* that it was almost insulting to me and to Miss McMakin. It was an inquiry as to whether *proper care* had been taken to see there was no flaw in the title!!

—an aspersion on the lawyers and on Mr. Washington. I enclosed
the letter to him, to reply. It was such an exquisite piece of irony
that I carried it to Dr. Dickson to enjoy, as I did! He let me into
the secret by informing me that Mr. R[uggles], Miss Hamilton's
counsellor, the gentleman who had conveyed her appointment to
her, and a friend of Mrs. Ritchie, was a rare specimen of *pompos-
ity,* one of those who thought nothing could be well done in
which he had no hand. I put all to his score after that, but Mrs.
Comegys tells me that Miss Hamilton battled hard to have Mount
Vernon turned over to the US, though our charter only allowed
the title to the Association as long as it kept up the place, and
reserved it to the State when it neglected to do so. I am not inclined after such an exhibition of principles to urge Miss Hamilton to *reconsider!*"

     She had not heard from Mrs. Eve in response to her invitation
to come to Rosemonte for a visit, and Miss Tracy knew of no way
to reach Mrs. Morse in New Orleans, and had had no reply to
a letter to Mrs. Walker of North Carolina. Of Mme. Murat, she
had heard that the Emperor had made a handsome donation in
consideration of the losses she sustained during the war, which
drew a caustic comment from Miss Cunningham—"What a pity
I am not cousin to him!" Mrs. Chesnut was dead, Mme. Berghmans was in Europe. "Where is Mme. LeVert? You tell me
nothing of your visit to her," she complained to Miss Tracy, and
unfortunately the first mention of that visit is lacking. "Has she
escaped ruin, that she is travelling about at leisure? She is so
bewitching and irresistible to the stern sex that I would gladly
leave matters to her. I knew her when I was in school in Philadelphia, met her at my cousin's, with whom she was intimate."
But before long, with her growing inconsistency, she was to remark that while Mme. LeVert could be very useful if she liked,
"she sees too much à la couleur de rose, and she *talks* too much!"
     Further discussing the secretaryship, Miss Cunningham wrote
in May that Mrs. Pellet had never been considered for any per-

manent position, beyond the early Richmond meetings, and that
therefore Miss Tracy could not have supplanted her, nor could
Mrs. Pellet now fill her place. And after the generous reference in
the following letter to an apparent request from Miss Tracy for
an increase in pay, the Regent's complete and unexpected reversal
on this matter less than two years later is more than ever incomprehensible.

"I did not know," she wrote, "that you had been appointed
secretary to the Executive Committee until your late letter came.
Of course this will make it necessary to refer the subject of salary
to them whenever they meet, but I should suppose that the power
of the Regent is ample to authorize your using your funds you
have for an increase in the interim. I have no fear that the Committee will not view the matter as I do, viz., as the rightful one.
Then too, no matter how low our finances, the sum paid you has
been accumulated solely by your own ingenuity and perseverance
and agency, you may say you have *made* it. I beg you to feel that
the Association will not feel ungrateful or indifferent when they
have it in their power. At any rate, *I* will not. I regard it as obligatory on me when Grand Council meets to place before them
our agreement, and if they award as I feel they will, $500, to see
it paid as soon as we get the means. That is, if my life is spared,
or poverty—for no one expects the freedmen to work next year
as they do this year, and it is not much over half work they do
now—don't put me hors de combat. Regard it, if there is greater
delay than you like, as a sum ready for old age!"

To an objection by the Regent that she used her "precious
time" for mending old sheets, Miss Tracy replied that she had
made up the new pillow-cases with a sewing-machine which had
been given to her, "fortunately, or I do not know what we would
do, for seamstresses are scarce as gold, and dress-makers are un-
heard of as far as we are concerned. As for mending, I consider
that when the ladies requested me to take charge and remain in

charge, the duties included everything necessary in the proper care of the place, as much mending as accounts, marketing, sweeping, and dusting, when everyone else was ill. The duties are comically diversified, but all are essential to one thing."

Mr. Herbert had had a chill ending in very severe fever, and was being dosed with quinine, and another servant man had gone down with it too. "I suppose there will be little rest from them now till June, then middle of July they will begin again," wrote Miss Tracy. "What a drawback to a lovely summer. Mary and I are very worried at the delay in your arrangements for coming North. We are afraid you will arrive at the very moment when imperative duty will take us both away. We cannot guarantee patience or toleration from our friends for more than five years, even if our own holds out. Pardon haste, but Mr. Herbert being ill throws all this boat-day preparation on me."

Casting about for some one to take Miss Tracy's place if she held to her determination to leave Mount Vernon, the Regent came to Edwina Marks, who had energy, firmness, and good sense. "She suits the place and if her mother were a widow, perhaps I might succeed in getting them to reside there a short period, for the property left to them is not remarkable," she wrote, the school at Barhamville having been put up for sale. "But of course, Dr. Marks being alive, the thing is impossible." However, the Marks family would come to Mount Vernon later on, with unhappy results.

In her own opinion, Miss Cunningham had developed an organic disease of the heart—the doctor said it was only nerves—and thought she should prepare for the worst. Meanwhile, she continued to beg off from starting North, and to discuss at long range what arrangements could be made "ere you and Mary take flight. I hardly know what I write, I have taken hartshorn, and laudanum to keep me up, but I must stop and let the pepper-plaster now applied to my forehead draw and see if that will help me. In my letter to Mary I expressed my deep regret at parting from her by a dissolution of ties which were dear to me, ties which had made you both wind yourselves around my heart. I told her I should never feel content when you both left me."

Entangled once again, Miss Tracy now wrote of Mary's belief that she owed her life to Sarah's quick action on the wharf in '63, and so had persuaded her family that she must remain at Mount Vernon long enough to allow Miss Tracy to go to New York for a summer holiday, in view of the Regent's delay until autumn. "As for hiring anyone to assist us, it is no easy matter," she explained. "We would any of us rather do double duty than to take for the sake of assistance any one into our circle who is not perfectly congenial to us all, and it is very difficult to find persons we can trust. I tried to get a boy to sell photographs, but was finally obliged to take one of old West's grandsons who can count money. I pay him 75¢ each boat day. He comes early, helps to sweep and clean the grounds, before and after the boat, and sells the pictures while the boat is here. But one of us must prepare them, that is, stamp them with the Association initials on each stamp, and the description of the card on the back of each picture. I always do it, and keep the rather complicated account myself. As soon as Mr. Herbert can get a trustworthy man, I am going to teach my Robert how to make bouquets, he has taste and can learn, but it is so hard to get a faithful assistant that except when it was necessary to have him drive us to town I have given him up to Mr. Herbert. We have a good gardener, but he cannot make a bouquet that will sell, so we have it to do. Old Jim sells them, but he cannot count, so he stands under the window and one of us makes change through the blind. The roses are just commencing to bloom. If we only had a greenhouse we could make a good deal by the sale of cuttings. Could you not give Mr. Herbert authority to take down that old summer house? It is a terribly unsightly thing, and makes a very bad impression on visitors. I wonder that every high wind does not bring it down, but he says that much as he wants to take it down, you have never said that he might, although there is no doubt but that Judge Washington built it. Do say Yes. Do not put off coming any longer than you are obliged to. I feel sure that if you had the energy to make a move, then rest a while, the change would strengthen you."

The summer house was to survive, like the South porch, at some expense, well into the twentieth century.

13

In the effort to get Miss Cunningham to move, Miss Tracy had suggested that Mary might come to meet her, as far as Columbia, making a visit to friends on the way, the only drawback being the expense of her fare. "I am not entirely selfish in wishing you to come," she wrote at the end of May, '66. "I consider it very important for Mount Vernon, and I feel if you were obliged to stay South for two or three years afterwards, things could be managed, but *this* year it is imperative, and you ought to do all you can to gain strength while waiting for the time for the division of crops. I have no idea who I can get after Mary leaves. I may have to take some plain person for propriety and let all outside business go. I would be unwilling to take everybody, and the danger of sickness is so great it would be no easy matter to find anyone willing to come at that time, and I would not want anyone who had not been exposed, for it would only add to my cares and not help me in the least. But I am not going to borrow trouble. I thought you would surely be here by the last of July, and one of Mr. Herbert's cousins has promised to come and stay a part of that month with me. She will not linger."

Meanwhile she was laying plans for her holiday in New York, and her June 7th letter is the third one cited by Miss Cunningham in 1868. "I intend to have as perfect a rest as possible, and have written them all not to *mention* Mount Vernon to me," she wrote, expressing a reasonable enough wish after five years without so much as a fortnight away, except for the Carolina journey in '63, but to the Regent it gave deep offense—eighteen months later. "I want to leave the whole behind me. I begin to feel this tax on mind and body very much. I feel this rest is absolutely necessary if I am to keep my promise to you to remain till the first of January. I think you write much more than is good for you, particularly when you are obliged to take laudanum to do so, and this Dr. Hodge told me was the worst thing for you, for the reaction is so great. You write the whole history of the first years of the Association, all the details of which you had told me over and over again—then the whole Christie Johnson business, when if you remember my first duty was the disagreeable one of being obliged to attend to the settlement of that affair, and went far to making me decide after the first month to have nothing to do with the Association which was dependent for friends upon such vulgar men as Forney and David Paul Brown. Forney was the first specimen of this kind I had ever come in contact with, and I did not like even the possibility of encountering any more such. Dr. Dickson, I believe, saved me from utter disgust, and I do not think there are any circumstances or individuals connected with the Association that you may not take for granted I have heard all about."

Miss Tracy's patience was again wearing thin. She was in the middle of a letter to Mrs. Comegys about her proposed holiday with her sister in New York, and was planning to leave on the Friday, when a telegram arrived for Miss McMakin to say that her mother was alarmingly ill. "Of course this changes all my plans and for the present at least I am stationary," the letter to Mrs. Comegys resumed after an interval consumed by Mary's hurried departure. "Of course I am much disappointed, but dare not murmur when Providence so decidedly interferes. I may go later for a few days."

Providence, said Miss Tracy, with a sigh. And continuing her letter to Mrs. Comegys, she stated her belief that unless the Regent's expenses were paid by the Association they would not see her for another year or two.

"I wish she had said so frankly before, but I am almost in despair," she added. "If it were not impossible for her to resign before she has been here and settled up some matters that no one else can, I would say she would do well to resign, but if she did in the present state of the country the whole thing would go to pieces. Well, where is the money to come from? I think Mrs. Farnsworth and Mrs. Mitchell and Mrs. Chace and Mrs. Van Antwerp would help, but could enough be gathered? I feel very sorry for her, but not in the least alarmed for her life at present. I have seen her in the very state she describes and she, like all nervous people, aggravates her troubles by enlarging on them. I think her expenses ought to be paid, and surely it is a small sum for them to raise.

"Of course it seems easy for me to say so, and yet mine is not the easiest task in the world—to make both ends meet—to contrive that peas, beans, cabbage, and flowers shall pay for rakes, hoes, etc., that flowers and photographs shall pay for a gardener, that bricks shall pay for little odds and ends of plastering, bricklaying, etc., and then when these fall short and the corn has failed, or been stolen from the field as it was last year, and seed is to be bought, to contrive where we can pinch out the means, where we can foot the bill without drawing extra—but we do edge along, and the fixings up we have done amaze me. Mr. Herbert is very good at managing these things."

Letters like that one were not part of Miss Cunningham's indictment against Miss Tracy in 1868. The one Miss Tracy wrote on August 3d, having seen Mary McMakin depart for New York instead of herself, has disappeared except for the extract preserved by the Regent.

"I had very severe fever since I wrote you last," it reads. "I was utterly prostrate, but Mary was absent and matters had to be attended to, and I staggered around as well as I could until I had a chill, and then it was decided I must leave whether I would or not. I saw myself that it was almost life or death. Her mother was still very sick, but in her kindness she sent Mary back to me as soon as she was out of immediate danger, as my friends feared I could not live in the state I was in.

"I presume I shall have my hands full for the next two months, but I am feeling so much better that I intend to try to take things easily and not again wear myself out. If I were to fall ill again, I think some of my friends would put me in a private lunatic asylum, for they think it madness in me to remain, and as they call it, sacrifice myself for nothing."

Miss Tracy's friends, whoever they were, would seem to have the same oddly shaped joke as hers were likely to be. But even if it were not meant as a joke, to the Regent's literal mind the mention of the lunatic asylum could be magnified into a threat amounting to a form of blackmail for her own dilatory course.

Miss Tracy was past fooling, anyway, when she wrote at the end of August, after another bout of bilious fever which attacked her after Miss McMakin had returned again to New York. Full of quinine, and feeling very weak, and down-stairs for the first time in many days, Miss Tracy really let fly on August 31st, and this is no extract:

"The truth is, we ought all of us to have left here and given up this spring, and let the place go—or rather last fall," she wrote desperately. "The past year has been too much for anyone after the previous four. But we hated to do so, and hoped against hope that you would come and settle matters. It was foolish, I am now satisfied, to sacrifice so much, but I do not know how to *half* do anything.

"I hope you will come as soon as possible, and that you will appoint a Grand Council and not an annual meeting, on account of the voting. There are too many people want to meddle and it would make trouble. I hope you can find some one who can write, otherwise I do not know what you will do, for I am good for nothing and it is doubtful whether Mary can return. I shall be glad when I can give some sort of definite answer to the incessant query, When is Miss Cunningham coming? And, When is there going to be a meeting? I have no doubt you will get more ladies together late in October or early November than later. December would be too unpleasant, it is one of the most disagreeable months here.

"You can get clothes here, everything is dear everywhere."

There is another extract for September 8th, brief and to the point, touched again with her mordant humor, which the Regent did not appreciate. "I am very glad you have at last concluded to try to come," it read. "I was beginning to fear that you would delay till we were all wearied out, and you would find no one here if we were alive. Now I hope everything will go straight."

By October, '66, they had got down to ways and means for the Council, and the Regent was inquiring about precedent and procedure. Miss Tracy replied that Mrs. Riggs promised to lend household equipment, if necessary, and the Mount Vernon servants were always ready to do anything that was wanted. She proposed that the Vice-Regents should all go down to Mount Vernon the first day, see everything, talk it over, have lunch there, and go back to Washington, and on the second day hold Council in Mr. Riggs's library, where they had met in '65. A few days later she sent another hasty letter.

"I have but a moment to say, Do not shorten your dresses that are intended for house or dress, at least not in the back! Small hoops but long trails are worn. Mr. Herbert and I have sheets and pillow-cases and table-cloths enough, and towels, so do not encumber yourself with anything of that kind. We have bedding of all kinds ample for the beds we have. I have only one dozen and a half nice napkins. Mr. Herbert brought nearly all his things here, and from time to time I have sent for all of mine. I have a dozen handsome towels and a dozen common. The Association has two dozen.

"There is nothing gained by your writing so many letters now, do let them alone till you come on and see us here. You will change your mind about many things. I have a very sweet letter from Mrs. Walker. She thinks she cannot come, but if you go there I presume she will. I think you can come from Richmond by the Aquia Creek boat and land at our wharf, which would save you so much fatigue and discomfort. I should think Mrs. Eve could buy you a cap better than Mrs. McMakin. Everybody has been sick, and I have not a carpet down in the house. We always take them up during the summer. I have more than I can do in a short time."

The Regent's letter of October 23d is disarming in its feminine flurry.

"I made you a miserable scrawl on Sunday night in a most despairing mood, for I just found that by a mental hallucination I had lost a number of days and was not half ready. I have made up my mind to go just as I am, and to risk the calling of Council for the 15th, if I get to you only four days in advance. You must do the possible to see that my head and neck gear are comme il faut. I have before me Mme. Demarest's Fashion Book for October. What a change in styles within a few years! The world is going back to ancient costume, especially in style of dressing hair. What I am to do I can't tell, unless I use false hair. I am going with threadbare flannel, and fear I shall suffer much, but I wish to get thick Northern flannel which I have never found at the South. They bring it very fine, but not thick and heavy unless it is very coarse, so I must risk until I can get the right sort. I lined and dressed my bonnet today, the first time I ever did such a thing. I am living on laudanum, and feel I can't keep up under such pressure."

Her maid had been taken ill, and she had to make do with a very young and delicate girl as a travelling companion. There was trouble on her plantation, and her brother was away, and she would be absent at the time when she ought to be engaging labor for the coming year. But at last, at last, she was on her way, dislodged from her cocoon at Rosemonte, and about to meet, for the first time, the assembled ladies of the Mount Vernon Association.

III

THE VICTORY
1866–1876

I

So few had gathered to greet her. So little remains of what took place that great day when the Regent, frail, aging, and undeniably ill, for the first time took the chair.

Looking round at them, she missed faces she longed to see, from the old days before the war began—Mrs. Ritchie, the brightest and dearest, was in London, too ill to travel; Lily Macalester Berghmans was abroad too, with her Belgian husband; Mrs. Goodrich, to whom the Association owed the invaluable Miss Tracy, was in a hopeless mental breakdown; Mrs. Fitch, veteran of the Washington campaign of 1860, had not made the journey from Indiana, nor Mrs. Eve from Georgia, nor had Mrs. Walker from North Carolina.

But Mrs. Comegys was there, faithful as always, everybody's confidante; and Mrs. Riggs, who had been Miss Tracy's rock and refuge all through the war; Mrs. Mitchell, another staunch friend to Miss Tracy, and Mrs. Van Antwerp, all the way from Iowa again; and for the first time, Mrs. Morse of Louisiana, recently widowed, and about to settle in Baltimore; only five, and the Treasurer and the secretary.

The Minutes of that 1866 Council, kept presumably by Miss Tracy, are brief and barren. There is no record even of the trip to Mount Vernon which must have been made before they sat down in Mr. Riggs's library to hear the Regent's opening address.

She rose and stood before them, and began to speak. It was the moment she had lived for, for how many years?

"Ladies of the Mount Vernon Association," she began. "It is with feelings whose peculiar depth and intensity I must fail to clothe in fitting words, that I greet you, sister guardians, on this proud, long-hoped-for day. Looking back from our present assured stand-point of an *accomplished fact,* my memory cannot fail to recall the early vicissitudes, the oft-discouraging progress of our labor of love, in redeeming from oblivion and sure decay the home and grave of the immortal Washington! Then we lived on hope! We *would* not yield to despair! Now we can rejoice, with intense satisfaction, to know that *Mount Vernon is ours*— the Nation's! And well may I feel almost overpowered to find myself, at this moment, in the midst of ladies representing the varied sections of our country, pledged to guard that sacred spot *forever! . . .*"

There was more, of course, in long rehearsed, much rewritten sentences, re-adapted now to the occasion as it finally arrived. Then came the financial report, with due credit rendered to Mr. Everett, and the proud statement that the entire purchase money, with interest on deferred payments, had now been paid to Mr. Washington's heirs, and an additional expenditure of over $20,000 had been made on upkeep and repairs. Miss Tracy's salary was raised to $600 a year, and an additional $300 a year was voted to pay a private secretary to the Regent. This would seem to recognize Miss Tracy's appointment as secretary to the Association made by the committee in 1864—and to acknowledge the need of a separate personal secretary to the Regent. Yet one of the points she would insist on in '68 was that the Association had no secretary and needed none, besides her own, which would demote Miss Tracy to her original status—although the November 8th extract quoted Miss Tracy as having said that nothing would induce her to return to the position she occupied before the war. And it may have been a dispute in Council on this point which precipitated disaster a year later.

The appointment of Mrs. Sweat as Vice-Regent for Maine was announced, to succeed Mrs. Little. Mrs. Pickens was named for South Carolina, Mrs. Chesnut having died. Miss Harper had at last accepted for Maryland, but was abroad. Miss Hamilton was to be replaced by Mrs. Brooks, wife of a New York Congressman, apparently suggested by Mr. Graham. These were the first new appointments made since 1860, and Connecticut, Massachusetts, and New Jersey were still vacant.

The most important result of this 1866 Council was that Miss Tracy was somehow persuaded to remain at Mount Vernon for another year, enabling the Regent to return almost at once to Rosemonte to wrestle with her labor problems there. In the 1868 correspondence Miss Cunningham wrote to Miss Reyburn of Missouri that she had made the journey North in 1866 because she had felt "in honor bound to come and release Miss Tracy without regard to the cost to myself," and it had so taxed her strength that she was taken out of the cars at Richmond "in a state of insensibility"—she was again Mrs. Pellet's guest there— and "suffered tortures for a week" after she reached Mount Vernon. At her request Mrs. Mitchell and Mrs. Comegys had come to Mount Vernon in advance of the others for consultation, and she explained to them that while she herself could not ask Miss Tracy to make further sacrifices, she implored them "in pity to me," to vote for all things to remain as they were for another year—"to give me time to recruit." Her 1868 letter went on to say that Miss Tracy could not then shut her eyes to the fact that the Regent was unequal at that time to the effort of making changes at Mount Vernon, and out of consideration to her, she supposed then, had agreed to maintain the status quo until the next Council meeting, allowing another year for winding up the work which no one else could do so well, and possibly training her successor, when Miss Cunningham should again have returned to Mount Vernon. To Mrs. Farnsworth in 1868 she stated her conviction—her very recent conviction—that while she had supposed her feeble condition had obtained the further concession from Miss Tracy, yet even before she left Mount Vernon in '66 she had "perceived that I had been brought on at such cost to myself principally to raise her salary"—an increase which had long since been agreed upon in their friendly correspondence.

The Regent's stay at Mount Vernon in '66 was in any case brief, and it remains cloudy. On November 29th she lamented in a letter to the elusive Mrs. Comegys that she had been deprived by Mrs. Comegys's early departure from Washington of "a full unburdening" between the Comegyses and herself, which would have done her more good than medicines or tonics, and wistfully recalled her 1860 visit to Dover. Mrs. Van Antwerp had accompanied her from Washington back to Mount Vernon and remained for a few days' visit, the Regent being prostrated from exertion and excitement. Dr. Hodge's wife was ill, so he could not come to Miss Cunningham, and she could not make the journey to Philadelphia to consult him. The news from Rosemonte was so bad that she felt pressed to return there as soon as possible—"my poor old mother just gave up when I left her," she wrote, and Mrs. Cunningham was threatening to rent out and board, in her despair over managing the Negroes. The Regent may have spent Christmas, 1866, at Mount Vernon, but very early in January she was on her way South again, paying another visit to Mrs. Pellet at Richmond on the way.

It must have seemed to Miss Tracy most unjust that January of 1867 should have brought to Mount Vernon the most severe and pitiless winter weather she had yet experienced there. "I never saw such a succession of storms and cold," she wrote to Miss Cunningham on the 25th. "These violent winds sift in everywhere about the house, there is very little variation in the thermometer, it goes up two or three degrees one day and down three or four the next. One night last week at 11 o'clock the mercury stood at 22° in the little entry between the sitting-room and dining-room. [This would be between the present diningroom and the library.] The snow is very deep. I suppose you have a mail now quite as often as we do. It is quite a treat with us, for I have not courage to send Robert very frequently to brave these terrible northwesters."

Two months later—

"There is at present one thing all absorbing—the weather," she wrote. "I do not think there was ever anything like it. I do not presume you are entirely exempt from the rain which has so nearly flooded the country, if you are away from the snow. We are in despair. We have had no boat since a week Tuesday, and then only seven persons came down. We have had but one mail since, for the roads are so much worse than ever known before that Mr. Herbert is unwilling to risk animals and wagons, but when the boat did not come on Tuesday we were in trouble— nothing to eat for ourselves or horses, and hot-beds not finished for want of glass. Everything was at a standstill, but it was pouring rain, and it seemed impossible to send anyone out for anything but wood.

"Early Wednesday morning Mr. Herbert sent word to me that Robert said it was not raining and he thought he had better try to get to town. There was no time to write any letters for he must of course go immediately to get back before dark. The day was very cloudy and looked like rain every minute, but did not till about ten minutes before Robert came back, and since then it has never stopped doing *something*—all Wednesday night and all day Thursday it poured in torrents—yesterday it snowed all day, rained and snowed all night, and then this morning it is raining as violently as if it were the first rain of the season.

"Robert brought me no letter from you, but one from Mary, saying she had just received eight pages from you, so you must have exhausted yourself on her. A very pleasant letter from Mrs. Chace, who had answered some one of my previous communications but it had been lost. One from Mrs. Sweat, who says that she has inquired and can find nothing of Mrs. Little's accounts.

Mrs. Little is going abroad this summer. I think you had better go and appoint a meeting in Paris for October, you will have a larger attendance there than in this country!

"Mr. Herbert and I are in a worry over the small amount of money this month. We are determined to do without a gardener and thus save that much. Since Mary left I have not had to pay anyone for staying with me, and have made arrangements for cousins of Mr. Herbert's and my nieces to be with me till the last of June. That with the gardener's wages saved will more than cover the additional salary the ladies voted me. Then all we have for the many little repairs is what we make in the garden. I see no help for it, no one is going to raise or give us any money, and we must do our best to save and make; notwithstanding the imperfections of our greenhouse and the terrible winter on plants, we have saved a number of cuttings and plants ourselves, and I have spent hours every day that it was possible to wade out there. I hope we make something by it when the sun shines, we have not seen his majesty since last Sunday.

"We are planting all kinds of vegetables in boxes, and the dining-room and sitting-room are full, much to Nathan's consternation, but they will get started, and there is no chance of working the ground. But we cannot plant corn or potatoes in the house! I am not saying all this to complain, only to show you that we may have harder work to make both ends meet than ever before. We will try to do our best. I regret the loss of this month by the boat, for all that we would have made would have been clear gain, as Washington was full of people, most of whom will be gone the first of April. But we have many blessings left, and the accounts of the floods stop all murmuring from those who are sheltered."

There was a Monday evening postscript.

"One glorious sunshiney day, and the promise of one equally fine tomorrow. We hope for the boat. The snow is almost gone, and we trust the storm is fairly over. It has done us severe damage, washed the hillside down into the road near the wharf on the carriage drive just after the turn from the wharf. It was a very bad slide. Mr. Herbert has had the men at work all day clearing the road. Otherwise our sufferings are only in the delay of every kind of outdoor work.

"I think you had better let me send you that merino dress before long, I am afraid the moths will get at it if I keep it. Did you intend to leave your silk mantilla here? You know you gave it to me to put away, and I think you forgot it. I did. Mrs. Riggs has been about three weeks in New York hoping the change would do her good, but she has had such dreadful weather there I am afraid she had not much chance of getting out. I have never been such a prisoner as for the past two weeks, and now it will be some time before the roads are sufficiently dry for me to drive to town."

There could hardly be a more friendly letter, quite in her usual vein, with no hint of recrimination for having been let in for another trying time at her post, and with evidence of a more than usual inventiveness and cheerful acceptance of the necessity to cope with discomfort and lack of funds. Nor was there anything but good will and affection in Miss Cunningham's reply from Rosemonte in April.

"If I could laugh, though I am too sick and troubled for that, I would have done so over your vegetable boxes, but it is a good idea. Mrs. Hopkinson [Massachusetts] urges my going to Washington and exerting the influence I have ever exercised over gentlemen to get a donation from Congress, but I have as little will for that as money, so I am getting gloomy because I see no officer qualified or willing to lead a new movement.

"We are having wretched times. I can just manage to get food to eat, and am in dread of getting out all the time. I am yet without a servant, mother has only a little girl, and a half-witted white woman who is beyond being taught anything save the drudgery to which she has been accustomed all her life, yet through her I get some little attention. Mrs. Eve has wound up her affairs, rented her home, and goes to live mostly with her daughter in New York, who after being childless for five years after marriage expects to become a mother in July."

And then, another tantalizing reference to Alabama—"Have you appeased Mme. LeVert?" There is no clue. But Mme. LeVert never came to Council.

The Regent wrote in June that her eyes were giving trouble, confining her to a dark room and making the days seem endless, without sewing, writing, or books to fill the time. The vacancies continued to worry her, and she exhorted Miss Tracy to write the prettiest sort of letters to various candidates in the hope of getting an acceptance—she had never taken in that between the sectional feeling and the unjustified newspaper attacks on Mount Vernon and the Association, the office of Vice-Regent was no longer considered the prize it had once been. "Do air the dyed dress and don't let the moths get into it," she wrote. "I am and shall be as poor as a church mouse until July, not a dime for anything." In a January, 1868, letter, she was to say that she had not purchased a new dress, bonnet, or cloak for eight years.

The season at Mount Vernon continued wet and cold into July, when another letter from Miss Tracy to the Regent reveals her renewed dedication to the daily round, without a sign of repining.

"We have none of us been really ill, but Mr. Herbert has not been well for a long time and I have been miserable for ten days. Mr. Herbert insists upon my going away but if I can keep from being ill I shall not. It costs so much to go anywhere, and at this season a few weeks absence does no good. I prefer to wait till September and then I can stay till it will be possible to return without so much danger, if I must go at all. I am so anxious to do all that is possible towards paying expenses, and I know if I go things will get crooked, with no one to leave in my place, that I shall not go unless obliged. I presume Mr. Herbert dreads to see me go down with one of those frightful fevers that I have had two seasons, but I hope to escape with care.

"We have paid expenses and a little over again last month. I have not drawn an extra dollar for anything, but have paid for manures, seed, garden tools, etc., out of the bouquet money, depositing photograph money with Mr. Riggs towards paying expenses. There are nothing like the number of visitors there have been the past two years. Everybody has gone to Europe.

"I do not wonder you want to go to Cape May, whether you can afford it or not. I think it is so natural a feeling, you sigh for it as I do for mountain air, but the expense to you I suppose would be enormous, for you have learned how impossible it is for you to get along with an indifferent maid. It does seem hard that there should not be found another like Grace, yet every time I speak of a maid to anyone they always say, a thing almost impossible to find."

Miss Tracy did however give in and go to "the Springs" during August, when letters again went astray, and the autumn Council was looming when she wrote from Mount Vernon early in September to urge the Regent not to leave it till too late in the year, as the Vice-Regents were planning on October and many of them would find it impossible to come at any other time. Both Mrs. Mitchell and Mrs. Sweat were going abroad for the winter, and there might be difficulty about a quorum. Nieces and cousins were available to help her send off the notices quickly as soon as the Regent could fix on a date.

As the fatal 1867 Council approaches, the historian's hindsight becomes more and more incredulous, in view of the apparently cloudless relationship between Regent and secretary. "Do not feel any anxiety about my health," Miss Tracy was writing in September. "I am perfectly well, I have followed my wise doctor's advice in giving way before I was too much run down and exhausted by the attack. I have been home three weeks and feel exceedingly well. Both Mr. Herbert and myself feel we are acclimated, and the systematic manner in which we have arranged things seems to keep everyone well. The first of this month we finished paying expenses—that is, so far had met all expenses since the last meeting, and a little over, and that without drawing one extra dollar from Mr. Riggs. We have worked hard for it, but feel quite proud of our performance. I have made with my own hands over 800 bouquets, which has paid for the super-phosphates, farm tools, etc., and we have nearly enough to put a new zinc roof on the tomb, which is an absolute necessity, the mending which we did last fall not being sufficient, and this without costing the Association an extra cent, for all the new plants and flower seeds requisite to keep up a supply of flowers I bought with my own money. We rarely hear complaints, but always wonder and admiration at the neatness and order of the place."

Besides Miss Tracy's natural veracity implicit in her character, it would have been impossible for her to present a false impression of the situation at Mount Vernon in view of the Regent's imminent arrival there and the necessity to make good her statements. Yet within a few months' time Miss Cunningham was attempting to discount the whole of Miss Tracy's post-war conduct of Mount Vernon affairs, in letters written both to Vice-Regents who had and had not been present on that unaccountable day in Council.

Meanwhile the Regent had a spell of fever, and her quinine ran out, and until her wagon could return from Augusta she was left in excessive weakness and confusion of mind, as she began to count up the probable attendance, which this year might come to nine. The lady they wanted for Connecticut would not reply to letters—then sent a belated refusal. Miss Cunningham wrote that she was "desperate" over the Association, and felt their only chance was to get the indemnity claim from Congress—$7000 was the figure they had decided upon to represent their losses by the interrupted boat. It was not enough, but they dared not ask for more. (She paused to take laudanum, and her pen struggled on.) Caterpillar had appeared at Rosemonte, but rust did more harm in the cotton, cutting down her prospects by twenty bales or more. The whole South Carolina country was infested with fever, the worst in twenty years. The nieces who had been keeping her company at Rosemonte were leaving tomorrow and would post the letter. "I am very much obliged for the information of the latest fashions," she added, "and shall be only too thankful if my wardrobe can serve me, for God knows the affairs of poor Southerners are desperate enough. Pray lay in the coal for the winter at once—also sugar if it is rising."

The year of grace was nearly past. The indemnity claim must be made. Once more, she must go and do battle for Mount Vernon.

2

Miss Tracy sent the accounts up to October 1st, and called the Regent's attention to the fact that the day appointed for the Council, which after all had fallen back into November, and was to recede still further, was also a boat day, and would involve complications with the public visitors. She enclosed a pathetic inventory of Mount Vernon's household assets —two pair blankets, cotton comforts, three counterpanes—she had bought six sheets and pillow-cases for the Association, and a dozen towels. Mr. Herbert had his own linen, etc., and she had her own mattress and blankets. The Regent had left her air-bed there last year—but its screw was missing and it could not be inflated, and no one had any idea where a featherbed—as requested by Miss Cunningham—could be found nowadays. Mr. Herbert had four bedsteads in the house, and mattresses, "such as they are. We had the use for three or four years of three very nice hair mattresses, belonging to a relative of Mr. Herbert's, but this spring they were returned to the owner."

Once again, the Regent's indestructible interest in feminine adornment had raised a question which Miss Tracy took pains to answer. "I inquired the price of jet sets such as are worn now. They are from $10 to $20 a set. They are very handsome. There are cheaper kinds, but they are not worn by ladies, of course. The $20 are the handsomest, but the others are very pretty." The reason for the query is pitifully clear—a new set of jet jewelry would perhaps set off a dyed, made-over dress. The Vice-Regents were women of means, with New York or Paris clothes. She had had nothing new since 1860, and she must face them again from the Regent's chair.

Mount Vernon too was "poor in goods—one table-cloth!" she

lamented. "But, mon amie, it was not right to be using your own articles out! Well, if I live and we ever get the money, you shall have them replaced. It would be but just. Are the sheets you bought linen? It would be dreadful for me to have to lay in sheets and table-cloths for a short use, and yet the Association is too poor to buy. What is the price of good table damask napkins? Bed covering is the worst, for I am so chilly that I sleep under three blankets."

The drop in attendance depressed her, for she could not realize that the country was settling into a peace-time pattern, the displaced Army people had all got home, European travel was being resumed—it was no one's fault that there was no novelty about Mount Vernon now. Mrs. Morse of Louisiana, a Senator's widow, was sure to be helpful about the indemnity, and she was taking up a residence in Baltimore, which would be handy. Quite suddenly, in mid-October, the Regent began to get ideas. Council must wait till Congress was in session. There must be another campaign— an excursion—her mind went back to the old days, the grand days, before the war, when she and Mrs. Fitch had enveigled a boatload of Congressmen to Mount Vernon, with speeches, and refreshments, and a band, and a grandstand built on the lawn in front of the piazza—reporters must be invited—the Vice-Regents must bring their friends—perhaps a picnic at White Point— oysters and chocolate, cake and wine—Miss Tracy must see the captain of the boat at once and arrange it—"You know your powers of pleasing when you try them, as you managed the men in power in Washington so admirably during the war—" And then, with a dizzy drop to reality— "I wonder what I should do if the Vice-Regents vote to give up and refuse to do anything! Sometimes I get very low down, but you must not let anybody but Mr. Herbert know that. I can't shake depression off. Can't you give me some pleasant news of some sort, it would be charity!"

But for what was apparently the first time in 1867 Miss Tracy threw cold water. She had not the Regent's flair for social crusade, the deliberate display of femininity and charm which in the hands of Miss Cunningham and Mrs. Ritchie had already served the Association well. "I am sorry you have so decidedly made up your mind to *my* getting up an excursion," she wrote, "for I must entirely decline. I am surprised that after so many years you do not understand me better. I am entirely unfitted for anything of that kind. When necessity required I would quietly and without a fuss see any of the people in command from the President to the quartermaster, but that necessity is over, and I am not adapted to getting up a flourish of any kind. Mr. Riggs says that as Congress and the President are in the midst of a deadly quarrel and do not speak, each party would consider such an invitation an insult, and would not accept. There is nothing attractive in the White Point in the dreary last of November, and it has during the summer been the picnic ground for the freedmen."

The quarrel between President Johnson and Congress was to run on into impeachment proceedings in May of the following year, which were decided in Johnson's favor by only one vote. The indemnity bill, Miss Tracy had learned, was required to go before a committee and be appended to some other bill, which the chairman of the committee had the power to prevent. She had bought linen sheets, and damask napkins were from $4 a dozen to as much as you chose to pay.

The Regent now expected to leave for the North on the 20th of November, with stop-overs at Columbia, Greensboro, and Richmond on the way. She would be accompanied by an inexperienced maid and a timid young niece called Lizzie—and by Mrs. Walker of North Carolina, who this year would attend Council for the first time, and could do some shopping for Miss Cunningham in Baltimore before coming on to Mount Vernon. The impoverished Regent was still in a flurry over her personal appearance, confronting the cherished, well-to-do wives and widows who comprised the Association, and Miss Tracy was requested to engage a seamstress named Kate to be at Mount Vernon for two days:

"I have my bombazine to alter, for on trying it on I saw it would not be presentable. I have sent express to Philadelphia for material to make a train, and for trimmings, to meet me at Greensboro," she wrote.

"Do advise me what to do about the fashion of dressing my hair. Mine is falling out since my fever, and if it goes on I shall have none to dress. What kind of false hair could I get to help modernize me? Let me know, as I can talk over all shopping with Mrs. Walker and give her a bill if I know before hand what to do. She is a relation of Miss Harper [Maryland] and I am sorry the latter has not yet returned for them to meet, as they are yet strangers. By the way, we must arrange to get Mrs. Walker down to Mount Vernon the earliest moment possible. She only wishes to be two days in Baltimore, and I shall want my things before Monday night. Two days will be too little time to fix me up."

She had just discovered that the latest date chosen for the Council fell on Thanksgiving Day, and yet if they delayed again they would lose Mrs. Farnsworth, who was visiting her daughter at Lynchburg, but would not wait there forever. Mrs. Mitchell had written that they were not to expect her this year. And as the time of the journey drew near the Regent's heart was behaving badly again, so that she must be sure to have a few days' rest after reaching Mount Vernon.

It was all an old familiar story to Miss Tracy. She would have begun to look forward now to her own escape—to reunion with her sister and friends in New York—to the brisk mountain air of Mr. Graham's Cumberland place. There is no mention of a date set for her departure. She was doubtless prepared for several weeks' work after Council, getting out the copies of the Minutes, settling the accounts, acquainting the Regent with the established household routine so that she could take the reins. Mr. Herbert's feelings about the impending changes will never be known. Mary

McMakin had already gone for good, so far as anyone knew, and was with her family in New York.

There is no indication that the Regent and Miss Tracy were not on good terms during the few days which intervened between her arrival at Mount Vernon in late November and Council—but something must have been brewing in the Regent's mind even then. The Vice-Regents met at Mount Vernon on the 2d of December for an inspection tour and luncheon served in the library. Apparently all went well that day. Three Vice-Regents from last year's group were absent about their own affairs—Mrs. Van Antwerp, Mitchell, and Morse. Two made their first appearance—Mrs. Hunt of Missouri, one of the eldest members and reputed to be a millionaire in her own right, accompanied by her secretary and companion, Miss Reyburn, without whom she could not travel—and Mrs. Walker. Mrs. Farnsworth, Mrs. Comegys, and Mrs. Riggs made five.

Lack of sufficient accommodation at Mount Vernon necessitated an adjournment to the greater comfort of Washington City, where the next day they met again in Mr. Riggs's library. And that was when it happened.

3

Miss Tracy's account of the December 2d cataclysm is the simplest—and the most maddening, in all that it does not say. And yet it must come closest to the basic facts. On February 1st from Washington, where she was again a guest in the Riggs household, she wrote to Mrs. Chace of Rhode Island, who had not been present at Council:

"Enclosed is a copy of the Resolutions passed at the late meeting of the Grand Council of the Mount Vernon Association. Miss Cunningham thinks they are incorrect, but wherein lies the fault I do not know. Mr. Riggs took them down during the meeting, and it was from his copy that I had them printed, to save me so much copying. Mr. Riggs says they are perfectly correct, verbatim, but as Miss Cunningham made objections and I was anxious to do what was right, I wrote to Mrs. Farnsworth, who worded most of the Resolutions, and enclosed a copy requesting her to say if they were correct. Her reply is, they are correct. I therefore send them, as is my duty.

"This is my last official act for the Association, as I have left Mount Vernon! As you will perceive, I have resigned my position and Miss Cunningham is at Mount Vernon for the present. There has been some feeling, I do not know why, manifested by Miss Cunningham against me. I attribute it to my refusing to be her private secretary—I resigned that position before the war, and at her earnest entreaty retained it temporarily. She now denies my appointment by the ladies in '64 as the secretary of the Association being legal, says she needs a private secretary, and there is no need of a secretary for the Association, and as I resigned being private secretary I am nothing. Then, too, I wrote repeatedly during '65 to urge her coming on and arranging matters on something like a settled footing. I had the care of Mount Vernon, the work of secretary, and she was overwhelming me with other work which was too much for me. She now quotes those letters to prove I was unwilling to remain at Mount Vernon, although at the meeting in November, 1866, the whole matter was apparently arranged, and I was requested by her through the ladies to remain, and nothing more was said about it.

"During the summer [of '67] I had several curious letters from Miss Cunningham which I did not quite understand, and while I heard through third parties of very curious statements she was making, there was nothing either in her letters to me or in these others to which I as a lady could reply. At the meeting Miss Cunningham took everybody by surprise by reading a paper embodying pretty much what I have told you, evidently showing a determination to get rid of me. There was much feeling shown, and I shall never forget the kindness with which all the ladies stood by me. They tried very hard to make some compromise with Miss Cunningham, but finally she threatened to resign. Of course I could not allow that, for whatever she may think, or whatever idea may now have possession of her, too much is due her for the past, for me to stand in the way.

"The whole thing was very sad. All our meetings heretofore have been so harmonious that it grieves me very deeply that I should have been, however unwillingly, the cause of uncomfortable feeling. I have written you rather a long explanation, but I felt it due to myself to represent the facts to some of the ladies whom I had met, and from whom I had received every kindness and consideration while staying at Mount Vernon and during our meetings. Mrs. Riggs, who was ill last winter and was in Europe during the summer for her health, was made ill by the fatigue and excitement of the meeting, and has resigned as Vice-Regent. Mr. Riggs has also resigned. This last is much to be regretted, but he did not approve of Miss Cunningham's course, and said he could not continue as Treasurer when he did not agree with her.

I am at present at his house, where I shall probably remain during the winter. Pardon my long letter, and receive, if you please, my thanks for the uniform kindness with which you as well as most of the other ladies always met me. . . ."

That is Miss Tracy's case, as submitted in finished form—her only comment now available. The "curious" letters from Miss Cunningham alluded to are not now in the files for '67, when the tone of the remaining correspondence appears to be more friendly than in '65, nor is there any evidence of the derogatory statements by the Regent to third parties to which Miss Tracy felt she could not reply. But the conclusion might be drawn from Miss Tracy's letter to Mrs. Chace that during the Regent's brief stay at Mount Vernon in '66 there was some sort of ferment which was somehow resolved at the time, and allowed to go on simmering.

Infinite speculation is possible. But holding firmly to the evidence in hand, which is like bits of a jigsaw puzzle which do not fit into each other to form a recognizable pattern, a few clues can be found on which to base conjecture which may not be altogether wild, though one remains baffled, dissatisfied, and in dire need of a few pages from Mrs. Comegys, who heard all, saw all, and as usual has said nothing.

The Regent's case is buried in the prolix verbiage of interlined, crossed out, and unfinished drafts of two papers read to the Council, and of several subsequent letters to Mrs. Farnsworth and Miss Reyburn, who were there, and to Mrs. Sweat, who was not. The letters as sent, or if sent, have disappeared. But it is time to see what can be made of the first impulsive, white-hot self-justification which Miss Cunningham felt called upon to make as a result of what must have become a truly agonizing scene for all concerned, that day in Mr. Riggs's library.

"I fear I shall never be able to recall the 3rd of December without a feeling of bewilderment and astonishment at the unexpected developments made on that day," she wrote from Mount Vernon on January 1st to Miss Reyburn, who had accompanied Mrs. Hunt of Missouri to Council, "and the effect on me, so familiar with all concerning the history of the Association I had myself started and labored for with absorbing devotion, without cessation for seven years. How strange it must all have appeared to other officers present whose knowledge of affairs was mostly restricted to the local history connected with their immediate labors. I feel it due to these, therefore, to place before them facts connected with Miss Tracy's position towards myself which will show that it was she herself who left me no other course to pursue! Indeed, I was so astounded at the aspect given to the affair in Council that I sought a private interview with her on my return here, to try and find out the cause of the inexplicable course pursued towards me, but I gained no further insight than that she considered herself injustly treated, and as I glean now, having some illimitable claim on the Association. As I had never felt *I* had any such claim, it had never occurred to me a paid secretary simply, whose services are supposed to be equalized by the monetary reward attached, could entertain such an idea.

"The unaccountable position taken by Miss Tracy in Council makes it due to myself to send extracts from her letters to such Vice-Regents as may have been connected with the matter, or become cognizant of it. All her letters have the same tone. These extracts are enough to show that she not only felt a disgust to her position as secretary, but such disgust to the life at Mount Vernon, which she described as the opposite to all she liked, that she demanded to be released from it, that she did not wish to die for the place, that others ought to take their turn at sacrifice. She included Mr. Herbert in this positive determination to leave.

"When she found I was now looking forward with comfort to the thought or expectation engendered by her apparent devotion during the war to Mount Vernon, that I would continue to have her to lean upon, not only to assist in arranging the very business which she had promised before the war to remain long enough to do, and the same which had compelled me to come here to attend to this winter, but for an indefinite future, she wrote me the emphatic letter of November 8th, '65. This letter was a terrible blow to me, for with her so capable and so familiar with the routine of business I felt I could still serve the cause. To attempt it with a stranger seemed then impossible, and it more than anything else brought on the illness I spoke of, for I was in a very critical condition of health. . . .

"After what I have written you will be surprised to learn that she states she was turned out, without warning, in the dead of winter, when in reality it was two years and one month after her refusal to remain with the Association in any capacity any longer, that I could effect her release. In conclusion, my dear Miss Reyburn, I must add that the claim set up at Council by Mr. Riggs was extraordinary. The Mount Vernon Association was created to serve the home and grave of Washington, to have it cared for and protected as a public shrine. The best plan to do this is the one sole object of the Association, not to create sinecure offices for anyone, no matter what part taken in bringing about the existence of the Association. I had felt the presence of some woman during the war connected with the Association was a necessity. It entailed heavy expense, but it was better to meet it than to strive for possession of the place by contending parties. As soon as war ceased there was no real necessity for continuing this state of things, but if the lady who had been—"

And here the draft of the letter to Miss Reyburn peters out on an unfinished page.

It is easy to take instant exception to several aspects of Miss Cunningham's argument. After a six years' residence at Mount Vernon, during which time she had transferred there most of her own personal possessions to eke out inadequate household arrangements, it would not have been possible for Miss Tracy to pack up and depart overnight. And the "expense" entailed by her presence there at an often overdue salary of $400 a year was more than compensated for by the housekeeping she did and the many small expenses, like her flower seeds, that she paid out of her own funds—to say nothing of the original, basic "presence of a lady" which was believed essential to Mount Vernon's safety, and her diplomatic excursions into Alexandria and Washington to maintain it. As for any allegation that the office of secretary to either the Association or Miss Cunningham was a well-paid sinecure— it is to die laughing.

The Regent's letter to Mrs. Farnsworth, who was also present at Council, gives a glimpse into the tensions of the session itself, as she went into a hair-splitting discussion of the Minutes as Miss Tracy had had them printed. There were no regular Minutes kept, she admitted, except that Mr. Riggs had jotted down certain Resolutions, which Mrs. Farnsworth herself had suggested that Miss Tracy might prepare for circulation. "The Minutes of all meetings of the Association are usually prepared during the meeting, read and approved, and if correct ordered to be printed and circulated," Miss Cunningham reminded her. "The irregularities attendant upon our late meeting made this impossible. According to our Constitution, on the Regent is imposed the general direction and order of affairs in the interregnum of meetings. Upon the Regent therefore devolved the responsibility of seeing the Minutes were correct and properly filed and circulated. While Miss Tracy granted a favor in drawing them up, she had no authority to print or to circulate. I could not but express my surprise. She seemed to realize that the proceeding was not exactly justifiable, and said that if on inspection I was not satisfied, the circulars need not be used, as she had printed at her own expense, to avoid the trouble of writing."

Apparently Miss Tracy, accustomed to her own authority for six long years, had in the Regent's view overstepped. This too could have led to hasty words in circumstances which were already surcharged.

The paper read by the Regent in Council which Miss Tracy said took everyone by surprise was summarized by Miss Cunningham to Mrs. Farnsworth as relating to the future of Mount Vernon and the Constitutional clauses which she insisted made it evident that there had not been and was not a legal secretary of the Association—which had in its turn overstepped by appointing Miss Tracy to that post in the Regent's absence during the 1864 meeting. "I suggested on the score of economy as well as necessity that the Association discontinue the housekeeping department at Mount Vernon and return to the plan adopted by all the Vice-Regents before the war, viz., to leave the place in charge of the Superintendent only, he to maintain his own establishment," she wrote to Mrs. Farnsworth. "I stated, however, that there was official business which ought not longer to be neglected, that it could only be attended to at Mount Vernon where the papers were, and it was most convenient to procure the services of a secretary. I asked that the Vice-Regents delay putting my suggestion into operation long enough to permit me to do so."

The ladies had found a decision difficult on so unexpected a proposal, and asked the Regent by all means to remain at Mount Vernon till the next meeting, and with a reference to the neglect of her own interests at Rosemonte, she consented. "Then you, my dear Mrs. Farnsworth, suggested my making Mount Vernon my future home, which I assured you I had never thought of, and would consider anything but an attractive idea to a confirmed invalid. It would indeed be a prison life," concluded the Regent, who had thought it quite good enough for Miss Tracy so long as she was useful there.

Casting back into her relationship with Miss Tracy before the war, the Regent wrote, "I soon saw that she did not, perhaps could not, do the amount of writing a secretary ought to do, but she possessed uncommon administrative ability, and this I felt the Association needed even more than the other. In my enfeebled state, in short, I let her hold the reins a great deal more than any other secretary might ever be allowed to do, for my experience has taught me that sooner or later one suffers from obliterating the lines of official distinction. Miss Tracy, however, did not like the position even with the uncommon latitude given her, she considered it hurtful to her health as it was uncongenial to inclination, and tendered her resignation in July, 1860, having received the offer of a most agreeable and congenial situation with old friends in Louisiana. I had become attached to Miss Tracy, reposed unbounded confidence in her, and dreaded to give her up."

And so Miss Tracy had allowed herself to be caught in the coils, and her administrative ability had indeed been called upon.

"While I have felt I owe to myself to give you, my dear Mrs. Farnsworth, to whom all is owed for the result of our meeting, and which prevented me from resigning, so astounded and hurt was I at much I had to meet there, I feel it best to treat this matter as lightly as possible, otherwise Miss Tracy will never rest till she creates dissension among us," Miss Cunningham's letter continued. "At least, I fear so. To our officers cognizant of the matter I will present these extracts, and to any friend wishing to know facts, but the public will have to receive Miss Tracy's version, for I shall abide the result which comes to those who do their duty with a single eye to God.

"I have striven to introduce economies since Miss Tracy ceased to direct matters, a difficult task to perform at all times, and under all circumstances, particularly so with colored people long suffered to use things ad libitum. I would change the servants, but I find it impossible so far to get any one person even willing to come into the country, and this place is sickly as well as lonely.

"So few are our visitors that only $14 have been made since the 1st of December by entrance fee by land. Yet, my dear Mrs. Farnsworth, my courage and Mr. Herbert's have risen with extremities. We are determined to remain and do our duty under all circumstances but that of starvation, and we do not quite anticipate that. Do not, therefore, be too much distressed by Mr. Riggs's desertion, to punish me, I suppose, for refusing to be instrumental in creating a sinecure office at a salary of $600 as he wished to have done, though our treasury was empty. I am but a feeble woman, nevertheless it is not in Mr. Riggs's power, I am happy to say, to annihilate me quite, nor to injure the cause very seriously. I think both it and we will survive the ordeal of this winter, though it will not be very pleasant.

"Did you not understand Miss Tracy to say in Council soon after taking her seat by you, which she did on first entering, that she was authorized to say that Mr. Herbert would resign on certain contingencies arising? It was also whispered to me that the servants would leave if she did. I returned here after the Council expecting both contingencies. Some days later, in a conversation on matters during the war, I drew Mr. Herbert out on this point, but with no hint as to an intention on his part of resigning, and he assured me that he was too much of a gentleman ever to do so without giving timely warning. Since then I have found out he was ignorant of the statement made about him in Council. Ditto with servants. So far from leaving, there was a fear that they would be turned off. Yet the house servants do not relish the restrictions economy has provided."

The imputation of a vindictive character to either Miss Tracy or Mr. Riggs is certainly unfair in view of their past loyalty, and shows the Regent hitting out recklessly in all directions, while giving the mild-tempered Mrs. Farnsworth credit for averting an even worse crisis in Council than did occur. As long ago as the 1864 meeting, in the awkward situation created by Miss Hamilton which did not in any way involve the absent Regent, Mrs. Riggs had written Mrs. Comegys that she and her husband would not remain in the Association if Miss Tracy was interfered with, and the November 8th extract from Miss Tracy's letters to the Regent indicated the same. No one knew better than the Riggses what Miss Tracy had endured for Mount Vernon, in circumstances which the Regent had never fully appreciated, though she had more than once expressed the most affectionate gratitude in writing to Miss Tracy before 1867.

Mr. Riggs's no doubt heated defense of Miss Tracy may have
been perversely construed by Miss Cunningham as a criticism of
herself for allowing the ordeal to run on so long when the war
had ended. A guilty conscience often shortens the temper, and
when other voices joined his in taking the secretary's part, the
Regent reacted angrily in self-defense, instead of recalling that
she herself had credited Miss Tracy with doing "far more than
the duties of a secretary" and that she herself had written that
she owed a "debt of love and gratitude." To feel herself at fault
before them all, in Miss Tracy's presence, was not a thing the
high-handed Regent would easily assimilate.

Miss Tracy's servants, who had remained faithful to her through
many trials, and were always treated as friends, must have found
South Carolina ways something of a shock, when the Regent took
over. Poor Mr. Herbert's position as either pawn or pivot between
the two women was not enviable, and the fact that he elected to
remain at his post under Miss Cunningham's supervision raises
questions—such as the possibility that the five years' interval between Miss Tracy's departure from Mount Vernon and her marriage to him may have been due, at least in part, to an estrange-
ment which began at this time. And while with Miss Cunningham
there was always much talk of being a lady, a true gentleman,
which Mr. Herbert certainly was, does not point to himself as
such, and the Regent must have embroidered a little there.

"I believe you are aware," the letter to Mrs. Farnsworth went
on, "that I invited Miss Tracy to remain here as long as her
convenience required it. Of course my experience during my stay
here during the previous autumn made me confident that I should
have a very unpleasant time of it, though now she was to be the
guest and not as before the mistress of the Mansion. As guest, she
must have for her use the only carpeted room, and thus the new
secretary was delayed in coming, though her services were needed.
But I supposed she would see the delicacy and propriety of turning
over the house keys, etc., no longer in her charge—also the desk

of the Association, and all other places made especially for the arrangement of my business papers. Far from it. She ignored the change in her position, indeed my presence, as far as possible, and went on directing the domestic ménage as before, until the want of resources financially compelled a gradual change, after some weeks, and a relinquishment of control.

"It has been with the deepest pain, my dear Mrs. Farnsworth, that I have been forced to realize I have been mistaken in the opinion I had formed of Miss Tracy. When duty forces me to come to an issue with anyone, I can do it firmly and immovably, as you saw in Council, but when it does not, I will let anyone ride over me, as the saying is, rather than meet what I feel is more disagreeable to the feelings of a lady, so I gave Miss Tracy full latitude, and I had much to call forth forbearance. Nevertheless, it was exercised whenever I met Miss Tracy, which was not often as I seldom left my room. I treated her sociably and kindly as before, and when she left to take up her abode at Mr. Riggs's, I invited her kindly to visit here when mild weather permitted.

"I dare not attempt to read this over. It has been written off and on, several days and nights. I trust our severe weather invigorates you, it is very trying, this is the coldest house I was ever in, and almost impossible to keep near being comfortable. Warm, I never am, with all the fires we can make."

Yet these were the conditions, straitened by the war, which Miss Tracy had endured for six years.

Miss Cunningham had apparently lost no time in arranging for Edwina Marks to come to Mount Vernon in Miss Tracy's place, and may have had some such move in mind heretofore, having realized that Miss Tracy, entrenched as she was, might find it difficult or inconvenient to surrender instantly all authority to some one not familiar with the Mount Vernon household routine, which had evolved by trial and error under stress. A more tactful woman than the Regent would have been willing, if not glad, to profit by Miss Tracy's experience, observing her methods, and thus ensuring a smoother transition. Edwina, coming green to the post, and no doubt in awe of her surroundings and employer, could be counted on not to offer opposition to the Regent's ideas of reform and economy.

By Miss Cunningham's own account, Miss Tracy took her time about handing over the command, perhaps in an attempt to prepare the way for what threatened to become a palace revolution, and the Regent was quick to resent the delay. In Chinese calligraphy, the character for trouble shows two women under one roof-tree, and both Mount Vernon's women were strong-willed, highly-strung, and at this time very much overwrought. It must have been a truly explosive atmosphere during the month which elapsed before Miss Tracy left the house for the last time, on her way to Washington City. And when she had gone—actually gone—everyone, including the Regent, must have felt rather aghast, as though some integral part of the place had gone with her, leaving a cold draft.

Writing to Mrs. Sweat, who had been appointed to the committee on the indemnity bill in absentia, Miss Cunningham said they had $107 in the treasury for the coming winter, with coal laid in and the November bills paid—and she had got credit extended by the tradesmen till the boat receipts began again in the spring, as they could only expect their income to decrease till then. A large part of their profit before the war was from travellers going from South to North, who were now kept at home by poverty, and Washington was not the social center it had been. The land purchased from Mr. Washington was very poor, and they had only 25 acres in cultivation, and it would require a larger outlay than the Association could afford to make this profitable.

"Americans are more destructive as visitors than any other nationality," she wrote unequivocally, "so more men are needed here to watch our visitors than Mount Vernon would require if located in France or Germany. Do what we will, however, with the force we have kept, we cannot prevent clippings outside and pilferings inside, in the rooms shown to visitors. The cornices are constantly broken off, even the ivory on the keys of the celebrated harpsichord are taken off, though a man stands in that room to protect the things exhibited there. The grounds here are very extensive, buildings also, repairs needed yearly, if we wish to keep the place as General Washington left it. We have tried to do so, but this must now cease entirely unless our country gives us further patronage, and we confine ourselves to the protection of the Mansion, its immediate surroundings, etc."

At Council she had proposed retrenchment in every way, and the immediate pressing of the claim before Congress for $7000, besides an appeal to the rich men of the country for contributions. The Resolution was passed—"more from my persistency, I fear, than from the hopeful spirit of the few present, who were inclined to be depressed, as Mr. Riggs opposed all but the do-nothing and no-changing policy he advocates."

Mr. Riggs, of course, had committed the unpardonable sin—he was on Miss Tracy's side. And indeed he could hardly have been elsewhere, after sharing with that dauntless woman the alarums and excursions of the war years. Mr. Herbert's position remains an enigma.

Neither of the other two women named with Mrs. Sweat for the indemnity committee had been present at the Council. Mrs. Brooks, with whom Mrs. Sweat was already acquainted through their husbands' Washington connections, though Miss Cunningham was not—and Mrs. Morse of Louisiana, whom the Regent did know as an energetic and practical woman, and who was conveniently beginning a temporary residence in Baltimore. But Mrs. Morse was now in deep personal distress, having been suddenly reduced to poverty by the failure of some large debts owed to her husband's estate, and she could not, the Regent feared, be relied on to aid. Owing to Mr. Riggs's resignation, which the Regent in this letter attributed to "pique because the Council had not sustained his views when he had not been called upon to give

them"—her characteristic imperiousness is very evident in all this
correspondence—they could not look for his influence, or his
wife's, in the Washington political scene. "I have engaged to remain here," the Regent wrote Mrs. Sweat, "until our next meeting in October, as there was important unfinished business to
arrange which the war prevented my attending to. Miss Tracy
sent me her resignation two years ago—"

Once again the letter peters away on an unfinished page of a
first draft.

There was one small, laughable repercussion from Miss Tracy's
resignation, in the form of a comment from Mrs. Pellet at Richmond, who so far as is known never set eyes on Miss Tracy. "You
know," she wrote the Regent, as though behind her hand, "I
cannot dispossess my mind of what you wrote of Miss Tracy, that
her movements involve an *affaire de coeur!*" If such an implication
was actually made, one is left with a choice of three very respectable gentlemen for the other party, and no way to guess at Miss
Cunningham's supposed nominee—Graham, Herbert, or Riggs.

Miss Tracy's intention was to spend the rest of the winter of '68
in Washington. After that she vanishes from the record until
February, 1873, when her marriage to Upton Herbert took place
in Philadelphia. They went to live in his house in Fairfax County,
and silence again envelops her, as would have been her wish, until
March, 1886. She then replied to a letter from the Association
which was sent to inquire if she would lend or give them whatever papers she might have in her possession relative to Mount
Vernon during the Civil War, which were wanted for one of the
spasmodic attempts to compile the history of the Association
which occurred every few years. She wrote from a house called
Muckruss, on March 25th:

"My dear Mrs. Comegys—
"Your kind letter of the 19th was forwarded to me here, and
on my return yesterday from a few days in Washington I found
it awaiting me. Our house burned the Friday before Christmas!

Since then, we have made our headquarters here, at Colonel Arthur Herbert's, about three miles from Alexandria. We are making arrangements to build again, but no other home can ever be to us what that pile of ashes *was!*

"We had no insurance. The fire was, we suppose, caused by a defective flue. It occurred in the middle of one of the calmest, loveliest days of that beautiful fall. Mr. Herbert was in Washington, and his most efficient man with him. I was alone with two house servants, and a lad of eighteen. A young lady friend and neighbor had come in a half hour previous to chat a little, and was of infinite service. The fire had doubtless been smouldering for many hours, if not days. The house was old, and when the air reached the flames it burned rapidly. We saved most of our silver, private papers, and clothing, the furniture of the parlor and our bedroom on the same floor was saved. Nothing from the second story, dining-room, or kitchen, or store-room! It has been a severe blow to us, this utter obliteration of so much that was precious. The pecuniary loss was great, but there was, of course, much that money could not buy, and money cannot replace.

"There were many mercies, much to be thankful for, to silence our murmurings, but the grief will long remain. In one small trunk were placed some old family letters from my grandfather and others, to the early years of my parents' wedded life. With these I had placed many private letters from Miss Cunningham and all the memoranda I had retained of Mount Vernon. It was burned. Therefore, I must depend upon my memory for the dates you wish. I will do my best. I went to Miss Cunningham as private secretary in September, 1859. . . ."

She says in this letter that when Miss Cunningham wrote her to go to Mount Vernon and wait for her there she told her to take the title of Secretary to the Mount Vernon Association, "as it was important that I should have a show of authority." This was only what Miss Cunningham later objected that the Council of 1864 had done illegally, when at that time it had actually only confirmed her own emergency appointment, or promotion, of Miss Tracy—which she apparently wished summarily to revoke on her return to Mount Vernon. Unfortunately Miss Tracy's letter does not go into the circumstances of her resignation in 1868. It is signed SARAH C. HERBERT.

There is no evidence that she ever saw Mount Vernon again.

4

The first months of 1868 would have been dreadful at Mount Vernon. The Regent found herself in possession, but without the friend and companion she had relied on so long. And no matter what her conviction of righteousness was, or her self-imposed sense of injury, or even her grounds for disappointment in Miss Tracy, if any existed, she must have been visited by a dire feeling of loss and by belated regrets. She was of course too proud and too worked up ever to ask Miss Tracy to return on any terms at all, and even apology would have been useless against Miss Tracy's own pride and spirit. The rift between them, which must have sprung from some quite trivial beginning, was fatal and final. But as the winter-bound days passed, in the cold, comfortless house, and there was no one but the inexperienced niece Lizzie and Edwina Marks to do the endless chores of secretary-ship and housekeeping, and only Mr. Herbert remained with whom it was possible to reminisce, or who could give any information on the past seven years' events, Miss Tracy's absence would have become an aching void.

A letter from the Regent's cousin Becky Mitchell of Philadelphia, who had accompanied her on that first sally to Mount Vernon in June of 1856, mentioned that Edwina Marks had arrived by the first of the year, and that at the Regent's request Mrs. Mitchell had sent a bottle of laudanum, and other medicines, to Alexandria by express to be collected by Miss Cunningham's servant. It is probable that from now on, with everything gone awry, Miss Cunningham became increasingly dependent on the sedative drug which was in the end largely responsible for her deterioration.

In April, '68, she wrote offering the Vice-Regency for New

Jersey to Mrs. Nathaniel Halsted, wife of a wealthy Newark merchant who had risen to brigadier-general during the war. It was promptly accepted, and one of the most vigorous and helpful women the Association had ever acquired began a long career of service to Mount Vernon. There was some connection between Mrs. Halsted and Mrs. Morse, by marriage. They called each other "cousin," but there was no blood relationship, and Mrs. Halsted was already acquainted with the Association as an assistant worker under the first Vice-Regent, Miss Ogden, who had died in 1865.

Mrs. Morse had been visiting the Halsteds at their handsome house called Hillside, and she left her youngest daughter Nina there when with another girl called Rosa she went to stay at Mount Vernon as the Regent's guest in the spring of '68. Her invitation there was obviously in connection with the indemnity claim, which Miss Cunningham had nominated her to introduce into the Congressional scene. She wrote to Mrs. Halsted from Washington early in May, having just arrived there from Mount Vernon. She was acting alone, as neither Mrs. Brooks nor Mrs. Sweat found it convenient to come to Washington at that time, and she found Congress absorbed in the approaching impeachment proceedings against President Johnson, but she felt confident that "when the agony is over, there is no doubt a handsome indemnity will be allowed us. I can give my time, eloquence, and influence to the Association, but not money. Therefore my expenses here are met by the Regent for the Association, and will be well spent if I succeed, which I think I will."

The boat was now running daily, which was due in some way to Mrs. Comegys, and had increased the number of visitors, according to Mrs. Morse, to as many as eighty a day, with a profit to Mount Vernon on each of 45¢. Recognizing the futility of attempting to collect funds for Mount Vernon in the present state of the country, she nevertheless suggested that Mrs. Halsted might get "McCormick the reaper man" to donate a mower for the extensive lawns at Mount Vernon, and a patent rake for the gravel paths. And she also requested letters of introduction to the Senators and Congressmen from New Jersey.

Writing again to Mrs. Halsted at the end of May, she said that if the Regent got the price for her cotton she expected to, she was anxious to spend a month or two at Cape May, and had asked Mrs. Morse to fill her place at Mount Vernon during her absence —and as she would take her secretary with her, there would be room for the Morse daughters to join their mother at that time. The Regent was preparing a new and very eloquent appeal for contributions. "She is a wonderfully talented little woman," wrote Mrs. Morse, "and will be a historical character."

Repairs to the roof, which was leaking again, were urgent.

There is some mystery about what happened next, but Mrs. Morse apparently accomplished nothing and got discouraged, or simply left Washington, without warning or explanation, and returned to Maryland on her private affairs, so that in June Miss Cunningham wrote to Mrs. Comegys: "If Mrs. Morse deserts her post, I shall have to go to Washington because the Members are quarrelling so, and the Rads are in such a stew about their politics that our bill will not be thought about without a lady there to urge its introduction. I have my hands full here, and ought not to have this put upon me."

But there it was, and July found her again in Washington, accompanied by Miss Marks. This last superb rally of the Regent's can be reconstructed by piecing together her letters to Mrs. Comegys and Mrs. Chace, when she had once more, almost single-handed, saved Mount Vernon.

She was now fifty-two, frail, fading, always ill, with a bad habit of dosing herself pitilessly for every symptom. She was almost alone in the world, except for an aged, complaining mother, a brother broken in health, and some young nieces and nephews, the family fortunes hopelessly damaged by the war and emancipation. She was dressed in cleverly contrived remnants and leftovers, her passé wardrobe a constant exacerbation to the pride and vanity of a woman once accustomed to the best, and to the admiration and indulgence of any gentleman she chose to charm. Her acquaintance in Washington, even in the old days, was small, and her former supporters there were scattered or alienated. The reputation of the Association had suffered, not only by sectional feeling but by the uncalled-for and unaccountable hostility in the press, and by unfounded, malicious rumor. The odds against her were astronomical. Somewhere she found the courage and the physical strength to undertake another fight.

Mr. Brooks of New York belonged to the wrong party, Mr. Blaine of Maine was "absorbed in party wire-pulling." Mrs. Morse before her abrupt departure from Washington had enlisted General Schenck of Ohio, a Yankee veteran of Bull's Run and Gettysburg who had entered Congress, and he had got the bill out of the Court of Claims and into the Committee of the Whole, where one ill-disposed opponent could with an objection hold it up indefinitely. This was being done by Elihu Washburne, known as "the watch-dog of the Treasury," whose particular hobby seemed to be a violent opposition to subsidies, appropriations, and what he called "logrolling" grants for public buildings, railroads, etc. Meanwhile, the early adjournment of Congress was announced, and "friends of the cause" urged Miss Cunningham to make a personal appearance at the Capitol. Perhaps animated by the example of Mrs. Ritchie at Richmond a dozen years before, she gathered her forces for the effort.

"I came," she wrote Mrs. Chace, "and though I had not for twenty years dared to walk up such a long flight of steps as those connected with the Capitol, I ventured—as I took restoratives with me. After they had revived me, and I had rested in the Speaker's Chamber, to which I had been especially invited, I sought an interview first with the Speaker and then with our able friend, General Schenck. The Speaker promised all his aid and zeal in the cause, as did General Schenck, but he frankly told me that our bill was lost for this season, though it had a decided majority in the House, as he had no time to overcome or wear out the vigilance of Mr. Washburne and others, who for the short period left could keep it down every successive Monday. He said there was but one hope left for us, to get it entered in the Senate and passed. That done, it returned to the House to be put on the Speaker's table, from whence it would come before the House. All would be safe, he would pledge himself to carry it through. I had left Mount Vernon with the expectation of simply spurring up General Schenck. You can imagine what I felt at this revelation. I who had been frightened at attempting that flight of steps *once!*

"I was almost an entire stranger in Washington, knew but one member of Congress—him slightly—Mr. Phelps of Maryland, the son of Almira Lincoln Phelps, the authoress. He was with me. After a few moments of utter dismay, I saw my duty very plainly, and giving an appealing look to Mr. Phelps, I said, If you will assist me to reach the Senate side and will promise to remain with me and bring out Senators to me, I will go now!

"Mr. Phelps conducted me to the beautiful Marble Chamber. I saw several senators, finally the Hon. Reverdy Johnson of Maryland. A few moments' conversation only were needed with him. He offered to take charge of our claim, and see it through the Senate. He thought that for so worthy a purpose as ours, the Senate would dispense with the delay of sending it to a committee and put the bill upon its passage at once. He tried to get this done, but failed. The bill was sent to the Committee of Claims, and Thursday July 2d, appointed for it to come up for discussion. I promised Mr. Johnson to be present, and returned to Mount Vernon.

"I came up Wednesday with my escort, Mr. Phelps, to whom by the way we owe more than to any other, if we triumph over all trials it will be because he helped me when no one else did. I appeared up to time in the Senate Reception Room, and sent in my card to Mr. Howe—senator from Wisconsin and chairman of our committee. He came to inform me that when they had called for the Mount Vernon bill a short time before, it was missing. The clerk had either lost or mislaid it. If not found in time, ere the morning hour expired, another bill would have to be drawn up and introduced and referred to the committee again. When Mr. Howe left me, Mr. Phelps exclaimed, 'This is too bad —your devotion to Mount Vernon seems destined to be tried to the utmost. I think I can help you and I will. Wait here till I return.' He went into the Senate, sat down by Mr. Johnson who is almost blind, drew up another bill and placed it in his hands, and had barely time to tell me to go to the gallery ere he was sent for to vote in the House. I mention all these particulars because I think our officers should know all things as they transpired, and what friends we had, and what they did for us.

"My secretary and I went into the gallery. I saw Mr. Johnson, paper in hand, standing to catch the eye of the President. Soon the paper went to the clerk's desk, thence to Mr. Howe. Seeing no more was to be done with it, I went to the Reception Room, to see Mr. Phelps and ask his opinion. He told me to come back in the morning, no doubt all would work well now. I returned to Willard's, and instead of resting, wrote some letters."

From here on, the story becomes an almost unbelievable mixture of melodrama and comedy. When she returned to the Capitol the following morning and sent in her card to Mr. Howe, he came out with a grave face, and told her that the bill was lost— not mislaid this time, but would fail of presentation. "How is that possible?" Miss Cunningham demanded. "You promised me to ask the courtesy of the Senate. Have they refused it to the memory of Washington?" No, said Mr. Howe, but to get it into the Senate without delay it was necessary that some members of his committee should ask him to introduce the bill "without further reconsideration." Those he had requested to do this had refused, and he could do nothing more.

"As he said this he looked into my face, which must have looked volumes, and a flash came over his, and he said, 'But *you* could do it—they will not refuse *you,* as they did *me!* If you can get three to make this request, I can act.' I couldn't help laughing at the turn things had taken. 'So,' I said, 'you wish me to diplomatize! Very well, I am ready. Tell me what to do!' He explained that he needed as many as three members of the committee to put the question named above to him, or rather to empower him to act. Miss Marks wrote down the names on the committee who he thought it was best to take first.

"I chose three—Willey of Virginia, Garrett Davis of Kentucky, Frelinghuysen of New Jersey—at a venture. Fortunately a neighbor of his touched him as he was leaving us and took him off to a sofa to have a chat, so he was at hand while I marshalled up the names of the committee.

"I sent first for Willey of Virginia, a most sleepy, die-away looking man, he seemed to need a dose from my hartshorn vial, but I soon stirred him, to the amusement of Miss Marks. He soon said, 'I'll do whatever you wish.' So I led him over, and said, 'Senator Howe, here is my first captive!' In the midst of smiles from all round, he went through the request to the chairman—Mr. Howe has plenty of mild fun in him—and I then sent in two cards, to Senator Davis and Frelinghuysen. The former came first, an odd-looking person, but in less than two minutes he said, 'Without explanation, I am ready to do as you wish.' I could scarcely keep from laughing, as I replied, 'This is just what I expected from Kentucky chivalry!' So I led him up, saying, 'Senator, here is captive Number Two! He yielded ere I said Deliver!' All enjoyed the joke. Mr. Howe declared that he and Senator Davis were too tender-hearted, that they were being captives all the time. Then Senator Frelinghuysen, a true gentleman, joined us—he avowed himself Captive Number Three, and then turned to Mr. Howe, remarking, 'Don't introduce the bill today, it is a bad time. Let it come up on Monday, first thing.' And he urged me to make sure that Senator Johnson was in his seat to respond to it."

Reverdy Johnson had recently been appointed Minister to the
Court of St. James's, and these were his final days in the Senate,
and she had noticed that he was often called out, and felt that
it was not safe to rely on him. She sent for a Mr. Sherman, who
wasn't in. And then, surprisingly, she tried for Sumner of Massachusetts—that humorless Harvard man, as tall as Lincoln, who
in 1856 had been beaten senseless in the Senate Chamber by a
representative from South Carolina, in retaliation for Sumner's
censure of his relative Senator Butler of that State. After four
years nearly incapacitated, Sumner had resumed his seat, and in
June, 1860, delivered a thundering speech on The Barbarism of
Slavery, and thereafter opposed any compromise as secession began. His influence now was tremendous, and somehow Miss
Cunningham knew it. Too much can hardly be made of this
triumphant last-ditch revival of the energy, the instinctive shrewd-
ness, and that irresistible something which had once captivated
Everett and John A. and the diverse women who called her
"chief." All the intervening years of tragedy and sickness and
despair were miraculously rolled back and, however briefly, the
Regent was herself again, a fragile, bewitching little woman so
alight with shining purpose that not even the short-tempered
fag-end of an irritable Congress was proof against her.

"I writhed under the necessity of sending for Sumner, but I
did it, and did not hold back my hand when he held out his," her
letter to Mrs. Chace continued. "Whether the touch of a South
Carolinian had some charm in the triumph of the thing I know
not, but he was charming! He told me he had the greatest interest
in the success of the effort, that he was always in his seat, and
would stand ready to respond and speak, but he would frankly
tell me that just now Reverdy Johnson was the man to disarm all
opposition. It was true that he was not keeping the run of the
business of the Senate, but was like a man preparing to die—i.e.,
making more preparation for the new world he was about to
enter than the one he was leaving. But the fact of his leaving the

Senate made him all powerful. He had only in his eloquent words to remind the Senate that this was the last favor he would ask from them, to carry all before him. Sumner urged that I go to see Mr. Johnson—though I told him *he* was regarded as the most influential man in the Senate.

"This was Friday, the 3rd of July. On Saturday I was so prostrated I could not raise my head, and passed the day in a dark room. Sunday intermittent fever came on. Still I went to the Senate on Monday, feeling ill. Was so late I only heard the remarks of Sumner and Frelinghuysen, and did not know till I saw the evening paper of the abusive controversy carried on by Senator Morrill of Vermont and others, uttering much that was as unjust as incorrect, arising from the supposition that the hottest secessionists had had charge of Mount Vernon during the war. The morning hour closed, before a vote was taken.

"Tuesday I was ill, but felt I must see Mr. Howe and give him the necessary information to enable him to reply to Mr. Morrill, so with the fever on me I went to the Capitol. It was well I did. Our bill would have been lost but for this! Our Senators were as ignorant of our Association whose deeds had filled the newspapers but a few years before as if America had not been the scene of our actions! I narrated all our history to Mr. Howe, explained our organization, showed him the charter, explained our constitution as drawn up by the ever to be lamented James Petigru, and informed him of the amount of money raised and how disbursed. I left the Senate Reception Room in a high fever, and I threw up till near midnight. About 10 P.M. Mr. Johnson left word for me at Willard's that our bill was fixed to come up Thursday, his last day in the Senate, and would pass! I knew by this that Senator Howe had fulfilled his promise to use promptly the information which had afforded him so much satisfaction.

"On Wednesday I was not needed at the Capitol and thankfully remained in bed, three fevers not having added to my physical strength. I drew up a paper for the use of Senator Johnson, in the event of not being able to see him, as a basis of reply in defence of our Association and of the residents at Mount Vernon during the war, from a most unjustifiable attack on them. I had damp chills and fever up to Thursday, and went to the Capitol with a shaking chill! I reclined on a sofa, but in such a manner as not to attract attention, and after the chill passed off I sent for Mr. Sumner (not finding Mr. Johnson) placed my paper in his hands, and received his promise to use it if debate permitted. He seemed so surprised to find that I had come to attend to the interests of our Association with a fever on me!— a species of patriotism which members of Congress do not often behold. No marvel, therefore, that he who is considered so brusque and rough generally to applicants, should have been so exceedingly gentle and courteous as I found him!

"I bore up through four long hours, and then returned to my room, rejoicing in the hope that victory was ours. The bill came up at the last moment, and as Mr. Johnson intimated that it was his last effort, on consideration of there being no debate the bill passed, without dissent!

"Think of such a triumph, we had no friends for our cause, and no party, and business is being pressed forward fearfully, yet in spite of all, it only took four days from the time it was taken up till the final vote! My friends say I ought to be very much elated. I do feel very proud that there was yet enough power in Washington's memory to make this feat accomplished in a time of intense political excitement.

"We have now to wait on the House. We have warm friends there, and in pity to me there have been several efforts made to get the bill up before its turn. I pleaded with General Schenck to do his utmost to encompass this, for my business is seriously interrupted, and the friends of the bill urge me not to leave till all is safe. After so many hairbreadth escapes, this seems prudent as the Clerk of the House may not be more careful than he of the Senate! General Schenck tried yesterday to get the rules suspended, but he told me it was hopeless unless the irrepressible

Washburne would be absent long enough to give him a chance to spring it on the House."

The opposition was successful. The bill did not pass the House in that session, and would require further strategy from the Regent early in '69.

5

She returned to Mount Vernon in hot weather which prostrated Miss Marks while the Regent was swathed in three shawls and shivering with chills. Her physician protested against her intention to live in the malarious Potomac atmosphere, but she felt too poor to travel.

She hoped for a visit from Mrs. Halsted, whom she had not yet met, and in a letter written late in July made a revealing reference to Mrs. Morse, whose erratic temperament had become apparent. "There is one subject I wish to discuss privately with General Halsted and yourself, and I will not venture to allude to it here, further than to say that while I am not angry with Mrs. Morse as you fear, her course towards me for months has been so unaccountable that it cannot be excusable except it arises from individual or family idiosyncrasy. Has there ever been anything peculiar in her family? If so, I must pass over what I have had to suffer, officially and individually, for some months past. From what I have observed, I think her daughters are better situated in the convents than they would be in any other arrangement their mother would make."

Possibly the supposed invitation to represent the Regent during her absence from Mount Vernon existed only in Mrs. Morse's imagination, for there is later evidence of her possessive attitude and her insistence on her prerogatives as Vice-Regent. She had tried to draw Mrs. Mitchell into her net, and the Vice-Regent for Wisconsin wrote from Newport during this summer suggesting, in all innocence of friction or intrigue, that they might dispense with a Superintendent "and get a gentlewoman, a widow, with her family to live at Mount Vernon, acting as our secretary and treasurer, a woman like Mrs. Morse, for instance, she could supervise the whole thing." This solution had obviously been proposed to her by the candidate for the post, as Mrs. Mitchell mentioned having had a letter from her, and asked if she was still at Mount Vernon, and inquired how the Regent got along with Mr. Herbert. "Your health will not permit you to remain long at Mount Vernon and you should not," Mrs. Mitchell wrote. "Neither are frequent meetings needed. Nearly all matters could be arranged by letters. If any of the ladies of the Association are in Washington they should consult with the resident officer and communicate with the Vice-Regents their own impression of affairs. The less machinery the better. But by all means do not let us neglect to hold together and keep the peace. I fear Government chances are not good, and I only hope there will be a change before election. I dread to see Grant in the White House! They think my husband will be elected, a small office, but if Government is defeated Washington will not be very agreeable to me." She had seen in the papers that the application for indemnity had been made to Congress "and the silly reception it received from men who should be above such petty twaddle."

In September, '68, Miss Cunningham, accompanied by Miss Marks, fled to Cape May after all, having been very ill since her return to Mount Vernon from Washington. From the Cape she wrote to Mrs. Halsted that her prolonged absence and disability had left an overwhelming amount of work to be accomplished before the autumn Council, which was called for November 17th at Mount Vernon. "Here they can see and learn for themselves what is needed," she wrote Mrs. Halsted, "and by being thrown together socially and without limit as to time, will not only be able to become well acquainted, but can consult and confer more advantageously. I suggested to each lady to put a knife, fork, and spoon and a change of towels and napkins in their trunk. As you are one of the nearest, let me suggest to add a blanket or anything you desire for your special comfort, for this is a cold house and all the fires in it will not make it like a furnace-warmed house as yours no doubt is. Our Mount Vernon boat will be at its landing a little after four o'clock the 16th, to bring the officers down here the afternoon before."

Her wisdom for Mount Vernon never failed her, however unwise she might be in personal relationships. The Council still meets annually at Mount Vernon, where the Vice-Regents can see and learn and get acquainted, as would not have been possible under Mrs. Mitchell's recommendation.

Miss Marks was now in better health and had agreed to remain at her post until after the Regent had got through "what you so aptly call dead issues, which though they are dead will call for long and tedious labor on my part." News of conditions in the South continued to be so alarming that she was advised not to return to Rosemonte during the coming winter, "where I could not live a day, nor lie down any night with a feeling of safety. With my heart affection, the life there would kill me."

Mrs. Morse also wrote to Mrs. Halsted about the November Council, which was the first during which the Vice-Regents would remain at Mount Vernon overnight, and she took it upon herself to invite General Halsted too, which later had to be vetoed by the Regent because if one husband came, they would have to invite them all, to avoid ill-feeling. What she didn't say was that to have gentlemen in the house in the circumstances would have caused considerable complication. Mrs. Morse furthermore instructed Mrs. Halsted as to the finances of the Association, the question of whether they should withdraw their application for redress from Congress—for some of the ladies, including herself and Mrs. Mitchell, objected to the terms on which it was to be granted—and indicated the names she wanted placed on the committees, and her own ideas as to how the money should be spent. She had engaged a room on the parlor floor at Willard's for the Halsteds, and would meet them at the depot and spend the evening with them, meeting the other Vice-Regents as they assembled at the hotel, "to cultivate an esprit de corps"—with which, apparently, to confront and dominate the Regent the following day at Mount Vernon. Mrs. Mitchell at the last minute found it impossible to attend, and, still ignorant that the busy Mrs. Morse was riding for a fall, had sent her proxy to her.

A few days later Mrs. Mitchell caught up with things, and was writing to the Regent—"How true it is that we must have familiar intercourse with people to know them thoroughly! I was terribly shocked when I read your letter this morning, for I supposed Mrs. Morse was the salt of the earth and that you had unbounded confidence in her. I am fearfully sorry to lose my good opinion of Mrs. M. We can as you say keep this to ourselves and not allow her to get any hold on the Association." The Mitchells were going abroad—"D.V."—and hoped to see Mrs. Ritchie in Italy. "Our plans are not made for travel on the Continent, but we shall go at once to London, from there to Scotland, and spend the remainder of the winter in the South of Europe. My husband was not elected, and I am so glad to have him to myself as I shall in going to Europe, I sometimes think this is such a blessing I shall not be permitted to enjoy it. I wish you knew my husband—maybe you will sometime." She was, as Mrs. Riggs had once said, "a mighty nice person."

There were two new faces at the 1868 Council—the Regent's old friend Mrs. Eve of Georgia, now residing with her married daughter in Brooklyn, who was attending for the first time, and Mrs. Halsted. Faithful Mrs. Comegys, Mrs. Chace, Mrs. Farnsworth, and Mrs. Morse made six. Once again, it was too late in the year for good attendance.

Writing her Reminiscences some years later, Mrs. Eve called it "a cosy little Council" with some unpleasant work to do. There were the objections, strongly voiced by herself, to the terms of the proposed grant from Congress, and she offered a Resolution "that we indignantly refuse this paltry sum, with its insulting qualification that it be expended by an agent appointed by Congress for that purpose, as if the women who had collected and paid out $200,000 and the interest thereon while it was being gathered could not be trusted." To everyone's surprise, "Mrs. Comegys said in a deep, distinct tone, 'I agree with Mrs. Eve, and

second the Resolution.'" But they were met by urgent entreaties
to withdraw it without even a vote. "Mrs. Farnsworth, the wise
woman of Michigan, and Mrs. Chace both spoke earnestly of the
disastrous effect which such a course would produce," Mrs. Eve
admitted. "Miss Cunningham was appalled. She had no idea that
such a mine would be sprung."

As Mrs. Eve had arrived at Mount Vernon, escorted from Washington by Miss Marks, in advance of the other ladies at the request
of the Regent, and had had time to rewrite and condense the
Regent's too prolix Address, it seems odd that she saw fit to
"spring" her Resolution at Council. And it is possible that the
known resignation of Mr. Riggs as Treasurer might have had
some bearing on the implied doubt of the Association's ability
to administer the funds. Feeling that she had backed down, and
still convinced at the time of writing that the Congressional
stipulations were an unmerited insult, Mrs. Eve did not insist
that her Resolution be acted on, and it was recorded only.

While in Washington the previous summer the Regent had met
General Michler, Superintendent of Public Buildings, who would
be in charge of the Mount Vernon operations—provided the
House passed the bill—and she assured the Council that he had
said he would place himself under the orders of the Association.
He had also explained that as he was working on the Potomac
forts he could use the same Government tug to transport materials to Mount Vernon free of cost, which would increase the
value of the grant. This proved to be only a temporary gallantry,
rendered no doubt to the Regent's bright eyes at their first meeting, because Mrs. Eve recorded that he later curtly refused to
show his bills or accounts, on the grounds that it was none of
their business, and his workmen tramped about the place pur-
suing their own course without regard to the Association's wishes,
until the money was suddenly all spent, with what the ladies considered not enough to show for it.

A grievous decision of this '68 Council was that their finances
were too low to afford any longer the salary of a Superintendent.

They already owed Mr. Herbert $3000, which he was not pressing for, but which they now voted to be paid. Their logic in then dismissing him, effective the first of the year, seems questionable. If the move to eliminate him began with the Regent there is a possibility that she found his continued presence there uncomfortable, even if there was no implied censure with regard to Miss Tracy. He belonged to the old régime, and she was now in full charge. It may have been necessary to her peace of mind to make a clean sweep, and demonstrate that she could run the place herself, with only a mere gardener to assist, at a much lower salary. There had already been some discussion in the correspondence of reducing the resident staff to a less expensive type of person than Mr. Herbert.

Mrs. Eve was delegated to break the news to him, and she described the interview as "painful." Mr. Herbert had been at Mount Vernon since 1859, to the exclusion of all other interests. He was now nearing fifty, and had no other occupation. From time to time he had transferred most of the furnishings of his house near Fairfax Courthouse to Mount Vernon, further to the comfort of Mount Vernon's occupants, and now, like Miss Tracy, he found himself obliged to uproot on a few weeks' notice. Whatever the state of armed neutrality between himself and the Regent, it would have been a blow. And he had never cared about the money.

The Association, or the Regent, would seem to have overreached themselves. More than half the furniture in the house, even to crockery, would depart with Mr. Herbert. It was Mrs. Halsted, the freshman Vice-Regent, who made the constructive suggestion that the old thirteen States, which included her own, should now furnish the Mansion suitably to the Washington period, by contribution, and said that if New Jersey were given a specific room and it could be done in blue, she would undertake it at once. This was an idea which grew and bore fruit. Of all the Vice-Regents, most of them women of considerable means, Mrs. Halsted was the first to whom it seemed to occur to spend substantial sums of her own money for the embellishment of Mount Vernon.

Although Mrs. Brooks of New York had been unable to attend, owing to the illness of her mother, she was appointed to the committee on furnishing. Mrs. Eve, and Mrs. Halsted, who was nearby at Newark, were to act with her in the project to buy at wholesale prices from well-disposed merchants.

Mrs. Morse was not mentioned at all in Mrs. Eve's manuscript reminiscences, even in connection with the Resolution against the indemnity bill, which she would have supported. But in the Minutes it is recorded that she presented a claim for a hotel account and travelling expenses in connection with her efforts for the indemnity, which were so abruptly broken off—it had been her understanding at the time that these would be paid, and after some discussion it was so voted, with the proviso that no precedent was thus established. Considerable rancor now existed, from this cause as well as others, for Mrs. Halsted in her own brief record of the 1868 proceedings set down one ungarnished sentence which leaves room for much speculation. "Mrs. Morse, Vice-Regent for Louisiana, was expelled from membership in the Association, because of a threatened attack on the Regent," she wrote. By the evidence, it had very little effect on Mrs. Morse, who seems to have ignored it until 1870, when it came up again.

Another financier, Henry D. Cooke, was appointed Treasurer in Mr. Riggs's place. Mrs. Chace moved that the Regent should continue to reside at Mount Vernon during 1869, which was the unanimous wish of Council, with an allowance of $150 a month for household expenses, and travelling expenses to leave Mount Vernon during "the sickly season" if desired, and $400 a year for a private secretary. The dean of the colored servants, Nathan, a most reliable man, was given a raise to $20 a month during the summer months, when extra duties fell on him. The house was to be insured, and the indemnity claim would be continued before the House during the spring session of '69.

Mrs. Eve, tried and true in her nebulous relationship to the Regent, and calling everybody "dearie," remained at Mount Vernon a fortnight after Council adjourned, and Miss Marks's parents arrived about this time to spend the winter there and assist with the arrangement of the Regent's papers. Edwina accompanied Mrs. Eve to Dover on a visit to Mrs. Comegys, and thence to the Halsteds at Hillside, near Newark.

Before the end of the month Miss Cunningham was writing to Mrs. Halsted to ask that the General lend his knowledge of markets, auctions, etc. to the purchase of a new cooking-stove, among other things. "We need crockery for the table, a hanging glass for the parlor, as the one now here is Mr. Herbert's, a set of bedroom furniture entire, besides sheets and towels, blankets, curtains, and shades for the windows, etc. The windows of this open cold house need curtains in every room, and this article brings less at auction than any other."

In the middle of this letter the boat arrived, bringing "dear Mrs. Farnsworth"—the affectionate adjective adheres to her in everybody's letters—and a party of her friends wishing to make the Regent's acquaintance and offer encouragement to the cause. "I was in my working dress," added Miss Cunningham, "pen in hand and surrounded with papers, and there was nothing for it but to put on company attire and give myself up to company till the boat carried them all off, our excellent and venerated Mrs. Farnsworth too."

She had decided to give New Jersey the "Lafayette Room," associated with the hero's visits to Mount Vernon, and occupied by Mr. Herbert during his entire residence there, hence soon to be destitute of furniture. "Mr. Herbert will begin to remove his furniture as soon as the boat can run, to avoid the risk of trouble and expense by land," Miss Cunningham wrote Mrs. Halsted. "Should the River freeze up again, we will be in straits indeed, with no table to eat off of, not a vegetable dish in our scanty amount of crockery, and no bed for Miss Marks when she returns.

The Association will have to take pity on me, and supply my room with a single bed and soft spring mattress. I do suffer from the hard beds we have here."

In December, '68, there was another scurrilous newspaper attack on Mount Vernon, which accused Miss Cunningham of "living on and by the Association, as an idle and penniless representative of a Southern family," etc. This brought her a letter from Mme. Berghmans, formerly Lily Macalester, Vice-Regent for Pennsylvania, who had recently returned to Washington with her Belgian husband, reassigned to his Washington post. The Regent spent the day writing for her a detailed account of Mount Vernon affairs since 1860. Mme. Berghmans' discretion did not permit this letter to survive, though in defence of the Regent she made a portion of it public, to Miss Cunningham's distress. The Regent laid the misrepresentations to Mrs. Morse, if not to Miss Tracy, but there had been adverse publicity long before now, as Miss Tracy herself could bear witness. This time it was fortunate, in that it brought Mme. Berghmans back into contact with the Association, with her personal prestige and Washington influence enlisted against the instigators of the rumors.

Christmas, 1868, found the Regent confined to bed from fatigue and exposure incurred, she alleged, because of the frequent absences of Mr. Herbert on his own affairs. Her mother was pleading for her return to Rosemonte, and she was too ill to contemplate the journey. Mrs. Halsted was trying to find a suitable woman to release Miss Marks from her secretarial duties, but the Regent was reluctant to take anyone in middle age. "In justice to her, the unattractive side of the shield must be presented," she wrote, "to prevent being dissatisfied after acceptance. This is anything but a comfortable house, in winter especially. We are nine miles from a church, a clergyman, physician, post office, and market. A stranger like myself coming to live here must make up their minds to the sameness of life imposed by never having a friend to visit, or a friend's house to procure a little variety from—all this without a library to afford mental food and companionship. My life of long confinement to a sick chamber fits me to meet this, but my nieces when here, and the Marks family, have felt these things so much, and at times seemed as though they could not bear up any longer under the monotony. There is a carriage to take persons to church, if they don't object to the ride."

Thus ended the eventful year of 1868.

6

1869 was to pass without a Council being called, but that is not to say that history was not made, as vigorous new blood among the Vice-Regents had its tonic effect, and—in the summer—the expenditure of the Government grant began. The Regent seems now to have found the childless Mrs. Halsted a more responsive correspondent than the enigmatic Mrs. Comegys on whom she had leaned so long, and whose happy domesticity absorbed so much of her time and thought, so that from now on Miss Cunningham's almost daily letters to the Vice-Regent for New Jersey provide a running chronicle of enormous interest.

She began the year with the worst neuralgia in ten, her head wrapped in woollen. The boat was laid up for repairs, and they were dependent on Robert and his wagon for supplies and mail. They were working on the gardener's house, "to make it habitable, I will not say comfortable," for the man who would, after a fashion, replace Mr. Herbert.

By mid-January this exceptional fellow named Craig was engaged—thirty-five and unmarried, though he had a girl in England. He had had some previous experience at the White House, and he proved to be a treasure, until after two years of the Mount Vernon climate failing health compelled him to take a job in the mountains. "Depend upon it, there will be no more sloth here," the Regent wrote enthusiastically to Mrs. Halsted, soon after his arrival.

The Minutes scribbled by Miss Marks during the 1868 Council were finally arranged to the Regent's satisfaction, and Dr. Marks was set to making the copies to be sent out to the Vice-Regents. Even Mrs. Marks was pressed into service for letter-writing, while her daughter was away with Mrs. Eve, and the search for a suitable secretary went on.

The "magnificent gift" of a new cooking-stove arrived with a variety of fixtures, which Miss Cunningham listed with delight to Mrs. Halsted, who had chosen them—two kettles, a boiler, dripping-pan, griddle, frying-pan, dipper, two baking-pans, three pots, etc.

Mr. Sykes, who now ran Willard's Hotel and the Mount Vernon boat, came down himself with a load of contributions and purchases collected and shipped from New York in his care by the committee on furnishings, of which Mrs. Halsted was the most active member, and there was Christmas in January at Mount Vernon.

"We have the bedroom furnished," wrote Miss Cunningham in childlike excitement and went on to count her blessings—"the dining-table, crockery, clock, blankets (they are so cheap I wish I had said three pair instead of two) cloth for the Association table-cloths and towels, tools for the garden, in short, we are quite rich. Mr. Sykes thinks you have procured bargains, he has just returned from New York where he went to buy new furniture for his hotel, and he declared he couldn't get such a nice set of cottage furniture under $50–60. Chairs ditto. The Association has reason indeed to be grateful to your influence and exertion. I was sick, but felt I must leave my room to look after our treasures. I had my bed down in a trice and the new bed up, for I intended not to let the night pass without the comfort of a soft spring bed. Pray accept my thanks for all, as well as that of all the Vice-Regents who feel so pleased at your success. Enclosed is a note of thanks for the enameled cloth. Mr. Craig measured the ambulance, and he thinks there is a great deal more cloth than will be needed for it, so we may abound in table-covers. [This was the old army ambulance purchased for $34 by Miss Tracy early in '66 to carry infirm visitors up the steep slope from the wharf to the Mansion, and to convey guests to church on Sunday, and it was in need of a new top.]

"You mention the little glass, a gift, which could be used in any bedroom," the letter went on. "None came, save the glass to the bureau for the oak set of furniture. We ought to make our parlor as presentable as possible, what say to securing a glass in a nice frame large enough to look well—the space between the windows is one yard and ten inches. I am so glad you bought so many chairs. The most of what we had had become broken, or so loose they are not comfortable, and though I had all mended they will not stay mended, it seems.

"The white girl I have is already at work sewing. Towels are now fringed and brushed and ready for use. We were so destitute that I used dispatch. The quality is excellent and I hope they will last. A lot of new hucks bought a year ago are in ribbons now. The quilt you spoke of as a gift did not come. I will have to put the dark table sent by the fireside in the parlor, and would be so grateful for a nice cover (woollen) for it. The carpet is red and oak.

"My plan is to go to Washington as soon as Miss Marks returns, and I can get a little fixed up, to see about starting our claim in the House. If I could get General Schenck to pay a visit here, and stay over Sunday, and General G's brother-in-law, I think we could push the bill forward, and that is the reason I am so anxious for the table-cover and the glass, if we can get one on reasonable terms. I must get better, however, before I dare expose myself again, as spleen and liver are both disordered, and a course of calomel is a necessity."

The Regent's 1869 campaign to get the indemnity bill through the House was almost as hairbreadth an affair as with the Senate the year before. "I am here leading a forlorn hope," she wrote Mrs. Halsted on February 27th. She had had the support of "dear Mrs. Farnsworth" at the beginning, but thinking all would be well the Farnsworths left Washington. The bill was blocked

again by Mr. Washburne, and there were two tie votes. The
strategy suggested by Mr. Brooks of New York was to get the
bill attached to an important Senate bill, so the House would not
attempt to defeat the whole thing for one undesirable item. She
got hold of Sumner again, and Howe and Frelinghuysen, and
best of all she resumed her friendship with Lily Macalester Berghmans, who would soon return to her neglected Vice-Regency for
Pennsylvania. The Senate stood by her, and she got the money.
To disarm the enemy, she and Mrs. Brooks acquiesced that it
should be disbursed by General Michler, who would be in charge
of the work.

She returned to Mount Vernon to find the Marks family overwhelmed with distress. "Barhamville, the palatial home which
cost a fortune to build, and for which they had an offer in New
York of $20,000, which they intended to accept, is burnt to the
ground," she wrote Mrs. Halsted. "They bear it beautifully, but
for all that it may kill these old people. They idolize their daughter, and thought the property would enable them to die with the
surety that she was provided for. Now they know that with her
delicate health she must labor for her and their support. It will
go very hard with them. I am in despair about a secretary, as
Miss Marks intends to remove her parents to a more cheerful
residence, fearing the loneliness on their spirits, and I have no one
to stay with me."

Only a week later the Markses had gone, and except for Craig
and the colored servants she was actually alone at Mount Vernon.
Alone and ill. Sarah, the dependable Nathan's dependable wife,
was also ill, and the Regent wrote Mrs. Halsted; "I had had
mostly to wait on myself, meet all the duties arising from the
great crowds, and with former fatigue and a fearful cold result-
ing from being tempted out into the mild air and warm sunshine
of yesterday."

Mrs. Eve had proposed that the Marks family should take up
permanent residence at Mount Vernon, and the Regent's reply to
that was caustic. "Its members revolve around the father, who

after passing eighty years under the influence of impulses, cannot now be governed solely by reason and prudence. These lessons he'll never learn. The solitude, monotony, and absence of books here affected him so that twenty times in the past year he was on the eve of leaving, and his family found it very difficult to restrain him. Now he declared that his reason would go unless he could be removed to a situation where there could be something to divert or occupy his mind. We did fear loss of life or reason, so completely did he give way to it. The family dared not show depression, for fear of its effect on him. I urged their staying. I hope to hear today of a companion. I do not feel solitude, I am used to it, but I do need assistance."

Even against her strong will, her thoughts must have turned back to Miss Tracy and Mary McMakin—not strangers, not old and selfish, but capable, cheerful, and fond of her. And a sense of loss, a backwash of regret, was inevitable. What had gone wrong? How had it happened? Too late now, for mending. She had let even Mr. Herbert escape. "Bear in mind," she wrote Mrs. Halsted before their promised visit to Mount Vernon early in April, "that Mr. Herbert owned half and more that was in the house, and it shows the loss of his things."

She acquired a companion and secretary pro tem, who would stay until she could get a place as a Treasury clerk—the goal of many self-supporting women now—or until Miss Cunningham could make a permanent arrangement with someone else. Where Miss Finney came from is not known, but "It is well I have such an affectionate and gentle one with me, though she is too kind for the cares and responsibilities here," wrote the Regent.

General Michler came down to inspect the place, and remarked helpfully that he needed four times $7000 to do all that was waiting to be done. Because of the quantity of good bricks the Association owned, he decided to rebuild the greenhouse, and with the happy prospect of raising grapes to sell as well as flowers, the Regent failed to realize at the time that the Mansion repair work should have been done first.

The Halsteds' visit did her good, as it was bound to do. Then Mr. Herbert, who seems to have made frequent friendly visits with no hard feelings, brought the worrying news that the beautiful hill overlooking the River beyond Mount Vernon was up for sale, and they feared that some one might buy and build on it before the Association would be able to acquire it.

Early in April the Regent received a letter from a cousin of Miss Finney's:

"Learning that your present secretary is about to leave, I do hereby make application for the position for myself," it read. "I was born and educated in Vermont, where my relatives now reside. My health is tolerable, and I am accustomed to an energetic and systematic mode of life. My circumstances are peculiar in this, that I am thrown entirely upon my own exertions, there being no male member of my family whose duty it is to provide for me. So far as I know the duties of the situation, I believe that I could satisfactorily discharge them, and do therefore ask you to give me a trial. Mr. Everett's late attorney-general is my first cousin, and I doubt not would recommend me. Rev. Mr. Spriggs of Alexandria is acquainted with me and I have asked him to forward testimonials direct to you to avoid delay. Should you grant my request the widow and fatherless will daily ask God to bless you and will thank you for giving me work to do. With sentiments of regard—"

That was Mrs. Tiffey, and she arrived simultaneously with Michler's workmen, who began at once to tear the place apart. She kept a sort of diary, and wrote often to her two young daughters, and while it is easy to laugh at her expansiveness, there was a lot of sense in Mrs. Tiffey, and she left a valuable record of her daily impressions, having succumbed without a struggle to the Mount Vernon magic.

"The day has passed quietly and we have read most of the time," she wrote on the first Sunday after her arrival. "The place, the house, all seems still and solemn. I have a feeling of awe. I feel the deepest thankfulness at being led to this place, and trust it is for good. I shall endeavor to do my duty and earnestly pray for strength to bear and forbear.

"We have a good room, nice parlor, and dine in what was Washington's library. Excellent board and good attention from servants. Miss Cunningham is an elegant lady but an invalid, she is from South Carolina and a warm Southerner. It is because I was born at the North and a relative of Mr. Everett's that she was anxious to secure me. She expects to go to South Carolina soon, also to Cape May. Then I shall be sole manager. We have a mail every day, Post Office box in Alexandria, sent down in a little satchel. The steamer runs from Washington daily except Sundays. I do not see the visitors to speak with them. I send you a leaf of the magnolia tree known to have been planted by Washington."

If Miss Cunningham had not already laid her plans for a trip to Rosemonte before taking refuge at Cape May for the hot weather, the invasion of workmen would soon have decided her on some such move, though it meant leaving the responsibility —and the unpleasantness—to some one so lately come on the scene as Mrs. Tiffey.

"We are in the midst of such confusion," the Regent wrote Mrs. Halsted, "there is but one bedroom left us on the second floor. Such heaps of plastering as the workmen are tearing down would gladden your eyes. The greenhouse walls are levelled, Mr. Craig's house is being repaired, the plastering from two bedrooms on the second floor has been taken down, and the first coat given; all on the third floor but one room will be entirely replastered, and in that room a portion will be renewed. On examination the beams are found to be perfectly sound, only swayed. But Mr. Follinsbee, the boss, will have the floors taken up and relaid, so as to be even. The roof is not much damaged, the dormer window being the cause of leaks, so we will not need a new roof.

"I long to fly away from this incessant hammering and clouds of lime dust which penetrate everywhere. Whether my incessant headaches are owing to these causes I do not know, but I am very miserable, and do but little, even towards initiating my new secretary, important as that duty is, leaving her as I must in charge here while I am absent.

"I crawled up the staircase since I wrote you last and examined the papering in the room above me. There are seven layers. The one next to the plastering is a solid color. You remember I sent you a copy of a paper in General Washington's handwriting about the bedrooms, in which two were spoken of as the blue room and the yellow room, and the others the River room and the Lafayette room. The room over me was the yellow room. The inside paper is the yellow paper, solid color; that is a guide, I think, for the bedrooms, at least.

"There are only three bedrooms to be papered, the one you occupied being in good repair, having been refitted by the last proprietor. The paper on the ceiling of the entrance hall is in tolerable repair. We ought to leave all things here untouched as long as we can. The paper on the ceiling of the passage of the hall on the second floor is much defaced. It is in a square block pattern. That on the walls where the staircase runs is much defaced. It is a column paper, I enclose a slip. These pinkish columns are a little over a third of a yard apart, the paper in between was white originally. Do you not think the style in vogue not unlike? I am too isolated to know."

This places Miss Cunningham's room as the one still furnished as a downstairs bedroom, the present dining-room being her sitting-room, and the library had always since Judge Bushrod's time been used as a dining-room. This gave her a private block of three rooms in the heart of the house, with a door giving on to the kitchen colonnade. The rest of the house, even the secretary's room upstairs, could be shown without intruding on her, an arrangement which was of course bound to cause complaints, by people who felt that too little of the house was open to visitors.

On the 26th of May she left for South Carolina, worn out with what Mrs. Tiffey called "the agony of dress-making," and the necessity to finish up the accounts. A Miss Arnold who was left with Mrs. Tiffey until her eldest daughter could arrive, so that she would not be alone at night, cannot be identified. Miss Cunningham had for a travelling companion only a young Scottish girl with no experience as a lady's maid, but it was better than going entirely alone.

There were lawsuits pending in South Carolina, and her mother was wailing as always. Their mill had burned down the previous year, and her brother had been badly injured in the fire. She carried with her an acute anxiety about the possible sale of the land adjacent to Mount Vernon, and many doubts as to the capabilities of Mrs. Tiffey, who had cheerfully undertaken the making of bouquets for sale, and the separate accounts for the photograph sales, canes, fruit, and milk to visitors.

Mrs. Tiffey wrote long, happy, gossipy letters, from which it might have seemed to the Regent that they were getting along a little *too* well without her. There was distemper among the hens, however, and the wet weather retarded the potato planting, and the plasterers went away and didn't come back for days, and the library closets would have to be tinned—but the Regent was not to worry. "Try and rest some. I will do my very best at Mount Vernon," wrote Mrs. Tiffey.

Her daughter arrived, to her joy, and took over the tying of the bouquets. Nathan was patient and good about trying to keep the Mansion presentable for visitors in spite of the workmen, and West Ford was helping him clean up the plaster tracked into the floors each day. Some elegant wall-paper arrived from Mrs. Halsted—buff, with a gilt and green figure—and would not of course be hung until the Regent returned. The banquet hall looked like a lumber room, but they had pointed up the plaster and mended the broken places. Old Daddy Jim was sick, and Sarah ailing. The quinine requested by the Regent had been sent. "Do pray don't take too much calomel, it will prostrate you," wrote Mrs. Tiffey.

They were selling strawberries out of a big yellow bowl at 25¢ a saucer. Ice was a problem, and the boat captain said the best thing would be for him to bring it down in hogsheads of sawdust at 50¢ a hundred. The milk wouldn't sell otherwise, and people wanted ice-water in the heat. The Buckeye mower which had been donated through the Halsteds was "the most splendid one" Craig had ever seen, and was a sensation with the visitors, who gathered to watch it while it mowed the lawns around the house, worked by the Mount Vernon mules. Craig had sold a calf for $10. Mrs. Halsted was sending wire for mosquito screens, and Michler's men would build the frames. A party of orphans had come down, and were driven into the piazza by a shower, where they sang hymns very sweetly while it rained. Mrs. Tiffey was making cherry bounce and currant jelly. The plasterers had finally finished, leaving the house "one enormous daub" and Nathan had had to clean all over again, from cupola to cellar. Michler had not come near the place for three weeks, and his workmen were neglecting to make the Mansion look well in favor of the greenhouse, which didn't show up as much as a coat of paint and varnish would have done inside. The colonnades and cellar had not been touched, and money would soon be running low. There was "something dead" in the well, and they had had it cleaned out. Mr. Craig's fiancée had come out from England to marry him, and he had brought her home to Mount Vernon, and she was "a nice little woman, perfectly unobtrusive and as quiet as possible." Craig reported that the land in question had not been sold after all, because the offer was not high enough. They had made enough money by the sale of fruit, butter, milk, flowers, and photographs to pay all the June bills, without drawing anything extra. "Be assured, we are taking good care in every way. Don't prostrate yourself with too much medicine.

Cheer up, cheer up, good seed has been sown, and you are the sower, the ball is in motion," wrote Mrs. Tiffey.

And yet Miss Cunningham complained that she didn't hear often enough. Mrs. Tiffey replied in obvious distress that she had written thirteen letters, and they had seemed to her very repetitious. Everyone had gone to the Springs for the hot weather, and Washington was emptier than it had been for years, and visitors to Mount Vernon were naturally few. General Michler had finally turned up again, sampled the cherry bounce, and promised that the painting should be done inside the Mansion.

The Regent returned to Mount Vernon on the 8th of August.

7

August 15th was her fifty-third birthday, and for the first time in her life, Mrs. Tiffey recorded, she *walked* to the tomb and the wharf— "Poor woman, she is so full of the work to be done, so worried and harassed, and no one can help her."

The matter of colors for the walls of the rooms to be painted and papered so perplexed the Regent that she had started inquiries among people whose knowledge of the house antedated her own, and in this way gathered in "Mrs. Judge Mason," of Culross, near Alexandria, who had been a friend of Nellie Custis Lewis, Martha's granddaughter, whose childhood and youth had been spent in Washington's household. Mrs. Mason had heard from Mrs. Lewis that the banquet room had had wall-paper, and that one of the parlors was blue. There was now no blue parlor, both rooms being "an ugly shade between brown and slate," and a delicate pink or pale lemon was being considered for the banquet room.

General Michler came down to consult with the Regent, and was again wrought upon by Southern charm. "You ought to have seen the Regent's eyes," wrote Mrs. Tiffey, "as General Michler in a glass of cherry bounce gave 'A happy turn to her success at Mount Vernon,' and the readiness with which she responded, 'To the elasticity of your funds!' Her face was lit up after he said he would paint the whole house, and put up the colonnade, and said he hoped to have a little left. She took this opportunity to remind him of a furnace for the cellar." But General Michler had not lately examined the accounts. When he did, he found that so far from money to rebuild the colonnade, it had barely held out for the greenhouse.

Disappointment and perpetual headaches drove the Regent to Cape May before the month of August was out, from where she continued her correspondence with Mrs. Halsted. If the Government funds should fall short of the necessary finish to the interior of the Mansion the Association itself could afford to cover that expense, in order that the public should appreciate what had been done, but the colors were still a matter of debate. And there was another vexation, as the mysterious feud with Mrs. Halsted's "cousin" continued.

"I am sorry to tell you that I believe Mrs. Morse to be at mischief again," the Regent confessed to Mrs. Halsted. "She wrote or caused to be written an article which appeared in the *Republican* in Washington. When Mr. Sykes read it he at once said she wrote it. Malice to me shows its source. I suspect Mrs. Morse will give us much trouble yet, unless as in the past you possess the power to keep her quiet. We hope so, for it is vital not to let the public know we have any black sheep amongst us. I am so thankful she has not a drop of your blood in her veins! While I was absent she visited Mount Vernon several times and resumed the former habit of making herself conspicuous as to being an officer, etc. to visitors. She would send for the gardener and give orders as to what she wished done, ditto to Mr. Follinsbee, and it seems that neither gave any heed to her, which offended her, no doubt. Shortly after I returned she was down again with several daughters, to see me, just before time for the boat to leave, and I declined to see her, as I wished her to realize that I would have no social intercourse with her. If she had shown she was sorry for the past, as she professed to be, I would have acted differently. I presume that, added to her state of mind, induced her to give vent to this recent most unpardonable attack on me in part, and the Association in general, as to management, etc. She has signed a feigned name, but she shows her hand too plainly for the initiated not to recognize it."

The basis for this breach with the Vice-Regent for Louisiana is not known, beyond the sudden departure of Mrs. Morse from Washington with the indemnity bill left dangling, for which no reason was assigned. Miss Cunningham added in this letter that her latest visit South had left her feeling ten years older. Ill luck pursued her. The seaside hotel where she was staying burned, and she had a bad fright, but managed to save her baggage. After that she stopped writing to Mrs. Tiffey, who became increasingly anxious lest she was seriously ill. "Something is all the time occurring to disturb her," Mrs. Tiffey lamented to Mrs. Halsted. "Waiting for a decision about the color of these rooms has held everything back and is a serious matter. The house is kept in confusion and in an unfinished state so long, many persons see it thus who will never see it again. It would be a very small matter to change the color of the large room at some future time. Only the walls is there any doubt about. All the rest is done and beautifully, but it cannot be seen well for the scaffolding, and general confusion."

Finally Mrs. Tiffey received three letters from the Regent dated from the 13th to the 19th of September, all postmarked the 20th —somebody had forgotten to mail them, possibly the Regent herself. Mrs. Tiffey's reply to these is illuminating—Miss Tracy would have felt for her. "Of course I did not read the letter of the 18th without great pain," she wrote. "I am as innocent as the smallest child of any intentional neglect of duty either at Mount Vernon or towards yourself. What possible motive can I have to neglect you? It is no burden to me to write a letter. Be assured I have not deserted Mount Vernon nor in any way neglected my duties. I have written you six times, this is the seventh, since you left here, and have forwarded all your letters properly directed. Nothing but extreme sickness or death will make me negligent of duty when left in charge, and I confess to a feeling of mortification that you conceive me capable of leaving Mount Vernon in your absence, unless death had called me away. If I had an enemy,

I would think some one was poisoning your mind against me."

The poison was in the Regent's own unnatural existence, her loneliness, her shattered nerves, her many disappointments and harassments, her hypochondria and the effects of the laudanum, all of which had now begun in earnest to overbalance her judgment, so that a day without a letter probably seemed like a week to her, and letters received were mislaid and forgotten. But always the rally came, for Mount Vernon. On her way back there, in October, she was able to stop in Philadelphia to get expert advice from the foremost firm on interior decorating, and arrived home in a high fever, having had a chill in the cars, so that the conductor had made her lie down in the parlor car.

"*The* room is painted—rejoice!" she wrote Mrs. Halsted, meaning the Lafayette or Jersey Room. "The east parlor stone color, nearly done and looks well. This afternoon we get a finishing coat to our parlor. The carpet is pulled to pieces to try to get the dingiest breadths from the inside, though this kind of patching and mending is very disagreeable work, and I am not experienced, yet by the time it is finished, the dull furniture varnished, and your beautiful glass and curtains in place, you will acknowledge that the sitting-room is more attractive than when you sat in it last. *I* shall be the only thing not improved!" And Mrs. Tiffey completed the picture by writing that "Miss Cunningham is down on her knees making a new carpet for the parlor out of the old."

Her neuralgia came back, and her head "had to be wrapped in woollens, like an old woman's." Mrs. Mason, who in Mrs. Tiffey's opinion was a "charming old lady," came down for a visit and recalled many interesting little things from her acquaintance with Nellie Custis Lewis, which would be useful to know. Before long, when Mrs. Ritchie sent in her final resignation from London, Mrs. Mason would become the second Vice-Regent for Virginia.

"I wish you could see Miss Cunningham when she receives distinguished visitors," Mrs. Tiffey confided to her Diary in November. "She is elegant, graceful, dignified, and says just the right thing at the right time. I hope I shall learn some of her graces."

The autumn Council was given up, largely so that the Regent could hurry back to South Carolina, "to save herself from ruin." The overseer she had engaged during the past summer to see her through 1870 was giving trouble, her brother's family had become entirely dependent on her and her helpless mother, and they feared he would not long survive. Mrs. Mitchell was in New York on her way to Florida, and it was hoped that the Regent could travel with her, but Mr. Mitchell was taken ill in New York and could not be left. At the end of November Mrs. Tiffey accompanied Miss Cunningham to Washington and saw her set out, entirely alone, on the long journey. She lost her spectacles on the boat, and though the captain offered a reward of a dollar, they were never found. This must indeed have seemed to her the last straw.

Mrs. Tiffey continued to write her affectionate letters, and contributions continued to arrive from Mrs. Halsted. The Lafayette Room was completed, even to a Bible, from which Mrs. Tiffey read aloud to the colored servants on Sunday evenings. She and Mr. Craig opened and decorated the tomb for December 14th, the anniversary of Washington's death. There were only three visitors by the boat and two by land, and she noted in her Diary that the house seemed unusually still and solemn that night. "I stood in the grand porch this morning as the mail boat passed, and the tolling seemed unusually solemn," she recorded. "Imagination, of course, yet to me a reality. No steamer with tolling bell or shrill whistle jarred on *his* ears in those days, but the scene could not have been unlike this that his eyes last rested upon, for it is the same grounds and river, and many of the trees are the same. Nothing to me is more touching than this tolling bell. Twice in twenty-four hours we know that some one is reminded of this hallowed spot. Considering the engrossing power of present events, the wonder is not that so little interest is felt, but that an interest has been kept up so long. The fact is an emphatic tribute to the memory of Washington."

Yet on the last day of the year the Regent was writing to Mrs. Halsted that she was "greatly disappointed" in Mrs. Tiffey and did not expect to retain her long, "capable as she is with her pen," though she was thought equal to anything which might transpire now in the dull season during the Regent's absence. The letter went on to enumerate the difficulties at Rosemonte, where servants were so impossible to obtain that until some other arrangement could be made for her aged mother and her invalid brother's seven children it would be impossible for her to return to Mount Vernon.

Mrs. Mason, writing to Mrs. Tiffey that winter, expressed herself as "mortified" that she could not have invited Miss Cunningham to share her home at Alexandria, but doubted that she could have made her sufficiently comfortable, owing to alterations or repairs to Culross then in progress— "and there is something so ethereal and dainty in Miss Cunningham's style and habit that she looks to me as if the angels had charge concerning her, lest any time she dash her foot against a stone, whereas you and I belong to another sisterhood and have to buffet with the world in widowhood until we are humbled into the consciousness that in these days the cruse is not replenished nor the beloved dead given back." Mrs. Mason's first impressions of the Regent are valuable, in view of the events of the next three years.

She was also concerned about the fact that Lewis Washington, who was descended from the General's elder half-brother "Austin," and had married Ella Bassett, who was descended from Martha's favorite sister Nancy, was offering some Washington relics for sale, having suffered a reverse of fortune in consequence of the war. The Washingtons lived in the Kanawha District of Virginia which refused to secede and became a separate state as West Virginia in 1863. Mrs. Mason was annoyed that Colonel Washington, "corrupted by the necessities of his situation," had seen fit to employ a mercenary agent to assist in their disposal, which placed the price well out of reach for the Association. Before the year was out, however, Mrs. Washington was to make the Regent's acquaintance and become the Vice-Regent for West Virginia.

On February 14th Miss Cunningham was writing to Mrs. Comegys from Mount Vernon.

"I am here at last, sick in body and weary in mind. I left in a rainstorm and arrived here in a snowstorm, and am still confined to my bed with a fearful cold, of a kind which affects my eyes and nose and head, so I have to keep unseen until I can breathe without keeping my mouth open.

"I am sorry to tell you that nearly all my labor to make my poor mother comfortable was in vain, though I travelled over 200 miles through mire and mud, and failed to procure such house servants as were suited to her, which is the general condition of things from the determination of the Negro women not to work, especially as house servants. My duty here compelled me to return, and it is too bad to be laid up as soon as I got here, nevertheless I have kept Mrs. Tiffey busy and much work has progressed, towards filling vacancies and sending off letters to distant Vice-Regents to inquire what time is most convenient to attend Council.

"I rejoice to find you still working and still successful, the oil cloth for the second story hall is beautiful, but not put down, the invaluable clock is stationed on the stairway but not running because as yet we cannot get workmen to come down here. The wood wagon broke down yesterday, and has been mended so often it will bear no more, so I will have to assume the responsibility of purchasing, as that cannot wait for Council."

Mrs. Tiffey's Diary records the Regent's renewed endeavor to raise interest in Mount Vernon in the hope of funds for its support.

"On Monday Miss Cunningham and I, with her maid Jessie, went to Washington. I went to hear Mr. Lossing's lecture. After the lecture I delivered a message from Miss Cunningham, and the next morning he came to Willard's Hotel to see her. He is much interested in Mount Vernon, and will do all he can to interest others. The next day I went to the Smithsonian to deliver a message to Prof. Henry. Yesterday I went with Miss Cunningham to the Capitol. One of the gentlemen who were there told Miss Cunningham to ask for the Sergeant-at-arms. He paid us every attention. Went to the Senate a while, then he took us to the lunch-room where we had stewed oysters, cold turkey, tea, etc. and he gave us the use of his carriage from one to six. We went to Georgetown to see Mrs. Kennon, where we were beautifully received, treated to cake and wine, and shown the most exquisite miniature of General and Mrs. Washington, and many interesting relics. Nothing could exceed the sweetness of Mrs. Kennon, and we were cordially invited again. I am sure I have Miss Cunningham's entire confidence and approbation, I have persuaded her to see more persons and thus she will do away with prejudice and increase interest in Mount Vernon. We had some agreeable people on the boat today as we returned."

Benson Lossing's three-volume *Pictorial History of the Civil War*, a companion work to his invaluable Revolutionary travels, both illustrated by his own sketches, had been published in 1868, and his friendship with George Washington Parke Custis of Arlington and Mrs. Lee had brought him the job of editing Custis's *Reminiscences*. Miss Cunningham may have hoped that he would prove to be another Edward Everett, but while he labored honestly and with enthusiasm among a wide acquaintance, the results were never spectacular.

The widowed Mrs. Kennon was the great-granddaughter of Mrs. Washington, through Martha Parke Custis Peter, and had inherited the magnificent mansion called Tudor Place which was built by her father in 1815. She had saved the house from Arlington's fate during the war by renting it to Union Army officers, and had received it back in good condition at the end of the conflict. Stored away somewhere in safety she had kept the Washington relics of her own inheritance as well as many which had been removed from Arlington before its occupation by Federal troops, and her home was now a museum containing all sorts of treasures from the miniatures to Mrs. Washington's lavender satin bridal slippers. Mrs. Kennon lived on into the twentieth century, "very tall, very slender, with the figure and grace of a young woman." Mrs. Tiffey was indeed fortunate to witness the meeting between two such remarkable ladies.

In March the roof was leaking again, so that the new plaster in the banquet room and the General's bedroom was stained, and water dripped under the cupola. "What are we to do?" the Regent wailed to Mrs. Halsted. "The Government workmen thought they had made all safe against even driving rains. When you and the General come he will no doubt find out where the trouble lies and remedy it." Miss Tracy could have warned her to retain Mr. Herbert while the Government men were at work.

In April Mrs. Tiffey's Diary again fills in the picture.

"Mrs. Eve, a charming lady, Vice-Regent for Georgia, is here and will be here until Council meets in June," she wrote on the 14th. "She is a noble woman, has great tact and great influence with the Regent.

"Mrs. Washington has been here. We all liked her so much. She was appointed Vice-Regent for West Virginia. Miss Cunningham is now in Washington, is expected home tomorrow and will bring company with her. I have seen some very agreeable persons, and Mrs. Underwood, daughter of Rembrandt Peale, an old lady of 70, and her sister who is 66, are to visit us soon. They are both very pleasant."

The Regent had returned to Washington in the company of Mrs. Mitchell, who had paid a visit to Mount Vernon— "The more I see of her, the better I like her," Miss Cunningham wrote Mrs. Halsted. She hoped now to interest President Grant in her project to acquire the Washington relics and to establish an endowment fund for Mount Vernon. As in 1868, she encountered a political tempest, this time as a result of the ratification of the Fifteenth Amendment—the one which guaranteed the right of suffrage "without regard to race, color, or previous condition of servitude." Government indifference, which with regard to Mount Vernon seemed inevitable, persisted. Even though she was accompanied by Mrs. Washington, who had some acquaintance with the President, they were unable to get an appointment to see him.

The visit of Mrs. Underwood to Mount Vernon furthered a project which was not completed until three years later—the loan and finally the gift of Rembrandt Peale's mammoth painting called "Washington Before Yorktown," which would be for a time lodged in the banquet hall, until the damp from the window whose light it obscured so damaged the canvas that it was removed to the Corcoran Gallery.

The Council of 1870 was called for June 21st at Mount Vernon. Mme. Berghman, who had come down to Mount Vernon during the spring and was resuming the Vice-Regency for Pennsylvania, wrote an affectionate letter to the Regent regretting that a severe attack of her "old enemy, neuralgia" would prevent her from attending. Mrs. Farnsworth wrote her favorite correspondent, Mrs. Comegys, that the journey from Michigan would be too much for her during the summer heat, and urged the Vice-Regent for Delaware to be present, as there was a general feeling of impending crisis around the meeting for this year.

Nineteen months had elapsed since the last Council, and many problems and uncertainties had accumulated. Gardener Craig, although apparently a conscientious man, was no Upton Herbert to control the help and keep the place up to scratch, and had by now somehow run afoul of the Regent— "These foreign gardeners are notoriously self-willed, and soon become very assuming and very unwilling to receive any directions," she wrote of him to Mrs. Halsted, indicating another conflict of authority—and had allegedly gone slack with ill-health and family cares, so that the crops had suffered as well as appearances. Mrs. Tiffey was also in the Regent's opinion inadequate and must be replaced by a more capable secretary. Mrs. Morse had not bowed to discipline and meant to attend Council again as though still in good standing. The work done by Michler with the Government funds, largely in Miss Cunningham's absence, was insufficient and unsatisfactory. The drive for an endowment fund to supplement the daily income, for running expenses, was not going well. There were too many vacancies among the Vice-Regents. The hostility of the press continued, and with some reason, for the place now showed signs of neglect and unfinished work. Worst of all, malicious rumors flew about the Regent's frequent absences, her lack of system and economy, and even her personal habits and weaknesses, including her dependence on drugs and—an inevitable rider—whiskey. There is no conclusive evidence of over-indulgence in the latter, and it must be remembered that laudanum—without which she could not now have borne her condition at all— was a mixture of opium and morphine soluble in alcohol, and could have produced a reaction sufficiently similar to intoxication to deceive even a well-intentioned servant or chance visitor into the more obvious conclusion. Mrs. Mason wrote Mrs. Hudson that although she had visited Mount Vernon several times unexpectedly, and had sometimes found Miss Cunningham in bed, she had always appeared promptly and had been entirely in possession of herself. It was the Regent's further misfortune that some of the newer Vice-Regents were ambitious and impatient of her jealously maintained power, and her conviction that at Mount Vernon she and she alone had the right to rule, while even some of her elder colleagues were beginning reluctantly to place the dignity and interests of Mount Vernon above their sympathy and affection for the Regent.

8

The Minutes for the 1870 Council exist only in Mrs. Tiffey's handwriting, well watered down by the Regent's vigilant supervision. Mrs. Sweat, who this year attended for the first time as Vice-Regent for Maine, was one of several who in the ensuing years assembled notes and memories preparatory to compiling the history of the Association which was never accomplished. She was of course a junior officer in 1870, but in acknowledgment of her more than amateur writing experience she was then elected to the newly created office of permanent secretary of Council, which she held until 1885, when the labor of copying Minutes which then extended to some forty pages became too much for her. Her recollections of the session of 1870 depict the growing concern and embarrassment of those present, confronted with the necessity somehow to impress upon the Regent that things could not go on as they were. At this grave turning point in Mount Vernon's affairs, the account of an eyewitness is best left in her own words.

"At the Council of 1870 the relation of the Association to the American public was just beginning to be understood," she wrote. "For the Regent it remained the shrine at which she had romantically worshiped, the altar at which she had lighted the torch of patriotism, the jewel for which she had raised the price of purchase, the possession for the control of which she had sacrificed health, youth, almost life itself. In fulfilling the official duties of the Regent she could not coldly calculate the prosaic claims of the outside world. To her, sentiment was a finer thing than an account book and patriotic fervor outweighed a possible balance at the banker's. As is not unusual, her organizing talent was much

greater than her executive ability and administration. Her feelings
would not allow of any deep respect for the unfeeling multiplica-
tion table. For a time much of this impression dominated the
sincerely grateful and admiring Vice-Regents, and at Council
only gentle remonstrances were made when hard facts were met,
and only timid suggestions were proffered as to more businesslike
methods. But the germ of reform was planted. Enthusiasm developed into responsibility. The object for which so much labor had
been wrought became the institution which implied a public trust,
and demanded an administration open to public scrutiny.

"The vividness with which the incidents of those early days
imprinted themselves upon the memory, the tragic force with
which the troubles and dangers which menaced us took hold of
our imaginations, the piteous struggle which took place between
our tender and somewhat romantic loyalty to our chief and the
imperative demand of conscience to fulfill the trust committed to
us—all these experiences stamped an indelible image upon those
who endured them, and it is neither right nor fitting that they
should be forgotten or underestimated.

"The only Report made that year was made up by the Vice-
Regent from Maine with many misgivings, for the public was
becoming interested to ask specific questions. The newspapers
were hostile and sensational, and our Regent impervious to entreaties and warnings of threatening catastrophes."

This report, she confessed, was of necessity composed of "glit-
tering generalities," in default of documents, accounts, and even
of correct information, though Mrs. Tiffey had certainly sent to
the Regent during the latter's absence, itemized monthly statements of the sales of produce to visitors—milk, flowers, fruit,
photographs, etc.—in her charge, which may have been wilfully
withheld.

Even more awkward than the situation created by the Regent
was the arrival of Mrs. Morse, who had been read out of meeting
in 1868 for threatening to state in the public press her belief that

"the Regent was incapacitated by her infirmities to fill her place."
At that time Mrs. Chace of Rhode Island had indignantly replied
that she would deny it over her own signature, and the fact that
Mrs. Morse had not acted, at least publicly, entitled her in her
own estimation to hold her position. Now, a year and a half later,
none of the Vice-Regents could have honestly denied the accusa-
tion, but they were agreed that Mrs. Morse was not the one to
handle it, and could not be allowed to represent the Association
in any way.

As before, it was only Mrs. Halsted who left any reference to
a curious scene which was never explained. She wrote that while
Mrs. Tiffey was reading the Minutes of the last meeting Mrs.
Morse "interrupted her," so that the Regent left the banquet room
where they were assembled, and retired to her own room, and
declared her intention not to return till Mrs. Morse had left the
house. Mrs. Sweat and Mrs. Chace went into conference in an
upstairs room, and summoned Mrs. Halsted to sign a paper ex-
pelling Mrs. Morse from Mount Vernon. Mrs. Halsted demurred,
as Mrs. Morse was her aunt by marriage, but when they told her
the Council would be at an end unless the action was unanimous,
she yielded.

The paper, devised among them, is of a brutal brevity, and there
is no indication whether it was read aloud in Council or handed
to Mrs. Morse in tactful privacy. And because such a document is
unique, it is quoted here in its entirety:

"The ladies of the Association perceiving your determination
to endeavor to retain possession of the position of which you have
been regularly and decisively deprived by the action of Council,
deem it proper to request you to retire at once from Mount
Vernon. It is impossible for you to retain any authority among
them, and though you might disturb the deliberations, you will
have no effect and will not be reported in the proceedings, except
if necessary by a brief reference. The ladies beg that you will take

advantage of the opportunity now afforded you of retiring quietly and without publicity."

It was signed by Mrs. Chace, Sweat, Mitchell, Eve, Walker, Brooks, and Halsted. It was not signed by Mrs. Barry, or Mrs. Comegys, or by Mrs. Washington, who was making her first appearance at this Council. It accomplished its purpose, for when the Council gathered on the piazza to have a group photograph taken, the first of these, Mrs. Morse was not among them, and nothing more is known about this sole instance of a Vice-Regent somehow failing to measure up to the standards set by her colleagues—nothing, that is, but a letter from Mrs. Farnsworth to Mrs. Comegys dated July 7th, and containing a reference to *l'affaire Morse* which is unexpectedly tart, in view of the gentle character of the Vice-Regent for Michigan. "I shall be happy to receive Mrs. Sweat's report and the photograph of the 'vices,' although minus the 'Marquise,'" she wrote. "Is it not a relief to be at quits with the Louisiana representative! I can heartily respond to the remark of the late Bishop Chase of Ohio in reference to an offending person— 'I never wish to behold that man again until I meet him a glorified spirit in the Kingdom of Heaven.'"

Mrs. Morse, we are happy to learn, was not at all crushed, and during subsequent years made more than one visit to Mount Vernon on her own, conducting parties of her friends.

From ensuing correspondence it can be gathered that a certain amount of more conventional business was got through at this extraordinary session. The question of fire protection was raised, and a committee was appointed to get advice about fire engines and extinguishers, and raise contributions towards the purchase of the apparatus recommended, and to tackle the problem of providing water for it and for the greenhouse. Another committee appointed itself to secure the services of a competent male superintendent to undertake the difficult assignment of managing Mount Vernon in spite of the Regent and reducing her as nearly as possible to a figurehead—at the same time somehow retaining her good will. They had learned too late that they should never have let Mr. Herbert go, but there is no sign that they attempted now to get him back. A third committee, including Mrs. Halsted, was to investigate the advisability of installing a furnace in the cellar, for the comfort of visitors and the preservation of the mansion from damp.

Returning to Mrs. Sweat's narrative of a later date, she wrote:

"After the adjournment of the Council of 1870 the Vice-Regent from Maine set about the task allotted her, viz., to raise her portion of an amount destined to procure protection from the constant risk of fire while the mansion was occupied as a dwelling-house. It is interesting to observe the way in which the clouds were gathering about Mount Vernon and to note the indomitable courage of the Regent. Her diplomatic skill, her untiring energy, her grasp upon the straws that are apt to be within reach of the drowning, make an absolutely pathetic picture. She had so identified Mount Vernon with her own personality that even financially she had come to regard them as one."

This is one of several vague allusions to what was to become a malicious conviction on the part of several of the more recent Vice-Regents, aided by the fact that Miss Cunningham's accounts were sketchily kept if at all—a belief that she had appropriated for her own use divers small sums contributed to Mount Vernon; a complaint which thoughtlessly ignored the unrecorded amounts she had in times past poured into Mount Vernon from her own diminishing resources, until the war ruined her entirely, and she had nothing more to give but her febrile energy and powers of persuasion. Mrs. Mitchell wrote in this connection that as lately as 1869 the Regent had added (from heaven knows where) $500 of her own to the Government's inadequate $7000, in order to eke out for essential work which otherwise would have gone unfinished.

It was a hot summer on the Potomac, and in July the Regent wrote to Mrs. Halsted: "I am broken down, and Mrs. Tiffey is more inefficient than ever, between groaning under the heat all day and about her children, who are now in Alexandria, and repining at her fate, I have a very uncomfortable time." Mrs. Halsted's plumber was to come to Mount Vernon to prepare his estimates and plans for installing the furnace as advised by General Halsted, but the Regent pleaded a sudden feminine ignorance of all such things, offered to house and board his workmen, and was preparing to escape again to the sea breezes of Cape May when she was prostrated by the news of Mrs. Ritchie's death in London. Mrs. Tiffey, always sympathetic, wrote that she suspected the Regent had loved this brilliant, warmhearted, devoted woman "better than any living being." Although ten years had passed since Mrs. Ritchie's departure from America, the Regent had always hoped for her return, and believed that the first Vice-Regent for Virginia was the one who could best write, or help her to write, the history of the Association. After a few days in bed, trying to recover from shock and grief, she went on to Cape May, leaving Mrs. Tiffey to cope with the furnace as she had the year before with the Michler job.

Mrs. Halsted spent the summer at Saratoga for her health. In September, having returned home, she received two letters from the Regent at the seaside to say that her affairs in South Carolina were in chaos and required her presence there, but she could not go until she had been again at Mount Vernon, and it was impossible for her to go there till frost had lessened the danger of malaria. She was therefore about to leave for Philadelphia, where she could consult Dr. Hodge, and where Mrs. Comegys was to join her, having made arrangements for the Regent to sit for her portrait to an artist named Lambdin. Mount Vernon was still more than usually sickly. Craig's wife and baby had been very ill, as well as Sarah, who was supposed to be immune, and Craig was not likely to remain at Mount Vernon for another season. Even the plumber's workmen could not yet be sent there to install the furnace until the weather changed. "What *are* we to do about the sickness at Mount Vernon!" she wrote despairingly. The colonnades were still a sight to behold, and the dormer windows must be tinned before winter. The boat was doing miserable business, and if the River froze over during the coming months, reducing their income still further, they would not have funds for a fire apparatus.

Mrs. Tiffey, who doubtless was feeling very poorly along with everyone else, got another raking over, as the Regent blamed her "inefficiency and non-adaptativeness" for her own relapse in health before leaving Mount Vernon in July. Poor Mrs. Tiffey's letters, which seem full of spunk and humor, along with the sentimentality, somewhat belie the criticism by the Regent and by Mrs. Barry, who wrote to Mrs. Comegys after the 1870 Council that they must find for secretary a person "more capable officially and more agreeable socially. I should die in a month, shut up with that Niobe!" she added. Miss Cunningham's niece Lizzie had promised to join her after her return to Mount Vernon, but was of course completely inexperienced in the work which would be required of her.

The Regent's current attendant, a raw, kind-hearted Irish girl named Bridget, went down with chills and fever when they reached Philadelphia at the end of September, and Mrs. Tiffey wrote that everyone was ill at Mount Vernon and she herself must go to Alexandria to consult a doctor. Miss Cunningham took calomel and passed a sick week-end, awaiting Mrs. Comegys's arrival which was unaccountably delayed.

Dr. Hodge conveyed the Regent in his carriage to her second sitting with Lambdin, "for I could not have gotten up the staircase without help," and Bridget was too ill to accompany her. He also prescribed a new medicine called chloral, also in the laudanum family, and a tonic, and assured her that she did not have an organic disease of the heart, but only neuralgia.

She sat to Lambdin for two hours at a time and enjoyed it— "We have gotten to be very sociable, for I like him." The artist

was a man in his early sixties, a pupil of Sully's, and had painted
Chief Justice Marshall, John Quincy Adams, and Presidents
Jackson and Tyler, besides being an accomplished miniaturist and
a very travelled and amusing gentleman. He doubtless found his
subject interesting and charming, and in a mistaken effort to
soften the lines of pain and grief in the Regent's face, he rounded
and smoothed it till she complained that he had made her look
dropsical—her father's aunt had died of it—and she sent for an old
photograph taken in her girlhood with a pathetic wish to show
him how she ought to look. The Lambdin portrait is now at
Mount Vernon in the Little Museum, and shows her with her
usual black lace mantilla drawn over her hair.

Mrs. Comegys finally arrived, to spend a day with her, and
Lizzie Cunningham, to remain indefinitely at Mount Vernon.
Mrs. Halsted invited her to come for a visit, though her household
harbored chills and fever like all the rest in this worst season in
years. Miss Cunningham was feeling "fainty" and oppressed, but
feared to return to the Potomac until the first frosts had come.
She therefore set out on a surprising jaunt which took her from
the Halsteds at Newark on to New York as Mrs. Brooks's house
guest—where she was to appear in society on behalf of the endowment fund. The usual panic over her inadequate wardrobe at once
began.

"Now there is to be a grand party on Friday night, given
nominally to raise political funds, but a few others are to be admitted," she wrote Mrs. Halsted. "I pleaded to run off to Brooklyn
[to Mrs. Eve] but Mrs. Brooks will not let me, though I cannot
make myself appear in party trim. The truth is she intends to
invite certain friends on my account, or rather that of the Association, hoping this will give us a chance to act on them at some
future day, and she expects me to play the agreeable and make a
good impression!! So I am up to my eyes to get ready, as I find
it almost impossible to get a mantua-maker. I was up last night
till after midnight sewing on a dress a mantua-maker—she could

only give me one day—had basted for me, and ditto tonight, for such is the excessive trimming in vogue that there is no end of work in a dress. I threaten to hide myself. Mrs. Brooks offers me the rotunda to hide in and look down on the crowd, but I suppose there is to be no escape. If good results to our cause in the future I shall feel repaid. As it is, I wish it was over. What a whirl New York life is! Don't ever come here to live!!"

From New York she went to Baltimore, where she stayed with an unidentifiable "cousin," and met the Vice-Regent for Maryland, Miss Emily Harper, who had just returned from more than two years abroad, and had never yet attended Council, but was now ready, wrote the Regent, "to go to work."

At Mount Vernon Craig had been too ill to leave his house for five days, and the weather was so unseasonably warm that the tenderest plants were still blooming. Miss Cunningham went as far as Washington, intending to take the boat down from there and return the same day to avoid the night air—a fearful waste of time and energy, she admitted, but her Washington physician forbade her residence at Mount Vernon now, saying the malaria had got into her blood, and she had taken cold on the way from New York, and her neuralgia had come back, so she had lost all the gain and stimulus of her happy visits.

It was some time during this protracted absence of the Regent that Mrs. Tiffey suddenly departed—Miss Cunningham wrote that it was on "less than ten days' notice"—probably defeated by the effects of the Mount Vernon climate, the unfriendly attitude of the Regent, and an opportunity for employment in the Treasury, which was one of the coveted ways in which a woman could support herself in those days. Nearly two years at Mount Vernon, much of it spent alone in its unhealthy atmosphere complicated by the confusion of extra workmen on the place, had apparently increased her tendency to eccentricity—Miss Cunningham used the word "crazy"—and she probably had no desire to present her resignation or receive her dismissal in person. The Regent was of course much annoyed, though she had often expressed the wish to be rid of her—and Mrs. Tiffey did promise to return on her days off until the accounts, correspondence, etc. were wound up.

Young Lizzie Cunningham was therefore elected to remain at Mount Vernon as the Regent's representative during the installation of the furnace, which began at last during November, while her aunt journeyed to South Carolina to try and solve the increasing problem of Mrs. Cunningham's future, and to find a reliable overseer for the coming year.

From Rosemonte in December the Regent wrote Mrs. Halsted that the drought and the fall in the price of cotton had brought increasing distress on the South, and she was forced by circumstances to ask the Halsteds to use their influence to get Lizzie a job in the Treasury Department, as she could then board with the Marks family, who were living in Washington, and be under the protection of Edwina. "Nothing but the hardship we endure has nerved me to ask this favor, but you who live in affluence cannot form the remotest idea of what those here accustomed to affluence have to endure since '65," she wrote. "I am glad you like her. Poor child, what a hard fate hers has been, and promises to continue to be. War came just after she and her sister were removed from elementary school to a fashionable French school in Charleston, the family soon became refugees in a very plain and unimproved section affording no society, where they were soon burnt out, losing almost every article save the clothes they wore. When the war ended they were penniless and we, my mother and myself, so utterly ruined that we could do but little for them. I was overwhelmed with debt not of my own making, but I had almost lifted the weight of misfortune and hoped to be able to do something for my nieces when the utter ruin struck the cotton and plunges me into such an abyss that I see no way out of it, for the people in this State.

"Dear old Mrs. Farnsworth will spend the holidays near New

York. Would you not like to see her? She was promised $50 from three persons a year ago for the endowment fund. She thinks she could get it now for our fire department if preferred. Mrs. Emory is willing to try to collect in Washington. This is all our prospect, except what Miss Harper may do. There are few or no sales about the place, and I fear 1871 will yield but poorly. . . ."

9

With the departure in the autumn of 1870 of Mrs. Tiffey, the Regent, and finally Lizzie Cunningham, the entire responsibility for Mount Vernon devolved on the ailing gardener Craig and Nathan and Sarah, and it is not surprising that before long the visitors were complaining of a lack of supervision and care.

At Rosemonte Miss Cunningham continued to be dogged by misfortune. In January she wrote Mrs. Halsted that her hands were burnt and scarred and painful from having put out a fire which her mother had started by her habit of reading in bed— "which no remonstrance will induce her to forego"—at the age of seventy-seven. "My mother is ruined," she added, revealing a situation which must have been peculiarly hard for her to bear. "She reproaches me with being the cause of it, and says that if I had remained at home those around her would not have defrauded and ruined her by their bad management. This may be true, and may God forgive me if I have erred in judgment, but I could not realize when she seemed so active that her balance of mind was so destroyed, or that my brother's mind was affected by that fearful fire some years ago. Suffice to say that now I am striving to stave off the worst. I cannot leave here till my duty is over, I have sacrificed everything for Mount Vernon, now Mount Vernon must wait on me, and as the ice in the River interrupts visitors I am fortunately not needed there yet. Do not go to Mount Vernon till I get back. I would so grieve to miss you."

Mrs. Halsted wrote offering the futile long distance advice which affection and sympathy prompts and which is usually so exasperating to the recipient in the grip of circumstances which of necessity can be only half comprehended by the most willing friend. After a vain effort to find board and lodging for her mother among their acquaintance in the neighborhood, Miss Cunningham was contemplating removing her to a nursing home in Washington, which had been established by Mr. Corcoran in memory of his dead wife, but this entailed so much expense that it was not an immediate solution.

"If I live a thousand years I can never forget what I have endured here this winter," she wrote in March, "from a perplexed and harassed mind trying to save my mother's remnant of property from being seized, and all danger is not over yet. I cannot in duty to her leave here till danger is over, I trust by the end of this week, but oh, how am I to reach Mount Vernon without a balloon! Three weeks ago I began to strengthen, to be able to sit up, and commence walking about my room, as I knew I must by degrees begin to bear exertion. But alas, as I increased effort in order to prepare my system for that long, dreadful journey I soon found how poor and wretched I was. I am in bed again suffering agonies with my back and limbs. I cannot get much better here, but how am I to bear travelling? I am pining too to get away. My heart is kept so on the rack that it will be a mercy to change the scene and get to occupation which can enable me to forget sometimes sorrows which are so consuming.

"Poor mother, she is as much absorbed with interest in our vines and flowers as though it could be her home while life lasts. I am afraid of the effect at her age when she learns that she must give it up forever, but what can I do? I have not yet succeeded even in getting board for her—everybody is so troubled about servants that it is not easy to get even friends to take a boarder. In a few days I will know. I am also not even sure of the place, I hope for Washington City, but can't be sure till I go on there, and even if I were I am now too poor to bear the expense of removing her there until another season yields me something. Poverty is hard to bear when you are not born to it, where you are not trained to its exactions. We in this State can't even have hope to strengthen us. Our destiny is darker each year under Negro rule and carpet-bag stealing. Each year our taxes increase and our labor gets worse. Will you come to Mount Vernon after my return? I hope so. My hand gets more and more tremulous, and if I stay here much longer I won't be able to hold a pen at all!"

It is small wonder, surely, that the Regent's mental and physical deterioration were increased during this terrible winter at Rosemonte. She returned to Mount Vernon in April, accompanied by another niece, named Floride, who wrote to announce their arrival at Mount Vernon to Mrs. Halsted. In May Mrs. Eve arrived to make a visit at Mount Vernon, just as the finished portrait by Lambdin was delivered, and wrote that they were on the whole pleased with it. Mrs. Farnsworth, advised of its arrival, wrote from California, where she was visiting a married daughter, that she hoped they "would not be restricted in the price of a frame" —but with the almost universal obtuseness of the Vice-Regents, she did not send a check to cover same. "Has anyone been found for secretary?" she inquired. "It can be no sinecure if Mrs. Tiffey's report is reliable, and the duties of secretary are very necessary in the Regent's precarious health."

Some time during the summer of 1871 Mrs. Cunningham came up to Mount Vernon on her way to the Louise Home in Washington. How she made the journey and with whom does not appear. The first indication of the change is a letter from Mrs. Farnsworth, expressing gratification that the Regent's mother had found "so desirable an asylum at the North. I had not heard of the Louise Home, which reflects such honor on Mr. Corcoran's head and heart."

In August Miss Cunningham wrote Mrs. Halsted from Philadelphia of yet another misfortune which had been visited upon her. "I know you will be surprised to find me here and not at Cape May, where for my health's sake I ought to have been a month ago. I tried to, but alas, I know not when I wrote you but I think it was before a series of events made it impossible for me to get away from the now deadly atmosphere of our dear old charge." She had gone up to Washington to arrange matters at the Home, presumably leaving her mother in Floride's care at Mount Vernon, and as her carriage was driving away from the building it was "pitched into" by an oncoming fire-engine. Miss Cunningham was badly shaken up, but providentially escaped severe injury, and after being carried back to the parlor for a rest she was able to proceed to the Marks's house where she was staying. That night the dreaded chills and fever came on, and lasted twenty-four hours, and nothing but the necessity of getting back to her mother, who had just recovered from an attack at Mount Vernon and was "imploring to be taken away" enabled her to leave her bed. The Washington physician had pronounced it malaria, and advised the seashore as soon as possible.

Returning to Mount Vernon, she found there a telegram to say that her brother's wife had died suddenly that morning from apoplexy. This was the mother of Lizzie and Floride, who had several married sisters and young brothers, among these Clarence, a promising student at Princeton, thanks to the Halsteds' influence there. Surrounded by new grief and distraction, Miss Cunningham escorted her mother to Washington and saw her installed at the Home, spent the night again with the Marks family and returned to Philadelphia, whereupon Bridget the maid went down with the fever, requiring a further delay before they reached Cape May —from where she wrote again to Mrs. Halsted, a letter so poignant that it can only stand in her own words:

"I feel like one in a bewildering dream," she wrote, "or as one benumbed, so great, so rapid, so fearful are the changes of the past year. I think that I do already realize all, yet there is a feeling that I cannot banish that some day, *some day* I shall be as one fully wakened, shall take it all in, the height and depth of its reality, and that then it will kill me! Our home no home for us any more—oh, how I felt it when on that last Sabbath at Rosemonte I went round the grounds, my mother by my side, supported by her walking-stick, and a little girl bearing a chair for me, to rest every few steps. I took a long look at each turn in walks and shrubbery, a farewell—for I felt that I could never again bear to go over these spots to be given up to desolation, till some one more fortunate than our family claimed them as their own. Could you have known me in other days, days of untamed, unbounded pride, you would realize what I suffered then.

"I looked at my mother again and again, and while I wished never to come to it, forever thankful that old age and trials had done their work and prevented her from realizing that soon this would be no more her home, that she would never have a home of her own any more! If I could only have taken a farewell then on that Sabbath evening—but it is my sorrowful fate to be compelled each year to go back to that desolate house in order to make a support for myself and others, when in the order of nature it would seem that the feeble invalid ought to be sustained and cared for by those stronger in sex and younger in years.

"I don't improve, and I fear I never can while weighed down with pecuniary cares which are so distasteful to me, and keep my nerves on edge, and if I don't improve I cannot hold out till my nephew Clarence is old enough to take my place, to the family at least. I have reason to be thankful indeed that my mother bears the change better than I expected. I was not aware of the exact arrangement of things in connection with the Louise Home when I applied for a place for her, for when Mr. Corcoran pointed out the place to me during a drive with him in July, I was left under the impression that a small amount for board would by his memoriam obtain a home of refinement and comfort for those who had met with adversity. I only found out the change in his plans after he had given her a place, and I did not dare tell her the real terms until after she joined me at Mount Vernon, and so she was so shocked that I feared the result. I do not believe that anything but the fact that I was there, and to the utmost extent I could bear gave her the power to conquer her pride and go there. I had to leave her there so abruptly, as I went from Mount

Vernon to come here, and with such a heavy heart. You can imagine the relief I felt to learn that she was contented, quite satisfied, and that the ladies already there seemed to vie with each other in their kind attention to make her feel at home.

"I thought last winter that my cup was so full that it could not bear another drop, when the sudden death of my brother's wife brought calamity on calamity. Another home broken up forever, none of our family now it seems are to know the word *home* any more, and I think the saddest affliction in life probably can be borne when there is one hearth where the family can gather sometimes to keep the heart warm. My two single nieces—you have seen one, Lizzie—are to be pitied, homeless, penniless, and so proud. If only the sons could get employment, but there is no opening in the South, and strangers in the North don't find it easy to make their way, where the applicants for office are so much greater than the offices. My nephews are ready to do anything that is honest and reputable, to keep them from being dependent, which goes very hard with them. My nieces feel the same, and each is hoping to get a place in the Treasury next winter, but I know they cannot. The Presidential campaign is intensifying sectional feeling in the party in power in Washington already. If they were older, one resource would yet be open to them, that is, keeping a boarding-house, and by this a home. That used to be the last resort in case the male members of the family did not succeed sufficiently.

"As you say, *change* is written on everything, but changes of home and property come harder to me. And you can imagine what trials are mine now, with more limited means and those so uncertain from year to year that nothing can be counted on, to see myself called on to be the mainstay of a large and helpless family, with little power to meet their necessities, yet with the knowledge that if I can't, there is no one for them to turn to. . . ."

This letter is certainly ample evidence of the unrelenting strain and emergency which pressed upon Miss Cunningham from every side, and which would have taxed a more robust nervous system than hers. Where Lizzie and Floride Cunningham spent the summer is not known—probably in Washington with the Marks family.

Mrs. Halsted made the only possible reply in the circumstances —she wrote inviting the Regent to come to them for a visit on her way back from Cape May. She accepted gratefully, and at the same time suggested a meeting of the Vice-Regents in New York for consultation—not a Council, she emphasized, just a sufficient number to be considered a quorum, "without any authority except such as the good sense of the Association at large would confer." She asked Mrs. Halsted to accompany her after the Newark visit, as they could be Mrs. Brooks's guests, and Mrs. Eve could join them there from her daughter's residence in Brooklyn. This she was convinced would be better than to try to convene a Council at Mount Vernon before next year, as the captain of the Mount Vernon boat had advised her that the sickness on the Potomac seemed only to have worsened with cool weather. "There is a new trouble before us all, which worries me quite as much as my family trials," she wrote in late September. "That is, Craig is going to leave us, as far as I can see before we can get any reliable person to fill his place. He will stay as long as he will be permitted, but I know how it will turn out. You can imagine the shock to me, although I had felt that the poor man ought to leave unless he could free himself from chills and fever." While she was still at Mount Vernon in the summer, Craig had had an offer to manage a beautiful estate in the mountains near Winchester, with a greenhouse and 100 acres to cultivate in vegetables, the use of three cows, and $1200 a year in salary. She had allowed him to go up for an interview and he returned enraptured.

Even if the Association could have afforded to meet the offer in money, it could not have met the chief problem—the sickliness of Mount Vernon, where for two years the climate had been particularly deadly. Mrs. Craig was willing to go to a wilderness to get health, and when the Regent urged on Mr. Craig the hope of acclimatization, "he laughed," she reported sadly, "and said, 'Miss Cunningham, I have inquired about that in all the region around for ten miles off the River, and the settlers from ten to twelve years have chills and fever every year. How can I hope?' I left no argument unturned to work on him," she continued in this jeremiad to Mrs. Halsted, "knowing full well the trouble to be encountered by me in losing him, and having a stranger to take charge who had to be proven."

Mr. Craig had now sent word to the Regent at Cape May that he was leaving the first of October, before she could possibly return, "and with the prospect of sickliness before us everywhere on the Potomac as last year, I could not expect the ladies to risk their health by coming to Council before frost has made it safe," she added, with her request for a New York meeting. When she asked him if he knew of a reliable man to take his place, Craig had only shaken his head helplessly. "He seems to have this place near his heart," she wrote, "to take pride in it, and I do believe it will cost him a struggle to leave it, and I do not think he will ever be as satisfied anywhere else. But what will not a man give for his life? For another such year as he has passed will certainly leave him a wreck in health. When I left Mount Vernon he had a high fever and was delirious. It would take a very prudent person to have any health at Mount Vernon, as well as one not subject to these fevers. I am very depressed about our chance of finding the right person to replace him, and if we could, the sickliness of Mount Vernon is becoming so notorious, how are we to induce persons whose health is their fortune to risk it there?"

Meanwhile Captain Stacpole, a helpful man, had found a possible substitute whose name was Watt, and who was willing to go down at least temporarily and take over Craig's basic duties, as Craig was now so debilitated that he was unconscious some of the time, which left his keys and supplies at the mercy of less responsible people. As usual, the ultimate emergency had brought the requisite rally from the Regent, and she had even done some sea-bathing, which she always considered a sovereign remedy, and

wrote Mrs. Halsted that her ambition was now to climb a staircase again.

Details are scanty on this October meeting in New York, her
second visit within a year to Mrs. Brooks's home, and many questions are left unanswered. But it was to have two far-reaching
results—the selection of a competent superintendent, and the unfortunate return to Mount Vernon of Mary McMakin.

IO

It has not been possible satisfactorily to trace the choice of Colonel James McHenry Hollingsworth for the second superintendent at Mount Vernon. Like Mr. Herbert, he was a veteran of the Mexican War, and more lately of the Civil War, where he had commanded Federal troops at Alexandria. He had a wife, but no children, and lived in an old house at Georgetown. Miss Cunningham wrote afterwards that circumstances had induced him to take summer boarders, among them Mrs. Brooks and Mrs. Hudson (the second Vice-Regent for Connecticut, who first attended Council in 1872) and that he was recommended by them for the position—Mrs. Hudson was not present at the October meeting in New York—and that Mr. Corcoran approved and offered to be Hollingsworth's bondsman. There is certainly no doubt of his tact, courtesy, and good breeding as evidenced in the almost impossible situation in which he soon found himself—for although the Regent apparently consented at this time to the appointment of a superintendent who was to relieve her of the onerous duties of Mount Vernon's daily management, which were admittedly too much for her or any woman to discharge alone, when it came to the point of recognizing any authority in him, or relinquishing any of her own almost absolute power at Mount Vernon, she resisted in every possible way.

While in New York Miss Cunningham seized the opportunity to look up her former secretary Mary McMakin, who had sat out the war at Mount Vernon with Miss Tracy and Mr. Herbert and then returned to her family's home in Harlem. So far as can be seen, there had been no correspondence between them preparatory to this visit, in which case the Regent descended like a bolt from the blue. She was determined that Miss McMakin should rejoin her at Mount Vernon and resume her old post as secretary. There is no indication of Miss McMakin's age, but as an unmarried woman she was still dominated by parental authority, and her mother obviously dominated the household, which consisted of Mary's father and a somehow handicapped if not deformed young brother. The confectionery and restaurant which in 1865 Miss Tracy had reported as doing well, was no longer a success if it existed at all, and the family had fallen on hard times.

Beset by the necessity to return again to Rosemonte on her own affairs, the Regent swept aside all objections, put forth all her considerable charm and persuasiveness for Mrs. McMakin's benefit, and "after three mortal hours" believed that she had reached an agreement to transport without expense to them the entire McMakin family to Mount Vernon, so that Mary could manage the place for her during her impending absence and remain with her on her return. A vague project to establish a restaurant lunch-room at Mount Vernon to be run by Mrs. McMakin on some sort of profit-sharing basis was concocted, probably on the spur of the moment, and may have helped to win her over.

Back at Mount Vernon on October 23d, Miss Cunningham reported to Mrs. Halsted, who probably had had no knowledge of the McMakins prior to the New York meeting, which had been followed by a hurried note from the Regent along the way, asking for assistance to move the family, "for the Association had not the ability to pay the expense, and neither had the parties in question," she wrote. "Miss McMakin would be an invaluable assistant here, and I believe her mother would be too, in time, in several ways, for she is a woman of energy and needs only to take an interest in matters here. We must work promptly if we wish to succeed, for poor Mary is out of work, and the sooner I go South the less my loss there, and the better for me, so as to get that fearful journey over before the rigors of winter. Mr. Sykes is away and cannot help. I am quaking in my shoes in hourly dread of chills and fever. Bridget is down. I read in the papers that there had been frost at the North, and of course I felt sure there had been enough here to make it safe to return, it was wintry the day I left Philadelphia, but alas, I find the frosts here are so slight that the tenderest flowers are still untouched. I have the furnace going to try by heat to drive out the malaria, but Bridget's seizure makes me fear for myself."

Craig had gone, leaving the new man, Watt, in charge. As usual, the Regent found fault with the supposed transgressor and praised the new broom, who was soon to prove unworthy, and wanted more money besides.

There is a bewildered, exasperated letter from Miss McMakin written from Harlem on October 25th, which plainly shows that the Regent had convinced herself that she had got her way, while many problems still remained to be solved.

"I am more than surprised that you have been expecting a letter from me, when I have been waiting every mail for the letter promised in your note to give me some idea of how much money will be needed to get us there if we go," Mary wrote. "Remember we are penniless, and well-nigh friendless, as far as pecuniary help goes, and in all your planning, at which you are so ingenious, you have overlooked the important item of the considerable sum of money it will take to move even the most essential furniture. Even if we could get transportation free, it would cost more than I can imagine how to raise, just to move our things to the wharf. Then at the very least, $25 would be needed just to make me decently presentable, my wardrobe having been so terribly run down.

"If we could raise all this money to go, we could as well raise it to stay, and save Ma from the trials of such an upturning. The matter seems so thoroughly impracticable that I am amazed Ma has even thought of it. If the Association were to advance me the means of getting there, my family would starve before I could overtake the advance, and it seems more cheerful to starve

here than there, if they must. Everything but rent and fuel would
have to be found, for of course the vegetables in winter would
have to be confined to potatoes, of which we do not use a half
peck a week. You see, the move is too serious to us to undertake
it precipitately. I am very sorry for the situation in which you
are placed, and would come at once if I could see the way to do
it. I could not leave my mother the burden of packing, even if
the way were clear to come.

"It is not worth while for me to trouble Mrs. Halsted about
it. I suppose she will communicate the result to you when she
can attend to it. It would cost nearly a month's wages only to
take our four selves, and it would be rather too much to ask Ma
and our old friend to go by sea, even if Andy and I could stand
it. You see, your offer looks all very tempting at first sight, but
won't bear analyzing for such poor folks as we. I hate to seem
so meanly calculating, but I cannot help it.

"I thought you were not to risk sleeping at Mount Vernon before frost. It is a great risk for you. I am sorry your maid has gone
too. Didn't I understand that the lunches were to be furnished to
the profit of the Association and Ma was only to superintend?
Still that would not make much difference as it does not help to
bridge the distance between Harlem and Mount Vernon. I do
not see any way to the end of this matter now, in such a way as
to meet your wishes. If it is the will of Providence that we go,
He will open a way, no doubt."

And so He did, though the means are not clear, for these
letters have not survived. But the McMakins were somehow installed at Mount Vernon before Christmas, and the Regent got
away southward. Apparently—the word is becoming tiresome,
but where only conjecture and deduction are possible it should
be so indicated—the family at once set up housekeeping in the
building first on the left of the North colonnade, facing the West
front [now the offices of the Resident Director] which had been
guest quarters in Washington's time, and was also known as the

servants' hall. There are two large rooms downstairs, and two above, with commodious fireplaces, and if in sufficient repair it could have been quite comfortable. They brought with them at least some of the no doubt shabby contents of their home in Harlem, and with the presence of the invalid boy it was soon obvious that the establishment was going to be no credit to the Association. Mrs. Eve was at Mount Vernon briefly before the Regent left, and the Halsteds paid a visit there in her absence by a confusion of dates. What they saw then may have been the basis for an immediate reaction among the Vice-Regents that the McMakins must be eliminated as soon as possible. A letter from Mrs. Halsted in reply to an inquiry from the West throws some light.

"At the informal meeting in New York on October 10th, Mrs. Eve, Mrs. Brooks, Regent, and self were present, to decide whether we should hold a Council in November or not until May next. After hearing pros and cons it was decided to be postponed until spring. The Regent then spoke of Miss McMakin as a secretary. No objection to the proposal was made by anyone and no one present appeared to know anything about her except the Regent. She spoke of her highly. I assure you it is a great mistake that the Vice-Regents present made no opposition to the Regent's choice in a secretary. Mrs. Eve was to have accompanied the Regent on the following day to Harlem to make the proposal to Mrs. Mc-Makin. The day being unpleasant, and Mrs. Eve asthmatic, the Regent took her nephew with her, and found the lady out of employment. I know that the mother was to be with the Regent at Mount Vernon, but that was to be a consideration in giving less salary, the particulars of which I did not hear, as salary was not spoken of at the meeting.

"I am disposed to think well of the new secretary from one circumstance that has come to my knowledge. Soon after the Regent left for South Carolina, Mr. Watt, the new gardener, became drunk and neglected his work and went to bed. The secretary went to Washington and reported to Mr. Sykes, as one of the advisory committee. Mr. Sykes wrote to Mr. Halsted and I presumed to Mr. Comegys also, to know what to do. I thought the secretary in that instance acted wisely, and if she has no company there but her mother it is all right, she cannot remain there without her. But if she has other visitors, she must be kindly informed that it will not be allowed. If they are dismissed now, Mount Vernon will be the loser, for Mr. Sykes said in my presence that he had forwarded $100 for the McMakins' expenses in moving to Mount Vernon. Of course that was to come out of her salary. If she should leave, the Regent's heart would be almost broken. Her earthly happiness is almost built up on having that lady for her secretary.

"Clarence wrote that his aunt had been very ill at Rosemonte, and could not get on before February. In going South the poor little lady lost her satchel with her medicines and her purse with some money, and all her little by-the-way conveniences. I felt very sorry about it—all but the medicines!"

Even Mrs. Halsted. From now on, the Regent's road could only lead downward.

By January 30th, Mr. Watt had been dismissed. "A much less pretentious and apparently able person named Chauncey is now in charge and seems very much at home in the varied duties of the place," Miss McMakin reported to Mrs. Halsted, the vacancy having been filled with Mr. Sykes's assistance. "The conservatory is looking very well, and I think the ladies will not fail to be pleased with his labors. I am getting along very quietly, with only a constant sense of responsibility, and looking forward to the Regent's return with earnest expectation."

It must have been an odd sensation for Miss McMakin to find herself back at Mount Vernon, after nearly ten years, and more or less in Miss Tracy's shoes, without Miss Tracy's advantages and capabilities. The situation there had obviously deteriorated to a serious degree by the time Miss Cunningham arrived exhausted from Rosemonte again in March, '72, to take up a somewhat macabre existence with only the McMakins, Nathan and Sarah, and a man named Chauncey, the servants already upset and unhappy under the McMakin invasion. Three full years had elapsed since the firm, experienced hand of Mr. Herbert had been withdrawn, and even the Regent had been absent more than half of that time, leaving the place to Mrs. Tiffey, Lizzie Cunningham, Mr. Craig, Watt, and finally Mary McMakin. In Mrs. Sweat's later account, she said that after the 1870 Council, with increasing dissatisfaction on the part of the public and the Vice-Regents, "matters went on very awkwardly until another Council convened in 1872"—which was another lapse of two years between Councils.

The Regent could hardly have deceived herself that things were going well. Mr. Sykes, her mainstay at Washington, was now at odds with the McMakins, and was threatening to resign from the advisory committee, which Mrs. Halsted felt would be a fatal loss to the Association. The Washington Press was hostile, and published an article alleging that Miss Cunningham held Mount Vernon "for her own uses, without rendering any account of expenditures and receipts" which recently appeared only too true, and caused considerable agitated correspondence among the Vice-Regents, who were brought to a realization that they had very little knowledge or evidence with which to deny it. Mrs. Sweat wrote to Mrs. Chace, that they had no right to sit still and let this matter alone, and that some force should be brought to bear on the Regent to bring her to her senses. She also wrote to Miss Cunningham entreating that for her own sake, as well as that of the Association, she should present at the next Council a careful and thorough accounting of the receipts and expenditures since the last Council—which it was hardly possible to do. "Nothing short of a clear account of our management can, and permit me to say, *ought* to satisfy the public that we are not only honest in intention but capable and successful in the trust committed to us," she added. "We are all only the agent of those who furnish the money and are responsible to them for the proper and eco-nomical use of the estate."

Miss Cunningham wrote a sharp reply to the Washington paper, which gave very little satisfaction anywhere, and called Council for June 11th at Mount Vernon.

Ten Vice-Regents answered the summons—of the old guard, Mrs. Comegys, Barry, Farnsworth, and Berghmans—the perma-nent Secretary of Council, Mrs. Sweat, and her friend Mrs. Brooks —Mrs. Walker, all the way from North Carolina—Mrs. Cutts of Vermont, making her first and only appearance at Council—Mrs. Mason, taking up her duties as Vice-Regent for Virginia—and Mrs. Hudson on her first appearance as the second Vice-Regent for Connecticut.

Mrs. Mitchell, so active heretofore and hereafter, is unaccounted for, as is Mrs. Eve. The death of Mrs. Halsted's father prevented her from attending, Mrs. Chace had gone abroad, Miss Harper was still to seek, though she had sent a check for $200 to be ap-plied to the infant endowment fund, which had received $500 from Mrs. Sweat's father.

Mary McMakin was present, as private secretary to the Regent, who in her opening address made reference to her declining health, and a desire soon to be relieved of her duties as manager and superintendent, which she had assumed in 1869 at the re-quest of Council in order to save the cost of a salary, as she now wished to devote herself to the compilation of a history of the Association. Thanks to Mrs. Sweat, the first real inventory of the place was now accumulated, and a respectable parade of accounts was made, which showed the Association to be solvent, with a balance of over $1000, due, it was pointed out, to the Regent's economies as supervisor. No accounting could be given of the Government indemnity, as that money had never come into the hands of the Association, and it was never accounted for to them. The furnace was installed, the Lafayette Room was furnished by Mrs. Halsted, the greenhouse and grapery were prospering. Their main source of income was still the boat, the "Arrow," which had been recently overhauled at some expense by Mr. Sykes, whose contract was extended to five years. And a committee was appointed to select a suitable person for the Regent's approval as Resident Secretary and Superintendent, and to define his duties. He was of course, already selected, in the person of Colonel Hollingsworth, who since the October meeting in New York had been waiting in the wings, and his name, at least, was already known to the Regent. His salary as voted by the Council, was $1500 a year. The same sum was set apart for the use of the Regent, "to meet the various expenses incident to her historical labors."

"It is proper to add," Mrs. Sweat's Report concluded, "that the services of all the Council are gratuitous; that several of them have been engaged in labors for the Association, bearing all their own expenses of travel and otherwise, more than sixteen years, and most of them more than twelve; first in the arduous work of making collections for the purchase of the estate; and since, in striving to create means, by every legitimate device, for its care and renovation. It is but just to Miss Cunningham for the Council to state that she has never desired or received any compensation for her services."

Those are the facts of the 1872 Council. What transpired behind the scenes is more difficult, but can in some degree be arrived at by a study of subsequent correspondence.

By Mrs. Sweat's reminiscences the Council broke up without actual adjournment, and without satisfactory results, but with the hope that the pressure of events would continue the reformation. "Special work was assigned to special Vice-Regents whose personal relations with the Regent were most intimate and of longest duration," she wrote—whatever that means. Everyone left the Council ill, in varying degrees, from fever and diarrhea probably from contaminated water supply, and in Mrs. Barry's case with serious and long-lasting effects.

Mrs. Sweat also recalled that "every effort was made to secure an amicable arrangement by which to place the Resident Secretary quietly in the practical care of the estate, and at the same time to retain for the Regent all the prestige of her position, and to pay her all the respect due her many services, and her really great personal worth."

The exact circumstances of Colonel Hollingsworth's first arrival at Mount Vernon are lost, but with his introduction onto the scene that summer of 1872, two more new figures emerge from obscurity into the limelight—Mrs. Mason and Mrs. Hudson.

Mrs. Mason was the "charming old lady" who came down from her house called Culross near Alexandria during Mrs. Tiffey's time, with valuable recollections of Nellie Custis Lewis, and she had now attended the 1872 Council as the second Vice-Regent for Virginia, following Mrs. Ritchie. Her letters to Mrs. Sweat, for whom she formed a quick, motherly attachment during that brief session, are lively, literate, and revealing, for she was a cultivated, well-read lady of the old school which practiced letter-writing as an art—and she was also the nearest Vice-Regent to Mount Vernon, the member of the Superintendent's committee to whom he was advised to turn when in difficulty, and as a native Virginian she best understood the inevitable complications at Mount Vernon.

Her original admiration for the Regent as once expressed to Mrs. Tiffey had suffered considerable disillusionment, as her first letter to Mrs. Sweat after Council, dated June 26th, showed:

"I thought your active duties as well as your responsibilities were enough to tire, and so you looked often—for there was no consolation to be found in the temperament of your Regent," she wrote. "She is a difficult subject to treat with, and Mrs. Walker and I, who were sent down to manage her upon the subject of

Mr. Hollingsworth, had to take what we could get and leave the rest either to Mr. Hollingsworth's address and tact, or to another coaxing interview. She would not permit me even to use the word *appointment,* but erased it with her own hand and wrote *employ.* As to the removal of the McMakin family, I thought it better to leave that with Mr. Hollingsworth, and give them a little time, as they said the mother was lying critically ill. But it was requested that Mr. Hollingsworth should have an office and other such apartments as would make him comfortable.

"I cannot fatigue you with all the details, but I was perfectly aware that we had left many points to be gained and secured by Mr. Hollingsworth himself when he once entered on his duties. But strange to say, I have not seen him—nor do I know if he is at Mount Vernon. She seemed in a fever of anxiety to have him there, and maybe he has gone. I intended seeing him so as to give him some judicious hints so as to get matters under his control. I think she will be very glad to get away. She certainly understood that Miss McMakin is in no way official to the Association. She was quite sharp with me about somebody saying she could not spell, but I took no notice of it."

It remains something of a mystery how Mary McMakin, with whom the fastidious Miss Tracy lived so long at peace, contrived in such a short time to put up the backs of every Vice-Regent she encountered during this Council, but they seem at once to have united in a deadly determination to oust her. Her family were unquestionably a blot on the Mount Vernon landscape, and her mother was admittedly not a very high class type, but Mary in the old days had mingled with the best without discredit to herself. Possibly she had risen to Miss Tracy's standards by emulation, and then after years of misfortune in a vulgar environment had reverted. Or possibly she possessed a single-minded devotion to Miss Cunningham so blind and blundering that she resented too savagely what she recognized as criticism of, if not hostility to, the Regent among the ranks. It was said that she used unbecoming language to the ladies, and accused them of engaging a superintendent to do their "dirty work" in getting rid of Miss Cunningham—for the salary granted the Regent by the Council was conditional on her departure from Mount Vernon, so that the whole house could be thrown open to visitors, while she wrote her history in lodgings elsewhere. In any case, Mary McMakin was to stand by the Regent staunchly to the very end, even against the needs and wishes of her own demanding family. And she was one of very few people the Regent never turned against or doubted.

Meanwhile the McMakins occupied the quarters which were intended for Colonel Hollingsworth, whose wife remained at Georgetown, and it is a question where he lived when he first began his duties within a short time after the Council. The Regent herself was in no hurry to leave Mount Vernon, and in July Mrs. Mason wrote to Mrs. Sweat:

"I have just received your letter and enclosed copy of yours sent to Miss Cunningham. It so happened that I had this morning written her myself, though in a different vein—it would be unbecoming in one so new to the Association to say all or much that you have so well said. I entreated her to consider the peril of losing the support of such friends as I had seen rally to her lately—begged her to yield in time; that though I never could forget that the Great Idea had originated with her, the *accomplishment* of the object was through her able associates.

"As to the McMakins, the simple way to rid the place of them was surely to tell Miss McMakin of the determination of the Vice-Regents that she must leave there, and surely her own gratitude to Miss Cunningham would induce her to go. I also entreated her to give her faith to Colonel Hollingsworth, permit him to assume all details, and leave her only to represent the dignity of the position—I hardly hope she will yield. Colonel Hollingsworth, however, is working his way discreetly. I wrote to him to come to me, and he called yesterday evening—and says things go a little better. Miss Cunningham has at last felt able to see him, and has given him a good room. The servants approach him differently, and he thinks in eight or ten days he can effect the removal of the obnoxious family."

Under Hollingsworth, things were being pulled together—the water ram installed along with the furnace had been put in order, and the hay had been saved. He had found the dairy in bad condition, "for how," remarked Mrs. Mason, "could Miss Cunningham supervise all outdoors when she is au lit half her time!"

The Regent's impulsive plan for Mrs. McMakin to open a lunch-room had of course fallen through without the sanction of Council, and Mrs. McMakin had taken to her bed, where she remained allegedly too ill to be moved. The Regent also was ill, if only from the incessant nervous turmoil, but Colonel Hollingsworth was temporarily in her good graces, for she wrote Mrs. Barry that "no one could be more deferential and kind, and he has judgment—I like him."

But at the end of July she was still at Mount Vernon, and the McMakins were still in possession of his designated quarters, and Mary was said to have a bad influence over the Regent—perhaps this was to say that she encouraged the Regent's natural wilfulness and insistence on her prerogatives, and perhaps too she made no effort to curb the increasing use of stimulants or sedatives which had now begun visibly to affect Miss Cunningham's behavior. Moreover, the Regent had not signed Colonel Hollingsworth's commission, which had been left with her at the end of Council. Instead she had drawn up another paper, very different in content, depriving him of all authority, and compelling him to turn over all moneys into her hands, which was just what they had all been trying to obviate, and which, as he pointed out when he sent the new document to Mrs. Comegys, would involve much trouble as she was not to be at Mount Vernon and he would be subjected to considerable inconvenience in not having access to funds to pay the daily expenses and labor costs. He had refused to sign this revised paper until the committee had acted on it, and a painful deadlock had been reached.

Mrs. Mason's gentle nature and abhorrence of scenes induced her to proceed too cautiously to suit some of the more impatient Vice-Regents, and the necessity somehow to impose the will of the Council on the Regent and compel her to leave Mount Vernon once and for all in Colonel Hollingsworth's hands, brought to the fore the hitherto unknown second Vice-Regent for Connecticut, Mrs. Susan E. Johnson Hudson.

II

Mrs. Hudson, it is safe to say, was not afraid of anybody. She was presumably a widow, as no mention is ever made of her husband, and the record is silent as to how she was chosen, though at the time of Mrs. Goodrich's appointment in 1858 Mrs. Ritchie and Mr. Everett were recommending a Miss Johnson for that State, and it is possible that the Regent looked back and found her as a replacement. She had been for some years a close friend of Mrs. Brooks of New York and Washington, who preceded her into the Association, and they were both acquainted with Colonel Hollingsworth before his appointment. Her letters at this time demonstrate that she had a long advantage over Mary McMakin for aggression, and at the same time a proprietary attitude towards the hapless Colonel Hollingsworth which transcended the maternal, though she never neglected to send her love to his wife.

All this summer of 1872 she bombarded him with long letters of advice, admonition, and concern, written in a singularly undecipherable spiky script on grey paper, which assumed without sufficient cause that he was quite unable to act for himself in the most rudimentary obligations of his post. She adjured him to get a little notebook which would go into his pocket and have it always with him so as to jot down his little expenditures as they occurred—to write at least once a week to the members of his committee and confide to them his difficulties and successes—to be very careful about keeping his records, and to answer letters promptly, so that the other ladies would think as highly of him as she did—to take every precaution for his health lest he catch the deadly Mount Vernon malaria, and to destroy her informal letters to him, which was not always done—and above all to turn off the McMakins and make himself comfortable in the house which was rightfully his. "Sign nothing not presented to you by the committee, Mrs. Mason, Mrs. Mitchell, Mrs. Comegys, and myself," she directed him, in her customary explicit fashion. "Don't desert us now, we will all, and we all *do,* stick by you. Overt acts of the Regent will only hasten the final and inevitable collision between Regent and Council. All the Vice-Regents have written the Regent plainly that she is to leave Mount Vernon to you and behave herself. You are entirely authorized to turn the McMakins off. Give them notice to quit on a certain day, and have a police officer to eject them."

Mrs. Mason did not approve of Mrs. Hudson's roughshod viewpoint, and felt that even her "sweetest Mrs. Sweat" was pressing a little too hard, when she wrote to the latter from Loudoun County, where she was paying a visit, on August 10th, to report on her latest interview with the Regent, who had been in a reasonable mood and "professed her desire for a perfect understanding."

"I then rated her on the McMakin family," Mrs. Mason continued. "I told her she was imposed upon, that the mother was a horror—not fit to be on the place, and knowing the objections of the ladies to her being there, if she had been a woman of any sense of propriety she would relieve her of trouble by voluntarily going away. She admitted that the old woman had been *'fast,'* etc., etc., and had had a timely fit of sickness, but like Mr. Jefferson's officeholders, she would neither die nor resign! Colonel Hollingsworth had not remained at Mount Vernon as much as I could wish, going home every other night, but I suppose when he gets his quarters he will remain there more as he can, now and then, have some of his family with him. I saw him just before I came away, and he said they (the McMakins) had taken a house in Alexandria, and by this time I hope they have left.

"I would say to Mrs. Hudson if I knew her, Doucement, doucement, my young friend, you are comparatively young in years and official duty—wait, and let others lead. For myself, I found

her very pleasing, respectful to me personally—and not a doubt
would have crossed my mind in any way injurious to her if I
had not been told soon after we separated that her life had been
one of painful experience, etc., etc. When Colonel Hollingsworth
mentioned to me that he had had a letter from her, I said, 'You
know Mrs. Hudson?' and he replied, 'Oh, yes, I know her well,
she lived in my family for some months.' Now, I will not tell you
from whom I received the other side, it is so painful to hear anything prejudicial to a person you are willing to know and esteem
that I felt very glad my conversation with Colonel Hollingsworth
turned on that subject.

"It was a great matter in my mind to get Miss Cunningham
away, and when away to try to detain her—for I do not think,
with her bad habits and her naturally haughty temperament,
that she is the right person in the right place. As to her secretary,
she is odious, and I have spoken to her quite plainly, hoping she
would tell Miss Cunningham. Another point I have gained is,
Miss Cunningham now wishes to give up entire control of *all*
money matters to Colonel Hollingsworth, and begged me to
write to some of the ladies to ask for a legal transfer of all funds
to him. Now, if we have gained the Treasury, and the direction
of all active duty at Mount Vernon, and the most complimentary
expressions towards Colonel Hollingsworth, isn't that *something?*"

Mrs. Comegys has as usual left little comment as a member of
the Superintendent's committee. Mrs. Mitchell had a house in
Washington, as her husband was now in Congress, and although
she was not at Council she must soon have made Colonel Hollingsworth's acquaintance. It is interesting that even this eminently
sensible woman was not proof against whatever it was about the
tall, bearded veteran of two wars which inspired in the Vice-
Regents the protective anxiety and affection which illumines all
their letters to him. Everyone mothered him. And because his

replies were seldom preserved—he must have replied sometimes —there is created on his part an amusing effect of enigmatic, if not embarrassed, silence.

He did inform Mrs. Hudson that the Mansion was often full of visitors who apparently came on the McMakins' invitation, and that the mother was there nearly all the time, and that so many rooms had been closed that the paying public were indignant. He had had the notices to keep off the grass repainted, and the magnolia tree fenced round to prevent people from tearing off the bark, and the houses of the gardener and old Warner white-washed. He said that Mrs. Mason was very kind and wise, and was making progress with the Regent.

By the end of August Miss Cunningham was at Berkeley Springs and the McMakin family had removed to Alexandria, though they had all left belongings at Mount Vernon to main-tain the right of return, and the Regent had not turned over her keys to Colonel Hollingsworth—possibly an oversight. "There must be no doors closed to you," Mrs. Hudson wrote to him, "and if they are, you must use force." The mail-bag was ordered to be addressed to him and to him *only,* and he was to buy a new lock and key. Mrs. Sweat wrote him that the Regent's bedroom and parlor, "taken in the heart of the house and rigidly closed, and sometimes I believe a room upstairs for the private secretary besides, have caused us more trouble than would seem possible. As soon as she leaves, I would open both and let the crowd trail through them at its own sweet will."

Relief at the Regent's departure was at once complicated by what seems an exaggerated apprehension of her return and a sort of cabal concerned with preventing this on any pretext at all in-cluded Mrs. Hudson, Sweat, and even Halsted and Mitchell. The words "impeach" and "depose" were used in their hardening de-termination to exclude her henceforth from the sacred soil which owed its preservation to her tireless initiative, however able her lieutenants had been. Mrs. Barry took the long and charitable

view, in a letter to Colonel Hollingsworth, showing that the feeling was by no means universal among the Vice-Regents.

"Many of the older ladies have been in the work from the beginning," she wrote, "and they know what has been done, and
what the Regent is when she is *herself*. For my part, when I take
any other view, I throw over her the veil, and turn away silent
and sorrowful. I think of her delicate health from the beginning
of her existence, which precluded her from the accustomed joys
of life, I look at the great enthusiasm which filled her soul, her
masterly labors—then her father's death, throwing family cares
and anxieties upon her, and no strong arm to lean upon. Then
came the loss of property through the war, and she came back to
Mount Vernon to find things in a sad state there after the war.
Then she stayed there alone, sick and suffering, and gradually
was led to seek relief, as we know!

"You may depend upon it that she will not return to Mount
Vernon—upon this the ladies are all united, and it must be so,
but I think Miss Cunningham will voluntarily decline to go.
There could not but be leakages, which she could not prevent
and which your vigilant eye will detect, but she did what she
could, and angels can no more."

In September Miss Cunningham wrote to Mrs. Halsted that
she would go from Berkeley Springs to Philadelphia to consult
Dr. Hodge. "I shall not risk any residence again at Mount Vernon
to add to injury already endured, from which I can never entirely recover," she added, influenced as much by malaria as by
the Vice-Regents' wishes. "I dread even to go there to arrange
my papers and remove my effects. Where to go I do not yet know.
I will leave it to Dr. Hodge to decide. I ought to be under his
care for the coming winter."

But however much she might inveigh against Mount Vernon's
climate and her disillusionment with life there, she had still not

signed Hollingsworth's commission nor turned over to him the
funds in the bank, and though she wrote him she had given Miss
McMakin the keys to be delivered to him, he had never received
them, while a letter from him to Mrs. Mason indicates that the
McMakins were "still hanging about the place." He was directed
not to allow Mary to come there unless with the Regent, and to
remember she was only the Regent's "servant" and had no official
connection with the Association.

In October she was with Miss Cunningham in Philadelphia,
and wrote Mrs. Halsted for her that the doctor had advised
Florida for the winter, which was of course impossible, and that
they were looking into lodgings at Georgetown, as being near
enough to Mount Vernon for her to carry on her work, yet beyond the area of worst infection. This did not suit the cabal,
which were determined on nothing less than the Regent's resignation, and the appointment of a new Regent in her place. Mrs.
Mitchell, as chairman of the committee, had written her a severe
letter on the subject of the funds in the Washington bank which
still could not be touched without her order, and the matter of
Hollingsworth's official position, still unconfirmed by her—reminding her that he was not employed until after she had been
advised with and had given her consent at the New York meeting the previous autumn. The Regent was hurt and offended,
and it was obvious that the situation could not be clarified without another Council at which she could be induced or forced to
resign and allow the machinery of the Association to turn in a
more normal manner under the superintendent's sole control.

Meanwhile the committee came together with several other
Vice-Regents in Mrs. Mitchell's rooms at the Hoffman House in
New York on November 8th, '72—Mrs. Eve, Sweat, Hudson,
Brooks, and General and Mrs. Halsted. There a paper was drawn
up "of a more forcible import than the indulgent arguments
previously employed to persuade the Regent to extricate herself,"
and was signed by all present and by the subsequent assent of

the other Vice-Regents. This requested her to "refrain from all interference with the administration of finances and the management of the estate," not to reside at Mount Vernon, and to at once confirm the appointment of the superintendent, giving him complete jurisdiction over Mount Vernon—while retaining her nominal position at the head of the Association. In the event of her continued refusal to consider their wishes, they took the ultimate step of threatening unwelcome publicity and the withholding of her salary until she complied. Detailed instructions were then written out for Colonel Hollingsworth, for her signature.

These papers were carried by Mrs. Mitchell to Philadelphia, where she was met by Mrs. Comegys, and together they went to see the Regent. It must have been a tragic, difficult hour for all concerned. In Mrs. Mitchell's account of it to Colonel Hollingsworth she said that the Regent had at first insisted that she must go back to Mount Vernon to get her things, and was persuaded by Mrs. Comegys to let Miss McMakin go in her place. "I see no other way out but that you should tell her plainly that the ladies have instructed you to keep open all the rooms, and as no provisions are made for entertaining anyone at Mount Vernon at present, for the Regent's good as well as ours she should not remain at night," Mrs. Mitchell wrote. "There are people watching what we do and ready to publish anything they can get hold of against us."

With the Regent's promise not to go down to Mount Vernon herself—she pointed out the face-saving fact that she had already signified to Mrs. Halsted her decision against any further residence there anyway—they left Philadelphia in hopes that the matter was at last amicably settled. But when Miss McMakin went to Mount Vernon in December to bring back the Regent's clothing and private papers, she was rude to Colonel Hollingsworth, spoke darkly of legal rights, and refused to undertake the removal of McMakin belongings which still occupied at least a part of the building he was supposed to have as his quarters.

The Regent had released some funds for his use, and he was advised simply to retain those which came into his hands on the place, and so with a sensible desire not to make a martyr of her, the Vice-Regents hoped, as Mrs. Mitchell wrote, "to hitch along" until a Council could convene in the spring.

12

They met in May of '73, at the Imperial Hotel in Washington.

During the winter the situation had remained vexed, for Miss Cunningham still held the reins from Washington. Mrs. Mitchell went to Florida, and wrote from there that the Regent would "outwit them yet," for she was right in her contention that the '72 Council had authorized neither the Treasurer nor herself to sell bonds or make investments or any financial change in the disposal of the idle funds in the Washington bank. Dissatisfied with Cooke & Co., they wanted Riggs back as Treasurer, but could not get him while Miss Cunningham was in office, and it would take another Council to make any financial readjustment.

The undue agitation among some of the Vice-Regents lest Miss Cunningham should set foot again at Mount Vernon continued, and Colonel Hollingsworth was authorized to forward to her the boxes of papers still stored at Mount Vernon which she wanted to refer to in her task of writing the Association's history —after he had opened them and made sure of their contents. Their uneasiness arose partly from their distrust of Mary Mc-Makin—who, Mrs. Mitchell wrote, was "without any idea of right or wrong, and never was a lady." Yet when Mrs. Halsted called on the Regent in Washington in March, Miss Cunningham reiterated her determination never again to live at Mount Vernon. The ginning mill on her plantation had burned down, and Dr. Hodge had died—two more in a long list of catastrophes. "I did my best to persuade her to resign, but she said 'Not yet,'" Mrs. Halsted reported to Mrs. Hudson. "Our Regent is of that disposition that she will never be driven. I think the only way now is to wait and see if she will not of her own accord resign at the coming Council."

That was, of course, what she was waiting for. Heaven knows how many sleepless hours had gone into the preparation of her farewell address, which she meant to read to them then—rehearsing her endless work, her ruinous generosity with money in the early days, her present success (was not Mount Vernon theirs forever?) and her failing health and the necessity for rest. The heirs of Rembrandt Peale had decided to present to the Association the picture of Washington at Yorktown, valued at $10,000, which would call for appropriate ceremonies, which she as Regent had the right to attend, in a last triumphant gesture. The date of the Council soon came under discussion—it was the Regent's prerogative to name it, and she was urged to make it early in the spring before people began to go abroad.

Noticeably absent from the correspondence all this time was Lily Macalester Berghmans. It is not just a matter of missing letters —her name was never mentioned by the others as having been written to or heard from, except once when Mrs. Hudson wrote Hollingsworth in March, '73, that Mme. Berghmans was coming to Washington and would visit Mount Vernon, and added: "She keeps on good terms with the Regent—somebody must—but she agrees that the Regent must not return to Mount Vernon." Her friendship with Miss Cunningham had probably been strengthened during the past autumn when the Regent was in Philadelphia. Mme. Berghmans had attended the Council in June, '72, the first for her since 1865, but had somehow held aloof from the subsequent furore and anyway would never have approved the hammer-and-tongs tactics of the Hoffman House meeting. After her visit to Mount Vernon this spring, which was cut short by the fatal illness of her brother at Philadelphia, she did write to Miss Cunningham suggesting an April Council, which she hoped to be able to attend.

Miss McMakin replied to her for the Regent—who had waked that morning to find that her maid had decamped with $25 and some clothing. They were anxious to have the Peale painting in place before Council—it was to occupy the west wall of the banquet room, obscuring the window, and a railing would be placed in front of it for its protection—so to allow time for its conditioning and transportation Council had been called for the middle of May, when Mrs. Underwood would make a formal presentation. "Miss Cunningham says she cannot contemplate your not being present at the meeting," Miss McMakin's letter went on. "Your judgment and business ability, in which you so far exceed many of the ladies, are no less indispensable than the gentleness which made Mrs. Mason style you 'the sweet petitioner.' No doubt there will be need of oil on stormy waters."

It was plain that Mount Vernon was in no condition to accommodate the Council over night, and they were therefore to go down by the boat for a day's inspection and the ceremony, and return to Willard's or the Imperial, each to pay her own bill. Mrs. Hudson wrote Hollingsworth that another good reason for not staying at Mount Vernon was that "we were all made ill there last year."

Although only seven Vice-Regents attended this 1873 Council, it was a memorable gathering in several ways. Mrs. Mitchell can only be said to have reneged at the last moment, writing from Florida to ask Hollingsworth to cancel her reservation at Willard's. Mrs. Comegys was not present either, and it will be remembered that these two ladies had carried the ultimatum to Philadelphia after the Hoffman House meeting, and that the painful memory of their last encounter with the Regent may have made it impossible for them to face what promised to be the final tug-of-war between Regent and Council. Mrs. Sweat, one of the most articulate members of what may be called the cabal, had long planned to go to Europe at this time, and Mrs. Chace was already there. A dangerous injury to Mrs. Eve's son had called her to Georgia, the death of Mrs. Farnsworth's daughter kept her at home, the illness of Mrs. Brooks's husband detained her, and Mrs. Mason had died.

This left only Mrs. Hudson and Mrs. Halsted as the chief opposition. Mme. Berghmans and Mrs. Washington had both attended in '72 and taken no part in the aftermath. Miss Harper now appeared for the first time in Council, as did Mrs. Barnes replacing Mrs. Emory for the District, and to everyone's surprise, Mrs. Fitch, who had not attended since 1865, arrived from Indiana. As the Regent was still in South Carolina in '65, this would have been her first meeting with Mrs. Fitch since the lively Washington winter of 1860. Mrs. Fitch left no record of her reaction to the changes a tragic decade had made in Miss Cunningham, and she found only one familiar face from '65—Mme. Berghmans. What these two said to each other we will never know.

On May 14th the Council, with many invited guests, assembled at Mount Vernon for the ceremony of receiving the Peale painting from Mrs. Rosalba Underwood, daughter of the artist, and the mammoth canvas was unveiled in the banquet room. On this day the Regent stood again under Washington's roof, no doubt at her best, and shared with Mrs. Underwood the honors of the occasion. Her thoughts, as she returned to Washington that afternoon to prepare for the opening session of Council at 1:00 P.M. the following day, will not bear dwelling on.

Mrs. Hudson was appointed secretary of Council pro tem for the absent Mrs. Sweat, and read the Minutes of last Council. Then the Regent, taking the chair, read an address which caused some embarrassment and no little pity.

"Ladies," it began, "I greet you with peculiar gratification—since I fear it is the last time I shall be able to meet with you to consult together on the patriotic responsibilities we have assumed, for unless my health improves I shall be compelled to resign, and at your next Council you may be called upon to choose another to fulfill the duties assigned to the Regent of your Association. Although it may be known to you all that I no longer reside at Mount Vernon, still it is proper to make an of-

ficial statement that I have left the place as a residence. Our
Vice-Regents paid me the compliment of asking me to make it
my home for life, and while deeply grateful for this mark of
their affection and confidence in me I never designed to avail
myself of it but temporarily, and then only for the interests of
the Association till certain hoped-for results could be obtained—
as the publicity of the place and the necessary restrictions in a
house open to the public made a residence there extremely uncomfortable, to say nothing of the unhealthiness which has so
poisoned my system that it may soon end my life. I prepared a
paper to convey this fact to you at the last Council, but by some
oversight it was not read. . . ."

She was right, of course, to save her face and theirs, even at the
cost of the truth, and the long resumé which followed of her
accomplishment since the war, and of the financial operations
she had conducted, verged on the fanciful. When the Council
came to present business, the Regent actually balked again at
signing Hollingsworth's commission, and required it to be rewritten—after which she wrote her name and handed it to him
herself, in formal abdication.

Mrs. Washington, many years later, recalled in a letter to Mme.
Berghmans the tense minute when Miss Cunningham was asked
to name her successor, or at least the one who would act pro tem
until next year when the second Regent would be chosen and
would assume the full office: "I remember so well her look of
affection and confidence, as she said, 'You, Lily.' "

And it was Mrs. Washington who years later wrote her account
of the Regent's ordeal in making the decision that was so long
overdue. "In this stringent emergency Miss Harper's gracious
dignity of presence, sound judgment, wise and practical advice
combined with sympathy for the Regent in her deep distress and
feeble health, was in its steadfast purpose like the 'shadow of a
great rock in a weary land.' It was to her, in a private interview
requested by the Regent, that she first spoke of her resignation

(the writer was the only other person present), lamenting the physical disability caused by long illness, but feeling how hard was the struggle to resign the work she so loved, which had crowned her life with its greatest pride and happiness, at the same time appealing to her friends for guidance and advice. Gathering the frail hands into her own, and looking tenderly into the tearful eyes, Miss Harper spoke words of wisdom firmly and gently, but so clearly, so convincingly reviewing the conditions, and with an almost lofty eloquence pointing the way it seemed best to pursue, that the painful agitation of her listener was calmed, and she whispered brokenly, 'Yes, my strength is all gone; I must resign my work, but my heart will die when I give up Mount Vernon.'"

13

So little is known about Lily Macalester Berghmans, who was to be Regent for the next eighteen years, until her sudden death in 1891. More than ten years younger than Miss Cunningham, she was now in her forties, small in stature, and not robust. She had one daughter, named Camille, by M. Berghmans, and she would marry again, after his death in 1874. Motherless herself from childhood, she was the close companion of her financier father, and from him she had acquired a more than feminine business head, while from her husband she had learned professional diplomacy on top of a natural social grace. As usual, Miss Cunningham had chosen the best.

The hiatus in Mme. Berghmans' Vice-Regency during the '60's made her deferential to those who had served continuously, and she consulted Mrs. Halsted and Mrs. Eve, agonizing over her first duty, which was to prepare the written Report, and to suppress the rambling and sometimes inaccurate Farewell Address which Miss Cunningham wanted printed. "The pro tem dignity is no sinecure, I assure you, and I feel I am rapidly degenerating into a mere writing machine," she wrote Mrs. Halsted in June, "with still enough vitality, however, to be in a condition of waking nightmare over that same dreadful Report. Dear sister of New Jersey, why did you not consent to undertaking writing it?"

But a firm hand was soon noticeable at the helm of Mount Vernon. The new Regent's letters, written on black-bordered notepaper, were brief and clear, in a tall, bold script easily read, and seldom exceeded the single fold for four square pages. Colonel Hollingsworth was at once authorized to remove the McMakins' abandoned furniture from his quarters, saying he wanted to paint the house, and he was to have for his own use the cottage furniture from the room he had occupied in the Mansion in Miss Cunningham's absence (now the downstairs bedroom which had also been hers) and from the room next the Lafayette Room which Mme. Berghmans intended furnishing as the Pennsylvania Room. This would be enough to make his two upstairs rooms comfortable in the building at the end of the north colonnade, and the Vice-Regents would furnish for him the downstairs sitting-room. The "cottage furniture" was probably that sent down by Mrs. Halsted in '69, which had been united to that purchased by Miss Tracy in 1860, in order to furnish the Regent's rooms and the secretary's room after Mr. Herbert's departure had stripped the house of his possessions. Hollingsworth was also authorized to purchase two new mules. And immediate plans for the furnishing of the rest of the Mansion by the Vice-Regents of other States were undertaken.

During this summer of 1873 Mrs. Cunningham left the Louise Home in Washington and returned to Rosemonte. As long ago as the previous autumn Miss Cunningham had written to Mrs. Halsted that the Home was no place for her mother, and that Mrs. Eve had scarcely known her, she was so changed. "No servant attention is allowed," she explained, "and no one is allowed to hire any service from the outside, as I had hoped to do. The ladies are very kind to each other and wait on each other like sisters." It seems a very unlikely state of affairs, and probably Mrs. Cunningham simply longed to go home. There is no indication of how or with whom she made the journey, though Miss Cunningham is silent long enough to have accompanied her and returned to Washington before her next surviving letter was written from there. There is no reference to any such trip, and no indication either of what provision was made for her mother's care at Rosemonte, which had previously been of such concern—possibly one of the nieces was pressed into service.

In any case, Miss Cunningham was in Washington, working on her history, when her mother died in October of the same year, and she then began preparations for her own return to South

Carolina, presumably to settle whatever estate remained. This entailed an endless sorting of papers and effects, some to be stored at the bank in Washington, some to go South with her—and it meant parting from her sole remaining anchor, Mary McMakin. It was not a severance of all ties that she contemplated—she meant to come back, and Council had voted $1000 for her to draw on while writing her history of the Association, but there was always in her mind the possibility that her strength might fail for the last time.

She fell ill, of course, of grief and exertion, and wrote a long, affectionate letter to Mme. Berghmans, asking to see her again before she set out: "The Association and myself owe you a great deal for coming to our assistance at a critical time, and I, dear Lily, fully appreciate the kind sympathy for me which caused you to listen and yield to my appeal to take my place pro tem. You have been more than you realize to me, the two past Councils— oil on the troubled waters—a true and faithful friend to me, for which you have my blessing." So many things still worried her, which she must leave in Mme. Berghmans' hands—the credential cards for new appointees, which had run out—the vacancies waiting to be filled—the *Records* stored at Mount Vernon, of which each new Vice-Regent should receive a set—so many things left undone, so much depending on her successor. "Farewell, dear Lily, if we do not meet, remember that you are one of the sweetest memories of Mount Vernon now left me, in the strange havoc death has made in our ranks. I love the Cause, and I believe you do, and if you do, cultivate such truly unselfish and trustworthy officers as Mrs. Barry, Mrs. Comegys, Mrs. Walker—gems, each and all. . . ."

It can be seen that she knew quite well which of the Vice-Regents were still her friends, and the strongest in the Association.

This was to be her last sad departure from the scene of her many disappointments and despondencies, and her hard, embittered victory. She left behind her the place she held dearest in the world, and turned her back on the little warmth and love which still sheltered her. So far as is known, she travelled alone —and there was no one waiting to welcome her at the end of the journey. She returned to an empty, run-down house, on a poverty-stricken plantation, deserted by all the best of its once loyal servants. But it was her home, the only one she had, and her life in the North had failed her, and she did not know where else to go. Confused in mind and ill in body, she made her way back to Rosemonte, still cherishing her remaining task, which was to set down on paper in her cramped and painful handwriting the long, exhausting, triumphant story of what she had done for Mount Vernon. There was no one else now, who could remember as she could, what she had done.

Before the year was out, she wrote from Rosemonte her condolences for the death of Mme. Berghmans' idolized father, who had recently given $1000 to the endowment fund. She had been attacked by gout—"a family affliction"—from which she expected little relief. In the spring of '74 Mrs. Comegys received from her the last letter which remains. Like so many others, it has been butchered by a pair of shears which cut out the middle of the page, destroying both sides, but it tells of painful illness endured without adequate nursing care, as she had only a "trifling woman" who neglected her so that she subsisted for days on a few spoonfuls of milk. She recalled that her mother had first suggested the rescue of Mount Vernon, and asked that now that she was dead, credit should be given. She had still so much to do, so many things to put straight—and it was such an effort to write. Squeezed in around the edge of the page was her last appeal: "Do write soon. I am so lonely."

Lonely, and sick, and alone. But not defeated. She had won. She had accomplished what she had set out, twenty years before, to do. Mount Vernon, thanks to Ann Pamela Cunningham, is still there today, standing cherished and serene as she longed to see it, with over a million visitors a year.

It had already turned the corner when the next Council met in 1874. There had been another inauguration—Grant's second term

—which always brought extra visitors, and the endowment fund was slowly increasing, and the air was cleared of the malicious rumor and mystery which had gathered over the recent years. Mrs. Halsted was collecting contributions for rebuilding the south colonnade, which had apparently been down since the storm mentioned by Miss Tracy in 1861, and there was a project to restore the south porch outside the library windows, while Mrs. Eve complained that it dated only to Judge Bushrod.

Mme. Berghmans presided with grace and dignity—though in the past year she had lost, one after the other, an only brother, her father, and her husband, by unexpected death. Mrs. Ball of Leesburg had succeeded Mrs. Mason as Vice-Regent for Virginia —the third. Her husband was the great-grandson of Washington's brother Charles, and her sparkling wit, especially when it encountered that of Mrs. Washington of West Virginia, enlivened many a Council to come.

Mrs. Eve, Halsted, Hudson, Barnes, and Miss Harper gathered round the long table in the library-dining-room where the Council assembled, and Mrs. Eve as the senior Vice-Regent and oldest friend of Miss Cunningham, read the announcement of her final resignation and her regrets at not being able to attend once more, and nominated Mme. Berghmans as her successor. The vote was unanimous, and the new Regent expressed her earnest desire to prove worthy of the office. She then read a letter from Miss Cunningham, which ever since 1907 has been reprinted in each annual Report and Minutes of the Association, for here once again the first Regent had found herself. The interlined first draft of this message in her own handwriting was left among her papers, and is now in the files at Mount Vernon. The final paragraphs have the authentic ring and challenge and inspiration of her earliest efforts in the Cause before illness and disaster took their toll:

"Ladies, the home of our Washington is in your charge. See to it that you keep it the home of Washington! Let no irreverent hand change it; no vandal hands desecrate with the fingers of—

progress! Those who go to the home in which he lived and died, wish to see *in what he lived and died!* Let one spot in this grand country of ours be saved from *'change!'* Upon you rests this duty.

"When the Centennial comes, bringing with it its thousands from the ends of the earth, to whom the home of Washington will be the *place of places* in our country, let them see that, though we slay our forests, remove our dead, pull down our churches, move from home to home till the 'hearthstone' seems to have no resting place in America; let them see that we do know how to care for the Home of our Hero!

"Ladies, I return to your hands the office held—since December 2d, 1853."

She died at Rosemonte in May, 1875—not quite alone, for Floride wrote Mrs. Comegys that the nephew Clarence was with her. As she had desired, she "held out" long enough to leave in his youthful hands the family responsibilities she had carried so many years. Her will named Mrs. Comegys and Mrs. Walker and a Charleston friend to take charge of her papers, those in storage in Washington and those she had brought home with her. Her history of the Association was unfinished and no trace of it exists —the task was beyond her strength, but she still hoped that some one would one day carry it through to its inspired conclusion.

Council was due within a month of the time the news of her death reached the Vice-Regents. Mrs. Comegys was so saddened that she thought of resigning. Mrs. Farnsworth, who could not attend, wrote to Mrs. Hudson, "I can never cherish any sentiment towards her memory but sympathy and kindness." And to Mrs. Halsted Mrs. Fitch, who had one of the longest memories, wrote, "You who did not know her in her palmy days cannot of course feel towards her as those who knew her then. The winter she spent with me in Washington, her first winter there, she was received and honored by the first in the land." And "dear Lily" wrote simply, to Mrs. Comegys, "I always loved her."

As Miss Cunningham anticipated, the American Centennial of 1876 brought unprecedented prosperity to Mount Vernon, and new faces to the Council—Mrs. Pickens of South Carolina, "lovely Lucy Holcombe," wife of the fire-eating "secesh" Governor, the famous beauty whose picture adorned the Confederate $100 note, and whom young Mrs. Chesnut in her war-time *Diary* accused of "looking love into the eyes of men at every glance"—Mrs. Broadwell of Ohio, who single-handed furnished the "little parlor" or music room with eighteenth century reproductions worthy of Nellie's harpsichord which stood there, and of whom a colleague wrote, "I have never known a sweeter woman. Antagonism seemed to fade away in her presence."

So the story of Mount Vernon is never a melancholy chronicle of old friends dropping away, but rather a perpetual acquaintance with fresh personalities arriving to fill the gaps left by death or resignation—Mrs. Hearst of California, Miss Longfellow of Massachusetts, Miss Comegys of Delaware, Miss Herbert of Alabama, Mrs. Leiter of Illinois, Mrs. Goldsborough of Maryland, Mrs. Townsend of New York—and that most beguiling character, Harrison Howell Dodge, the third superintendent, who served more than fifty years, and from 1885 kept his own Mount Vernon journal in little pocket-sized note-books rather like those which Washington had used a hundred years before him, and who lived well into the memory of his successor, the present Resident Director, who had the good fortune to work under Colonel Dodge before, as it were, inheriting—all spending their energy, zest, and devotion to preserve Mount Vernon, as Miss Cunningham said a hundred years ago, "*forever!*"

THE REGENTS AND VICE-REGENTS OF THE MOUNT VERNON LADIES' ASSOCIATION OF THE UNION SINCE ITS ORGANIZATION IN 1853

REGENTS

MISS ANN PAMELA CUNNINGHAM, *1853–1874; resigned 1874; died May 1, 1875*

MRS. J. SCOTT LAUGHTON (*formerly Madame Berghmans*), *1874–died 1891*

MRS. HOWARD TOWNSEND, *1891–1909; died April, 1912*

MISS HARRIET CLAYTON COMEGYS, *1909–1927; resigned May, 1927; died July, 1927*

MRS. ALICE HALIBURTON RICHARDS, *1927–died 1936*

MRS HORACE MANN TOWNER, *1936–died 1942*

MRS. LUCIEN M. HANKS, *1943–1948; died December, 1959*

MRS. ALBERT HARKNESS (*formerly Mrs. Thomas Ives Hare Powel*), *1948–1958*

MRS. FRANCIS F. BEIRNE, *1958; re-elected 1963*

VICE-REGENTS

ALABAMA

MRS. HENRY S. LE VERT, *1858–1877*

MRS. HILARY HERBERT, *1882–died 1884*

MISS LEILA HERBERT, *1894–died 1897*

MRS. ROBERT D. JOHNSTON, *1900–died 1934*

MRS. MORRIS WILLIAMS BUSH, *1946–resigned 1959*

MRS. PRESTON H. HASKELL, JR., *1963*

ARIZONA

MRS. ARTHUR NEWTON PACK, *1962*

ARKANSAS

MRS. ROBERT WARD JOHNSON, *1859–died 1866*

MRS. C. L. SCOTT, *1872–resigned 1878*

MRS. CELSUS PRICE PERRIE, *1919–resigned 1922*

MRS. J. FAIRFAX LOUGHBOROUGH, *1932–died 1962*

445

CALIFORNIA

MRS. WILLIAM BLANDING, *1859–resigned 1884*
MRS. GEORGE HEARST, *1889–resigned 1918; died* **1919**
MRS. CHARLES S. WHEELER, *1920–resigned 1940*
MRS. LOCKWOOD DE FOREST, *1956*

COLORADO

MRS. NATHANIEL P. HILL, *1889–died 1908*
MRS. HORTON POPE, *1919–resigned 1947*

CONNECTICUT

MRS. SAMUEL G. GOODRICH, *1858–resigned 1864; died 1868*
MRS. SUSAN E. JOHNSON HUDSON, *1870–died 1913*
MISS ANNIE BURR JENNINGS, *1915–died 1939*
MRS. WILMARTH S. LEWIS, *1942–died 1959*

DELAWARE

MRS. JOSEPH P. COMEGYS, *1858–died 1888*
MISS HARRIET CLAYTON COMEGYS, *1888–1909; elected* **Regent,** *1909*
MRS. ANTOINE LENTILHON FOSTER, *1911–died 1934*
MRS. THOMAS F. BAYARD, *1937–resigned 1958*
MRS. C. LALOR BURDICK, *1961*

DISTRICT OF COLUMBIA

MRS. GEORGE W. RIGGS, *Acting Vice-Regent 1858; appointed 1867–resigned 1868; died 1871*
MRS. JOSEPH K. BARNES, *1873–died 1912*
MISS JANE A. RIGGS, *1912–died 1930*
MISS HELEN LOUISE SARGENT, *1931–died 1948*
MISS CONSTANCE ELLEN TYLER, *1952–died 1963*

FLORIDA

MADAME ACHILLE MURAT, *1858–died 1867*
MRS. DAVID LEVY YULEE, *1868–died 1884*
MRS. JAMES M. BAKER, *1888–died 1901*
MRS. THOMAS PALMER DENHAM, *1913–resigned 1948; died 1950*
MRS. LE ROY COLLINS, *1961*

GEORGIA

MRS. WILLIAM J. EVE, *1858–died 1889*
MRS. JOSEPH JOHN WILDER, *1891–died 1914*

MRS. JEFFERSON RANDOLPH ANDERSON, *1919–resigned 1949; died 1956*
MRS. BARNWELL CUBBEDGE, *1958*

ILLINOIS

MRS. WILLIAM BARRY, *1859–died 1883*
MRS. LEVI Z. LEITER, *1885–died 1913*
MRS. GEORGE A. CARPENTER, *1916–resigned 1947; died 1948*
MRS. HENRY PORTER ISHAM, *1949*

INDIANA

MRS. GRAHAM NEWELL FITCH, *1859–died 1880*
MRS. CHARLES DENBY, *1901–died 1906*
MRS. BENJAMIN D. WALCOTT, *1914–resigned 1932; died 1933*
MRS. BENJAMIN D. HITZ, *1936*

IOWA

MRS. VER PLANCK VAN ANTWERP, *1858–died 1870*
MRS. JOHN F. DILLON, *1872–resigned 1873; died 1898*
MRS. HORACE MANN TOWNER, *1913, elected Regent 1937; died 1942*
MRS. DOUGLAS NELSON GIBSON, *1955*

KANSAS

MRS. MILAN LESTER WARD, *1876–died 1910*
MRS. JOHN V. ABRAHAMS, *1916–resigned 1921*
MRS. JOHN REYNOLDS SHELTON, *1923–resigned 1930*
MRS. EARL K. LORD, *1930–died 1956*

KENTUCKY

MRS. ALEXANDER JEFFREY, *1858–resigned 1885; died 1894*
MRS. GEORGE W. WOODWARD, *1885–resigned 1889; reappointed 1891–died 1897*
MRS. WILLIAM F. BARRET, *1901–died 1920*
MISS MARY MASON SCOTT, *1923–died 1934*
MRS. MASON BARRET, *1938–resigned 1953; died 1955*
MRS. WALTER N. HALDEMAN, *1960*

LOUISIANA

MRS. ISAAC E. MORSE, *1858–resigned 1872; died 1893*
MRS. DAVID URQUHART, *1873–resigned 1876*
MRS. TOBIAS G. RICHARDSON, *1880–died 1910*
MISS ANNIE RAGAN KING, *1912–died 1933*

MISS SARAH DUNCAN BUTLER, *1936–resigned 1960*
MRS. FRANK G. STRACHAN, *1963*

MAINE

MRS. JOSIAH S. LITTLE, *1858–resigned 1866; died 1893*
MRS. LORENZO M. SWEAT, *1866–died 1908*
MRS. ALICE HALIBURTON RICHARDS, *1911, elected Regent 1927; died 1936*
MRS. HAROLD LEE BERRY, *1930*

MARYLAND

MISS EMILY L. HARPER, *1866–died 1891*
MRS. GEORGE R. GOLDSBOROUGH, *1893–resigned 1904; died 1906*
MRS. HENRY W. ROGERS, *1905–died 1931*
MRS. DE COURCY W. THOM, *1935–resigned 1946; died 1963*
MRS. FRANCIS F. BEIRNE, *1948, elected Regent 1958*

MASSACHUSETTS

MRS. HORATIO GREENOUGH, *1858–resigned 1865; died 1891*
MISS ALICE M. LONGFELLOW, *1879–died 1928*
MRS. NATHANIEL THAYER, *1930–died 1934*
MRS. JOHN TEMPLEMAN COOLIDGE, *1940–resigned 1948; died 1964*
MRS. SAMUEL CABOT, *1949*

MICHIGAN

MRS. ELON FARNESWORTH, *1858–resigned 1877; died 1879*
MRS. JOSHUA HENRY RATHBONE, *1885–resigned 1918; died 1923*
MRS. EDWARD H. PARKER, *1923–died 1924*
MRS. BENJAMIN S. WARREN, *1925–resigned 1958*
MRS. ALEXANDER L. WIENER, *1964*

MINNESOTA

MRS. HENRY H. SIBLEY, *1859–died 1869*
MRS. CHARLES EUGENE FLANDRAU, *1889–died 1911*
MRS. CHARLES ELIOT FURNESS, *1914–died 1935*
MISS ANNA E. RAMSEY FURNESS, *1940–died 1964*

MISSISSIPPI

MRS. WILLIAM MC WILLIE, *1858–1873*
MRS. WILLIAM BALFOUR, *1873–resigned 1885*
MRS. KATE WALTHALL FREEMAN, *1885–1888*

MRS. BENJAMIN SHERROD RICKS, *1907–resigned 1914*
MISS MARY GOVAN BILLIPS, *1916–resigned 1963*

MISSOURI

MRS. ROBERT R. WALTON, *1858–resigned 1858; died 1867*
MRS. WILSON PRICE HUNT, *1860–died 1878*
MRS. ROBERT CAMPBELL, *1879–died 1882*
MRS. BENJAMIN GRAHAM, *1893–died 1915*
MRS. CHARLES NAGEL, *1916–resigned 1943; died 1951*
MRS. MARVIN E. HOLDERNESS, *1948–resigned 1959*
MRS. ROBERT NEILL, JR., *1964*

NEBRASKA

MRS. ROBERT H. CLARKSON, *1894–resigned 1900; died 1902*
MRS. CHARLES F. MANDERSON, *1900–died 1916*
MRS. ALEXANDER C. TROUP, *1923–died 1950*

NEVADA

MRS. M. E. HICKMAN, *1866–resigned 1874*
MRS. JOHN P. JONES, *1875–resigned 1876*

NEW HAMPSHIRE

MRS. SALMA HALE, *1858–resigned 1861; died 1865*
MRS. ONSLOW STEARNS, *1866–resigned 1873*
MRS. ABBY GODWIN WINDER, *1890–died 1906*
MISS HARRIET L. HUNTRESS, *1914–died 1922*
MRS. GORDON WOODBURY, *1929–resigned 1949*
MRS. JOHN LAWRENCE SULLIVAN, *1952*

NEW JERSEY

MISS PHOEBE A. OGDEN, *1858–died 1865*
MRS. NATHANIEL NORRIS HALSTED, *1868–died 1891*
MRS. FRANCIS S. CONOVER, *1893–died 1914*
MRS. WILLIAM HALL BRADFORD, *1915–resigned 1939*
MRS. THOMAS TURNER COOKE, *1946*

NEW YORK

MISS MARY M. HAMILTON (*later Mrs. George Lee Schuyler*), *1858–resigned 1866; died 1877*
MRS. JAMES BROOKS, *1867–resigned 1876*

MRS. HOWARD TOWNSEND, *1876, elected Regent 1891; resigned 1909; died 1912*

MRS. PHILIP SCHUYLER, *1893–resigned 1894*

MISS AMY TOWNSEND, *1894–died 1920*

MRS. HENRY GOLD DANFORTH, *1922–resigned 1948; died 1961*

MRS. THOMAS STILWELL LAMONT, *1952*

NORTH CAROLINA

MRS. P. K. DICKINSON, *1858–resigned 1859; died 1881*

MRS. WILLIAM RICHMOND WALKER, *1859–died 1908*

MRS. ALEXANDER BOYD ANDREWS, *1909–died 1915*

MRS. WILLIAM EWEN SHIPP, *1919–died 1936*

MRS. JOHN WITHERSPOON LABOUISSE, *1944*

OHIO

MRS. GEORGE H. PENDLETON, *1858–resigned 1863; died 1886*

MRS. EMILY R. MC ILVAINE HEWSON, *1866–resigned 1873*

MRS. SAMUEL J. BROADWELL, *1875–died 1890*

MISS MARY LLOYD PENDLETON, *1893–resigned 1897*

MRS. JAMES E. CAMPBELL, *1897–resigned 1902*

MRS. LEWIS W. IRWIN, *1907–died 1916*

MRS. CHARLES J. LIVINGOOD, *1919–resigned 1935; died 1936*

MRS. CHESTER C. BOLTON, *1938*

OKLAHOMA

MRS. RUSSELL STORY TARR, *1947*

OREGON

MISS MARY F. FAILING, *1907–died 1947*

PENNSYLVANIA

MISS LILY LYTLE MACALESTER (*Madame Berghmans, later Mrs. J. Scott Laughton, Second Regent*), *1859–died 1891*

MRS. J. DUNDAS LIPPINCOTT, *1893–died 1894*

MRS. CHARLES CUSTIS HARRISON, *1896–died 1922*

MRS. WILLIAM R. MERCER, *1924–resigned 1928*

MRS. BENJAMIN FRANKLIN PEPPER, *1929–resigned 1948; died 1955*

MRS. HENRY NORRIS PLATT, *1948*

RHODE ISLAND

MRS. GEORGE I. CHACE, *1858–died 1893*
MRS. WILLIAM AMES, *1894–died 1904*
MRS. JOHN CARTER BROWN, *1907, Honorary Vice Regent 1935; died 1936*
MRS. ALBERT HARKNESS (*formerly Mrs. Thomas Ives Hare Powel*), *1936, Regent 1948–1958*

SOUTH CAROLINA

MRS. JAMES CHESNUT, *1860–died 1864*
MRS. FRANCIS WILKINSON PICKENS, *1866–died 1899*
MRS. JOHN JULIUS PRINGLE, *1901–died 1921*
MISS VIRGINIA LEIGH PORCHER, *1924–died 1940*
MRS. BENJAMIN ALLSTON MOORE, *1948*

TENNESSEE

MRS. FRANCIS B. FOGG, *1858–died 1872*
MRS. AARON V. BROWN, *1874–died 1889*
MISS MARY POLK YEATMAN (*later Mrs. Thomas Shapard Webb*), *1893–died 1917*
MRS. HORACE VAN DEVENTER, *1920–died 1956*
MRS. MARVIN E. HOLDERNESS, *1959*

TEXAS

MISS ELLA HUTCHINS, *1866–resigned 1872*
MISS MARY E. MAVERICK, *1873–resigned 1873*
MRS. THOMAS S. MAXEY, *1896, Honorary Vice Regent 1937; died 1938*
MRS. JOHN MIRZA BENNETT, *1940–died 1963*

VERMONT

MRS. HAMPDEN CUTTS, *1859–resigned 1878*
MRS. J. GREGORY SMITH, *1878–resigned 1884*
MRS. CORNELIUS LOW KING, *1885–died 1896*
MISS MARY EVARTS, *1911–resigned 1923; reappointed 1924–died 1928*
MRS. HORACE BROWN, *1930–resigned 1940; died 1943*
MRS. JAMES DENNIS, *1946–died 1946*
MRS. A. JOHN HOLDEN, *1961*

VIRGINIA

MRS. WILLIAM F. RITCHIE, *1858–resigned 1866; died 1870*
MRS. THOMSON FRANCIS MASON, *1872–died 1873*
MRS. CHARLES B. BALL, *1874–died 1918*
MRS. WILLIAM RUFFIN COX, *1921–died 1925*
MRS. FAIRFAX HARRISON, *1927–died 1943*
MRS. EDWARD CLIFFORD ANDERSON, *1947–resigned 1960*
MRS. JOHN H. GUY, JR., *1963*

WASHINGTON

MRS. JOHN LEARY, *1907–died 1935*
MRS. STANLEY D. LYLE, *1944–died 1955*

WEST VIRGINIA

MRS. LEWIS WILLIAM WASHINGTON, *1870–died 1898*
MRS. EUGENE VAN RENSSELAER, *1900–died 1923*
MISS CONSTANCE LEE PETERKIN, *1924–resigned 1946; died 1948*
MRS. AUGUSTINE JAQUELIN TODD, *1955*

WISCONSIN

MRS. ALEXANDER MITCHELL, *1858–died 1902*
MRS. LUCIEN M. HANKS, *1914, elected Regent 1943–1948; resigned 1956; died 1959*
MRS. JOHN CUNNINGHAM LOBB, *1960–resigned 1962*

WYOMING

MRS. THOMAS F. TALIAFERRO, JR., *1936–resigned 1950; died 1953*

ACKNOWLEDGMENTS
and BIBLIOGRAPHY

As has been mentioned elsewhere, the most valuable source materials for this book consist of the letters which passed between the founding sisters and the early Minutes of Council, all unavailable except at the library of the Mount Vernon Ladies' Association, and quoted only by their express permission. Additionally, I must render my usual thanks to Miss Helen Ruskell and the staff of the New York Society Library, whose membership mailing system makes research possible to a writer who prefers not to be nailed down in New York City during the preparation of a book of this kind, and the tedious historical double-check required. My thanks are also due to Dr. Woodhull S. Hall of the Putnam Memorial Hospital at Bennington, Vermont, for his patient consideration of, and necessarily handicapped opinion regarding, the effects on Miss Cunningham's overly punished heart and nervous system of the continued reckless medication by the physicians of her time; and for the loan from the hospital library of Dr. Thomas A. Gonzales' massive volume on *Toxicology* (Appleton, 1954) which confirmed my own conviction that without her habitual overdosage of laudanum and kindred sedatives, prescribed and made available to her, though apparently against his own better judgment, by Dr. Hodge, the end of the story might have been different, even in the tragic circumstances imposed by the war and the subsequent chaos of emancipation in the South.

The State Historical Societies, notably those of Alabama, Florida,

Ohio, and Tennessee, have been very helpful in replying to letters
of inquiry, as were the descendants of some of the early Vice-Regents.
Among the many volumes consulted during the course of the work
were:

Appleton's Cyclopaedia of American Biography. New York, D. Appleton & Co., 1898.

CHESNUT, MARY BOYKIN, *A Diary from Dixie,* edited by Ben Ames
Williams. Boston, Houghton Mifflin Co., 1949.

ELLET, ELIZABETH FRIES, *The Queens of American Society.* New York,
Scribner & Co., 1867.

ELLIOTT, CHARLES WINSLOW, *Winfield Scott, the Soldier and the Man.*
New York, The Macmillan Co., 1937.

FREEMAN, DOUGLAS SOUTHALL, *Lee's Lieutenants.* New York, C. Scribner's Sons, 1942–44.

———, *Robert E. Lee.* New York, C. Scribner's Sons, 1934–35.

FREEMAN, JULIA, *Women of the South Distinguished in Literature.*
New York, C. B. Richardson, 1866.

FROTHINGHAM, PAUL REVERE, *Edward Everett, Orator and Statesman.*
Boston, Houghton Mifflin Co., 1921.

LEECH, MARGARET, *Reveille in Washington, 1860–1865.* New York,
Harper & Brothers, 1941.

LE VERT, OCTAVIA WALTON, *Souvenirs of Travel.* Mobile, 1857.

LOSSING, BENSON JOHN, *The Home of Washington.* Hartford, Conn.,
A. S. Hale & Co., 1870.

———, *Pictorial History of the Civil War in the United States.* Philadelphia, G. W. Childs, 1866.

MYERS, WILLIAM STARR, *A Study in Personality, General George Brin-
ton McClellan.* New York, D. Appleton-Century Co., Inc., 1934.

PEACOCK, VIRGINIA T., *Famous American Belles of the Nineteenth Century.* Philadelphia, J. B. Lippincott Co., 1901.

PRYOR, MRS. ROGER A., *Reminiscences of Peace and War.* New York,
The Macmillan Co., 1904.

SWANBERG, W. A., *Citizen Hearst.* New York, Charles Scribner's Sons,
1961.

———, *Sickles the Incredible.* New York, Charles Scribner's Sons, 1956.

INDEX

455

MOUNT VERNON

1. Mansion
2. Greenhouse and Quarters
3. Flower Garden
4. Icehouse
5. Museum
6. Botanical Garden
7. Spinning-House
8. Storehouse
9. Gardener's House
10. Office
11. Courtyard
12. Bowling Green
13. Kitchen
14. Butler's House
15. Smokehouse
16. Laundry Yard
17. Washhouse
18. Coachhouse
19. Kitchen Garden
20. Stable
21. Paddock
22. Park
23. Potomac River
24. Vineyard Enclosu

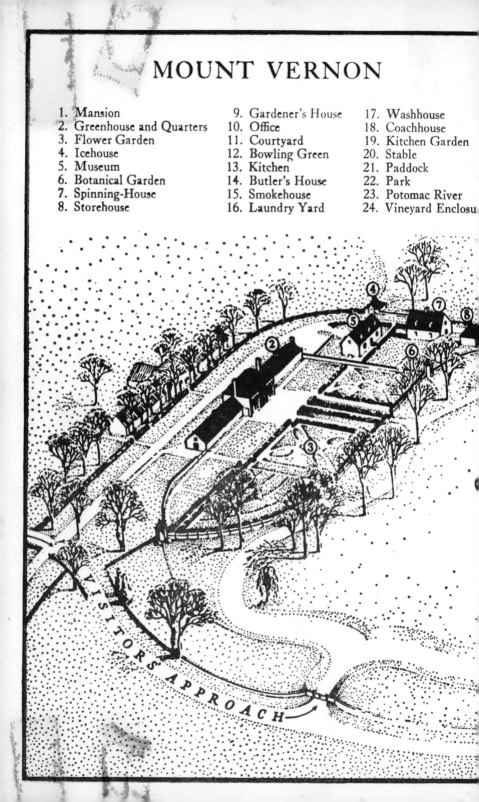